One Bible...
And Yet, So Many Beliefs

Exploring the Doctrinal Chaos

By
Steven A. Carlson

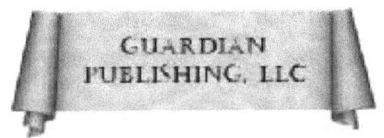

GUARDIAN
PUBLISHING, LLC

Copyright © 2014, Steven A. Carlson
All Rights Reserved
ISBN: 978-0-9827915-5-4
Printed in the United States of America

This edition published in July 2014 in association with

Guardian Publishing, LLC
Holt, Michigan

guardianpublishingllc.com

Unless otherwise indicated, the biblical passages cited in this book are from the Holy Bible, New American Standard Bible (NASB). Scripture taken from the NEW AMERICAN STANDARD BIBLE®, Copyright © 1960, 1962, 1963, 1968, 1971, 1972, 1973, 1975, 1977, 1995 by The Lockman Foundation. Used by permission.

Acknowledgements

This work is dedicated to the members of my Sunday school class at Holt Christian Church. For more than a decade I have taught an adult Sunday school class that has exceeded expectations. Taking time to study diligently many books of the Bible, these men and women have been unbelievably faithful in attendance and amazingly industrious, taking care to help me consider the truth of God's Word.

They have also been surprisingly encouraging where my writing efforts are concerned, urging me onward and often taking the time to read my work and offer substantive feedback. Many probably do not even realize how deeply they influence my studies and biblical perspective. I do not believe I could offer works like this were it not for their loyalty and support.

I would like to thank my son, Adam, and daughter, Crystal, who were responsible for the editing of this work. They did an exceptional job, and it can be said unequivocally that the book was substantially improved when they were finished.

I would also like to mention my dear Christian brother, Dr. Ed Cook. He has been a consistent friend for many years, always willing to lend an ear and an independent perspective when I approach him, as I often do, to assure that I am gleaning from a chapter or verse what the author intended. I would also like to thank my sister, Naomi Nash, who was able to offer substantive feedback on the topic of election.

My undying gratitude goes to my brother, Tim Carlson, who is a minister of the gospel and whose grasp of doctrinal truth far surpasses my own. Over the years I have relied heavily on his biblical knowledge and this work is no exception. He deserves enormous credit for his part in the development of much of the doctrinal analysis and application of interpretive principles contained in this work. Without his help, this book would undoubtedly fall short of the goal of full and honest exegesis.

Finally, I would like to thank my wife, Denise. At some point in time, she must have prayed for God to help her develop more patience in her life and God answered by calling me to write. She has been incredibly understanding over the past dozen or so years as I have sought to put thoughts on paper. Thank you, dear. You are my rock.

Table of Contents

TITLE	PAGE
PREFACE	8
Doctrinal Conflicts	*8*
The Cause of Doctrinal Conflicts	*9*
Freedom in Christ	*11*
The Timing of Doctrine	*12*
Individual Doctrinal Issues	*13*

------SECTION I: APPROACHING GOD'S WORD------

CHAPTER 1: SOLA SCRIPTURA	16
Evidence of God	*16*
Evidence of the Sufficiency of Scripture	*16*
Scripture as God's Word	*17*
The Principle of Sola Scriptura	*18*
Internal Scriptural Conflict	*21*
CHAPTER 2: SYSTEMATIC THEOLOGY	23
The Science of Theology	*23*
Disciplined Theology	*24*
Understanding Context	*25*
Discerning the Author's Intent	*26*
Considering the Results/Audience Response	*27*
Where Systematic Theology Falls Short	*28*
CHAPTER 3: PRINCIPLES OF INTERPRETATION	30
God Communicates Through Language	*30*
Understanding and Applying Principles of Interpretation	*31*
Objectivity – The Heart of Biblical Understanding	*33*
The Objective Use of Inference	*34*
Words Have Meaning	*38*
Difficult Biblical Passages	*39*
Handling Difficult Passages	*39*
Proof Texting	*41*
Literal vs. Figurative Use of Language	*42*
Common vs. Uncommon Use of Language	*44*
Apostolic Repetition and Biblical Harmony	*46*
The Holy Spirit and Scripture	*46*
CHAPTER 4: DOCTRINAL SIGNIFICANCE	48
The Weight of Doctrine	*48*
Managing Essential and Non-Essential Doctrine	*49*
Abundance of Biblical Instruction	*53*
SUMMARY ON APPROACHING GOD'S WORD	55

------SECTION II: SPIRITUAL GIFTS------

CHAPTER 5: NOW CONCERNING SPIRITUAL GIFTS	58
The Continuation/Cessation Divide	*58*
A History of Spiritual Gifts	*58*

TITLE	PAGE

CHAPTER 5: NOW CONCERNING SPIRITUAL GIFTS (CONT'D) **58**
   The Nature of Spiritual Gifts in the Church *61*
   The Apostolic and Early Church Fathers *67*
   Spiritual Gifts and Essential Doctrine *67*
   Biblical Harmony *69*
   The Day of Pentecost *69*

CHAPTER 6: SIGNS OF AN APOSTLE **75**
   Distinguishing the Apostolate *75*
   The Apostolic Signature *78*
   Identifying the Signs of an Apostle *78*
   The "Super Apostles" *87*
   Bestowal of Miraculous Gifts *90*

CHAPTER 7: WHEN THE PERFECT COMES **97**
   Partial Cessationism *97*
   Partial Knowledge and Understanding *100*
   The Perfect *101*
   Complete vs. Incomplete Understanding *102*
   Obscurity vs. Clarity *103*
   Parallel Pauline Passages *109*
   Faith, Hope, and Love *111*
   Identifying "The Perfect" *112*
   Spiritual Gifts and the Parousia *113*

CHAPTER 8: SPIRITUAL GIFTS AND BIBLICAL HARMONY **116**
   Miraculous Episodes in Scripture *116*
   Acts 6: 8 .... *116*
   Acts 8: 5-8 .... *117*
   Romans 8: 26-27 .... *118*
   Romans 12: 4-8 .... *119*
   1 Corinthians 1: 4-9 .... *120*
   1 Corinthians 12: 27-31 .... *122*
   1 Corinthians 13: 1-3 .... *123*
   1 Corinthians 14: 1-5 .... *125*
   1 Corinthians 14: 14-16 .... *125*
   1 Corinthians 14: 39 .... *127*
   Ephesians 6: 18 .... *127*
   1 Timothy 4: 14; 2 Timothy 1: 6 .... *128*
   Jude 20-21 .... *130*

SUMMARY ON SPIRITUAL GIFTS **132**

------SECTION III: ELECTION AND FREE WILL------

CHAPTER 9: THE DIVIDE CONCERNING ELECTION **136**
   Elect vs. Elected *136*
   Early Church Fathers *137*
   Augustine (A.D. 354-430) *137*
   Pelagius (A.D. 354-420/440) *141*
   The Middle-Ages *142*
   John Calvin (A.D. 1509-1564) *143*
   Jacob Arminius (A.D. 1560-1609) *144*

TITLE	PAGE
CHAPTER 10: THE PRINCIPLES OF CALVINISM	**148**
God's Sovereignty	*148*
The TULIP Philosophy	*149*
Total Depravity of Man	*149*
Unconditional Election	*152*
Limited Atonement	*154*
Irresistible Grace	*156*
Perseverance of the Saints	*159*
CHAPTER 11: GOD AND PREDESTINATION	**161**
The Doctrine of Predestination	*161*
God is Sovereign	*163*
God Is Omnipotent (All Powerful)	*164*
God Is Omniscient (All-Knowing)	*164*
Predestination vs. Free Will	*165*
CHAPTER 12: RIGHTEOUSNESS AND REFORMED THEOLOGY	**167**
The God of the Bible	*167*
God and Righteousness	*168*
Godly Righteousness and Reformed Theology	*171*
CHAPTER 13: UNCONDITIONAL ELECTION: MAJOR PASSAGES	**172**
The Dynamics of Unconditional Election	*172*
Acts 13: 48	*173*
Romans 8: 28-30	*183*
Romans 9: 1-13	*193*
Romans 9: 14-18	*198*
Romans 9: 19-24	*204*
Ephesians 1: 3-6	*208*
CHAPTER 14: UNCONDITIONAL ELECTION: MINOR PASSAGES	**213**
John 6: 37-39	*213*
John 6: 44-45	*214*
John 6: 64-65	*215*
John 13: 18	*216*
John 15: 16	*217*
2 Thessalonians 2: 13	*217*
2 Timothy 1: 9	*218*
1 Peter 1: 1-2	*218*
Jude 1: 4	*220*
Revelation 17: 8	*221*
SUMMARY ON ELECTION AND FREE WILL	**223**

------SECTION IV: BAPTISM------

CHAPTER 15: THE BAPTISM DIALOGUE	**226**
The Baptism Debate	*226*
Salvation by Immersion in Water	*226*
Salvation by Immersion, Sprinkling, or Pouring	*227*
Baptism as a Sign of Salvation	*228*
Baptism Is Spiritual – Not Physical	*229*
Baptism in Water Is Irrelevant	*229*
Is Baptism an Essential Doctrine?	*229*
Baptism and the Principles of Interpretation	*230*

TITLE	PAGE

CHAPTER 16: THE EFFECTS OF BAPTISM 232
   Baptism and Forgiveness of Sins (Justification) 232
   Baptism and Regeneration 234
   Baptism and Sanctification 235
   Baptism and Adoption/Inheritance 236
   Baptism and the Body of Christ 237
   Baptism and Salvation 237
   Baptism and the Holy Spirit 238

CHAPTER 17: CHRISTIAN BAPTISM IN THE GOSPELS 240
   Matthew 28: 18-20 240
   Mark 16: 15-16 242
   Luke 23: 39-43 244
   John 3: 3-5 247

CHAPTER 18: CHRISTIAN BAPTISM IN ACTS 255
   Acts 2: 38 255
   Acts 10: 44-48 261
   Acts 16: 30-34 262
   Acts 19: 1-7 265
   Acts 22: 16 266

CHAPTER 19: CHRISTIAN BAPTISM IN THE EPISTLES 271
   Romans 6: 1-4 271
   1 Corinthians 1: 12-17 272
   1 Corinthians 12: 13 275
   Galatians 3: 23-27 278
   Ephesians 5: 25-26 280
   Colossians 2: 11-14 282
   Titus 3: 5-7 284
   Hebrews 10: 22-23 288
   1 Peter 3: 21 290

CHAPTER 20: BAPTISM AND THE REFORMATION MOVEMENT 293
   The Historical View of Baptism in the Church 293
   The Reformation and Faith Only 294
   Baptism as a Covenant Sign 297
   Synecdoche 299

CHAPTER 21: BIBLICAL CLASSIFICATION OF BAPTISM 302
   Salvation by Grace Through Faith 302
   Baptism Is God's Work 303
   Baptism Is Fundamental to the Faith 306
   Baptism as the Time of Regeneration 308
   Baptism and Christian Unity 309
   The Witness of Baptism 311
   The Biblical Measure of Baptism 312
   Baptism – A Unique Calling 314

SUMMARY ON BAPTISM 316
APPENDIX A: THE GIFT OF APOSTLE 319
APPENDIX B: THE SINNER'S PRAYER 322
BIBLIOGRAPHY 325

Preface

Doctrinal Conflicts

Over the past two millennia, humankind has been inundated with an assortment of claims about the lessons of Scripture. This has resulted in so many doctrinal differences that it is often difficult to recognize the truth of God's Word. Since the authors of the Bible teach that Scripture reveals how mankind might be saved and receive an eternal heavenly reward (2 Timothy 3: 15), the fact that conflicting views have developed about the substance of that message is no small matter.

Where God's Word is concerned, not every difference of opinion is critical to eternal life. Much biblical instruction comes in the form of guidance about how a believer can live a life that most effectively honors God. Still, differences often arise over issues that are fundamental to a person's relationship with God. For instance, Roman Catholics maintain that the pope has been specially ordained by God to speak on his behalf – a view that is not shared by members of the evangelical community. This doctrinal departure comes primarily, although not solely, from conflicting views over Jesus' words to Peter after he had given his confession of faith (Matthew 16: 13-18). While everyone reads the same words spoken by Jesus and Peter, some of the doctrines that have developed from those words are openly contradictory.

Gnosticism, which grew in popularity in the early church, involved some challenging views of the lessons of Scripture. For instance, Gnostics denied the virgin birth and believed that Jesus did not assume the role of Messiah until he was baptized by John the Baptist in the Jordan River (Matthew 3: 13-17). Yet, those who adopted these positions read the same apostolic instructions as those who trusted that Jesus was the Messiah in physical form from the moment he was conceived.

Baptism is a sensitive topic among various groups with a multitude of views surrounding this rite. The differences generally involve disagreement over the mode (immersion vs. sprinkling) and/or purpose (efficacy vs. sign) of baptism. These conflicting doctrines have brought about something Paul continually warned against, which is division in the church (1 Corinthians 1: 10).

The Cause of Doctrinal Conflicts

Understanding that there are doctrinal conflicts begs the question: *Why do these conflicts exist?* Most who accept Scripture as God's Word generally agree that the Bible does not contradict itself, so why should people contradict one another in determining the lessons of Scripture? The fault is not God's. He is not the author of confusion (1 Corinthians 14: 33). The only possibility, then, is that the responsibility for the doctrinal chaos that exists lies with man's treatment of God's Word.

These differences cannot necessarily be attributed to a lack of intelligence or education. Saul, who later became the Apostle Paul, was neither unintelligent nor uneducated. On the contrary, he was exceptionally intelligent and received his education through very elite sources. However, prior to his conversion in Damascus, Saul traveled the country on a misguided quest to persecute Christians. He was sincere, although wrong, in his beliefs; but his error was not due to stupidity or inferior training.

The Pharisees were some of the most clever and well-educated men of the first century. Yet, Jesus often rebuked them for their flawed teachings and their manipulation of Scripture. While they knew the words of the Old Testament, they fell short in their application of what they read. For this reason, they failed to recognize Jesus despite the fact that he fulfilled the Old Testament prophecies concerning the Messiah. While he was here on earth, Jesus warned his disciples about the doctrine of the Pharisees, identifying it as false doctrine (Matthew 16: 5-12).

There are two basic reasons for differing doctrinal views. The first is simple ignorance. While some may feel offended by this statement, it is not intended in a derogatory sense. For instance, Paul admitted that he had persecuted the church out of ignorance (1 Timothy 1: 13) and Peter recognized that the Jews had also "...acted in ignorance" (Acts 3: 17) when they crucified Jesus. In that same sense, many people cling to certain man-made beliefs simply because they lack the biblical insight necessary to distinguish between scriptural and human teachings.

Although the Bible is the best-selling book historically, the number of people who spend quality time in God's Word is very meager. Those who devote significant time to biblical study tend to include professional theologians (professors and authors), ministers, and some church leaders. It is these men and women who end up being the primary source of doctrinal instruction for the vast majority who open their Bibles only on occasion, if they open them at all. Therefore, most do not derive their doctrinal views from Scripture. Rather, their beliefs are founded upon what they have been taught by others about what the Bible says. Like the Apostle Paul prior to his conversion, they believe what they believe out of ignorance.

The second source of doctrinal inconsistency is not quite as easy to excuse as is the ignorance mentioned above. While ignorance carries with it a sense of naivety, in that a person may not know what the Bible teaches and has been misled, the second cause of doctrinal divergence carries with it a deeper sense of responsibility for those involved. In a word, it is pride.

Pride has been the source of mountains of innovative doctrine that has been developed by teachers and theologians who dive into the words of Scripture on a very deep level. At times, those who take seriously their study of God's Word, in seeking to distinguish themselves from all others (generally as a matter of self-importance), inadvisably choose to develop a private (new) interpretation of Holy Writ that will differentiate them. In that quest, various passages of Scripture are assigned meanings that the author(s) never intended. Paul and Peter warned against this.

> [3] If anyone advocates a different doctrine and does not agree with sound words, those of our Lord Jesus Christ, and with the doctrine conforming to godliness, [4] he is conceited *and* understands nothing; but he has a morbid interest in controversial questions and disputes about words, out of which arise envy, strife, abusive language, evil suspicions, [5] and constant friction between men of depraved mind and deprived of the truth, who suppose that godliness is a means of gain. (1 Timothy 6: 3-5)

> [20] But know this first of all, that no prophecy of Scripture is *a matter* of one's own interpretation, [21] for no prophecy was ever made by an act of human will, but men moved by the Holy Spirit spoke from God. (2 Peter 1: 20-21)

God's Word harmonizes fully, but also very intricately. Consequently, someone who becomes inventive in his/her analysis of a verse of Scripture to support *new and improved* doctrine must, sooner or later, begin re-characterizing other verses so that they will conform to this enhanced interpretation. This ultimately leads to a revision of many of the lessons of the New Testament writers. These beliefs then make their way to the masses where they are often embraced with misguided sincerity.

Freedom in Christ

Not every religious issue is a salvation issue. According to the Apostle Paul, believers have freedom in Christ when it comes to life decisions (1 Corinthians 6: 12; 10: 23). Paul provides examples of freedom when discussing which foods are acceptable for consumption – a focal topic particularly among those Jews who had lived under the Mosaic Law. According to the apostle, there is nothing inherently evil about eating meat sacrificed to idols (1 Corinthians 8: 4-13). Sacrificing an animal to honor the deity of a stone or a piece of wood has no effect on the meat itself. However, he pointed out that it is important to consider others when it comes to decisions like this, since weaker believers may struggle with the choices of seemingly stronger and wiser Christians. He also noted that some people eat meat while others do not (Romans 14: 2-8). This is also a matter of freedom.

Many of the choices Christians face fall within the scope of the freedom that Paul discusses in these passages. Some things really are a matter of personal preference. When a subject is not specifically addressed in Scripture as either a *requirement* of those who follow Christ (e.g., belief in Jesus) or something that is *prohibited by God* (sin), it is important to recognize freedom in those matters. While it is important to avoid becoming a stumbling block in exercising individualism, it is equally important to respect each other in matters of freedom about which the apostle wrote. It seems wise to teach only what the Bible teaches and remain flexible in matters where personal differences are permitted.

This freedom allows individuals to make choices based on personal preferences while maintaining close relationships with God and other people. Each individual can develop a unique personal relationship with God without the encumbrances of the law that the Israelites faced. This allows believers to worship him the way he desires to be worshiped – "...in spirit and truth" (John 4: 24).

The freedom discussed by Paul is often misconstrued. Freedom in Christ does not extend to every area of doctrine. For instance, no person can choose to be saved other than through the blood of Christ. This creed was established and confirmed in the first century with the intent that it should remain a stalwart teaching throughout the life of the church (1 John 1: 7; Hebrews 10: 19).

It was a practice of the Pharisees to teach rules and to establish rituals that were not endorsed by God (Mark 7: 1-4; Luke 6: 1-2). This is why Jesus often rebuked them (Matthew 5: 20; 23: 13; Luke 11: 42). Similarly, some relatively modern doctrines have been developed despite scriptural silence or contradiction. However, like the Pharisees, modern men have not been given the authority to offer personal views as replacement for the doctrine of Christ.

As Christians, it is best to be non-judgmental where biblical instruction is concerned, understanding that not everyone will agree when it comes to matters of personal preference. This is the very point Paul made when he discussed eating meat sacrificed to idols. When the Bible is silent on a topic, humans have not been given license to speak or judge on God's behalf. On the other hand, where biblical commands are explicit (cf. Acts 4: 12), no human being is in a position to modify instructions clearly given. Biblical doctrine is intended to be firm and unchanging, especially with respect to the plan of salvation. Where redemptive instruction is concerned, a verse cannot mean different things to different people.

Where redemptive instruction is concerned, a verse cannot mean different things to different people.

The Timing of Doctrine

In modern times, it can be difficult to distinguish between *apostolic* doctrine and a doctrine generated from other sources. One of the reasons this is such a challenge is that, over the past few centuries, the way Scripture is read (and interpreted) has changed dramatically. This is the reason so many denominations exist today.

It can be helpful to consider *when* a doctrine first appeared historically. False teachers of the first century were rebuked by the apostles, such as when John confronted the Gnostics. However, the apostles were not around to address suspicious teachings that arose later.

It is generally accepted by Bible scholars that John was the last living apostle and that his death occurred late in the first century. If an individual doctrinal view did not appear on the scene until a significant amount of time had lapsed after John's death, especially when the teaching overtly challenges clear biblical instruction, it is likely that this doctrine was contrived by people who had developed a new approach to Scripture, an evil against which the apostles warned the earliest Christians (Acts 20: 30; Galatians 1: 6-7; 2 Peter 3: 16).

It may also help to consider the consensus regarding a doctrine among those who lived closest to the time of the apostles – namely, the apostolic fathers. That list includes men like Barnabas, Hermas, Clement of Rome, Ignatius, and Polycarp. They are called apostolic fathers because they lived during the apostolic age. This was a generation of men who had the opportunity to learn directly from the lips of the apostles. It is not unreasonable to believe that, on a topic where the apostolic fathers were fully united, and that doctrine harmonizes with God's Word, they were reflecting apostolic views. It is critical to remember that their words are not Spirit-inspired, but they do, at times, provide valuable insight into the apostles' doctrine.

It can also help to read from the works of the early church fathers – that group of men who, over the first few centuries of the church, sought to guide the believers in their quest to honor God. It is true that their writings are not Spirit inspired and they occasionally drifted away from pure apostolic instruction. However, their united views on certain doctrinal topics offer valuable insight into how the early church understood the words of the apostles.

Individual Doctrinal Issues

It is not the purpose of this book to address every doctrinal conflict that exists. These numerous debates date back centuries and they will, no doubt, continue until Jesus returns. Rather, it is an attempt to uncover the reasons for these differences, offering the reader the tools necessary to consider his/her personal doctrinal views and how they may or may not harmonize with God's Word. The focus will be on the rationale behind various doctrines, how they have come to be, and what might be done to garner from the words of Scripture exactly what it is that God intends for mankind to learn.

Certain individual doctrines will be discussed. The issues that will be considered – spiritual gifts, election, and baptism – have sparked some of the most contentious theological debates in modern times. While many will dispute some of the conclusions in this work, the hope is that each reader will appreciate the author's attempt to treat Scripture with respect. In each case, a sincere effort has been made to abide by the principle of *sola scriptura*, which is discussed at length in the first chapter, and employ principles of interpretation as evenly and objectively as possible.

Section I
Approaching God's Word

Chapter 1

Sola Scriptura

Evidence of God

A great number of men and women believe in God as the creator of the world and all that exists within that world. This creation includes everything from the one-celled ameba to the photosynthetic world of plant life, to the complex intricacies of the human body (physical, mental, and emotional), and even to the sophisticated and far-reaching gravitational interaction of planets and galaxies. If everything was created by God, this says much, not only about his unequaled power, but also about his authority over that which he has created. It is fair to say that what he has created, he owns.

Why do people believe that God exists and that he created the world? The answer, in a nutshell, is that they have faith in these truths. It is easy to scoff at the idea of believing in a seemingly invisible God; but those who scoff fail to recognize that faith in God is not blind faith. He has provided abundant evidence of his existence and his authority.

The first and most obvious support for the existence of God is life itself and the world that sustains that life. The very fact that life exists forces acknowledgement that it came from something or someone. Recognition of this truth leads to the realization that the source of life, whatever that may be, has always existed, since something cannot come from nothing. That is an impossibility that *would* require blind faith.

Evidence of the Sufficiency of Scripture

In complement to the existence of life as evidence of the role of God in creation, there are historical records about God's relationship with his creation. It is true that much of this history is found in Scripture, but that is sufficient for a couple of reasons. The first reason is that other historical writers stand as witnesses in support of the truth of Scripture. For instance, the *Babylonian Chronicles*, which were penned over a period of several hundred years beginning in the eighth century B.C., support the biblical account of Nebuchadnezzar's dealings with the Israelites in the sixth century B.C., as well as several other biblical records. In addition, the works of Cornelius Tacitus (A.D. 55-120), one of the best-known and most respected historians of first century Rome, served to reinforce the historical accuracy of Scripture. In his writings he told how the Roman emperor Nero:

> ...inflicted the most exquisite tortures on a class...called Christians. ...Christus [Christ], from whom the name had its origin, suffered the extreme penalty during the reign of Tiberius at the hands of one of our procurators, Pontius Pilatus....[1]

Similarly, Flavius Josephus, a Jewish historian (A.D. 38-100+), wrote about Jesus in his work entitled *Jewish Antiquities*. Countless historical works offer compelling support for the integrity of God's Word.

Beyond historical writings, strong archeological evidence speaks to the truth of Scripture. Sir William M. Ramsey (1851-1939) held several esteemed positions at Oxford University beginning in 1885 and was considered "...the foremost authority of his day on the topography, antiquities, and history of Asia Minor in ancient times."[2] He originally set out to challenge the reliability of Scripture. However, after a quarter century of travels and studies, he admitted:

> It may be stated categorically that no archeological discovery has ever controverted a single biblical reference. Scores of archeological findings have been made which confirm in clear outline or in exact detail historical statements in the Bible.[3]

Scripture as God's Word

For those who accept that the Bible is true, it is a simple step to believe that God created all that exists, since this is a claim found in God's Word (Genesis 1: 1-31). Scripture teaches that God is eternal (Psalm 90: 2; 93: 2). He is also all-knowing (Psalm 147: 4-5) and all-powerful (Revelation 19: 6), both of which are inevitable traits for the creator.

Scripture says much about God's character. It teaches that he is holy (Isaiah 6: 3; 1 Peter 1: 16) and that he loves (1 John 4: 8). The

---

[1] Tacitus, A. *Tacitus on the Christians*. http://www.livius.org/cg-cm/christianity/tacitus.html.
[2] Anderson, J. G. C. *Dictionary of National Biography 1931-1940*, "Sir William Mitchell Ramsey," 727.
[3] Glueck, Nelson. *Rivers in the Desert: A History of the Negev*, 31, citing Sir William M. Ramsey.

Bible teaches that God deeply loves his creation and that he has a special affection for mankind, whom he created in his own image (Genesis 1: 26-27; John 3: 16).

The Bible is self-described as the vehicle through which God has revealed his will to humanity. It is true that, in times past, he occasionally interacted with humankind in a more direct fashion; but the means available in the church age to know the will of God falls upon faithful study of his Word. It is there that he has provided direction concerning what he expects from those created in his image and how life can be lived in a manner that honors God.

If the Bible is God's Word for mankind, it stands to reason that the information found there must be error free. After all, it has been received from an error free God (Matthew 5: 48). Not only does Scripture provide an understanding of God's will, but the Bible offers complete revelation concerning those things God deems important. Everything a person needs to know about God and his relationship with mankind is available within the pages of Scripture.

The Principle of Sola Scriptura

Scripture is filled with warnings about false teachings. It is a lesson addressed in several books of the New Testament. For example, Jesus warned his disciples, "See to it that no one misleads you" (Matthew 24: 4). Similarly, John warned the early Christians, "…make sure no one deceives you" (1 John 3: 7), and the Apostle Paul cautioned the disciples in Ephesus, "Let no one deceive you with empty words" (Ephesians 5: 6). In his letter to the Colossians, Paul wrote, "See to it that no one takes you captive through philosophy and empty deception, according to the tradition of men, according to the elementary principles of the world, rather than according to Christ" (Colossians 2: 8). He told the Galatians, "But even if we, or an angel from heaven, should preach to you a gospel contrary to what we have preached to you, he is to be accursed! As we have said before, so I say again now, if any man is preaching to you a gospel contrary to what you received, he is to be accursed!" (Galatians 1: 8-9). As is obvious from these writings, the apostles anticipated that troublemakers would come along who would pervert God's instructions and attempt to lead believers astray.

Paul warned the youthful Timothy to beware of false teachings (1 Timothy 1: 3; 6: 3). He also told him to persevere when it comes to sound doctrine (1 Timothy 4: 16), a lesson he also shared with Titus, who was another of his disciples (Titus 1: 9; 2: 1). Paul's words lead to the undeniable conclusion that, when it comes to doctrine, true and false do exist.

Since Paul warned the first century disciples to not only avoid, but to rebuke false doctrine, they must have had the means available to distinguish between true and false doctrine. Consequently, there must be a resource available so that believers can know the difference. Such a resource must be both authoritative and understandable. That source, according to the apostle, is Scripture (2 Timothy 3: 16-17). The Bible is profitable for teaching that which is true and rebuking that which is false.

The Bible is not mankind's only source of knowledge about God. Holy Writ represents direct revelation from God, but there is also an abundance of indirect revelation concerning the Heavenly Father. According to Scripture, God's nature can be *clearly seen* in the created world he has provided.

> [18] For the wrath of God is revealed from heaven against all ungodliness and unrighteousness of men who suppress the truth in unrighteousness, [19] because that which is known about God is evident within them; for God made it evident to them. [20] For since the creation of the world His invisible attributes, His eternal power and divine nature, have been clearly seen, being understood through what has been made, so that they are without excuse. (Romans 1: 18-20)

God makes it clear that he can be known even without the Spirit-inspired words of the Bible. It is evident that he cares for his creation since he is a loving God who provides rain and sunshine so that even the flowers of the field may prosper. Yet, through the words of Scripture, there is much more to know about him than could ever be learned by studying nature.

Since the first century, the writings of the apostles and those under their guidance have been recognized as Holy Spirit-inspired. Unfortunately, even with the availability of apostolic instruction, over the course of time, many questionable traditions developed within the Roman Catholic Church. *Sola scriptura* (from the Latin, meaning *by scripture alone*) is a principle that grew out of the Protestant Reformation in the sixteenth century aimed at challenging what many considered unbiblical practices of the RCC. The goal was to end suspicious church customs that were not supported by God's Word. Yet, if information about God is available elsewhere, exactly what does *sola scriptura* mean?

The phrase does not suggest that the Bible is humanity's only source of information about God. *Sola scriptura* simply identifies Holy Writ as the sole and final authority concerning the things of God in relation to his creation (2 Timothy 3: 16). In other words, the Bible is the definitive Word of God *to mankind*. As such, it is the sole source of authority with respect to doctrine. Any belief concerning man's relationship with God that Scripture does not support must be considered unreliable and rejected accordingly.

The Apostle John, in his closing remarks in the book of Revelation, offers a somber warning to those who might consider altering the written word.

> [18] I testify to everyone who hears the words of the prophecy of this book: if anyone adds to them, God will add to him the plagues which are written in this book; [19] and if anyone takes away from the words of the book of this prophecy, God will take away his part from the tree of life and from the holy city, which are written in this book. (Revelation 22: 18-19)

While this passage seems to focus, to a large degree, on the words of the book of Revelation, in a broader sense, it complements other passages that address the sufficiency of Scripture as a whole. For instance, Moses taught the Israelites about the worth of Scripture (Deuteronomy 31: 9; 32: 46-47). Also, Jesus' teachings were based solidly upon Old Testament Scripture. He looked to the Old Testament as an unimpeachable source of authority (Mark 12: 10; John 7: 38), as did the apostles (Acts 1: 16; Romans 10: 11). Also, Paul emphasized the substantive character of God's Word in his words to Timothy, mentioned earlier (2 Timothy 3: 16).

Those books that comprise the New Testament were recognized as Spirit-inspired quite early. Peter wrote about the scriptural authority of Paul's letters, equating them with "…the rest of the Scriptures" (2 Peter 3: 16). In his first epistle to Timothy, Paul cited some of Jesus' remarks (1 Timothy 5: 18), as recorded in Matthew's and Luke's gospels (Matthew 10: 10; Luke 10: 7), treating those words as authoritative. Also, the apostolic fathers fully embraced the authority of the books that were eventually canonized. It may be argued that the New Testament consists of those works that *could not be denied inclusion*, given the apostolic support they received.

Those who embrace the principle of *sola scriptura* teach that Christian beliefs must be drawn from the Bible as the authoritative Word of God. The Bible has been provided as a roadmap to God. It offers directions so that people can lead lives that will honor him. Therefore, from this point forward, every discourse with respect to doctrine will be considered with the principle of *sola scriptura* in view.

Internal Scriptural Conflict

Respect for the consistency of Scripture is critical to the *sola scriptura* approach to doctrine. God's Word will not contradict itself when it comes to doctrinal instruction, although it does complement itself; so quite often insight into one passage will be enhanced or clarified by another. The foundation for the idea of biblical unity is the belief that God, through the hands and minds of men, ultimately authored the Bible from beginning to end. Since God would never disagree with himself, the lessons of Scripture must harmonize.

One of the challenges men face in light of *sola scriptura* and biblical harmony is the fact that, in a candid comparison, certain passages *could* be interpreted in such a manner that they appear to contradict one another. This has been the source of a host of doctrinal differences. When this happens, the dogmatic student of Scripture might pit the Bible against itself, insisting that one passage of Scripture is right, and the other is wrong. However, the better approach, in fact the necessary approach when considering what seem to be conflicting passages of Scripture, is to reason how the passages can harmonize. It is generally a matter of giving the context of a passage due consideration, since failure to recognize the biblical landscape can lead to much confusion.

One example of doctrinal conflict lies in the teaching of the doctrine of unconditional election. According to this view, God predetermined, before the creation of the earth, who would receive eternal life. In contrast to this view, others insist that God has given mankind free will to live life as each one sees fit, including whether or not to follow him and accept his offer of grace.

Some surface tension exists in Scripture where this topic is concerned, and people on each side of the debate can find verses to bolster their viewpoint. In this instance, God's Word includes passages that speak boldly of free will while others do, indeed, address the doctrine of election.

[18] "Speak to Aaron and to his sons and to all the sons of Israel and say to them, 'Any man of the house of Israel or of the aliens in Israel who presents his offering, whether it is any of their votive or any of their **freewill** offerings, which they present to the LORD for a burnt

offering-- ¹⁹ for you to be accepted--it must be a male without defect from the cattle, the sheep, or the goats.'" (Leviticus 22: 18-19) Emphasis added.

So then as through one transgression there resulted condemnation to all men, even so through one act of righteousness there resulted **justification of life to all men**. (Romans 5: 18) Emphasis added.

The Lord is not slow about His promise, as some count slowness, but is patient toward you, **not wishing for any to perish** but for all to come to repentance. (2 Peter 3: 9) Emphasis added.

²⁹ For those whom He foreknew, He also predestined to *become* conformed to the image of His Son, so that He would be the firstborn among many brethren; ³⁰ and **these whom He predestined**, He also called; and these whom He called, He also justified; and these whom He justified, He also glorified. (Romans 8: 29-30) Emphasis added.

⁵ He **predestined us to adoption** as sons through Jesus Christ to Himself, according to the kind intention of His will, ⁶ to the praise of the glory of His grace, which He freely bestowed on us in the Beloved. (Ephesians 1: 5-6) Emphasis added.

One might count those passages that discuss free will or the availability of God's grace to all of mankind and weigh that number against those that speak of predestination/election. Then, based strictly on volume, it could be argued that the principle addressed more often in Scripture must carry more weight, doctrinally speaking; but that would defeat the purpose. This is an example of setting Scripture in opposition to itself. The objective is to grasp the biblical harmony that exists in these seemingly conflicting passages to be true to God's Word. In light of the principle of biblical harmony, the use of the term *freewill* in the Leviticus passage (above) cannot frustrate the meaning of *predestined* in the eighth chapter of Romans. Similarly, in whatever manner God "predestined us to adoption" (Ephesians 1: 5), it cannot encroach upon Paul's teaching concerning "…justification…to all men" (Romans 5: 18) or Peter's claim that God does not want "…any to perish" (2 Peter 3: 9).

It is vital, when considering assorted doctrinal views and the biblical passages from which they are derived, to seek to discover the harmony that exists between various portions of Scripture. This is the only way men can fully and honestly receive the message God intends to deliver through his Word.

Chapter 2

Systematic Theology

The Science of Theology

To many readers, the title of this chapter probably sounds intimidating. However, the topic is not quite as overwhelming as one might imagine. Additionally, as much as is possible, the goal here is to help each person learn the best way to study God's Word and to provide those lessons in terms that are easily understood.

Like most words ending in *'-ology'*, the word *theology* can seem a bit daunting. Yet, as with other sciences like cosmology (the study of the universe), historiology (the study of history), meteorology (the study of the weather), paleontology (the study of fossils), and a number of other *-ologies*, theology can be gratifying even for the amateur theologian. What is theology? Here are some historical definitions of the term:

> ...the science about God and of the relations existing between him and his creation.[4]

> ...the science of God and of the relations between God and the universe.[5]

> ...any deliberate effort to learn and/or teach about God and his relation to his creation.[6]

The term *theology* comes from the Greek *theologia*, which itself is derived from two other Greek words: *theos* and *logos*. In the Greek language, *theos* means *god* and occasionally denotes man-made or false gods. For the purpose of this work, however, the word points to Yahweh, the God of creation and revelation, the Supreme Being. In the New Testament, this is the word that is used to identify God. Interestingly, the word *logos* can, in certain instances (John 1: 1;

---

[4] Byrum, Russell R. *Christian Theology, A Systematic Statement of Christian Doctrine for the Use of Theological Students*, 25.
[5] Strong, Augustus Hopkins. *Systematic Theology*, 1.
[6] Cottrell, Jack. *The Faith Once For All*, 9.

Revelation 19: 13), refer to Jesus himself. However, that is not how it is used when it appears in the word *theology*. In this sense it refers to using thoughtful reasoning to understand a topic.

Theology is essentially man's study of God, although it can be much more. After all, even if a person has complete knowledge about God, it is useless unless that knowledge can be applied effectively to some end. The best reason for seeking this knowledge is that it affords each individual the opportunity to develop a personal relationship with him. Thus, people cannot only know *about* God, but they can *know* God in a manner that is spiritually fulfilling.

God is not physical, but spiritual in nature (John 4: 24), so one must connect with him differently than that same person might interact with humans and other created beings. He has explained how each person can relate to him by providing detailed instructions (biblical doctrine) to follow. To affect that relationship, an individual must learn to respect and abide by the guidelines given. Therefore, an accurate understanding of his instructions is essential to achieve and maintain the kind of bond that he seeks with his creation.

The guidelines that God has established make clear that it falls upon each person to make certain decisions about their relationship with him. In fact, an individual can choose to forego such a relationship. However, if the choice is to have a loving relationship with God, which is what he seeks, it is important to fully grasp the nature of that relationship and honor any boundaries or conditions that have been established in order to fellowship with him. Proper understanding and treatment of the lessons of Scripture can make that happen.

Disciplined Theology

Now that a basic understanding of the make-up of theology has been attained, it is time to take this understanding to a higher level. That new level is the introduction of *systematic theology*. Ultimately, systematic theology is about what might be better termed *disciplined* theology that follows a reasonable *system*. In theory, the goal of systematic theology is to prevent personal bias and prejudices from playing an excessive role in the development of a belief system. If every person could study the Bible through an impartial lens, it is reasonable to believe that each one might come to similar conclusions about the lessons of Scripture.

Volumes have been written in an effort to establish a system of theology upon which all can agree. Sound systematic theology must be grounded in solid hermeneutics (the interpretation of scriptural texts). A reliable theological study should involve consistent application of the following hermeneutic principles:

1. When reading a passage of Scripture, the context of the material under consideration can dramatically affect the meaning of the text. Therefore, the immediate context, as well as the larger biblical landscape, must be given due consideration when determining the meaning of a statement or discussion.

2. It is important to consider the author's intent. In other words, what point is the writer attempting to make through a statement or the details of a biblical episode?

3. Reflecting upon the results and/or characters in a particular setting – especially the response of the audience involved – can help the student of Scripture understand what God wants him/her to take away from a verse or passage. No one should take away more, or less, from a passage of Scripture than the text has to offer. While inference is a legitimate tool of interpretation, one must avoid inferring something that is not found in the text.

Understanding Context

The context (situation/circumstances) of a biblical statement can dramatically affect its meaning. When it comes to understanding the complexities of the Bible, context can be quite involved. The literary context entails: 1) the subject matter of the chapter and book under consideration; 2) the situation behind the writing; and 3) the identity of those being addressed. For example, the focus of the gospels (the books of Matthew, Mark, Luke, and John) is on Jesus' ministry as well as his death, burial, and resurrection. Also, through his teaching that is recorded in these books, Jesus often provided insight into the character of the coming church age.

Following the gospels is the book of Acts. This book is unique in the New Testament in that it is transitional. It offers insight into the shift from the Abrahamic covenant to its fulfillment in the covenant of grace as Luke recorded the events surrounding the establishment of the church and the introduction of the Holy Spirit into the lives of Christians. The epistles, which are letters addressed to various churches or individuals, are intended to offer spiritual guidance to believers in the first century and throughout the entire church age. The context of each chapter and/or book, weighed against its surrounding biblical backdrop, is critical to the message it holds.

Paying attention to context is vital since, at times a verse may not mean what it plainly says. Context may fully alter the meaning of a verse, so no single verse or passage stands alone. For instance, following are some words from the narrative when Jesus and the disciples encountered a man who had been blind from birth:

> "Neither this man nor his parents sinned," said Jesus... (John 9: 3 – NIV)

Was Jesus making the claim that this man and his parents were sinless? Of course, that is not the case. He was responding to the following question from the disciples:

> His disciples asked him, "Rabbi, who sinned, this man or his parents, that he was born blind?" (John 9: 2 – NIV)

This is a case where the context of the statement radically affects its meaning. Jesus was not saying that this man and his parents had never sinned, even though that is a message easily derived from a candid reading of this single statement by Jesus. What he was saying is that their sins were not the cause of the man's blindness.

Discerning the Author's Intent

The Bible narrative has been given to humankind so that people can learn the lessons of God. In studying Scripture, it is important to consider the author's intent in a given setting. In other words: *What is the author trying to accomplish?* That message is generally linked to the overall theme of the letter/book that is being read.

Where the incident concerning the blind man (above) is concerned, fortunately the purpose of the story is spelled out twice. First, the objective of the gospel of John is revealed directly by the author:

> [30] Therefore many other signs Jesus also performed in the presence of the disciples, which are not written in this book; [31] but these have been written so that you may believe that Jesus is the Christ, the Son of God; and that believing you may have life in His name. (John 20: 30-31)

John's goal was to reveal to mankind the deity of Christ. He did this primarily through his presentation of the many miracles Jesus performed. The apostle also noted that he had only covered a small number of the works of Jesus.

And there are also many other things which Jesus did, which if they were written in detail, I suppose that even the world itself would not contain the books that would be written. (John 21: 25)

In the story of the blind man, Jesus explained to his disciples the reason this man had been blind from birth. The reason he gave is causally linked to John's purpose in writing the gospel of John.

> ¹As He passed by, He saw a man blind from birth. ² And His disciples asked Him, "Rabbi, who sinned, this man or his parents, that he would be born blind?" ³ Jesus answered, "*It was* neither *that* this man sinned, nor his parents; but *it was* so that the works of God might be displayed in him." (John 9: 1-3)

After speaking these words, Jesus healed the man. He spat on the ground and, mixing the saliva with dirt to make some mud, he placed the mud on the man's eyes. He then told the man to "Go and wash in the pool of Saloam" (John 9: 7). Once he had washed per Jesus' instructions, he received his sight.

Considering the Results/Audience Response

The purpose of the healing of the blind man is openly proclaimed by both Jesus and John. However, there are times in Scripture when the author's intent is not so clearly stated. On these occasions, it may be necessary to determine the intended lesson by considering the consequences or results of the incident. It is also wise to bear in mind the response of those involved when that response is made clear.

If Jesus and John had not plainly declared the purpose of Jesus' encounter with the blind man, it would still be relatively easy to identify John's intent in reporting this incident by reflecting upon what occurred as a result. The balance of the ninth chapter of John finds the apostle relating the reaction of the people in Jerusalem to the healing that had taken place.

Those who knew the man who had been healed were amazed at what had occurred. They were so amazed that they brought the man to the Pharisees. Noting that the healing had occurred on the Sabbath, the Pharisees were not amused (John 9: 16). Twice in the ensuing text they interrogated the man who had been healed, doing their best to counter the effect of the miracle among the people. However, the healed man was relentless in his support of Christ.

In the end, Jesus returned and affirmed his deity to the man he had healed as well as to the Pharisees who were with him (John 9: 35-41).

Since this is what occurred as a result of the healing, even if the apostle had not openly stated that intent, it could be reasonably inferred that it was his goal to reveal Jesus' identity to those involved in the narrative (the blind man and the Pharisees) and ultimately to all who read the gospel of John.

It is also possible to gain insight into the lessons of Scripture by considering how the audience responds to the written or spoken word when that response is documented. This is especially true in instances where the gospel message is presented. Some of these responses will be discussed in depth in an effort to gain insight into individual doctrinal issues. Most audience responses in the New Testament are reported in the gospels and the book of Acts, since these are *event* narratives. In contrast, the epistles are instructive letters that do not generally provide insight into the readers' responses.

Where Systematic Theology Falls Short

One of the inherent challenges presented by systematic theology is that theological systems are ultimately developed by human beings. It is fair to say that those people who are advanced sufficiently in their study of God's Word to devise a system of theology have already developed preconceptions and prejudices with respect to Scripture and the doctrine that is established there. In other words, a Baptist will fashion a method of theological study to fit Baptist beliefs. Similarly, a Methodist will write from the Methodist perspective, and a Roman Catholic will write from the RCC point of view. This is not meant to disparage the existence of these prejudices, but simply to acknowledge them.

> *One of the inherent challenges…is that theological systems are ultimately developed by human beings.*

In fact, the very work you now hold was penned by someone with certain admitted assumptions that have developed over time; but the goal is, as much as possible, to keep them in check and rely fully on God's Word for instruction. Still, it is important to recognize that these biases exist in any and every theological work.

Scripture contains many passages from which conflicting doctrines have developed. Some of these doctrines differ so significantly that harmony is not possible. Given the inerrancy and unified message of the Bible, it must be true that some of these views are not supported by God's Word. Hence, they must originate with people and their approach to Scripture. Yet, these conflicting doctrines creep into the various systems that so boldly claim to be unbiased. Therefore, most systems that exist fall short since they cannot be applied evenly across the whole of the Bible. Certain passages must be ignored, and others re-characterized because they do not harmonize with the doctrine that comes out of a particular system of theology.

The verses of Scripture can be manipulated to provide support for virtually any belief mankind can muster. However, the goal of honest students of the Bible is to learn what God wants to teach. A doctrine should be deemed acceptable only when the Bible *makes the case* for that doctrinal position. A person is on the right track when the doctrine he holds to be true harmonizes fully and freely with the entirety of God's Word.

Chapter 3

Principles of Interpretation

God Communicates Through Language

God has many forms of communication available to him, not the least of which is nature itself. Every day he can be seen in the beauty of the created world. History reveals that he also communicates through numerous events (e.g., the flood and the plagues). When it came to explaining his relationship with, and expectations for, mankind, he chose a simple form of communication. He selected the same tool he had established for men and women to communicate with each other. He used language.

God is the ultimate communicator. He knows and understands language better than anyone, since he is its creator. By inference, it is understood that he originally designed a language through which he and Adam could communicate (Genesis 1: 27-30). Later, he established assorted human languages and scattered those of like tongues across the globe (Genesis 11: 8-9).

Since God chose language as the primary means through which he would communicate his message of salvation to men, there is every reason to believe that he knows how to use words to make his point completely understandable. His use of both figurative and literal language is unmatched. When approaching God's Word, it is important to recognize that he has chosen words that best communicate what he wants to say and teach.

On the Day of Pentecost, God employed assorted languages to present his message to those in Jerusalem. Yet, each person who heard that message in his/her own language received the same lesson as those of other tongues. So efficient was God's use of language that day that he was able, via a host of languages, to present the gospel to everyone listening through the voices of twelve men.

Language is a form of science (linguistics) and, as with other sciences like mathematics and physics, has a distinct set of rules it must follow to be effective. For instance, if *eye* does not mean *eye* or *cloak* does not mean *cloak* (figurative language aside) any hope of communication is lost. Consequently, when reading the Bible, it is important to apply linguistic principles to the words that are written. It is also vital to understand that God, the very creator of language, wrote (through men) what he intended to write.

Understanding and Applying Principles of Interpretation

When it comes to understanding the Bible, it is necessary to approach Scripture with honesty and humility. If a man goes to God's Word to prove what he already believes, he will find a way to accomplish that goal, no matter how theologically sound or unsound that belief may be. A math teacher does not ask his students to add two and two together and *decide* on a sum. Instead, he wants them to *learn* that the unqualified answer to the equation is four. In that same vein, God did not provide the Bible so people could decide what it does or does not mean from a personal perspective (2 Peter 1: 20). The Bible was written so that people could learn what the apostles taught. That having been said, the first general rule to remember with respect to principles of interpretation is:

1. Interpret only when it is necessary.

In seeking to learn what God has to say, it is important to recognize that not every passage of Scripture requires robust interpretation. Part of the problem with conflicting doctrines is that people often spend their time vigorously interpreting a passage of Scripture when it is unnecessary. It is safe to assume, given God's unequaled capacity to communicate, that he has provided a book that needs little interpretation, particularly in matters of salvation. If God wants people to be with him eternally, as he says he does (2 Peter 3: 9), why would he force them to unearth a veiled message to know his will?

There is no reason to *force* interpretation upon the straightforward teachings found in the instructive writings of the apostles. While Jesus spoke mystically at times, that air of mystery applied primarily to those who lived prior to the covenant of grace (Matthew 13: 10-12). In modern times, the fullness of Scripture is readily available. Apart from the apostles, more recent believers have been offered a much clearer understanding of Jesus' teaching than those who listened to him while he walked the earth.

The words of the apostles provide considerable insight into the kingdom of heaven. Unlike Jesus' parables, the apostles' teachings are generally very direct. When an apostle introduces figurative language in Scripture, which happens quite often, its figurative nature is not that difficult to recognize (cf. Romans 11: 17-21; 1 Corinthians 3: 5-9; Galatians 4: 21-31). God placed upon their shoulders the task of *revealing* the kingdom to the nations, not hiding it from them. While Paul's epistles bear deep spiritual overtones, they are not written in cryptic code that only a few can understand, especially concerning matters of salvation.

Corinthians, Galatians, Ephesians, and other epistles were written to the general membership of the church body rather than an elite group of scholars and should be read with that in mind. Therefore, unless the context offers commanding evidence to the contrary, believers should embrace the apostles' words in the candid way they are written.

Men are not called to *interpret* the Bible. Instead, they are told to *study* God's Word (2 Timothy 2: 15). The word *interpret* appears in the New Testament nineteen times in some form (interpretation, interpreter, etc.). Yet, in none of these instances is personal interpretation of the Bible in view. Instead, the reader should let the Bible speak for itself. Most of Scripture is written in a manner that can be understood even by the young (2 Timothy 3: 15). For those who are prepared to commit the necessary time and effort, God has delivered his Word in a manner that makes clear those things he wants people to know.

That having been said, interpretation cannot be entirely dismissed since, at times, the Bible demands it. For instance, the parables call for a certain level of interpretation. However, when relying on the use of interpretation, it is important to apply sound interpretive principles in a reasonable manner. When interpreting a passage of Scripture, due consideration must be given to the context, the original intent of the author or speaker, and what the words would have meant to the audience at the time a statement was made. Personal beliefs must never be allowed to lead the way in interpretation. This leads to a second general rule of interpretation with respect to Scripture.

2. Be objective when applying interpretive principles.

Objectivity can be difficult to achieve. When someone views a passage of Scripture through a specific theological lens for a considerable length of time, impartiality becomes essentially impossible. For this reason, few are willing to revisit their doctrinal views, confident that their understanding of Scripture is right. To someone thoroughly entrenched in an unbiblical doctrinal view, a verse says what they believe it says. Other verses are then read through that same tinted lens and forced to agree while legitimate interpretive principles are set aside. This leads to the third and final general rule of interpretation relative to scriptural instruction.

   3. Do not try to force Scripture to harmonize. It will do this on its own.

The fundamental principle of biblical unity was discussed earlier. From Genesis through Revelation the Bible is unified. Scripture will not oppose itself despite the many voices claiming that scriptural conflicts exist. Consequently, biblical harmony does not need to be forced. Where apparent conflicts arise, it is generally a matter of various biblical authors writing from different perspectives. However, if it is necessary to rewrite a biblical author's words in order to force his teaching to harmonize with a personal understanding of other passages, it is safe to say that the view of one or more passages is flawed.

Objectivity – The Heart of Biblical Understanding

Maintaining objectivity can be a challenge since most people address the Bible with their doctrinal views fully intact. Considering certain passages without personal bias is a tall order, especially when conflicts arise over the meaning of those passages.

It should be obvious that certain passages of Scripture need no interpretation since the teaching is straightforward. Still, that does not mean that teaching should be taken lightly or just skimmed over without question. Every passage has meaning, and it is important to always consider how any scriptural teaching does or does not affect a person's relationship with God.

People are often taught lessons about Scripture by others, such as ministers and teachers. Yet how can someone know when to question those lessons? The answer is easy. Each individual should take personal responsibility and question every lesson they are taught. While Bible scholars and teachers can be a valuable resource in understanding Scripture, it is ultimately upon the shoulders of each person to learn the lessons God has provided in his Word. Is it possible, then, to know if these lessons are true? The truth can be found by asking oneself a series of *objective* questions about the text and reviewing the narrative to determine the answers to those questions.

The first question to ask when hearing and considering a lesson from the Bible is: *Does the Bible teach this lesson openly in the passage under consideration?* For instance, suppose a teacher proclaims that, according to the Apostle Paul, Christians are to love each other. In support of this teaching, he turns to the book of Thessalonians where Paul wrote:

> Now as to the love of the brethren, you have no need for *anyone* to write to you, for you yourselves are taught by God to love one another. (1 Thessalonians 4: 9)

Since the passage states explicitly that the Thessalonians are to love each other, the first objective question has been answered. However, that is not the only question to be asked. The next thing to consider is: *Does this teaching apply to all believers in the same manner that it applied to Paul's immediate audience?* This can be determined by examining whether the teaching is specific to the Thessalonians, or if it is a teaching that applies to Christendom in general. With the help of a good concordance, a relatively easy review of numerous passages about love can be undertaken. This exercise will reveal that Paul's lesson of brotherly love applies to today's believers just as much as it applied to the Thessalonians in the first century.

Lessons about love permeate the pages of Scripture. Therefore, the teacher has not led anyone astray. Believers are to love one another. This lesson could even be taken a step further by investigating what the Bible says about *how* that love might manifest itself. Still, because of the forthrightness of Scripture on this topic, there is no need for concern about the truthfulness of the teacher's comment.

The Objective Use of Inference

At times, people interpret the Bible in a manner that leads them to stray from the often-uncomplicated teaching found within its pages. Peter realized this would happen and warned the first century church to beware of those who would twist and distort God's message. Writing about Paul's epistles, Peter noted:

> ...as also in all *his* letters, speaking in them of these things, in which are some things hard to understand, which the untaught and unstable distort, as *they do* also the rest of the Scriptures, to their own destruction. (2 Peter 3: 16)

Confusion over the message of a given passage of Scripture often occurs when sound principles of interpretation are ignored or inconsistently applied. One way to wander from a reasonable interpretation of a passage is through what is known as inference; that is to say, a doctrinal conclusion may be derived from a passage even though it is not actually mentioned in a verse or passage. The use of inference in itself is not wrong. In fact, when applied correctly, it can provide additional insight into the message of a text.

Inference can take two distinct forms. First, there is *reasonable* inference. This means that, when reading a passage of Scripture, a truth can be reasonably determined even though it is not stated explicitly in the text. For instance, two thieves were crucified with Jesus. One thief ridiculed and mocked Jesus. The other, however, humbled himself before Christ, asking Jesus to remember him in the afterlife. Jesus responded by promising the man a place in his kingdom. Note, however, that nothing is said about the eternal fate of the other thief. Yet, despite this scriptural silence, it can be reasonably inferred (Luke 23: 39-43) that he did not share in the kingdom of God after his death.

There is also what is known as *necessary* inference. That is, a conclusion can be drawn that something *must* be true in a passage of Scripture even though it is not stated openly in the text. Consider the example of the woman named Lydia, to whom Paul taught the gospel message. Lydia was a woman who heeded the gospel (Acts 16: 14-15). Her immediate response to the message of the gospel, as spoken by one of God's teachers, was submission to baptism. The only possible explanation, the *necessary inference*, is that Paul directed her to submit to baptism as he presented the message of Christ, even though his specific words are not revealed in the narrative. She apparently considered baptism an act of faithfulness to God, freely noting that Paul could judge her faithfulness by her response to his teaching.

While inference can be an effective tool of interpretation, it can also be misused. Occasionally someone will assume something about a passage that cannot be reasonably drawn from the text and that does not harmonize with the balance of Scripture. Thus, it fails both the test of *reasonable inference* and *necessary inference*. This is unfortunately the source of much doctrinal disparity. To avoid the use of illegitimate inference, it is important to understand the sound principles respecting the use of this interpretive tool.

Once again, the reliability of inference can be determined through objective inquiries about the passage in question. However, when it comes to the use of inference, the questions might not be so easily answered as those concerning love that were mentioned earlier. Suppose, for instance, using the example of the Ethiopian eunuch, a teacher made the bold claim that, like the eunuch, an individual must repent of sins committed in order to be saved. He then offers the eighth chapter of Acts as evidence.

> [30] Philip ran up and heard him reading Isaiah the prophet, and said, "Do you understand what you are reading?" [31] And he said, "Well, how could I, unless someone guides me?" And he invited Philip to come up and sit with him. [32] Now the passage of Scripture which he was reading was this:
>
> "HE WAS LED AS A SHEEP TO SLAUGHTER;
> AND AS A LAMB BEFORE ITS SHEARER IS SILENT,
> SO HE DOES NOT OPEN HIS MOUTH.
> [33]"IN HUMILIATION HIS JUDGMENT WAS TAKEN AWAY;
> WHO WILL RELATE HIS GENERATION?
> FOR HIS LIFE IS REMOVED FROM THE EARTH."
>
> [34] The eunuch answered Philip and said, "Please *tell me*, of whom does the prophet say this? Of himself or of someone else?" [35] Then Philip opened his mouth, and beginning from this Scripture he preached Jesus to him. [36] As they went along the road they came to some water; and the eunuch said, "Look! Water! What prevents me from being baptized?" [37] [And Philip said, "If you believe with all your heart, you may." And he answered and said, "I believe that Jesus Christ is the Son of God."][7] [38] And he ordered the chariot to stop; and they both went down into the water, Philip as well as the eunuch, and he baptized him. [39] When they came up out of the water, the Spirit of the Lord snatched Philip away; and the eunuch no longer saw him, but went on his way rejoicing. (Acts 8: 30-39)

As before, this begins by asking the first in a set of objective question: *Does the Bible teach this lesson openly in the passage?* This time the text does not state, as the teacher has suggested, that the eunuch repented of his sins. In fact, the text does not state explicitly that the eunuch was saved, complicating the matter even more. In other words, using inference, the teacher has concluded not only that the eunuch repented of his sins, but that he received salvation.

---

[7] Verse 37 is not present in all Greek manuscripts, which is why it is missing from some well-known English Bible translations (e.g., ESV, NIV, NRSV, RSV).

This leads to a second question, which is: *Does the Bible at any time refute the claim?* In other words, does any passage of Scripture deny that the eunuch repented of his sins? A thorough search of God's Word will fail to unearth any such passage. While the Bible does not state explicitly that the eunuch repented of his sins, neither does it deny the claim. Therefore, the question must be asked: *Can one infer from either the immediate narrative or the scriptural landscape whether the eunuch was saved?*

In considering this question, the first thing to consider is the eunuch's response to Philip's teaching. The eunuch was baptized. Scripture defines baptism as the moment of forgiveness (Acts 2: 38; Colossians 2: 11-14) and salvation (1 Peter 3: 21). The narrative also states that the eunuch "...went on his way rejoicing" (v. 39). By considering scriptural instruction about salvation, and comparing that instruction to the current narrative, it can be determined that salvation was the cause of the man's joy (v. 39). Still, this says nothing of the man's repentance. Thus, the follow-up question must be asked: *Can one infer from either the immediate narrative or the scriptural landscape whether the eunuch repented of his sins?*

A study of repentance in the New Testament reveals the plain biblical truth that, short of repentance, a man cannot be saved (Luke 13: 3; Acts 2: 38; 3: 19; 17: 30). The teacher's understanding of Scripture has led him to infer, justifiably, that the eunuch repented of his sins even though this aspect of his conversion is not recorded in the text. This would have been an important part of Philip's message and a significant element of the man's conversion.

The final question is: *Does this teaching apply to other believers in the same manner that it applied to the eunuch?* Those passages that speak of repentance portray it as something required of every man, regardless of his station in life or the century in which he lives. The fact that no one can be saved without repentance explains the teacher's position that, like the eunuch, each one who hopes for eternal life must repent of sins committed.

Inference can be a valuable tool in studying and understanding the lessons of Scripture. However, inference must always yield to the plainspoken word. If a lesson that is derived through inference contradicts the clear message contained within a passage, or the inferred lesson does not fit the context, it is most likely due to interpretive bias. The use of inference requires objectivity in the study of God's Word. Doctrinal impartiality when addressing biblical teachings can help the serious student of Scripture to avoid misunderstanding the words and lessons of God's Word or inferring what the text does not permit. Asking the kinds of questions presented in this section affords Scripture the respect it deserves.

Words Have Meaning

The fact that *words have meaning* may seem to be an obvious and, therefore, unnecessary observation, but it is a principle that deserves earnest attention. In fact, perhaps this expression should be restated to say that *words have purposeful meaning*. The focus of this principle is on legitimate characterization of biblical words or phrases. Numerous theological slants have been born from the practice of discounting, amending, or disregarding uncomplicated biblical instruction.

One of the most troublesome aspects of this principle for the modern student of Scripture lies in the fact that God's Word was originally written in koine Greek and ancient Hebrew. This fact has opened the door to a deluge of creative biblical analysis. Often a seemingly knowledgeable individual will propose that a Greek or Hebrew word *could* take on a special (and often unfounded) meaning in a certain context and wonder of wonders, a new and unbiblical doctrine is born.

No word of Scripture is insignificant. When the apostles put ink to papyrus, they did so with confidence and purpose. That is the entire point of John's warning about adding to or taking from the written word (Revelation 22: 18). Scripture is Holy Spirit-inspired. Thus, any line of reasoning that compels someone to *improve* upon a single word or thought in a passage, straining the natural meaning of the text within the context of the material, automatically loses its biblical footing.

With respect to the New Testament, it is always best to determine the meaning from the original Greek text. However, most English-speaking people are unfamiliar with the language, so they must rely on English translations; but this is not an insurmountable obstacle for those who seek doctrinal truth. The foremost role of a translator, beyond interpreting words between languages, is to ensure that, once translated, the meaning of the text remains true to its origin.

While there are exceptions in certain instances, for the most part, English Bible translations are true to the original languages. However, it is always best to compare various translations, especially when it comes to complicated passages, to see if there is a consensus among the different versions. Where assorted translations are in harmony, it is generally safe to say that the wording rendered in English reflects what was written in Greek. Where these translations offer varying interpretations, deeper study is required.

Difficult Biblical Passages

Within the pages of Scripture, certain passages can be difficult to understand. This is partly due to cultural differences between the first century and the modern age. It also occasionally involves imprecise interpretation caused by language barriers, since some words and phrases do not translate well, but these are not the only factors. Paul was a colorful author as were others like James and John. Consequently, the Bible student will occasionally encounter verbiage that makes it challenging to fully grasp the author's or speaker's meaning. However, rather than seeking out complementary Scripture to provide greater insight into a complicated passage, some take the opportunity to invent a new doctrine. They superimpose a questionable meaning onto an obscure statement and walk away with a point of view that is inconsistent with the balance of God's Word. That is why opposing views have developed concerning things like original sin, the papacy, baptism for the dead, and a host of other doctrinal issues.

When encountering a passage of Scripture that seems difficult to understand, the proper response is to learn what Scripture generally has to say about the subject in question. Passages over which people tend to quibble include discussions about spiritual gifts (1 Corinthians 13: 8-13), election (Ephesians 1: 3-6), apostacy (Hebrews 5: 4-6), the role of women in the church (1 Timothy 2: 15), baptism (John 3: 5), and others.

Not one of these passages stands alone. The Bible is abounding with testimony on each of these topics. Therefore, no verse or passage should be considered *the* source of doctrine on any subject. When a verse is difficult to understand, it is best to set it aside and consider what the balance of Scripture teaches on the subject. The difficult verse should then be measured against those with less complicated wording to determine how *both* can be true. In this way, biblical harmony and doctrinal truth will prevail.

Handling Difficult Passages

Recognizing the existence of certain challenging Bible verses, it seems wise to set guidelines for how to deal with them. How can anyone be confident in their understanding of the author's intent where the meaning is difficult to grasp?

First, in a setting where the doctrine is not essential, everyone can relax a bit since it is not a redemptive matter. Even if someone fails to completely understand the teaching involved, it will not affect that person's salvation. Still, that does not make it any less puzzling or the reader any less curious. Thus, some guidelines might be helpful. Following are three tests that can help a student of the Bible avoid drawing conclusions from difficult verses that are well off the mark. A good place to start is 1 Timothy 2: 15 – a passage many people believe is one of the most challenging verses of the Bible.

> But women will be saved through childbearing—if they continue in faith, love and holiness with propriety. (1 Timothy 2: 15 – NIV)

It is easy to see why this is considered a difficult text. In English translations, given what is known about salvation and the birthing process, this passage makes no sense. Since so many views of the meaning of this verse exist, there will be no attempt to solve the mystery at this time. However, consideration will be offered to demonstrate how to apply interpretive principles to this verse in order to avoid false conclusions.

1. The meaning must be reasonable.

This is a common-sense test. For instance, since the statement in question is specific to women, no attempt should be made to derive any lesson about men from these words. That would be unreasonable. Paul has much to say to the young Timothy concerning men, but not in this verse. Conclusions about the lesson offered here should fit comfortably within the words. Drawing conclusions about males from a verse where they are not discussed stretches the fabric of the remarks beyond what is reasonable.

2. The meaning must fit the context of the passage.

When facing a challenging biblical text, it helps to consider what topic is under consideration by the author. In this instance, Paul is helping Timothy to better understand the distinctive roles of men and women in a congregational setting and why those roles exist. Therefore, Paul's point about women and childbearing must be related to that topic in some fashion.

3. The meaning must harmonize with the balance of Scripture.

This is critical. The fact that a passage of Scripture is difficult to understand does not give license to develop a doctrine from that passage or verse that conflicts with the general and specific themes in God's Word. It is always best to search for other passages where similar topics are in view. In doing so, the answer may be discovered. At the very least, however, no legitimate conclusion can contradict the whole of Scripture.

Even though scholars and laymen alike disagree about what Paul is saying in this verse, most agree on what he is not saying. He is not suggesting that women receive eternal salvation by having a baby. This kind of conclusion finds no support in Scripture and stands in stark contrast to biblical instruction about the path to eternal life (cf. Matthew 28: 19-20; John 3: 3-5, 16; Acts 2: 21, 38; 3: 19; 4: 12; 16: 31; Romans 10: 13; Ephesians 2: 8). Therefore, childbirth (at least in the common physical sense) can be ruled out as a matter of spiritual salvation.

For those who are interested, Paul gives greater insight into the role of women in the church in the fifth chapter of 2 Timothy. Still, it is unlikely that everyone will unite around a single meaning for this verse through the balance of life on earth, but when considering these words, it will be helpful to always apply the three criteria mentioned above. This will not always lead to *the* correct answer in a difficult text, but it can help the concerned Bible student avoid the pitfalls that have, over time, led to questionable teachings.

Proof Texting

When a debate over differing doctrines arises, it is not unusual, and has even become common practice, for each one involved to begin offering those passages of Scripture that appear to support his/her view. Each will offer passages that, when interpreted in a specific fashion, help to bolster their doctrinal stance. Both believers are equally confident in their doctrinal views.

> He chose us in Him before the foundation of the world, that we would be holy and blameless before Him. (Ephesians 1: 4)

> ...that if you confess with your mouth Jesus *as* Lord, and believe in your heart that God raised Him from the dead, you will be saved. (Romans 10: 9)

Proof texting has brought much division when it comes to doctrine. That is because, in every case, each person gives greater weight to his/her proof texts. Someone who sees election as God's unqualified pronouncement regarding who will be saved will place greater weight on passages like Ephesians 1: 4. However, for those who believe salvation involves the choices of men, Romans 10: 9 takes precedent. They may not say that one verse eclipses another, and they may not openly teach that one verse is more important, but that is the way these passages are treated when it comes to proving doctrine.

That is not to say that people should not turn to individual verses or passages to garner biblical doctrine. The very purpose of God's Word is to reveal his will to mankind. However, there is a considerable difference between *learning* and *proof texting*. Seeking understanding requires accepting all biblical teaching. Proof texting pits the Bible against itself. It entails accepting the teaching of some passages and denying/revising others.

Every verse – every word of Scripture is Spirit-inspired. It does not fall upon individuals to choose between them. Therefore, whatever lesson is taught in Ephesians 1: 4 is undeniably true. The same may be said about Paul's words in Romans 10: 9. They were even written by the same hand. Not only are both passages true, but they are intended to complement each other. That is the character of God's Word. It is not up to people to decide which passage is correct or which teaching should prevail. The goal must be to determine how they harmonize. Only by deriving a doctrine that fully expresses the spiritual truth of both passages without distorting what is written can a person be somewhat confident that they have gleaned from the text what the author intended.

Literal vs. Figurative Use of Language

Much literature is filled with figurative language and the Bible is no exception. From the poetry and hyperbole of the Psalms to the metaphoric eloquence of the prophets to the parables of Jesus, figurative language fills the pages of Scripture. Unfortunately, this has led many to presume the presence of such imagery in passages where it is not intended or insist that a figurative comment should be taken literally. This has, in turn, led to doctrines that are inconsistent with the lessons God intends to deliver through his Word.

In his work, *Principles of Interpretation*, Clinton Lockhart highlights several rules that are invaluable for those seeking to grasp scriptural truths. In that work, he mentions a couple of interpretive principles relative to figurative language that can help people avoid misunderstanding Scripture.

Rule: - Before interpreting a passage, determine whether it is literal or figurative.[8]

A prime example of figurative language is found in the varied uses of the word *circumcision* that appear in both the Old and New Testaments. Circumcision, which involves the physical removal of the male foreskin, was given to the Israelites as a sign of the covenant God established with Abraham (Genesis 17: 11). The Jews practiced this rite faithfully in keeping with the terms of the covenant. The following verses speak of the sign of circumcision that God gave to Abraham:

> [26] In the very same day Abraham was circumcised, and Ishmael his son. [27] All the men of his household, who were born in the house or bought with money from a foreigner, were circumcised with him. (Genesis 17: 26-27)

> And He gave him the covenant of circumcision; and so *Abraham* became the father of Isaac, and circumcised him on the eighth day… (Acts 7: 8)

However, consider the following passages that address circumcision in a much different way:

> So circumcise your heart, and stiffen your neck no longer. (Deuteronomy 10: 16)

> Moreover the LORD your God will circumcise your heart and the heart of your descendants, to love the LORD your God with all your heart and with all your soul, so that you may live. (Deuteronomy 30: 6)

It should be evident even to the layman that these verses from Deuteronomy represent a use of the word *circumcise* that sets aside its literal meaning. In the first passage, having one's heart circumcised is equated with *no longer being stiff-necked* (Deuteronomy 10: 16), suggesting that an uncircumcised heart reflects an obstinate attitude toward God. The figurative use of the word in the expression "circumcise your hearts" implies a heart that no longer resists God. Just as removed foreskin no longer impedes the seed of a man, the circumcised heart is unimpeded in its desire to fellowship with God. Because the literal meaning of the word does not, and cannot, fit the

---

[8] Lockhart, Clinton. *Principles of Interpretation Revised Edition*, 51.

context in Deuteronomy, diligence must be employed to understand what the writer has in mind. Here, as in most cases, the author has graciously provided the meaning he intended.

When imagery is employed in Scripture, its figurative character, as with other literature, is generally evident to the reader. The Apostle Paul was known for his use of figurative language and Jesus offered parables to explain the character of the kingdom of God to his listeners. Although a word or phrase can be used figuratively at times, that does not affect the import of that same terminology in a setting where the literal meaning is clearly intended.

Common vs. Uncommon Use of Language

Closely related to the *Literal vs. Figurative Use of Language* is the *Common vs. Uncommon Use of Language*. While the two are kindred when it comes to understanding the meaning of biblical words, they are not the same. The first weighs figurative speech while the second seeks to consider the most appropriate contextual use of words that can be applied in numerous ways. Lockhart addresses this point, stating:

> Rule: - The literal or most usual meaning of a word, if consistent, should be preferred to a figurative or less usual signification.[9]

Although words are often employed figuratively in Scripture, the figurative use of a word in one instance does not give anyone license to supplant a literal meaning with a figurative meaning in another instance when the literal meaning fits the context. For example, the Hebrew *kabac* refers to bathing in water for the purpose of purification in the Old Testament (Exodus 19: 10; Leviticus 11: 24-28). That is the literal meaning of the word. Yet, there are times when this word is used in a manner that depicts a spiritual cleansing, as in the following verses:

> Wash (kabac) me thoroughly from my iniquity and cleanse me from my sin. (Psalm 51: 2)

> Wash (kabac) your heart from evil, O Jerusalem, that you may be saved. How long will your wicked thoughts lodge within you? (Jeremiah 4: 14)

---

[9] Ibid., 160

The atypical use of the word with respect to spiritual cleansing does not alter the fact that *kabac* normally indicates a washing that involves the physical substance of water. That is the most common use of the word. Therefore, when *kabac* appears in Scripture, absent sufficient contextual reasons to insert an alternate meaning, the word's literal and most used meaning must be applied.

At times, a word may carry one common meaning in other settings (e.g., colloquial English) while the most common meaning in Scripture is completely different. For instance, *rent* is something that is paid in exchange for the right to use property that belongs to another; but, in certain versions of the Bible where this word is employed (KJV, NKJV, etc.), this is not the common meaning. In these Bible translations, the word refers to *tearing*, appearing as the past tense of *rend*, as depicted in the following excerpts:

And Joshua **rent** his clothes… (Joshua 7: 6 – KJV) Emphasis added

And, behold, the veil of the temple was **rent** in twain from the top to the bottom… (Matthew 27: 51 – KJV) Emphasis added

Since this reflects the ordinary usage of the word in these versions of the Bible, when *rent* is encountered in these translations, unless the context points to something different, it must be assumed that some kind of tearing is taking place.

The word *host* carries different common meanings even within the pages of God's Word since different Greek words are translated into English as *host*. It can refer to someone who is hosting an event (Gr. *ho keklēkōs*), or it may point to a group, esp. an army (Gr. *stratias*). The following verses portray these uses:

But when you are invited, take the lowest place, so that when your **host** (ho keklēkōs) comes, he will say to you, 'Friend, move up to a better place.'… (Luke 14: 10 – NIV) Emphasis added.

Suddenly a great company of the heavenly **host** (stratias) appeared with the angel… (Luke 2: 13 – NIV) Emphasis added.

In each of these cases, the Greek drives the meaning of the word *host* while the context explains the meaning. In the first instance, it would be unreasonable to assume that the word refers to a *great number*, since it clearly depicts an individual. In the next verse it depicts a *multitude* (an army) of heavenly beings. Honestly applying the meaning of a word in context can prevent an individual from overriding the author's meaning by inserting his own thoughts into the text.

Apostolic Repetition and Biblical Harmony

In Scripture, when a doctrine is addressed repeatedly by the same author, it stands to reason that his words in a particular passage will complement what he has written elsewhere on the same subject. In other words, he will not contradict himself. For instance, what Paul taught the Corinthians about spiritual gifts will not conflict with his words to the Romans on the same subject. The same holds true when two different biblical authors address the same topic. According to Lockhart:

> Rule: - Two or more statements by honorable authors relating to the same thing should, within reason, be interpreted harmoniously. [10]

The apostles have provided instructions that are not only intended to be clear, but fully supportive of each other. This idea ties in nicely with biblical unity that was discussed earlier. Recognizing the doctrinal harmony that exists especially among the apostles is vital to understanding the message of the New Testament. Thus, what Peter wrote about baptism and predestination must harmonize fully with Paul's words on these topics.

The Holy Spirit and Scripture

Men often misunderstand the Holy Spirit's role when it comes to understanding God's Word. It is reasonable to believe that, as people study Scripture, the Holy Spirit can help each one to learn and appreciate spiritual truths (1 Corinthians 2: 8-16). Identified by Jesus as the "…Spirit of truth" (John 14: 17; 15: 26; 16: 13), the Holy Spirit can provide an individual with a better grasp of Holy Writ that will enhance that person's walk with God. However, some believe the Spirit will also lead them to discover not just deep spiritual truths through diligent study, but *personalized* doctrinal truths through revelation. Thus, they have developed doctrines that eclipse the words of Scripture, insisting that they have been guided by the Spirit to take an innovative doctrinal stand.

The Roman Catholic position on baptism clashes with the Baptist view even though each group insists that the doctrine they teach is faithful to Scripture. However, it is not possible for *both* teachings to

---

[10] Ibid., 145

be biblically true. If *infant baptism* is scripturally sound doctrine, as Roman Catholics proclaim, the Baptist stance insisting that baptism is meant only for believers must be considered false. If *believer's baptism* by *immersion only* is biblically sound doctrine, the other view cannot be. They are at odds with each other.

The Holy Spirit does not assist individuals in developing *conflicting* doctrines through special revelation or exceptional individual insight into the words of the Bible. On the contrary, his role is one of unity, including doctrinal unity. In fact, the Holy Spirit is considered by the Apostle Paul to be a unique *unifying* element where Christianity is concerned (Ephesians 4: 3-4). He is not divisive. Furthermore, God would never author opposing doctrines (1 Corinthians 14: 33).

The Holy Spirit's function where doctrine is concerned was to reveal one truth to those men who authored the Bible (John 16: 12-15; 1 John 4: 6). They, in turn, penned the doctrine of God in terms that everyday people could understand. That doctrine, the doctrine of *the faith*, was then delivered to mankind once for all (Jude 1: 3). It is up to each believer to learn the doctrine of God through study and not through revelation. Therefore, the many incompatible doctrines that have captivated the minds of men cannot be attributed to the Holy Spirit.

Chapter 4

Doctrinal Significance

The Weight of Doctrine

Not every doctrine is created equal. There are both *essential* and *non-essential* doctrines. Essential doctrines are those causally linked to spiritual salvation. For instance, belief in Jesus as the Son of God is an essential doctrine since, according to God's Word, a person's salvation is reliant upon that belief (Acts 16: 31).

Prayer, on the other hand, is not deemed an essential doctrine in Scripture. The Bible offers instruction about prayer but does not dictate how much time a person should spend in prayer each day. Paul encouraged the disciples to pray continually (1 Thessalonians 5: 17), but his lesson is about a prayerful attitude and not about how long a person should remain on his/her knees in a twenty-four-hour period.

What distinguishes the weight of the doctrine of prayer from that of belief in Jesus? Prayer is a relational doctrine. In the Bible, prayer is not linked directly to salvation, but it is a significant matter when it comes to a person's spiritual well-being and his/her relationship with God. While those who spend more time in prayer will develop a closer walk with God due to their abundant contact with him, Scripture does not teach that the Christian who prays more than another receives a greater portion of eternal life.[11]

Similarly, believers are taught to do good works (Ephesians 2: 10). These works are also relational in that they tend to reflect a person's faith in God (James 2: 18). Perhaps the man who prays to God less than his brother actually performs an abundance of good works. No proportional rule for prayer and works is offered up in Scripture. Doctrine concerning prayer and works are about believers honoring God with their lives. They are not depicted as matters of salvation in God's Word (Ephesians 2: 8-10). That having been said, someone who has *no* prayer life and performs *no* righteous deeds as a matter of

---

[11] Many teach of varying levels of heavenly rewards. This statement concerning eternal life is not intended to address that particular topic.

honoring God would do well to consider strongly his/her measure of faith (James 2: 17).

This same line of reasoning can be applied to various other doctrines. For instance, some partake of the Lord's Supper weekly based upon the example of the early church that is found in God's Word (Acts 20: 7). Others participate less often, perhaps monthly, or quarterly. When biblical instruction surrounding this rite is given honest consideration, it becomes evident that no *command* to partake of communion on the first day of each week is given. Additionally, Scripture does not limit the observance of the Lord's Supper to that day. It is generally accepted that Jesus introduced this meal to his disciples on a Thursday evening. By and large, scholars agree that the purpose of meeting together on Sunday in the first century was to pay tribute to the Lord's resurrection, which had occurred on that day.

Scripturally speaking, no one can insist that observing the Lord's Supper every Sunday is an essential doctrine, since the apostles fail to give it that level of distinction. That means no one can judge too heavily those who do not partake on a weekly basis. However, it is plain to see that this was the practice of the early church as they were guided by the apostles. Therefore, while following their example may not be deemed vital to salvation, it seems that the apostles viewed this as a splendid opportunity to regularly honor Jesus' death on the cross (1 Corinthians 10: 16). Indeed, it is given as the very reason for their gathering (cf. Acts 20: 7). Since there is nothing to prevent it, following the apostolic model in this case seems both reasonable and proper and an excellent opportunity to honor God, modeling modern worship after the fashion of the early church.

Managing Essential and Non-Essential Doctrine

As discussed earlier, objective questions are essential to understanding the Bible from God's perspective. However, along with the need to ask objective questions, it is crucial to seek honest answers to the questions that are asked. Answering an objective question with a biased response defeats the entire purpose of the exercise. Honesty and objectivity must walk hand in hand when considering the words of Scripture. Following are some objective questions that might help when confronted with a doctrinal matter in a passage of Scripture.

The first question to be considered focuses on understanding biblical teaching about the significance of the doctrinal issue(s) under consideration. The question should generally be aimed toward New Testament instruction. The Old Testament provides a firm foundation for the covenant of grace. However, it is in the New Testament that instruction is received from Christ and the apostles concerning the church age. Therefore, the following question leads the query:

1. Is the teaching in question an essential doctrine?

When approaching any biblical teaching, the first thing to consider is whether the principle being discussed is a matter of essential doctrine or reflective of the freedom believers enjoy in Christ. How can the significance of a doctrine from a biblical perspective be determined? The first thing to consider is whether biblical teaching connects the doctrine to salvation in any way. If the teaching is tied to the words *saved* or *salvation*, in a spiritual sense, it is time to pay close attention to what is being said, since this most likely involves a study of an essential doctrine. A link to salvation can also be identified by the presence of other phrases that are salvation–related including, but not limited to, forgiveness, redemption, rebirth/renewal, eternal life, etc. Those points of doctrine that are scripturally tied to salvation carry significant weight.

As a matter of practical application, it might help to put the question concerning essential doctrine to the test. For instance, consider whether confession of Jesus as Lord is, in fact, an essential doctrine according to Scripture. Using a respectable concordance, it is not difficult to locate those passages where confession is discussed.

[32] Therefore everyone who confesses Me before men, I will also confess him before My Father who is in heaven. [33] But whoever denies Me before men, I will also deny him before My Father who is in heaven. (Matthew 10: 32-33)

Fight the good fight of faith; take hold of the eternal life to which you were called, and you made the good confession in the presence of many witnesses. (1 Timothy 6: 12)

[8] But what does it say? "THE WORD IS NEAR YOU, IN YOUR MOUTH AND IN YOUR HEART"--that is, the word of faith which we are preaching, [9] that if you confess with your mouth Jesus as Lord, and believe in your heart that God raised Him from the dead, you will be saved; [10] for with the heart a person believes, resulting in righteousness, and with the mouth he confesses, resulting in salvation. (Romans 10: 8-10)

The idea of confessing Jesus as Lord eclipses the notion of a singular statement and encompasses living in a manner that demonstrates that Jesus is Lord of one's life; but the biblical connection between salvation and open confession of Jesus before witnesses cannot be overlooked. According to Paul, a verbal confession is made "resulting in salvation" (Romans 10: 10). The connection between confession and salvation that is displayed within these verses could not be more direct. It is fair to say, then, that confession of Jesus as Lord must be considered an essential doctrine.

It is vital to first determine the essential or non-essential character of any biblical doctrine. When a teaching is determined to be essential, there is no excuse to ignore it. Once it is determined that a certain teaching is, in fact, essential to salvation, any studying surrounding that doctrine should be considered in that light.

2. If the doctrine in question is deemed essential, what does God expect from humankind relative to that doctrine, according to Scripture?

While God's Word offers much doctrinal instruction, it is also true that people manipulate the words of Scripture to develop views that are inconsistent with biblical teaching. Combating the tendency of spiritual leaders to *enhance* or *improve* biblical doctrine – even essential doctrine – with personal views is only half the battle, since teachers are not the only culprits. Paul explained that some of the blame for false doctrine lies with the listeners. He told Timothy that some would seek for themselves teachers who offer words and lessons they *desired to hear*, regardless of biblical accuracy.

> [3] For the time will come when they will not endure sound doctrine; but *wanting* to have their ears tickled, they will accumulate for themselves teachers in accordance to their own desires, [4] and will turn away their ears from the truth and will turn aside to myths. (2 Timothy 4: 3-4)

It is important to eagerly seek biblical instruction, but it is equally important to refrain from seeking out those who simply teach what is pleasing to the ear. Like the people in Berea, whom Luke described as "…more noble-minded than those in Thessalonica, for they received the word with great eagerness, examining the Scriptures daily *to see whether these things were so*" (Acts 17: 10-11), believers must take seriously the lessons of God's Word. The Bereans were respected because they not only hungered after the message of God, but they held to a lofty standard anyone who claimed to teach God's truth. They were unwilling to entertain any teaching that did not harmonize with the inspired words of Scripture, even scrutinizing thoroughly the teachings of the Apostle Paul.

Approaching any doctrine, especially one that is considered essential, involves, first and foremost, determining what the biblical authors had to say on the subject. Modern-day believers are blessed to have available a multitude of tools such as concordances and numerous Bible translations that can aid in a topical undertaking. However, one of the most valuable tools people have available is common sense. When reading a passage of Scripture, one's initial response to the words (not including footnotes) is quite often the most honest. Lockhart states this principle as follows.

> Rule: - The simplest and most natural interpretation of a passage must be preferred.[12]

If the wording in a passage is straightforward, and a certain meaning is easily drawn from the text based on that frankness, in most cases that view probably represents the author's intent. It is likely the same meaning that was understood by those to whom the words were originally spoken or written. This principle assumes, of course, that full consideration is given to the context of the passage as well as any figurative language (metaphor, hyperbole, etc.) that might be used. Additionally, no passage can be exempted from harmony with the balance of Scripture, which must always be given consideration.

Salvation (i.e., eternal life) is the ultimate result of faith in God and a primary motive for studying the Bible. Therefore, passages that provide instruction concerning redemption are essential and must be treated with the utmost respect when examining God's Word. These passages explain what God expects from mankind where salvation is concerned. Therefore, when it comes to essential doctrine, always follow the apostles' instructions.

Non-essential doctrines are those where people have flexibility, such as prayer and works. However, a doctrine's non-essential status does not make it irrelevant. When it comes to these doctrines, one must ask:

---

[12] Lockhart, Clinton. *Principles of Interpretation Revised Edition*, 81.

3. If the doctrine in question is deemed non-essential, how can I apply this doctrine in my life in a way that best honors God?

The more time spent with God in prayer, the more likely it is that a person will develop a deeper relationship with him. Similarly, abundant good works done for others in Jesus' name can provide a believer with greater opportunities to win people to Christ. Those two are relatively simple to understand. However, not all doctrines are so easily applied.

It is clear from Scripture that gluttony displeases God. King Solomon offers some particularly harsh language condemning gluttony (Proverbs 23: 2, 20, 21; 28: 7). Thus, it stands to reason that someone who wishes to honor God will avoid it. Yet how much is too much? What if someone overeats…just a bit? At what point has a person crossed over the line and dishonored God? It is issues like this where individuals must make decisions when applying biblical doctrine on a personal level.

Abundance of Biblical Instruction

Another tool that may be used to determine the importance of a teaching or topic is found in the abundance of instruction that is available in Scripture pertaining to that subject. For example, much of Jesus' teachings focus on man's relationship with money, wealth, etc. This is true of several of the parables (Matthew 13: 22; 18: 21-35; Luke 16: 19-24) as well as some of his more intimate teaching moments.

> And Jesus, looking around, said to His disciples, "How hard it will be for those who are wealthy to enter the kingdom of God!" (Mark 10: 23)

> For where your treasure is, there your heart will be also. (Luke 12: 34)

Similarly, the apostles spend much time in the epistles of the New Testament warning the early Christians about the danger of being seduced by earthly riches. While Scripture does not link wealth directly to salvation (or condemnation), Jesus and the apostles often talked of the dangers of greed and materialism.

> For the love of money is a root of all sorts of evil, and some by longing for it have wandered away from the faith and pierced themselves with many griefs. (1 Timothy 6: 10)

> [1] Come now, you rich, weep and howl for your miseries which are coming upon you. [2] Your riches have rotted and your garments have become moth-eaten. [3] Your gold and your silver have rusted; and their rust will be a witness against you and will consume your flesh like fire. It is in the last days that you have stored up your treasure! [4] Behold, the pay of the laborers who mowed your fields, and which has been withheld by you, cries out *against you*; and the outcry of those who did the harvesting has reached the ears of the Lord of Sabaoth. [5] You have lived luxuriously on the earth and led a life of wanton pleasure; you have fattened your hearts in a day of slaughter. [6] You have condemned and put to death the righteous *man*; he does not resist you. (James 5: 1-6)

The abundant biblical teaching concerning a person's attitude toward money (e.g., self-indulgence vs. generosity) provides important insight into the kind of character God expects to see in his followers. Therefore, due to the emphasis placed upon this topic in God's Word, each one should consider carefully all biblical instruction with respect to earthly possessions.

All scriptural instruction is important, since the Bible is God's Word to mankind, so the teaching offered there must never be diminished. Additionally, certain teachings are more causally related to eternal fortune than are others. All teaching must be kept in perspective, all the while respecting, and thanking God for the message he has delivered.

Summary on Approaching God's Word

The evidence of God's existence and his inspiration of Scripture is exceptionally reliable. If then, God is the creator and the Bible is his guide for individuals to have a relationship with him and gain eternal life, it is critical to consider seriously the guidance he has offered. Since the Bible is God's source of information to humankind concerning his will, treating both the source and the instructions with great respect is crucial. Believers must not only receive spiritual instruction from the Bible, but they must receive that instruction from the Bible *only*, rejecting teachings that do not harmonize fully with God's Word.

From cover to cover the Bible is harmonious and complementary. It is always wise to be cautious of teachings that set the Bible in opposition to itself – pitting one passage against another. This approach to Scripture most certainly results in skewed doctrine. Seeking harmony among various segments of Scripture will generally provide an individual a much better grasp of the lessons God intends.

It is easy, and even tempting, to derive teaching from the pages of Scripture that is biased, based upon what more learned people have taught. Yet, when it comes to biblical understanding, humans are a flawed species. Accepting teachings that conflict with instructions found in God's Word has become standard practice for many. In fact, people have arguably reached the point, and beyond, about which Paul wrote to Timothy, where many doctrinal teachings are offered in an effort to satisfy personal desires, teaching people exactly what they wish to hear.

The Bible was not written to an elite group of scholars, nor was it encrypted with a secret code that must be uncovered. It was written to average Christians and should be received in that light. When approaching God's Word, it is important to set aside doctrinal biases as much as possible. Each one must be willing to shun beliefs that conflict with apostolic teaching and accept instruction from the Bible, rather than superimposing personal doctrinal views onto the pages of Scripture.

God's Word was written to provide solid, demonstrable answers and not a variety of options from which people can choose. Much of the doctrinal disparity that has developed over the course of time has been driven by two basic elements. The first is that many, unsatisfied with the lessons of Scripture, seek out new meaning from the words of the apostles (2 Peter 1: 20). Once dissatisfaction sets in, so, too, does the second element, which is a disregard for honorable interpretation of God's Word (2 Peter 3: 16). Those who wish to glean from Scripture the lessons God intends must be watchful concerning misleading doctrine.

> [16] All Scripture is inspired by God and profitable for teaching, for reproof, for correction, for training in righteousness; [17] so that the man of God may be adequate, equipped for every good work. (2 Timothy 3: 16-17)

When it comes to addressing doctrinal issues, it is wise to be as objective as possible – setting aside preconceptions. No one should assume that a doctrine is true or false without knowing what Scripture has to say. Instead, in the spirit of *sola scriptura*, biblical instruction on the subject must be given serious consideration and beliefs must be built on that foundation alone.

Section II
Spiritual Gifts

Chapter 5

Now Concerning Spiritual Gifts

The Continuation/Cessation Divide

Before he ascended to heaven, Jesus promised to send the Holy Spirit to mankind as a helper and teacher (John 14: 26). When the Spirit arrived (Acts 2: 1-4), he provided the believers with some extraordinary tools known as *spiritual gifts*. These gifts enabled Christ's followers to perform incredible, miraculous feats so that unbelievers might be persuaded of the legitimacy of the gospel message they proclaimed (i.e., extraordinary works of wonder, miraculous healings, and speaking in tongues) and believers could receive instruction and edification (tongues and interpretation, knowledge, wisdom, discernment, and prophecy).

A fracture has developed among students of the Bible over the many spiritual gifts that are credited to the work of the Holy Spirit. The schism rests primarily on the question of whether these signs and wonders (e.g., prophecy, tongues, healing, etc.) were intended to outlive the apostles of the first century. Those who believe extraordinary gifts ceased with the apostles are labeled *cessationists*, while those who claim that the gifts continue even today are known as *continuationists*. Their differences are difficult to overcome given the deep-seated and emotional character of that divide.

The tension that envelops this discussion is further fueled by the fact that there is no middle ground. The positions held by these competing camps are irreconcilable since, by their very nature, they cannot coexist. If God's Word teaches that miraculous gifts ended with the apostolic age, the belief that they continue today is, by default, unscriptural. On the other hand, if it is discovered that these special gifts were intended to continue throughout the life of the body of Christ here on earth, then the view that they ended in the early stages of the church must be summarily dismissed.

A History of Spiritual Gifts

Extraordinary works were in play at various levels long before the church was established. For instance, Old Testament prophets spoke on God's behalf for centuries prior to Jesus' arrival on earth; although it would be more accurate to say that God spoke through the prophets. That is the nature of inspired prophecy. An additional characteristic of the Old Testament prophets was their inerrancy. Apart from certain eschatological prophecies that are yet to be realized, no prophecy from God fell short of meticulous fulfillment (Deuteronomy 18: 21-22).

Seventeen of the thirty-nine Old Testament books are considered prophetic, but even those deemed historical or poetic in character are riddled with prophecies and the fulfillment of those prophecies. On occasion, prophecies came directly from the mouth of God, such as those delivered to Adam, Eve, and the serpent (Genesis 3: 14-19) or his promise to Abraham that he would have a son (Genesis 15: 4). However, God commonly employed prophets to deliver his words to the people. From Abraham (Genesis 20: 7) to Malachi, the prophets testified concerning the things of God – at times proclaiming God's will and often declaring his warnings or punishments. Some prophecies were simply announcements while others concerned future events. Certain futuristic prophecies were given and fulfilled in short order. Other prophecies saw either partial or complete fulfillment in the first century with the coming of Christ (Isaiah 9: 6-7) and the establishment of the church (Joel 2: 28-32). Still others remain unfulfilled yet today.

While creation and the flood came directly from the hand of God, he also worked through Moses and the prophets to demonstrate his power by the myriad of miraculous works he had them perform. For instance, the plagues of Egypt were the tool God employed, through the hand of Moses (Exodus 7: 10-12: 30), to free the Israelites, not to mention the fact that he parted the Red Sea (Exodus 14: 21-31) and delivered water from a rock in Horeb (Exodus 17: 5-7). God worked a multitude of miracles through his prophet Moses for all the Israelites to see.

Through God's servant Joshua, the Israelite people witnessed the parting of the Jordan River (Joshua 3: 14-17) and the crumbling of the mighty walls of Jericho (Joshua 6: 6-20). They even watched as the sun stood still in the sky for an entire day at Joshua's command (Joshua 10: 12-14). Shadrack, Meshak, and Abed-nego were rescued from the fiery furnace (Daniel 3: 19-27), and the Lord sent an angel to close the mouths of the lions as Daniel sat helpless among them (Daniel 6: 16-23). Countless other miracles permeate the pages of the Old Testament as God used his power to influence the minds and hearts of men.

The Old Testament writers also bear witness to several healings. As an example, Naaman, a captain in the Aramean army, sought out Elisha, having heard that the prophet might possess the power to heal his leprosy. Indeed, Naaman was healed as he washed in the Jordan River seven times, per Elisha's directive (2 Kings 5:1-14). Additionally, Elijah (1 Kings 17: 17-24) and Elisha (2 Kings 4: 32-35) each raised a young man from the dead by the power of God.

Tongues (the speaking of unlearned languages) are also found in the Old Testament, but not in the same sense that they are experienced in the New Testament. The introduction of the multitude of human languages present in today's world is found in the Old Testament. The original empowering of tongues took place when God, angry at the pride exhibited by those who were created in his image, "…confused the language of the whole earth; and from there the LORD scattered them abroad over the face of the whole earth" (Genesis 11: 9).

Prophecy was also fulfilled when Jesus came to earth. While on earth he performed a host of miracles and healings among men. His ministry lasted only about three years, but during that time he turned water into wine (John 2: 1-11), cast out demons (Mark 1: 21-28), healed a great many who were sick (Matthew 8: 1-3; Luke 4: 38-40; John 4: 46-54), raised some from the dead (Luke 7: 11-17; 8: 41-55; John 11: 1-44), fed multitudes with virtually no food (Mark 8: 1-10; John 6: 5-14), and much more. The Bible records nearly forty distinct miracles performed by Jesus during his ministry on earth. Yet, other statements testify even more to the vast wealth of his miraculous works:

> …they brought to Him many who were demon-possessed; and He cast out the spirits with a word, and healed all who were ill. (Matthew 8: 16)

> Many followed Him, and He healed them all. (Matthew 12: 15b)

> [30] Therefore many other signs Jesus also performed in the presence of the disciples, which are not written in this book; [31] but these have been written so that you may believe that Jesus is the Christ, the Son of God; and that believing you may have life in His name. (John 20: 30-31)

> And there are also many other things which Jesus did, which if they were written in detail, I suppose that even the world itself would not contain the books that would be written. (John 21: 25)

The Nature of Spiritual Gifts in the Church

Before diving too deeply into a discussion on spiritual gifts in the church age, it is important to distinguish between *miracles* and *miraculous spiritual gifts*, since there is a significant difference. *Miracles* are those things beyond the natural capacity of human beings – things only possible through what could be considered unearthly powers. God has performed numerous miraculous works by his own hand, including creation and the flood. *Miraculous spiritual gifts*, on the other hand, constitute a subset of miracles in general. These gifts, or at least those involving inexplicable manifestations, represent God's empowerment of individual human beings, through the work of the Holy Spirit, to perform miraculous works of their own accord in the church age. These include speaking in unlearned languages, miraculous healings, the proclamation of godly truth through prophecy, and more.

For the purpose of this work, as the miraculous is discussed, the focus will be on the spiritual gifts that have been bestowed on men. Therefore, any phraseology that is employed here such as *spiritual gifts*, *extraordinary works*, *miraculous*, or similar terminology, unless otherwise specified, is focused strictly on *miraculous spiritual gifts* in the church age.

Numerous *lists* of spiritual gifts are found in God's Word. However, even these lists have tended to divide believers over the nature and use of these gifts.

> [1] Now concerning spiritual gifts, brethren, I do not want you to be unaware. [2] You know that when you were pagans, you were led astray to the mute idols, however you were led. [3] Therefore I make known to you that no one speaking by the Spirit of God says, "Jesus is accursed"; and no one can say, "Jesus is Lord," except by the Holy Spirit. [4] Now there are varieties of gifts, but the same Spirit. [5] And there are varieties of ministries, and the same Lord. [6] There are varieties of effects, but the same God who works all things in all persons. [7] But to each one is given the manifestation of the Spirit for the common good. [8] For to one is given the word of wisdom through the Spirit, and to another the word of knowledge according to the same Spirit; [9] to another faith by the same Spirit, and to another gifts of healing by the one Spirit, [10] and to another the effecting of miracles, and to another prophecy, and to another the distinguishing of spirits, to another various kinds of tongues, and to another the interpretation of tongues. [11] But one and the same Spirit works all these things, distributing to each one individually just as He wills. (1 Corinthians 12: 1-11)

Paul's phrase, "Now concerning spiritual gifts" (v. 1), must be qualified since, in the Greek, the word commonly translated *gifts* (Gr. *charismata*) is not present. The word *pneumatikon,* which is rendered "spiritual gifts" in this setting, essentially means *the spirituals*, which seems to encompass the general topic of *spiritual things*. This suggests that it is not Paul's intent to focus solely on spiritual gifts. Rather, he uses the topic of spiritual gifts as a backdrop for his discussion of spiritual things. For instance, he addresses division and jealousy in the church that had developed over the use of these gifts. He also discusses the unequaled value of love within the kingdom contrasted against the limited utility of spiritual gifts.

No single grouping of spiritual gifts in the New Testament should be considered exhaustive. In this instance, Paul omits some gifts mentioned in other passages. There are other times when certain gifts mentioned here are absent. Each listing of spiritual gifts given in Scripture has a distinct flavor. In this current setting, the apostle recognizes three categories (for lack of a better word) that were present in the church at Corinth, all identified under the umbrella of spiritual gifts (v. 1).

Fully grasping Paul's meaning in the first few verses of the twelfth chapter of 1 Corinthians is critical to appreciating his lesson concerning the character and application of spiritual gifts. For instance, notice that he mentions what appear to be three distinct categories of spiritual gifts (gifts, ministries, and operations).

Paul employs the Greek word *diaireseis* to distinguish between the gifts. This word has been translated as *varieties* three times in this passage (vs. 4-6). However, the idea that this word signifies is probably better represented by the English word *distributions*, or *apportionments*.[1] There are, according to the apostle, *distributions* (apportionments) *of gifts* (v. 4), which evidently result in various supernatural occurrences such as healings and tongues, that extend beyond the natural laws and bestow upon believers the ability to perform extraordinary feats (miracles) of some kind. There are also *distributions of ministries* (v. 5), indicating a ministry of service. The word translated *ministries* is a form of the word that is rendered *deacon* in other passages (Philippians 1: 1; 1 Timothy 3: 10-13). In this context in the KJV, this word is rendered *administrations*, while the NIV uses the word *service*. Finally, Paul states that there are

---

[1] The Scripture4All Online Greek Interlinear Bible (NT) translates this word as 'apportionments.'

distributions of effects (v. 6), or operations, within the church that are fulfilled through the working of the Spirit.

There is some debate about whether certain gifts that Paul mentions here resulted in inexplicable manifestations of the Spirit while others did not. These verses in 1 Corinthians seem to strongly indicate that not all spiritual gifts involved miraculous manifestations. Therefore, for the purpose of this work, and to avoid confusion, the presumption will be that Paul has both miraculous and more ordinary gifts in mind given the lines of distinction he has drawn here.

What Paul has identified in this passage is the various ways the Holy Spirit works through men. Each of the distributions Paul addresses, whether gifts, ministries, or effects, is, in its own way, a significant manifestation of the Spirit. According to the apostle, everyone in the body participates in "the manifestation of the Spirit for the common good" (v. 7). Every believer receives an endowment from the Spirit in some fashion – some through miraculous workings of the Spirit, some through service skills, and still others through participation in the operations of the church. A. Allison Lewis explains the distinction as "…those (gifts), that is, which were distinctively gracious, and those which were distinctly miraculous."[2] Paul does not preclude someone who participates in a service ministry (e.g., deacon) from also displaying a miraculous manifestation of the Spirit, but neither does he require it.

While all three pertain to things spiritual, Paul's focus turns from ministries and effects to the numerous issues that have arisen within the congregation with respect to miraculous spiritual gifts, since this seems to be the source of a certain degree of division in the congregation. In doing so, he identifies some of those gifts, noting that they are always distributed for the profit of the kingdom (v. 7). Among these gifts are *wisdom* and *knowledge* (v. 8), the gift of *faith* and the ability to *heal others* (v. 9), the authority to *perform miracles*, the honor of *prophesying*, the ability to *discern spirits*, the gift of *speaking in unlearned languages*, and the power to *interpret* properly what someone else has said in another language (v. 10).

It is safe to say that each extraordinary spiritual gift mentioned in these verses enabled the person so endowed to extend beyond what would be considered normal human capabilities. Grouped alongside healing and miracles, the wisdom, knowledge, and faith that Paul calls *gifts* are surely bestowed by the Spirit at a level that eclipses the

---

[2] Lewis, A. Allison. *The Ceasing of the Charismata*, http://www.christianbeliefs.org/books/cm/cm- charisma.html.

wisdom, knowledge, and faith men can anticipate experiencing in ordinary day-to-day life. Later in this same chapter (1 Corinthians 12), Paul offers a separate list of spiritual gifts that is distinct from the first, even though they are proximate in the epistle.

> [28] And God has appointed in the church, first apostles, second prophets, third teachers, then miracles, then gifts of healings, helps, administrations, various kinds of tongues. [29] All are not apostles, are they? All are not prophets, are they? All are not teachers, are they? All are not workers of miracles, are they? [30] All do not have gifts of healings, do they? All do not speak with tongues, do they? All do not interpret, do they? (1 Corinthians 12: 28-30)

Paul has, in these verses, broadened the spectrum of spiritual gifts. He has reiterated the gifts of *prophecy*, *miracles*, *healing*, and *tongues*, but he has also identified a few other gifts. Most notably, *apostleship*, which most consider to be a unique office in the kingdom, heads the list of gifts in this passage. Also included are some, like *teachers*, *administrations*, and *helps* (helpful deeds), that are not generally associated with supernatural workings of the Spirit. These would be more strongly associated with the *ministries* and *effects* mentioned earlier in the chapter. Thus, Paul has included here all three kinds of gifts he mentioned earlier.

As before, Paul notes that these gifts/abilities are distributed prudently among the membership by the Spirit. For instance, not all are apostles and/or prophets. Similarly, not everyone is a teacher or a worker of miracles (v. 29), and a variety serve as healers or speak in tongues (v. 30).

In his words to the Ephesians, Paul supplements his teaching concerning the make-up of spiritual gifts. He confirms here the roles of apostle, prophet, and teacher, while giving evangelists and pastors similar designation.

> [11] And He gave some *as* apostles, and some *as* prophets, and some *as* evangelists, and some *as* pastors and teachers, [12] for the equipping of the saints for the work of service, to the building up of the body of Christ. (Ephesians 4: 11-12)

While the roles of apostles and prophets are known to involve extraordinary works of the Spirit, this is not necessarily the case when it comes to evangelists, pastors, and teachers. The final list to be considered, also among Paul's writings, is found in his letter to the Romans. Here the breadth of gifts is expanded even more.

⁶ Since we have gifts that differ according to the grace given to us, *each of us is to exercise them accordingly*: if prophecy, according to the proportion of his faith; ⁷ if service, in his serving; or he who teaches, in his teaching; ⁸ or he who exhorts, in his exhortation; he who gives, with liberality; he who leads, with diligence; he who shows mercy, with cheerfulness. (Romans 12: 6-8)

The oft-mentioned gift of *prophecy* leads the way in this instance. The gift of *service* that is mentioned here may be comparable to the gift of *helps* that was named in the Corinthians passage. The gift of *teaching* is also revisited. Additionally, Paul has identified the gifts of *exhortation, giving, leading,* and *showing mercy*.

These groupings of spiritual gifts strongly suggest that the work of the Spirit in the first century did not result in *miraculous* gifts for every believer. For some, the apportionment of the Spirit was found in a form of service or administration, for others a propensity to teach, and for others a penchant for helping those in need. Still others received the ability to perform rather remarkable works such as healing and prophesying. Each spiritual manifestation served a godly purpose, miraculous or not.

Historically, the church body has been blessed with a veritable smorgasbord of spiritual gifts all aimed at advancing the kingdom and assisting the membership in their desire to honor God. Yet, these numerous gifts raise as many questions as they answer. For instance, how were the gifts distributed to the believers? How were the gifts to be used, according to Scripture? Are any, or all, of these gifts still active in the church? These questions are challenging and are debated honestly by a multitude of people who simply wish to honor God.

Spiritual gifts are how God, through the work of the Spirit, assists those who seek to help him further the kingdom. Paul calls them appointments (1 Corinthians 12: 28) and they truly are that. Common sense dictates that different people be given different appointments. If everyone had the same gift, for instance, interpretation of tongues, its usefulness would be lost, since no one would be speaking those tongues that were meant for interpretation. Therefore, men and women are gifted (appointed) for a variety of ministries to complement each other's work, a principle that lies at the heart of the doctrine of spiritual gifts.

Since Paul's discourse concentrates on gifts that involved some miraculous manifestation of the Spirit, it is safe to say that these were the culprits causing a rift at Corinth, so these will be the focus for a time. Certain conclusions can be drawn about gifts from Paul's instructions to the churches (Romans 12: 6-8; 1 Corinthians 12: 14-26; Ephesians 4: 11). For example, it seems each gift was a manifestation of the Spirit that was tied to a person who was free to use the gift responsibly. When someone received some form of miraculous gift, such as speaking in tongues, prophesying, or healing, as with the more ordinary appointments of teaching and service, it was the responsibility of the gifted person to use the gift for the benefit of the entire body (1 Corinthians 12: 7).

Each one had control over the gift received and could use it at will. For this reason, tongue speakers and prophets were told to discipline themselves to avoid confusion in worship (1 Corinthians 14: 26-33). Presumably, healers could heal at will since this was certainly true of the apostles (Acts 3: 1-10; 28: 8). From these examples, it is evident that each gift was subject to the control of the gifted individual.

Scripture also suggests that these spiritual gifts were unmistakably identifiable. There is no indication that the believers were confused about who had each gift. Paul's concerns seem to focus on the jealousy of those who had received seemingly modest gifts and the haughtiness of those with more intriguing gifts like tongues or healing. Those who spoke in tongues knew they could speak in tongues. Those who prophesied were fully aware of the gift. The same was true of the healers, and it stands to reason that this was true of those with the gifts of knowledge, wisdom, and miracles, just as Paul was fully conscious of his gift of apostleship.

Finally, the gifts were effectual for the edification of the membership in general. The gift of tongues, which served the dual purpose of a sign to unbelievers (1 Corinthians 14: 22) and a means of revelation (Acts 2: 6), allowed a person to speak in unlearned languages in a revelatory manner. The interpreter, in turn, explained the nature of the message given via tongues (1 Corinthians 14: 5). A prophet did not simply offer an opinion or personal interpretation of godly inspiration. Scripture indicates that God used the gift to disseminate inerrant revelation through the prophecy that was given (Ephesians 3: 5). Similarly, knowledge, wisdom, and discerning of spirits should be understood as gifts of extraordinary illumination, although their use is not specifically addressed in the Bible as are tongues (Acts 2: 4; 19: 6), healing (Acts 9: 18), miracles (Acts 6: 8; 8: 6), and prophecy (Acts 21: 10-11).

The Apostolic and Early Church Fathers

The apostolic fathers, who were directly associated with the apostles, were discussed early in this work. It would be nice to be able to turn to these men and draw some conclusions concerning continuationism vs. cessationism. The fact that they lived during the apostolic age and received some of their instruction directly from the apostles puts them in a position to effectively settle this dispute. However, in their many writings, they are completely silent on the subject. Even though some of their letters were written to churches like Corinth and Ephesus where these gifts were experienced, there is no mention of the gifts in any of their letters. It is likely that their primary reason for ignoring the gifts in their writings is that the debate over continuation of the gifts had not yet begun.

The early church fathers – a group of post-apostolic church leaders – were also discussed earlier in this work. While spiritual gifts are mentioned in some of the works of the early church fathers, apart from Chrysostom (A.D. 347-407), none of these men wrote anything definitive about their doctrine concerning these gifts. Chrysostom, who lived most of his life in the fourth century, stated in his *Homily on John and 1 Corinthians* that the gifts had ceased. While this is significant, the words of a respected evangelist of the fourth century do not necessarily resolve the issue of continuation of the gifts. It may be considered noteworthy, however, that none of the apostolic fathers or the early church fathers ever claimed to participate in the miraculous gifts of the spirit. A. Allison Lewis notes:

> And so we pass on to the fourth century in an ever increasing stream, but without a single writer having claimed himself to have wrought a miracle of any kind or having ascribed miracle working to any known name in the church, and without a single instance having been recorded in detail.[3]

Spiritual Gifts and Essential Doctrine

Is teaching concerning spiritual gifts an essential doctrine? Scripture does not say that the gifts possess any redemptive qualities. Some believers were bestowed with miraculous abilities quite early in their Christian walk. For instance, some men from Ephesus received the gift of tongues shortly after being baptized in Jesus' name (Acts 19: 1-6). On the other hand, Luke wrote nothing about the Ethiopian eunuch (Acts 8: 26-40) or the Philippian Jailer

---

[3] Ibid.

(Acts 16: 22-40) ever participating in extraordinary gifts. Similarly, some of the believers in Rome evidently lacked spiritual gifts – a situation Paul hoped to remedy (Romans 1: 11). Yet, those who did not participate in the miraculous were saved. Therefore, participation is not essential to one's salvation.

Not everyone who boasted miraculous powers was faithful to God (2 Chronicles 33: 6; Jeremiah 14: 14; Zechariah 10: 2; 1 John 4: 1). Jesus and the apostles offered warnings about false apostles and prophets who would lead people astray (Matthew 24: 11; 2 Corinthians 11: 13; 2 Peter 2: 1). It is safe to say that such agitators live outside the comfort of God's grace notwithstanding their *giftedness*. As Jesus concluded his first sermon to the Jews, he addressed that very point:

> [21] "Not everyone who says to Me, 'Lord, Lord,' will enter the kingdom of heaven, but he who does the will of My Father who is in heaven will enter. [22] "Many will say to Me on that day, 'Lord, Lord, did we not prophesy in Your name, and in Your name cast out demons, and in Your name perform many miracles?' [23] "And then I will declare to them, 'I never knew you; DEPART FROM ME, YOU WHO PRACTICE LAWLESSNESS.'" (Matthew 7: 21-23)

Some have suggested that those mentioned in these verses were once faithful believers who lost their way and turned from Christ. Yet, that view is difficult to reconcile with Jesus' words, "I never knew you" (v. 23). He portrays these false miracle workers, who apparently believed they were doing God's will, as pseudo disciples who were never part of his kingdom. Additionally, these workers believed they were saved and were astonished that they would not receive their eternal reward. It is evident from the retort, "did we not" (v. 22), that Jesus was talking about people who believed they had been faithful.

This passage from Matthew seems to raise the stakes when it comes to participation in the miraculous in that, clearly, false gifts exist. The exact source of miracles is not mentioned in this text, but it seems clear that they were not from the Holy Spirit, since Jesus did not recognize these individuals as God's faithful (v. 23).

Since participation in the miraculous is not a matter of salvation, this should not be considered an essential doctrine, but there is a caveat. In Matthew's account of Jesus' hypothetical exchange with counterfeit disciples, Jesus does not deny that these pseudo disciples had performed what they claimed were miraculous works. However, what they saw as miraculous works performed in Jesus' name, Christ identified as *lawlessness* (v. 23). It seems that participating in miraculous works that are not from God may very well impact one's eternal fortune. This raises the question: *What is the biblical doctrine concerning miraculous spiritual gifts in modern times?*

If continuationists are correct in their view that spiritual gifts continue even today, believers must be on the lookout for false gifts and false prophets who try to mislead. However, it also means that cessationists are overlooking what could be a significant matter in their relationship with God. In that case, to honor God, they should reconsider their cessationist stand and seriously seek these gifts. On the other hand, if cessationists are correct, then the miraculous phenomena so widely accepted in this modern age are not the same as the gifts practiced by the first century church. If that is the case, continuationists should reassess their position, since participation cannot honor God and constitutes lawlessness in his eyes. These are the two possible outcomes in a debate that has, over the past century, frustrated Christian unity.

Biblical Harmony

While the principle of biblical harmony has been addressed at length, nowhere does this need to be stressed more than with the examination of spiritual gifts. On both sides of the debate, each one interprets assorted Scripture (e.g., Acts 10: 44; 1 Corinthians 12-14) to buttress personal beliefs (proof texting). Unfortunately, this is often accompanied by a sense of pride and satisfaction that someone else has, in their view, been proven wrong, and not that God has been glorified. This approach does not describe the use, but the abuse, of God's Word. Therefore, seeking biblical harmony concerning these gifts is critical so that credit can remain where it belongs – with God.

Still, Scripture can legitimately support only one of these views. Hence, each passage that addresses this subject must harmonize with every other passage where it is discussed. If an interpretation of a portion of God's Word fails to harmonize completely with all biblical teaching concerning spiritual gifts, then such an interpretation must be flawed.

The Day of Pentecost

Following Jesus' death, resurrection, and ascension, his followers began experiencing the miraculous power of the Spirit on the Day of Pentecost. On that day, the Holy Spirit was poured out upon men – an account with which most are probably familiar.

> ¹ When the day of Pentecost had come, they were all together in one place. ² And suddenly there came from heaven a noise like a violent rushing wind, and it filled the whole house where they were sitting. ³ And there appeared to them tongues as of fire distributing themselves, and they rested on each one of them. ⁴ And they were all filled with the Holy Spirit and began to speak with other tongues, as the Spirit was giving them utterance. (Acts 2: 1-4)

The continuation/cessation divide over spiritual gifts begins with the events that took place on the Day of Pentecost. In the narrative leading up to that day, Luke describes a meeting of roughly one hundred twenty disciples who gathered in Jerusalem to witness the selection of an apostle who could replace Judas (Acts 1: 15-26). Continuationists tend to believe that it was the one hundred twenty disciples who "were all together in one place" (v. 1). As a result, they teach that the way the Holy Spirit fell upon those who were present is normative for believers in the church age. Cessationists, on the other hand, teach that the Spirit fell only upon the apostles and that it was a most uncommon experience.

> *The continuation/cessation divide over spiritual gifts begins with the events that took place on the Day of Pentecost.*

In order to understand exactly who gathered together on that day and received the outpouring of the Spirit, one must determine who *they* were in the statement, "they were all together" (v. 1) in Luke's narrative. Based upon this phrase alone, the word *they* could legitimately apply to either the apostles or to the entire company of disciples. While the word translated *all* (Gr. *hapantes*) is masculine, it is usually employed rather broadly such that in itself it does not rule out the presence of women (cf. Luke 7: 16; Acts 2: 14). Therefore, this single statement cannot answer the question, which means the greater context must be examined for further illumination.

Those who believe that this incident involved all of the one hundred twenty disciples who were in Jerusalem at the time have failed to note the relevance of the surrounding text, as well as some complementary insights that are offered throughout the balance of the New Testament. In the storyline leading up to the Day of Pentecost, the spotlight is fully on the apostles:

> ²³ So they put forward two men, Joseph called Barsabbas (who was also called Justus), and Matthias. ²⁴ And they prayed and said, "You,

Lord, who know the hearts of all men, show which one of these two You have chosen [25] to occupy this ministry and apostleship from which Judas turned aside to go to his own place." [26] And they drew lots for them, and the lot fell to Matthias; and he was added to the eleven apostles. (Acts 1: 23-26)

Following this clear focus on the apostles, the very next verse states that "they were all together" as the Spirit was poured out, but that is not all. In the succeeding verses, additional information is provided concerning those individuals who addressed the crowd through *other tongues*:

[6] And when this sound occurred, the crowd came together, and were bewildered because each one of them was hearing them speak in his own language. [7] They were amazed and astonished, saying, "Why, are not all these who are speaking Galileans?" (Acts 2: 6-7)

All Galileans? Yes, the Jews of Jerusalem recognized that *every person* who was speaking in various languages on that day was of Galilean descent. Since Luke does not argue the point, it can be accepted as scriptural fact. This begs the question: *Who among the disciples in Jerusalem were of Galilean heritage?*

God's Word indicates that the apostles were from the region known as Galilee. This can be presumed concerning Matthias also, since he would have been among the apostles mentioned here, along with the fact that he had been with Jesus "...beginning with the baptism of John" (Acts 1: 22), which occurred in Galilee. It is also true that certain other disciples were Galileans as their backgrounds have been revealed at other times in the New Testament. These include Mary Magdalene, Jesus' family, and probably several other individuals, since Matthew wrote concerning Jesus' crucifixion, "...many women were there watching from a distance, who had followed Jesus from Galilee." (Matthew 27: 55).

Is it not possible that *all* one hundred twenty of the disciples were from Galilee? This is an implausible proposition given the diverse character of Jesus' followers. Some of Jesus' disciples were from Galilee, such as the apostles. However, according to Scripture, many were not.

Mary, Martha, and Lazarus were some of Jesus' closest friends (this is the Lazarus whom Jesus had raised from the dead just prior to his own death). These three lived in Bethany, which fell practically within the shadow of the walls of Jerusalem (less than two miles away). It is difficult to imagine any gathering of Jerusalem disciples that did not include them. It would have been most difficult to keep Mary from this kind of fellowship (cf. Luke 10: 38-42).

Simon the leper also lived in Bethany. Most Bible scholars agree that this is the man who returned to thank Jesus for his healing while the other nine went on their way (Luke 17: 11-19). Living on the outskirts of Jerusalem it is *highly* likely that Simon, a Samaritan, was among the disciples in Jerusalem.

Scripture mentions one disciple by the name of Joseph who hailed from Arimathaea. This is a stretch of land located in the region known as Ephraim between Jericho and Joppa. Joseph had given his tomb as Jesus' burial place (Matthew 27: 57). Since he had purchased a tomb in the area, it is likely he lived in Jerusalem at the time of the crucifixion. Therefore, as with Mary, Martha, and Lazarus, he was probably among the one hundred twenty disciples. Yet, he was not Galilean.

A most convincing piece of evidence concerning the makeup of the one hundred twenty disciples is the fact that John Mark, author of the gospel of Mark, and his mother Mary, were residents of Jerusalem. They were not Galileans, yet they were among Jesus' early disciples. Scholars generally agree that these two were among the one hundred twenty disciples mentioned in the first chapter of Acts. Some also assume that the upper room that housed the apostles (Acts 1: 13) was located at Mary's home and that this was where Jesus celebrated the Passover with the disciples (Mark 14: 12-26) prior to his death. J. W. McGarvey remarks concerning John Mark:

> Thus it appears that from the very beginning of the Church, if not during the life of Jesus, John Mark enjoyed the company of the apostles in his home…[4]

Even if the room where the apostles were staying was not at Mary's residence, it must have been the home of another believer living in Jerusalem who had made his/her house available to them. Richard Longnecker has proposed that the early church was probably familiar with "the room" (Acts 1: 13; 9: 39) where the disciples stayed in Jerusalem, suggesting that this may be the same room where Jesus met with the disciples to partake of the Passover – the room where he introduced them to the Lord's Supper. He even supposes:

---

[4] McGarvey, J. W. *A Commentary on Matthew and Mark*, 258.

Perhaps it was the room where he appeared to some of them after he rose from the dead (cf. Luke 24: 33-43; John 20: 19, 26). Or, though this is more inferential, it may have been a room in the house of John Mark's mother, where the church later met. (Acts 12: 12).[5]

This is a lot of material to take in, but it is valuable when seeking to understand the events of Pentecost, especially in relation to spiritual gifts. What can be determined from such a flood of information? It can be said with confidence that not every disciple who was in Jerusalem prior to and on the Day of Pentecost was a Galilean transplant. In fact, it is much more likely that the majority were not Galileans since Galilee lay roughly eighty miles north of Jerusalem. This leads to the inescapable conclusion that not all of the one hundred twenty disciples were "together in one place" when the Day of Pentecost arrived (Acts 2: 1), since all who received the gift of tongues on that day were Galileans (Acts 2: 7).

Some have suggested that the apostles may have been gathered with only those disciples of Galilean descent. However, when Luke stated that "they were all together in one place" (v. 1), he limited the possibilities. He was either referring specifically to the apostles (Acts 1: 26) or he was pointing to the entire complement of disciples in the company of the apostles (Acts 1:15). The verse simply does not offer the option that *all* the apostles and *some* of the disciples were gathered. Luke has yet to explain *why* the experience was limited to the apostles, but the narrative supports the teaching that it was specifically the apostles who were empowered by the Spirit and spoke in tongues on that day.

Despite the overwhelming evidence, many reject this conclusion. Yet, additional evidence can be found in the fact that it was the apostles whom Peter defended against the charge of drunkenness that morning.

> [14] But Peter, taking his stand with the eleven, raised his voice and declared to them: "Men of Judea and all you who live in Jerusalem, let this be known to you and give heed to my words. [15] "For these men are not drunk, as you suppose..." (Acts 2: 14-15)

The antecedents for "these men" in verse fifteen are *Peter* and *the eleven* found in verse fourteen. It was not the one hundred twenty

---

[5] Longnecker, Richard N. *The Expositor's Bible Commentary, Acts*, 56.

disciples, but the apostles who were accused of inebriation so early in the morning. Furthermore, once the people were convicted in their hearts, they did not turn to the one hundred twenty for guidance. Instead, they turned to those to whom they had been listening – the apostles.

> Now when they heard *this*, they were pierced to the heart, and said to Peter and the rest of the apostles, "Brethren, what shall we do?" (Acts 2: 37)

Luke mentions only the apostles in his narrative concerning the Day of Pentecost. The one hundred twenty are noticeably absent from the text. Additional support for the Spirit falling only on the apostles is found in the fact that it was they who performed miracles after Pentecost (Acts 2: 43). No other miracle workers or tongue-speakers are mentioned in the earliest stages of the church. If others were involved in miracles beginning with Pentecost, it means that Luke has uncharacteristically omitted a critical feature of the earliest days of the church and gratuitously focused on the apostles in his account of these events.

Scripture teaches that miracles were performed only by the apostles in the days following Pentecost; a truth that is incompatible with the stance that the Spirit fell on the one hundred twenty disciples or that all spoke in tongues. The biblical facts overwhelmingly support the position that the Holy Spirit was initially poured out only on the apostles – a key factor in relation to spiritual gifts.

Chapter 6

Signs of an Apostle

Distinguishing the Apostolate

It is a commonly accepted view that, within Holy Writ, the term *apostle* carries two distinct meanings. On a generic level, it refers to someone who is sent (with a specific message or task in mind) to represent another individual (or group) with a level of authority that has behind it the full support of those being represented. That explains why, in the following biblical examples, the Greek word for *apostle* is interpreted as *messenger(s)*:

> But I thought it necessary to send to you Epaphroditus, my brother and fellow worker and fellow soldier, who is also your messenger (apostolon) and minister to my need. (Philippians 2: 25)

> As for Titus, *he is* my partner and fellow worker among you; as for our brethren, *they are* messengers (apostoloi) of the churches, a glory to Christ. (2 Corinthians 8: 23)

Another application of this term is found in its characterization of certain men holding a unique position within the kingdom of God. Apostleship, in this more formal sense, depicts those men who had received the gift of apostleship[6] and were sent as Christ's personal messengers/representatives with a level of authority that had behind it the full support of God himself. The word portrays these men as messengers just as it does in the generic sense. Hence, its meaning does not change. The formality that is attached to the word when it comes to the men who held this office is found in the nature of the one whom they were chosen to represent. These men were known as *apostles of Christ*, since they were specially selected by Christ as he set them apart for the task of establishing his spiritual kingdom (the church) here on earth once he had ascended to heaven.

---

[6] See Appendix A: The Gift of Apostle, 319.

> [13]And when day came, He called His disciples to Him and chose twelve of them, whom He also named as apostles: [14]Simon, whom He also named Peter, and Andrew his brother; and James and John; and Philip and Bartholomew; [15]and Matthew and Thomas; James *the son* of Alphaeus, and Simon who was called the Zealot; [16]Judas *the son* of James, and Judas Iscariot, who became a traitor. (Luke 6: 13-16)

> [19]So then you are no longer strangers and aliens, but you are fellow citizens with the saints, and are of God's household, [20]having been built on the foundation of the apostles and prophets, Christ Jesus Himself being the corner *stone*, [21] in whom the whole building, being fitted together, is growing into a holy temple in the Lord, [22]in whom you also are being built together into a dwelling of God in the Spirit. (Ephesians 2: 19-22)

It was the personal appointment of the apostolate by Christ in tandem with the foundational character of their authority that distinguished them from everyone else in the kingdom of God. Therefore, while others were designated as *apostles* in Scripture (e.g., Epaphroditus was a messenger (apostolon) of the church at Philippi), this more formal treatment is used to identify those who held the extraordinary office (or gift) of apostle in the kingdom of God. The significance of their office derived from the unique authority of the one by whom they were sent.

Scripture reveals that there are two exceptions to the original twelve apostles mentioned above. First, there was the replacement of Judas Iscariot who had betrayed Jesus. After Jesus had ascended, the eleven remaining apostles sought someone to take Judas's place among them. Given the importance of the role of the apostles, any legitimate candidate for the position was required to meet certain rather stringent qualifications. These were spelled out before the disciples in Jerusalem as candidates were selected. Interestingly, according to the narrative, this new apostle, like the other eleven, was also appointed directly by the Lord.

> [16] "Brethren, the Scripture had to be fulfilled, which the Holy Spirit foretold by the mouth of David concerning Judas, who became a guide to those who arrested Jesus. [17] For he was counted among us and received his share in this ministry." [18] (Now this man acquired a field with the price of his wickedness, and falling headlong, he burst open in the middle and all his intestines gushed out. [19] And it became

known to all who were living in Jerusalem; so that in their own language that field was called Hakeldama, that is, Field of Blood.)

[20] "For it is written in the book of Psalms,
'LET HIS HOMESTEAD BE MADE DESOLATE,
AND LET NO ONE DWELL IN IT';
and,
'LET ANOTHER MAN TAKE HIS OFFICE.'"

[21] "Therefore it is necessary that of the men who have accompanied us all the time that the Lord Jesus went in and out among us-- [22] beginning with the baptism of John until the day that He was taken up from us--one of these *must* become a witness with us of His resurrection." [23] So they put forward two men, Joseph called Barsabbas (who was also called Justus), and Matthias. [24] And they prayed and said, "You, Lord, who know the hearts of all men, show which one of these two You have chosen [25] to occupy this ministry and apostleship from which Judas turned aside to go to his own place." [26] And they drew lots for them, and the lot fell to Matthias; and he was added to the eleven apostles. (Acts 1: 16-26)

The condition that an apostle must have traveled with Jesus and the others during his ministry (v. 21) limited the field of candidates considerably. In fact, it was one element of the office that made it so unique and confined that office to the first century – a time known as the apostolic age. Still, there was a singular exception to that provision as God sought someone to take the message of the gospel into the heart of the Gentile nations.

Saul, a persecutor of Christians, headed toward the City of Damascus where he intended to seek out and take action against the followers of Christ. Along the way, Jesus intercepted Saul and eventually transformed him into the man who became known as the Apostle Paul. His own comment that he was "…one untimely born" (1 Corinthians 15: 8) as far as apostleship was concerned demonstrates his understanding that this office was, from the beginning, foundational in character and, therefore, limited to the early stages of church life. Although Paul had not traveled with Jesus during his ministry like the other apostles, consistent with his apostolic calling, he received his doctrinal instructions directly from the Lord (Galatians 1: 11-12).

The Apostolic Signature

Paul had proven himself to the Corinthians. He was, in every sense of the word, including its most formal meaning, an *apostle* of Jesus Christ. In defense of his own apostleship, Paul wrote the following to the Corinthians in his second epistle to that congregation.

> [11] I have become foolish; you yourselves compelled me. Actually I should have been commended by you, for in no respect was I inferior to the most eminent apostles, even though I am a nobody. [12] The signs of a true apostle were performed among you with all perseverance, by signs and wonders and miracles. (2 Corinthians 12: 11-12)

While he considered himself unworthy, he claimed apostleship equal with the twelve because he had been called to the office by the Lord (Acts 9: 15; Romans 1: 1). According to Paul, no one had reason to question his apostolic standing, least of all the Corinthians. He had, after all, demonstrated his authority by performing in their midst "signs and wonders and miracles" that were intimately associated with that office (v. 12).

Paul's words to the Corinthians raise some challenging questions not only about the distinction of the apostolic office, but also about such things as tongues, prophecy, healing, and other miraculous works. He claims here that signs, wonders, and miracles served to confirm his place among the apostles. He considered these to be evidence of "The signs of a true apostle" (v. 12) or, as it is stated in the NIV, "the marks of a true apostle." These signs were not only effective in confirming the apostolate, but in authenticating the message those men delivered. These signs proved to the people of that time that both the messengers and the message were from God. The following passage reveals the personal connection between the apostles and these signs, wonders, and miracles:

> Everyone kept feeling a sense of awe; and many wonders and signs were taking place through the apostles. (Acts 2: 43)

Identifying the Signs of an Apostle

The argument has been offered by some that, in his words to the Corinthians, Paul was not portraying miraculous works as apostolic signs. For instance, Wayne Grudem, Professor of Theology and Biblical Studies at Phoenix Seminary, contends that "signs and wonders and miracles" were not "the signs of a true apostle." His conclusion is based partly on the belief that Paul was simply trying to distinguish between true and false apostles. In that vein, he writes:

> In short, the contrast is not between apostles who could work miracles and ordinary Christians who could not, but between genuine Christian apostles through whom the Holy Spirit worked and *non-Christian pretenders to the apostolic office*, through whom the Holy Spirit did not work at all.[7]

In his explanation, Dr. Grudem has made a curious observation about the grammar of 2 Corinthians 12: 12, noting that the expression "the signs of a true apostle" reflects a nominative use of the word *signs* (the primary subject). In contrast, "signs and wonders and miracles," in this context, appear in the dative case (indirect object). According to Dr. Grudem, if Paul meant to depict miracles as *apostolic* signs, they should appear in the nominative case. In the dative case, as Paul has used them here, Dr. Grudem has proposed that they accompanied his ministry just as they accompanied the faith of other true believers. Thus "signs and wonders and miracles" were not intended to mark Paul's apostleship, but his Christianity. This is how they served to distinguish Paul from *false* apostles.

The difficulty with this explanation of the text is that it is based on certain English translations of the verse that employ verbiage like "The signs of a true apostle" (NIV, NASB). It appears from this interpretation that Paul's goal is to differentiate between true and false apostles. However, that translation is a bit misleading since the Greek text does not mention *true* apostles.

The most accurate English rendering of this verse is, "Truly, the signs of an apostle..." (KJV). Several other English translations,[8] as well as *all* Greek/English Interlinear Bibles, plainly express the meaning of the original Greek. Paul employs the word "Truly" (Gr. *men*) as a matter of emphasis to underscore the substantive character of his words. This is reflective of how this word is used elsewhere in Scripture.

> For indeed (men), the Son of Man is going as it has been determined; but woe to that man by whom He is betrayed! (Luke 22: 22)

---

[7] Grudem, Wayne. *Systematic Theology: An Introduction to Biblical Doctrine*, 362.
[8] The American Standard Version, The New King James Version, NIV-1984, The 21st Century KJV, The Amplified Bible, The Darby Translation, The Lexham English Bible, New Century Version, and the New Living Translation each use this wording.

And indeed (men) if they had been thinking of that *country* from which they went out, they would have had opportunity to return. (Hebrews 11: 15)

...and indeed (men) our fellowship is with the Father, and with His Son Jesus Christ. (1 John 1: 3b)

Paul was not attempting to distinguish between genuine and not-so-genuine apostles. In his words to the Corinthians, he expressly highlights the authenticity and authority of his role as an apostle of Jesus Christ. His use of *men* demonstrates the emphatic nature of his remark. He was disappointed that the Corinthians had not eagerly defended his apostolic status (v. 11).

As noted earlier, the argument that "signs and wonders and miracles" are not apostolic signs is grounded largely in Paul's use of the dative case in this verse (2 Corinthians 12: 12). On that point, strictly speaking, Dr. Grudem is correct in stating that these are not in themselves the signs of an apostle. This creates a bit of a quandary since, in this setting, they are plainly offered as evidence of Paul's own apostolic status. Consequently, the relationship between miracles and apostolic signs requires further investigation. If signs, wonders, and miracles are not the signs of an apostle, and if full appreciation is to be given to what Paul intended with his reference to miraculous works, it is necessary to 1) determine how Paul's use of the dative case, in this context, affects his message, and 2) seek to identify the signs of an apostle.

The function of a dative expression can vary significantly depending on the context. The purpose of the dative case is to provide support for the nominative figure in a sentence. There are assorted applications for the dative case; more than need to be discussed in a section where the focus is spiritual gifts. Still, a small sampling will help to shed light on Paul's use of this grammar. In considering the use of dative language, this study will be limited to the writings of Paul, hopefully providing a clear vision of his thoughts.

At times, the dative case denotes the recipient of an action by the nominative, or primary, subject of a statement. This use of the dative is known as *dative of recipient*. It signifies that those referenced by the dative case have a rather direct interest in the action being taken. That is the case in Paul's introductions in his many New Testament epistles. It is characteristic of his writing style to acknowledge the recipients of his work.

> **Paul** (primary), an apostle of Christ Jesus by the will of God, and **Timothy** (primary) *our* brother, **to the church** (dative) of God which is at Corinth... (2 Corinthians 1: 1) Emphasis added.

> ¹**Paul** (primary), a bond-servant of Christ Jesus... ⁷ **to all who are beloved** (dative) of God in Rome... (Romans 1: 1, 7) Emphasis added.

There are other times when the dative describes the manner or disposition (demeanor) with which something is done or not done. This is known as *dative of manner*.

> For our proud confidence is this: the testimony of our conscience, that **in holiness** (dative) and **godly sincerity** (dative)..., not **in fleshly wisdom** (dative) but **in the grace** (dative) of God, **we** (primary) have conducted ourselves in the world, and especially toward you. (2 Corinthians 1: 12) Emphasis added.

At times, the dative case describes a sense of accompaniment, or association. This is known as the *dative of sphere*, or *locative dative*, where it is only linked to the nominative in that they reside in the same realm (time or location). Paul often employs *dative of sphere* in relation to those who are *in Christ* or *in the faith*.

> ...if indeed **you** (primary) continue **in the faith** (dative) firmly established and steadfast... (Colossians 1: 23) Emphasis added.

> We proclaim Him, admonishing every man and teaching every man with all wisdom, so that we may present **every man** (primary) complete **in Christ** (dative). (Colossians 1: 28) Emphasis added.

The *dative of means,* also called *instrumental dative,* is also commonly used in Scripture. Such is the case in Paul's first epistle to the Corinthians when he explained their means of entrance into the body of Christ. In this case, the Holy Spirit is the *instrument*, or *means*, by which the transformation takes place. Similarly, he taught the Ephesians that grace is a *means* of salvation.

> For **by one Spirit** (dative) **we** (primary) were all baptized into one body. (1 Corinthians 12: 13) Emphasis added.

> For **by grace** (dative) **you** (primary) have been saved through faith. (Ephesians 2: 8) Emphasis added.

There is one additional, important principle that must be given consideration when it comes to the use of the dative case. It is undeniable that in every passage of Scripture where dative language is used, it introduces something that is germane to the topic at hand. In other words, when the dative case appears in God's Word, its presence is materially related to the subject that is being discussed. Hence, in the statement "For by grace you have been saved," grace, which is in the dative case, is *materially linked* to one's salvation.

Countless examples of the dative case can be found in the New Testament (more than twelve thousand), but these few are sufficient to address the text currently under consideration. How the dative case affects the narrative is dependent on the way it is used. Correct treatment of words appearing in dative case involves respecting the context in which they appear.

Which of these dative functions applies in 2 Corinthians 12: 12? Dr. Grudem's position, which is shared by many biblical scholars, is that this passage represents an example of *dative of sphere*. In other words, as with other Christians, the work of the Holy Spirit accompanied Paul's ministry. This would not have been true of the false apostles to whom the Corinthians had been listening. The difficulty with this explanation of the verse is that it does not offer support for Paul's apostolic authority – only for his status as a believer.

It is Paul's *apostleship*, and not his Christianity, that is in view in the narrative. Paul's goal was to defend his apostleship by reminding the Corinthians of those things that distinguished an apostle of Jesus Christ. The comments in this verse do not stand alone. His entire discourse, beginning with the previous chapter, directs his readers' attention to the legitimacy of his apostolic status.

Given the subject Paul is addressing, his use of the dative case must be related to the authenticity of his apostleship. If this is not true, his mention of miraculous works is gratuitous. However, it can be stated with confidence that this is not the case. The miraculous works Paul mentioned were *materially linked* to his point concerning the apostolate. In that vein, he wrote that miraculous manifestations of the Spirit served to substantiate apostleship *in Paul*. Thus, there must be a link between the apostles and these extraordinary works that is both inherent and exclusive, making them integral to Paul's claim of apostleship.

The most reasonable explanation of this verse is that the statement "signs and wonders and miracles" represents the use of *instrumental dative* with respect to the apostolate. If these miracles were not the means of apostolic authentication, which is what Paul was addressing, then they are unrelated to the discussion that is taking place. If that is the case, it means that Paul had no reason to include them in the text and, to avoid confusion, could have and should have omitted them.

As he was completing his second epistle to the Thessalonians, in his closing salutation, Paul drew his readers' attention to the fact that the letter before them was, in fact, his work. He asked his readers to take special notice of his mark (Gr. *semaino*) by which they could be confident of his authorship. The exact nature of Paul's *mark* is unclear, but it apparently served as the equivalent of one's personal signature in modern times. It appears that he may have been referring to the *closing remarks* of the epistle being written in his own hand, suggesting that the Thessalonians should recognize his handwriting. Paul knew that his *mark* would provide the Thessalonians with the assurance he believed they needed to accept the work as genuine.

> I, Paul, write this greeting with my own hand, and this is a distinguishing mark in every letter; this is the way I write. (2 Thessalonians 3: 17)

Paul used his *mark* (handwriting) as a matter of personal identification. This mark confirmed the authenticity of this work to his audience. In the same manner, the signs (semaino: the same word translated 'mark' in the Thessalonians passage) of the apostles served to confirm their authority to speak and act on God's behalf. These signs identified the apostles. Consequently, Paul was able to refer his readers in Corinth to his use of miracles as a demonstration of his apostolic authority.

When Paul drew the attention of the Thessalonians to his "distinguishing mark" as a matter of assurance, he noted that he had placed the mark there "with my own hand" (2 Thessalonians 3: 17), which is an example of the use of *instrumental dative*. Paul's hand was not the actual mark, but without his hand holding the utensil, the mark would fail to provide evidence of Paul's authorship. The apostle appealed to the use of his own hand as evidence that the mark was genuine. When Paul states, "Truly the signs of an apostle were wrought among you…by signs and wonders and mighty works" (ASV), it is in the same sense that Paul's *mark* was made *with his own hand*.

In the Thessalonians text, Paul's hand is the (dative) means by which the (nominative) mark, or signature, was delivered and the letter could be authenticated. Without his hand, the mark would have been a forgery and would not have served its intended purpose. The uniqueness of the three-way relationship between a dative vehicle, its nominative counterpart, and the target of validation is central to this principle. That is the case with the link between Paul's hand (the dative vehicle), his personal signature or mark (the nominative counterpart), and the letter he wrote (the target of validation). In short, if there was no unique relationship between these three, his claim that the mark could serve as proof of his authorship would be meaningless.

Paul's hand was intrinsic to the man. It was this relationship that gave his mark meaning. In the same way, if no unique relationship existed between the apostles and the miraculous works that Paul invoked, his appeal to them as evidence of his apostleship would simply fall short. Therefore, Paul had in mind a singular bond between them that validated his claim.

The signs and wonders that served to authenticate the apostolate were, to the signs of an apostle, what Paul's hand was to his signature. Miraculous episodes were, in essence, the *hand* that validated the *distinguishing mark* of apostleship. They were the means through which apostolic signs were delivered and could be authenticated. As with one's hand and signature, the relationship between apostolic signs and miraculous gifts must be intrinsic, such that those signs were evident *only* through these extraordinary works. Given his remarks, Paul seemed to consider them virtually indistinguishable, as though apostolic signs were embodied within miraculous works just as his signature was embodied within his own hand. These "signs and wonders and miracles" were, in essence, the visible manifestation of the "signs of an apostle."

Paul's hand was not his signature. It was simply the means used to deliver his mark. Similarly, these divine works were merely the vehicle used to convey the signs of an apostle. Thus, it is necessary to give serious consideration to the fabric of the apostolic signature. In other words, exactly what were the signs of the apostles to which Paul was directing his readers? If the apostles were unique within the kingdom, there must have been something that distinguished them from all others. This is the thrust of Paul's comment about "The signs of an apostle." If nothing dramatically differentiated the apostles, Paul's line of reasoning would collapse for lack of substance.

Many have eagerly jumped on the theological bandwagon, seeing this as an opportunity to downplay what was clearly a special union between miraculous works and the apostles. For instance, some quickly point to the patience Paul mentions in this verse, convinced that this is surely an apostolic sign, despite the fact that the word for patience (Gr. *hupomone*) appears in the dative case – the very line of reasoning employed to seek to disqualify "signs and wonders and miracles." However, this dative refers to disposition (or attitude), making it *dative of manner* as discussed earlier and affirmed by Jamieson, Fausset, and Brown. They note that patience was not an apostolic sign, but the demeanor with which apostolic signs were wrought, as a candid reading of the text intimates.

> **in all patience, in signs,** &c.--The oldest manuscripts omit "in." "Patience" is not one of the "signs," but the element IN which they were wrought...[9]

Others have argued that the apostolic signs Paul had in mind are not mentioned in the immediate text but can be found strewn throughout the Corinthian epistles for all to see. For instance, some believe the fruitfulness of Paul's ministry may have served as an apostolic sign. Paul told the Corinthians that he considered them the *seal* of his apostleship (1 Corinthians 9: 1-2), presumably seeing this as confirmation of his apostolic authority. Additionally, Paul's Christ-like example of holiness and humility (cf. 2 Corinthians 1: 12; 3: 4-6; 7: 2), as well as the persecution he endured in his witness for Christ (cf. 2 Corinthians 4: 7-15; 5: 4-10; 11: 23-28), are seen by some as apostolic signs.

Paul was a devout man. This is obvious from these examples of his faithfulness. However, other believers who were not apostles could make similar claims. These same things could be said of Barnabas or Silas, neither of whom held the formal *office* of apostle. Similarly, Philip, who served in Jerusalem under the apostles, successfully spread the gospel message (Acts 8: 5-8, 26-40), and Stephen, who also served the church in Jerusalem, was persecuted even to the point of death (Acts 7: 54-60).

The triumphs and persecutions Paul experienced did not prove, or serve as signs of, apostolic *authority*. They did not distinguish him or any other apostle from the faithful of that day. Most importantly – and this is critical – they fail to explain Paul's appeal to signs, wonders, and miracles as evidence of apostleship, since they are unrelated to miraculous works. Instead, the successes he experienced and the

---

[9] Jamieson, Robert, A. R. Fausset, and David Brown. *A Commentary on the Old and New Testaments, Volume 3*, 368.

hardships he endured simply offer evidence of the diligence and faithfulness Paul exhibited in that office.

When Paul mentioned "the signs of an apostle," he was discussing something unique to the apostles – something that *marked* them as apostles. Anything less would be the equivalent of offering *the signs of a Christian*. Paul's point was that the signs of an apostle verified apostolic authority, not one's diligence or faithfulness to Christ. Therefore, it is necessary to determine exactly what served to distinguish the apostles from all others. It is fair to say that this is what Paul believed was revealed through signs, wonders, and miracles.

To what spiritual apostolic attribute, then, do miraculous works of the Spirit point? It is not Christian character since that is the fruit of the Spirit (Galatians 5: 22-23). Many display Christ-like qualities without ever participating in wonders and miracles. It cannot be salvation, as previously noted[10] (Matthew 7: 21-24). Yet, something must have stood out that separated the apostles. Ultimately, there must have been something recognizable that was so strongly associated with the miraculous that, where these works were present, proof of apostleship was also present.

In modern times, when people claim to witness or participate in the miraculous, whether tongues, healing, prophecy, or a host of other extraordinary gifts, they maintain that these distinctively represent the power, work, and authority of the Holy Spirit, insisting that these manifestations are intrinsic to the Spirit. The same can be said of those who exercised these special gifts of the Spirit in the first century. In fact, this is Paul's very point. The miraculous works of the Spirit demonstrated the Holy Spirit's *power* and *authority* that was bestowed upon the apostles. This is what served to identify the apostles. Paul did reveal the signs of an apostle in his words to the Corinthians, but they were not the same signs that have been suggested, such as holiness and persecution. In fact, Paul confirmed earlier in his epistle to the Corinthians that these signs, wonders, and miracles effectively embodied and demonstrated the power and authority of the Holy Spirit:

> [3] I was with you in weakness and in fear and in much trembling, [4] and my message and my preaching were not in persuasive words of wisdom, but in demonstration of the Spirit and of power, [5] so that your faith would not rest on the wisdom of men, but on the power of God. (1 Corinthians 2: 3-5)

---

[10] See Chapter 5, Now Concerning Spiritual Gifts: Spiritual Gifts and Essential Doctrine, 68.

For the Corinthians, the demonstration of the Holy Spirit's power and authority through signs, wonders, and miracles, attested to Paul's apostleship, as these verses affirm. As a matter of confirmation, in a complementary passage in his letter to the Romans, Paul identifies miracles as a demonstration of the Holy Spirit's power and authority.

> [18] For I will not presume to speak of anything except what Christ has accomplished through me, resulting in the obedience of the Gentiles by word and deed, [19] in the power of signs and wonders, in the power of the Spirit; so that from Jerusalem and round about as far as Illyricum I have fully preached the gospel of Christ. (Romans 15: 18-19)

These verses unmistakably point to miraculous works as the demonstration of the Holy Spirit's power and authority, and that those works came to the disciples through Paul's ministry. The disciples at Corinth were fully aware of this fact, which is what gave Paul's appeal to miracles as evidence of his apostleship sufficient force to substantiate his claim. To them, "signs and wonders and miracles" were, in effect, the signs of an apostle.

While many individuals claim to experience and/or witness miraculous manifestations of the Holy Spirit today, this view fails to harmonize with teaching found in God's Word concerning signs, wonders, and spiritual gifts. In his words to the Corinthians as he defended his apostleship, Paul testified that the power and authority of the Spirit, embodied in signs and wonders, identified the apostles, not Christians in general. *The Bible in Basic English* and *Common English Bible*, respectively, combine to express the apostle's thoughts precisely:

> Truly the signs of an Apostle were done among you with quiet strength, with wonders and acts of power. (The Bible in Basic English)

> The signs of an apostle were performed among you with continuous endurance through signs, wonders, and miracles. (Common English Bible)

The "Super Apostles"

Some have become confused over Paul's use of the Greek term *huper lian apostolōn* (2 Corinthians 11: 5; 12: 11), which immediately precedes his comments about the signs of an apostle. Literally, these words mean *the highest apostles* or the *very chiefest apostles*, and it is to these that Paul compares his own apostleship. This phrase is translated into English in a variety of ways and some of those translations may seem perplexing. Below are a few translations of this expression, explaining exactly why there is so much confusion.

> ...for in nothing was I behind the very chiefest apostles, though I am nothing. (ASV)

> ...for I am not in the least inferior to the "super-apostles," even though I am nothing. (NIV)

> For I was not at all inferior to these superlative apostles, even though I am nothing. (RSV)

> ...for in no respect was I inferior to the most eminent apostles, even though I am a nobody. (NASB)

Some believe that, with these words, Paul is comparing his own apostleship to false apostles based on the presumption that he is mockingly referring to them as "super-apostles." This has led many to believe that he is distinguishing between true and false apostles where signs are concerned (2 Corinthians 12: 12). However, the term does not point to false apostles. Instead, Paul is comparing himself to the twelve original apostles, a fact that the greater context of the passage makes clear. In the preceding chapter (11: 5), Paul uses this same terminology. Once again, he compares his own apostleship to *huper lian apostolōn*. However, in that earlier setting, the idea of false apostles is incompatible with Paul's line of reasoning.

> [5] For I consider myself not in the least inferior to the most eminent apostles. [6] But even if I am unskilled in speech, yet I am not *so* in knowledge; in fact, in every way we have made *this* evident to you in all things. (2 Corinthians 11: 5-6)

Paul claimed apostleship equal with *huper lian apostolōn* (v.5). He then adds that "we have made *this* evident to you" (v. 6). The KJV offers a more precise rendering with the words, "we have been thoroughly made manifest among you." This translation is faithful to the Greek and more accurately reflects the point Paul was trying to make. The idea is that it was not the apostles who had made their apostolic standing evident to the Corinthians, but the Holy Spirit who had acted in witness of their apostleship.

It would represent the ultimate absurdity for *huper lian apostolōn* to depict false apostles in this context. If false apostles were in view, it would mean that Paul not only considered his own apostleship equal with that of counterfeit apostles, but that the Holy Spirit stood as witness on behalf of those false apostles. That is not what Paul intended. Since it is not possible that Paul would defend false apostles in this way, *huper lian apostolōn* can only represent "the most eminent apostles" (the twelve) as depicted in the NASB translation. W. Harold Mare and Murray J. Harris effectively make this point.

> In this verse, then, Paul claims to be in no respect inferior to the original apostles (see 1 Cor. 9: 1; 15: 5-8, 10) with whom he was being unfavorably compared and whose authority his adversaries illegitimately invoked in support of their Judaizing program in Corinth.[11]

Now that the meaning of *huper lian apostolōn* has been settled, it is time to return to the use of this expression in connection with the "signs of an apostle" (12: 12). Paul again compares himself to the twelve when writing to the Corinthians about apostolic signs, using the identical phraseology, *huper lian apostolōn*. In this setting, there is every reason to believe that these words carry the same meaning as in the previous chapter where the original apostles are in view.

> [11] I have become foolish; you yourselves compelled me. Actually I should have been commended by you, for in no respect was I inferior to the most eminent apostles, even though I am a nobody. [12] The signs of a true apostle were performed among you with all perseverance, by signs and wonders and miracles. (2 Corinthians 12: 11-12)

False apostles are mentioned by Paul in the previous chapter (11: 13). However, they are only peripherally connected with his claim about apostolic signs. Paul was concerned about the Corinthians' response to false apostles. This is what led to his disappointment. It was the Corinthians, and not some pseudo apostles, who had forced Paul's hand concerning his apostleship.

What is in view in this text is the distinctive character of the apostolate and the fact that these men (Paul and the twelve) could be recognized by the miraculous signs that accompanied them. These

---

[11] Mare, W. Harold, and Murray J. Harris. *The Expositor's Bible Commentary, 1 & 2 Corinthians*, 214.

signs served as the Holy Spirit's witness to the apostolic office. While it was completely against Paul's nature to *boast* of his apostleship by highlighting the uniqueness of the office, it was important for him to make these points to the Corinthians so that they would not be led astray.

Bestowal of Miraculous Gifts

In the Bible, beginning with the Day of Pentecost, the reader is privy to the actual bestowal of miraculous spiritual gifts on four occasions. On the Day of Pentecost, the Spirit filled the apostles, accompanied by tongues of fire, and they began speaking in numerous foreign languages (Acts 2: 1-4). In Samaria, the Spirit fell upon the Samaritans through the touch of the apostles' hands (Acts 8: 14-17). In Caesarea, Peter spoke to some Gentiles who had gathered at the house of a man named Cornelius. As he spoke, "...the Holy Spirit fell upon all those who were listening to the message. All the circumcised believers who came with Peter were amazed...For they were hearing them speaking with tongues and exalting God" (Acts 10: 44-46). Finally, as Paul approached Ephesus in Asia Minor, he encountered some disciples of John the Baptist who had "...not even heard whether there is a Holy Spirit" (Acts 19: 2). Once the apostle had immersed them in water in the name of Jesus, he "...laid his hands upon them, the Holy Spirit came on them, and they began speaking with tongues and prophesying" (Acts 19: 6).

What is noteworthy about these four occasions is that they all have two things in common. The first of these is, naturally, the presence of the Holy Spirit. Each episode involved the Spirit enveloping those present, filling them, and manifesting his presence in a way that was undeniable. The second common element is that each incident is marked by the presence of at least one apostle.

While the narrative does not identify the exact nature of the spiritual gifts experienced by the Samaritans, Bible scholars generally agree that they must have been comparable to what took place on the other three occasions where speaking in tongues and prophesying and/or exalting God ensued. The result was clearly discernible, since a man named Simon "...saw that the Spirit was bestowed through the laying on of the apostles' hands" (Acts 8: 18). In this passage, in the simplest of terms, Luke has revealed the way miraculous gifts, such as tongues and prophecy, were distributed. They were given through the apostles' touch. Still, certain exceptions are found in Scripture. On the Day of Pentecost, the Holy Spirit manifested himself without an apostle's touch. The same is true in Caesarea where the Gentiles received the Spirit.

It seems rather obvious that the initial outpouring of the Spirit upon the apostles would not have required an apostle's touch. Prior to that time only Jesus had instilled the Holy Spirit and bestowed humankind with the capacity for the miraculous (Luke 10: 1-9; John 20: 19-23). After Jesus ascended, no one on earth had this kind of power. Therefore, God entrusted that power to the apostles through the initial outpouring on the Day of Pentecost. That is what makes it such a special day.

Years later, in Caesarea, the Gentiles received the Spirit without Peter's touch. The reason for this is fully explained in Luke's narrative. The Spirit and gifts were given as testimony to the Jews, including Peter, that Gentiles were welcome in the kingdom of God (Acts 15: 8).

Prior to his journey to the house of Cornelius in Caesarea, it seems Peter had not seriously considered God's plan for the Gentiles, since God had to provide a vision just to persuade him to travel to Caesarea (Acts 10: 9-23). Though he went to the house of Cornelius, Peter seemed to question whether Gentiles were eligible for participation in the kingdom. When the Gentiles received the Spirit without Peter's touch, the incident is depicted as an exception to the way the gifts were normally distributed. This extraordinary delivery of the Spirit was performed that it might serve as God's directive to Peter concerning the Gentiles.

The phenomenal nature of the event is revealed in the apostle's own words. While the gifts had been an important post-Pentecost aspect of Christian life, this incident reminded him of the time they had received the Spirit "…at the beginning" (Acts 11: 15), which Bible scholars generally see as a reference to the Day of Pentecost. Peter did not view this as representative of the method by which spiritual gifts were commonly given, but an anomaly that vividly contrasted the normal manner of distribution (Acts 8: 18). Yet, on this occasion, as is true throughout the New Testament, the gifts were given in the presence of an apostle. It seems it was God's plan that the Holy Spirit would come to others through these twelve.

The author of the book of Hebrews offers some additional insight concerning the apostles and their unique relationship with miraculous works of the Spirit.

¹ For this reason we must pay much closer attention to what we have heard, so that we do not drift *away from it*. ² For if the word spoken through angels proved unalterable, and every transgression and disobedience received a just penalty, ³ how will we escape if we neglect so great a salvation? After it was at the first spoken through the Lord, it was confirmed to us by those who heard, ⁴ God also testifying with them, both by signs and wonders and by various miracles and by gifts of the Holy Spirit according to His own will. (Hebrews 2: 1-4)

To fully appreciate the magnitude of these verses, it is necessary to determine the precise lesson the author has in mind. A key component of that lesson lies in the identity of the people mentioned in these verses. Since only personal pronouns appear in the text (we, us, those, and them), the immediate context, along with the greater scriptural landscape, must be considered in seeking answers.

Bible scholars generally agree that the book of Hebrews was written to Jewish Christians between A.D. 65 and A.D. 70. The letter may have been addressed to a singular group of Jews, but the contents are general enough that it could have been aimed at Jewish Christians over a large geographical area. It is reasonable to conclude that when the author employs the words "we" (vs. 1 & 3) and "us" (v. 3), he has in mind himself and the recipients of the letter and, perhaps in a larger sense, the whole of Christendom. According to the author of the letter, they were the ones to whom the message of salvation was confirmed "by those who heard" (v. 3). Who, then, were *those who heard?* Their identity is important since God testified "with them" (v. 4) about salvation.

According to the author, the lesson of salvation came to certain people through Jesus' spoken word. The following literal Greek translation makes clear that the term "those who heard" is a pointed reference to those taught by Jesus while he was on earth (v. 3).

³ᵇ Which having received a beginning to be spoken through the Lord, was confirmed to us by the ones hearing; ⁴ God bearing witness with them by both miracles and wonders. And by various works of power, even by the distribution of the Holy Spirit, according to His will. (Hebrews 2: 3b-4)[12]

---

[12] Green, J. P., Sr. general editor, *The Interlinear Bible Greek English, Volume IV New Testament*, 587.

There is something very telling in the Greek wording of this passage that is not generally sustained in English interpretations. Although most popular English translations of the Bible (e.g., ASV, KJV, NASB, NIV) employ the phrase "gifts of the Holy Spirit" (v. 4) in this instance, the word that normally identifies spiritual gifts (charisma) does not appear in the Greek text. The accurate translation of verse four (above) does not read "gifts of the Holy Spirit." Instead, it reads *distribution* of the Spirit, as noted in the literal translation.

This passage falls into the category of *words have meaning*.[13] God provided testimony not only by signs and wonders, but by the *distribution* of (the) Holy Spirit as well. That is to say, the very manner by which the power of the Holy Spirit was distributed (Gr. *merismos*) was a matter of testimony for "those who heard." This is the lesson of these verses. The first century *gifts* of the Spirit were distributed to believers by the Holy Spirit (1 Corinthians 12: 11), but the *power* of the Spirit through which those gifts were delivered came via the apostles. As noted earlier, Luke confirmed this in his narrative concerning the events in Samaria:

> ...Simon saw that the Spirit was bestowed through the laying on of the apostles' hands. (Acts 8: 18)

These verses (Acts 8: 18; Hebrews 2: 3-4) complement each other in supporting the biblical principle that God worked through the apostles when it came to the distribution of the miraculous power of the Holy Spirit. Other early Christians were not witnesses in the same sense that the apostles were witnesses. These men were *apostles* (ones sent) of Jesus Christ in that the gospel message was entrusted to them. It is for this reason that "those who heard" has been recognized by Bible scholars as restrictive terminology that is meant to specify the twelve rather than the general discipleship. This is how the Jews of the first century would have understood these words.

Over the centuries, a host of Bible commentators from assorted theological backgrounds have recognized that the intent of the author of the book of Hebrews was to identify the apostles as "those who heard." These include: *The Expositor's Bible Commentary* by Leon Morris and Donald Burdick, *Barnes' Notes on the New Testament* by Albert Barnes, *Commentary on Hebrews* by John Calvin, and many, many more.

---

[13] See Chapter 3, Principles of Interpretation: Words Have Meaning, 38.

God joined with the apostles by providing them with the *power* of the Spirit. While other disciples listened to Jesus' teachings when he lived on earth in human form, they did not receive the depth of instruction or the power the apostles received. According to Scripture, it was the apostles who were sent to be witnesses on Christ's behalf. Therefore, they were given the fullness of knowledge necessary to carry out that task. The apostles were "those who heard." It was the apostles with whom God joined forces in testimony concerning the message of salvation (Hebrews 2: 3-4). It was the apostles to whom Jesus said:

> ...you will receive power when the Holy Spirit has come upon you; and you shall be My witnesses both in Jerusalem, and in all Judea and Samaria, and even to the remotest part of the earth. (Acts 1: 8)

The harmony that God's Word provides leaves no room for maneuvering when it comes to understanding the distribution of the miraculous gifts of the Spirit. Every post-Pentecost episode of the distribution of these gifts that is offered up in Scripture involved the presence of at least one apostle. This is consistent with Paul's claim that miraculous works provided an apostolic signature and Simon's witness that the Holy Spirit was given through the apostles' hands. That is surely why Paul wrote to the Romans, "For I long to see you so that I may impart some spiritual gift to you" (Romans 1: 11). It also explains why the apostles Peter and John traveled to Samaria to disperse these gifts (Acts 8: 14-18).

Many people maintain that the Holy Spirit continues to *fall upon* individuals in modern times just as he did in Jerusalem on the Day of Pentecost and in Caesarea as he came upon the Gentiles. However, those who insist that the Spirit distributes these same miraculous gifts today, absent apostolic authority, are making a claim for which there is no biblical precedent. It is a doctrinal position that openly clashes with fundamental apostolic instruction. This is a truth that bears up under intense biblical scrutiny. Given this reality, it is time to revisit Paul's comments concerning "the signs of an apostle."

The Holy Spirit bore witness to these men via signs, wonders, and miracles. Apostolic sanction was validated by the Spirit's power that was made evident through miraculous works. No others had authority equal to the apostles. Authority was bestowed upon them by God himself. Additionally, they received doctrinal instruction directly from the Lord. It was recognition of that apostolic authority that allowed

Paul to proclaim that the apostles were a vital element of the church's foundation (Ephesians 2: 20).

The fact that miraculous works were given to and through the apostles has been noted by several Bible scholars. Here are some observations from a few of these authors:

> Jesus Christ had promised his holy apostles that they would be able to perform miracles and that God would work with them, "confirming the word" (Mark 16:20); and Paul enjoyed that prerogative along with the other apostles.[14]

> **12. Truly, &c.**--There is understood some such clause as this, 'yet I have not been commended by you.' **in all patience** *(hupomene)*, **in signs,** &c..."Patience," *or enduring continuance*, is not a "sign," but the element IN which the signs were wrought: Translate, "IN . . . patience, BY signs," &c. His expression is modest, putting himself, the worker, in the background: "were wrought," not "*I* wrought." The first "signs" means the evidences; the second, miracles. As the *signs* have not been transmitted to us, neither has the apostleship. The apostles have no literal successors (compare Acts 1:21, 22). **mighty deeds** *(duname-sin)* -- works of divine omnipotence.[15]

> And you are without excuse in thus compelling me to defend myself by proving my apostleship, for it was proved long since among you by the miracles which I wrought among you as signs and evidences of it...[16]

The apostles were the source of miraculous works in the first century precisely because they were the vehicle for the distribution of the power of the Holy Spirit. These miraculous abilities were passed on to other believers *by* the Holy Spirit (1 Corinthians 12: 11), but always *through* the apostles (Acts 8: 18). It is this intrinsic, exclusive relationship between the apostles and the miraculous works of the Spirit that allowed Paul to proclaim to the Corinthians:

> Truly the signs of an apostle were wrought among you in all patience, in signs, and wonders, and mighty deeds. (2 Corinthians 12: 12 – KJV)

---

[14] Coffman, James Burton. *James Burton Coffman Commentaries, First & Second Corinthians*, 484.
[15] Jamieson, Robert, A. R. Fausset, and David Brown. *A Commentary on the Old and New Testaments, Volume 3*, p. 368-369.
[16] McGarvey, J. W., Philip Pendleton. Y. *A Commentary on Thessalonians, Corinthians, Galatians, and Romans*, 237.

While the miraculous phenomena of the first century served to demonstrate the unique office of the apostles of Jesus Christ, the same cannot be said of those gifts such as teaching, giving, leadership, and others where it is believed the Spirit did not manifest himself in *mighty works*. Given Paul's frankness about the connection between the miraculous and the signs of the apostles, there is no biblical reason to believe these other *apportionments* required an apostle's presence or touch. That is not to say that they were not provided by the Holy Spirit, since Scripture teaches that the Spirit resides with every believer (Acts 2: 38), but they involved more ordinary ministries that Paul did not associate with apostolic signs. Thus, it is not unreasonable to believe that these gifts have been maintained throughout the life of the church like the offices of elder and deacon.

Chapter 7

When the Perfect Comes

Partial Cessationism

Most believers who are at all familiar with the discussion concerning spiritual gifts are intimately acquainted with the following verse from the thirteenth chapter of Paul's first letter to the Corinthians:

> Love never fails; but if *there are gifts of* prophecy, they will be done away; if *there are* tongues, they will cease; if *there is* knowledge, it will be done away. (1 Corinthians 13: 8)

Paul's words are not blurred. He states with conviction that the gifts of prophecy, tongues, and knowledge will, at some point, come to an end (v. 8). Few would even attempt to deny this since the apostle writes with razor-sharp clarity. Anyone who reads the apostle's words and takes them to heart understands that he is teaching that these miraculous spiritual gifts will cease. That, however, is not the end of the debate. In fact, it is only the beginning since the question is not whether spiritual gifts will end – a point upon which believers commonly agree – but rather when they will end.

There is a sense in which many continuationists are partial cessationists and it rests in their view of the apostolate. According to the Apostle Paul, apostleship is a spiritual gift of the highest order (1 Corinthians 12: 28; Ephesians 4: 11). While certain sects insist that the office of apostle continues even to this day, this is a minority view. It is also a most difficult position to defend since God's Word is straightforward on the subject. It is a doctrine that simply fails to muster scriptural support.

The foundational role of the apostles (Ephesians 2: 20), along with the biblical qualifications for the office (Acts 1: 21-22), present insurmountable obstacles when it comes to any claim in favor of apostolic succession. In addition, since Scripture depicts each apostle being chosen personally by Jesus, including Matthias (Acts 1: 21-26) and Paul (Romans 1: 1), it seems the authority to select individuals for this position was never surrendered to men. Other offices such as elders and deacons (Philippians 1: 1; 1 Timothy 3: 1-13; Titus 1: 5) were by human appointment, but this was not the case for the apostolate. For these reasons, even many continuationists recognize that the office of apostle, which Paul identified as a spiritual gift, ended in the first century with the passing of the original twelve (plus Paul).

The special relationship between apostles and miraculous works of the Spirit that Paul affirmed (2 Corinthians 12: 12), in complement with the finite foundational role of the apostles, is central to the cessationist point of view. Given Paul's claim, it is not biblically feasible to separate the apostles from the miraculous works of the first century. These works of the Spirit were unique to the apostolate in that the Spirit worked through these men in a manner not afforded other believers.

Since the apostles served as God's agents for the miraculous power of the Spirit, which was Paul's point to the Corinthians, when the apostles died, the means for the distribution of these gifts also died. Other miraculous gifts ended alongside the gift of apostle. If these powerful gifts survived into the twenty-first century, it means that Paul was wrong in his assessment of signs, wonders, and miracles being indicative of apostleship. Reviewing the greater context of the earlier passage concerning the passing of prophecy, tongues, and knowledge, it seems Paul had considerably more to add.

> [8] Love never fails; but if *there are gifts* of prophecy, they will be done away; *if there are* tongues, they will cease; *if there is* knowledge, it will be done away. [9] For we know in part and we prophesy in part; [10] but when the perfect comes, the partial will be done away. [11] When I was a child, I used to speak like a child, think like a child, reason like a child; when I became a man, I did away with childish things. [12] For now we see in a mirror dimly, but then face to face; now I know in part, but then I will know fully just as I also have been fully known. [13] But now faith, hope, love, abide these three; but the greatest of these is love. (1 Corinthians 13: 8-13)

People on both sides of the debate find these words compelling, insisting that the apostle's remarks fully make their case. The fact that both camps employ the same passage of Scripture as proof text probably says much about why the issue remains unsettled and exceptionally divisive. Instead of resolving the issue, these words from the apostle have been a source of considerable wrangling in the religious community.

A thorough analysis of this passage of Scripture could easily fill volumes; in fact, it *has* filled volumes. However, since the exclusivity between miraculous spiritual gifts and the apostolate that was established by the Apostle Paul has been confirmed, this section loses much of its force in the debate over the cessation of spiritual gifts. Still, many continue to deny the teaching that miraculous gifts/works were designed for apostolic support despite Paul's clear affirmation. Therefore, brief consideration will be given to the lessons in Paul's renowned statement concerning the ending of these spiritual gifts.

The thirteenth chapter of 1 Corinthians is sandwiched between two chapters that speak extensively about the role and exercise of spiritual gifts. To help the believers in Corinth keep a proper perspective concerning these gifts, Paul waxes eloquent about the virtues of Christian love. Those remarks make up the thirteenth chapter of this epistle. Within the framework of Paul's discussion about love, he offers a simple contrast between the permanence of love and the temporal nature of spiritual gifts, which serves as a backdrop for the discussion. Still, in this section, there is no doubt that the apostle's point is to praise the ideal of love.

What is most ironic is that, although everyone realizes that Paul's focus is on Christian love, over the past century more papers have been penned, more debates have been launched, and more people have become emotionally charged over verses 8-12 than the balance of the chapter. Paul's comments about godly love have, for the most part, taken a back seat to what many are convinced is his veiled message concerning the duration of the extraordinary gifts of prophecy, tongues, and knowledge. They are confident that Paul was, in clandestine fashion, pinpointing for his audience the moment of their termination.

> *Paul's comments about godly love have…taken a back seat to what many are convinced is his veiled message concerning the duration of the extraordinary gifts…*

Paul had no need to provide a timeline for the passing of the gifts. Their intimate link to the apostles as a demonstration of their God-given authority (2 Corinthians 12: 12) denotes a reasonably short life span. The Corinthians had undoubtedly already connected those dots, which is why Paul was able to make a seemingly exceptional remark about their cessation in matter-of-fact fashion with little explanation. Nonetheless, the doctrinal implications of these verses cannot be ignored since, beginning in the early twentieth century, they have become a matter of serious division among believers. Therefore, it is important to determine how Paul's words (about love) influence the discussion on spiritual gifts.

Partial Knowledge and Understanding

Paul's statement that gifts will cease (v. 8) seems rather bold since he was addressing people who evidently cherished these gifts. While Paul's declaration concerning the gifts would not have been a complete surprise, the prospect of living without something upon which they had come to rely was probably not heartening news for the Corinthians.

Paul follows his pronouncement about prophecy, tongues, and knowledge with what he surely intended as comforting words. Knowing the Corinthians' fondness for spiritual gifts, he offers his readers reason to believe that the absence of these gifts should not be cause for dismay.

> ⁹For we know in part and we prophesy in part; ¹⁰but when the perfect comes, the partial will be done away. (1 Corinthians 13: 9-10)

The apostle begins verse nine with the word "for" (Gr. *gar*). This indicates that he is about to explain, or assign a reason to, his claim that "if *there are gifts of* prophecy, they will be done away; if *there are* tongues, they will cease; if *there is* knowledge, it will be done away" (v. 8). Why will they come to an end? They will end because of their shortcomings. Regardless of what one believes about *when* the gifts should come to an end, it is impossible to escape the fact that they would cease due to their limitations.

Paul notes, however, that the gifts would not simply disappear – they would be replaced by something better. The superior understanding offered by "the perfect" that was coming would eclipse the partial information/revelation provided through prophecy, tongues, and knowledge. This is exactly why, according to Paul, they could expect the gifts to cease.

The Perfect

A primary issue with these verses is the English translation of the Greek *to teleion* as "the perfect" (v. 10) that seems to distract so many. Applying an English definition to this word that is not intended has led many over the past century to erroneously assume that *to teleion* represents the believer's promised heavenly existence or, at the very least, the Parousia (Second Coming).

It is a mistake to presume that the Greek *teleios* expresses the same sense of flawlessness that *perfect* designates in English. The word *teleios* generally denotes maturity or completeness. In this case, *completeness* is the better interpretation, since it provides a natural contrast to *in part* that *perfect* does not. Perfect, as it is used in the English language, is considered a measure of quality while completeness generally denotes quantity or substance.

That *teleios* commonly points to maturity or completeness is evident in God's Word. For instance, Jesus told the rich young ruler, "If you wish to be complete (teleion), go *and* sell your possessions and give to the poor, and you will have treasure in heaven; and come, follow Me" (Matthew 19: 21). In his letter to the Colossians Paul wrote, "Epaphras, who is one of your number, a bondslave of Jesus Christ, sends you his greetings, always laboring earnestly for you in his prayers, that you may stand perfect (teleion) and fully assured in all the will of God" (Colossians 4: 12). Paul does not have in mind perfect (sinless) people, as the word *perfect* suggests in English, but rather those who have a fully developed (complete/mature) faith.

Since the goal is to apply legitimate principles of interpretation to Paul's words, the common biblical use[17] of *teleios* must be respected. Robert L. Thomas, who is Professor of New Testament at The Master's Seminary in Sun Valley, California, offers the following insight:

> No other use of *teleios* in Paul can possibly mean "perfection" in the sense of the absence of all imperfection…Utopian perfection was a philosophical notion, not a New Testament idea, for this word.[18]

Of note in this Corinthian setting is the fact that *to teleion* is neuter, rendering it a non-substantive, or a visionary concept, rather than an object (person, place, or thing). As such, it is not intended to identify a person or event, but a sense of maturity or wholeness, as it does in

---

[17] See Chapter 3, Principles of Interpretation: Common vs. Uncommon Use of Language, 44.
[18] Thomas, Robert, L. *Understanding Spiritual Gifts Revised Edition*, 124.

other verses (cf. Matthew 5: 48; James 1: 4; 3: 2). *The Scripture 4 All Greek Interlinear Bible* (NT) identifies *mature* (1 Corinthians 13: 10) and *finished* (James 1: 4) as the Greek meaning of *teleios*.

In the present setting, *to teleion* points to something (the identity of which is yet to be determined) that will offer what these spiritual gifts could not – superior spiritual knowledge. The "partial" that "will be done away" (v. 10) corresponds to prophecy, tongues, and knowledge (v. 8) and to "in part" (v. 9), each referring to a lesser degree of knowledge (*in part* suggests an emphasis on *quantity* of knowledge/revelation). It is evident from the text that *to teleion* (v. 10) points to something impressive that offers a spiritual perspective unattainable through the use of these gifts.

Complete vs. Incomplete Understanding

The apostle attempts to further enlighten his readers concerning this partial/complete relationship by following it with an analogy to which he believed the Corinthians would be able to relate.

> When I was a child, I used to speak like a child, think like a child, reason like a child; when I became a man, I did away with childish things. (1 Corinthians 13: 11)

Paul offers this statement with metaphoric eloquence. He compares the body of Christ (the church) to his own life that is encased within a human body. He then offers a contrast, within the framework of that metaphor, between his understanding and experiences as a child and his life as an adult. Thus, he depicts the human growth process that is intended to reflect the *in part* and *completeness* mentioned in the previous verse.

Humans experience various stages of life from infancy to adulthood. As one grows and learns, life can be seen much more clearly. In like manner, the apostle considers the limited information provided through the revelatory gifts to be fractional when compared to the wealth of knowledge and understanding available at the coming of *to teleion*. The Greek *ek merous*, which is translated "in part" in connection with knowledge and prophecy (v. 9), literally means that the information received through the gifts was coming *in pieces*, or *in installments*, much like the learning process from childhood to adulthood. That similarity makes the analogy effective.

Note that, in this metaphor, Paul does not identify the *end* of his journey (his eternal spiritual state) as that which is complete, but a comparatively advanced aspect of that journey (childhood vs. adulthood). Consequently, this is not the apostle's attempt to direct his readers' attention to the church's ultimate heavenly experience at the end of their journey. Instead, he pictures a more highly developed sense of understanding the church will experience along the way due to advanced revelation (when compared to the gifts).

Partial knowledge is being contrasted against *complete* knowledge (vs. 9-10) rather than *perfect* knowledge. That contrast is intended to correspond with the childhood (partial knowledge) and adulthood (the perfect) Paul mentions in the illustration. A meaning of the Parousia for *to teleion* (v. 10) fails the test as a correspondent to Paul's adult state (v. 11) that he saw as quite flawed (1 Timothy 1: 16). In fact, in this very section he points directly to the deficiencies of his adulthood, stating "now (as an adult male), I know in part" (v. 12). Yet, his adulthood (v. 11) is offered as a model of "the perfect" in the metaphor (v. 10). Those who consider *to teleion* a reference to absolute perfection have failed to recognize that it is, in this very setting, likened to Paul's quite imperfect manhood. Consequently, a *perfected state* (the Parousia or the believer's heavenly existence) or *perfect knowledge* (in the sense of flawlessness or lacking any imperfection) is a serious overestimation of *to teleion*.

Obscurity vs. Clarity

Paul seems to want to clarify his position even more, completing his analysis with yet another correlative. Beginning his comment with "For" (gar), Paul offers these words as further explanation of the portraiture in the previous verse:

> For now we see in a mirror dimly, but then face to face; now I know in part, but then I will know fully just as I also have been fully known. (1 Corinthians 13: 12)

Many view the "face to face" expression found here as a direct reference to either the Parousia or the eternal heavenly state, in keeping with their interpretation of "the perfect" (v. 9). In this case, "face to face" is seen as a literal encounter with Jesus beyond this earthly life. Yet, it is difficult to draw that conclusion when principles of interpretation are earnestly applied to the text.

Doing justice to Paul's words requires taking into consideration the figurative character of his statement. As with the child vs. man illustration (v. 11), the phrase, "For now we see in a mirror dimly" is a metaphor representing the depth of knowledge provided by the spiritual gifts mentioned in this passage (v. 9). Paul is not saying that the Corinthians were literally viewing themselves in a physical mirror. His point is that the knowledge they were receiving could be compared to a weak or distorted reflection. (Mirrors in antiquity were not of the quality of modern mercury-backed mirrors. They were made of polished brass or bronze and offered a reflection that was dim and unclear, which is what gives the metaphor of the poor image its effectiveness.)

The term "face to face" completes the metaphor Paul began with the image of the mirror. If the initial (mirror) terminology is figurative, there is no reason to take the second half of his statement literally. The idea is that the disciples will have knowledge and understanding (which is what Paul is talking about) such that obscurity will be done away. It will be like seeing with "face to face" clarity as opposed to the distorted image seen in a bronze mirror.

Paul is contrasting a *vague* image with a *clear* image, which is a logical distinction that flows smoothly within the narrative. He is not contrasting an obscure image in a mirror with the Parousia, which would be, at the very least, an awkward comparison. These are two completely different concepts with no natural contrast.

Metaphors offer colorful depictions that are comparative by nature. Consequently, upon encountering a metaphor in literature, the reader mentally (and often subconsciously) projects the words *as if* or *like* into the statement, knowing that it does not detract from, but accentuates the author's meaning. In fact, this is the point and personality of a metaphor. Therefore, it is difficult to argue with the stance that when Paul said, "For now we see in a mirror dimly," he was really saying *it is as if we see in a mirror dimly* – his way of saying that the knowledge and insight received via spiritual gifts did not always provide clarity due to the limited nature of the gifts. Like the mirror image, the message was incomplete, providing only a small glimpse into things spiritual.

The same can be said of the conclusion of Paul's metaphor. He is not referring to a literal face to face *meeting* any more than he is writing about a literal image in a mirror. Rather, he is writing about something that would provide superior definition. That is the nature of a metaphor and it is undoubtedly Paul's intent, given the figurative character of his remarks. Only a few Bible translations, some of which are mentioned below, have captured the true character of Paul's words.

Now we see a dim reflection [obscurely; *or* indirectly], as if we were looking into a mirror [through a glass darkly], but then we shall see clearly [face to face]. (Expanded Bible)

Now we see a blurred image in a mirror. Then we will see very clearly. (God's Word Translation)

Now we see a dim reflection, as if we were looking into a mirror, but then we shall see clearly. (New Century Version)

At this time, we see only a blurred image in a *metal* mirror. At the time of maturity, we will see plainly – as one person looking at another's face. (The Simple English Bible)

Paul completes his thought with "now I know in part, but then I will know fully." This comment constitutes a summarization of the meaning of the two metaphors of the text. It also speaks directly to the partial/complete character of the knowledge that is being discussed. If what the early Christians received through the spiritual gifts amounted to *pieces* of knowledge, one would expect to receive full (not perfect) knowledge when *to teleion* has come.

When Paul states "now I know in part," he is writing about the partial image in the mirror and about himself as a child. In contrast, when he says, "then I will know fully," he is writing about a clear mirror image and his adult state. Note that he does not say that he would know *God* fully – a meaning that has been offered as a matter of speculation by various commentators. He says he would *know* fully – or have full knowledge.

In the metaphor, the idea is simply that the first image is blurred and the second is not. Therefore, it is reasonable to conclude that both portions of the example make reference to the same image. The image that is in view is revelation from God. The first depicts distorted revelation while "face to face" indicates greater clarity when it comes to godly instruction.

In literature, including Scripture, mirror metaphors generally speak of self-reflection, or self-awareness. A strong argument can be made that this is the apostle's point since godly revelation is ultimately about individual relationships with God and with each other. The apostle explains to the Corinthians that the mirror image will become clear when *to teleion* arrives as a replacement for the gifts. At that time, believers can anticipate receiving complete insight into how to best honor God. James makes a valuable point concerning this principle as he employs his own imagery involving a mirror and the significance of self-awareness.

> [23] For if anyone is a hearer of the word and not a doer, he is like a man who looks at his natural face in a mirror; [24] for *once* he has looked at himself and gone away, he has immediately forgotten what kind of person he was. [25] But one who looks intently at the perfect law, the *law* of liberty, and abides by it, not having become a forgetful hearer but an effectual doer, this man will be blessed in what he does. (James 1: 23-25)

This is the only other passage in the New Testament where the Greek *esoptron*, translated as *mirror*, appears. Like the Apostle Paul in his words to the Corinthians, James has in mind the idea of one's self-awareness. He demonstrates, via the mirror imagery, the awareness and understanding available through God's Word. Scholars agree that "the perfect law" (v. 25), where *perfect* is translated from *teleion*, is a reference to Scripture since no other interpretation serves James's purpose. The difference is that, unlike the limited knowledge provided by the gifts, the knowledge that is available through God's Word is considered complete.

Paul often employs figurative speech in Scripture. When he does this, it is a consistent characteristic of the apostle to bring the metaphor full circle. He completes the figurative thought figuratively. Consider, for instance, his contrast between childhood and manhood (v. 11). Paul begins and ends the statement in figurative form. Like verse twelve, he contrasts these images within the construction of the metaphor. The same may be said of metaphors in other Pauline epistles:

> [16] Do you not know that when you present yourselves to someone as slaves for obedience, you are slaves of the one whom you obey, either of sin resulting in death, or of obedience resulting in righteousness? [17] But thanks be to God that though you were slaves of sin, you became obedient from the heart to that form of teaching to which you were committed, [18] and having been freed from sin, you became slaves of righteousness. (Romans 6: 16-18)

> [19] So then you are no longer strangers and aliens, but you are fellow citizens with the saints, and are of God's household, [20] having been built on the foundation of the apostles and prophets, Christ Jesus Himself being the corner *stone*, [21] in whom the whole building, being fitted together, is growing into a holy temple in the Lord, [22] in whom

you also are being built together into a dwelling of God in the Spirit. (Ephesians 2: 19-22)

In the Romans passage, Paul finishes the thought in the same manner as it began – as a metaphor – concluding with the imagery of slavery and freedom. Similarly, in his letter to the Ephesians, Paul remains faithful to the figure of the foundation that he had introduced, identifying Jesus as the cornerstone. Paul always completed his figurative thoughts in this manner.

Paul was an expressive writer. Each of these passages, written by the apostle, contains a natural flow within the metaphor itself. Given the consistency with which Paul developed and concluded his figurative remarks, it is unlikely that 1 Corinthians 13: 12 is the single exception to this principle in the Pauline epistles. There is no reason, literary or exegetical, to believe that Paul broke with consistency in this passage and, instead of comparing *vagueness* to *clarity*, which offer a natural contrast, switched from the figurative to the literal in mid-sentence by introducing the Parousia. This is not only an unwieldy rendering of the text, but it is uncharacteristic of Paul the author. This assortment of biblical metaphors (Romans 12: 4-5; 1 Corinthians 3: 6-9; 9: 24-27; 12: 12-27; 2 Corinthians 5: 1-5) provide a number of examples of Paul's writing style along with his inspired use of figurative language.

While discussing interpretive principles, Clinton Lockhart offered a basic rule in that, prior to interpreting a verse, it is important to first recognize whether it is intended as figurative or literal. In this case, there can be no doubt, and it is accepted by scholars of all doctrinal persuasions, that the mirror imagery Paul employs is intended as a metaphor. His "face to face" comment is meant to complete his statement that began with looking, figuratively speaking, into that mirror.

Despite the host of scholars who insist upon the eschatological significance of "face to face" in 1 Corinthians (which seem to be a majority), given the figurative nature of Paul's remarks, that approach to the passage is unfounded. It requires splitting the statement into a half-figurative/half-literal remark. The well-established truth about metaphoric language, and a basic rule of grammar, is that if it is not concluded in figurative mode, the metaphor loses its effect. The famous grammarian Lindley Murray (1745-1826) demonstrated this principle as follows:

...we should be careful, in the conduct of metaphors, never to jumble metaphorical and plain language together. An author, addressing himself to the king, says:

To thee the world its present homage pays;
The harvest early, but mature the praise.

It is plain, that, had not the rhyme misled him to the choice of an improper phrase, he would have said, *The harvest early, but mature the crop*; and so would have continued the figure which he had begun. Whereas, by dropping it unfinished, and by employing the literal word "praise," when we were expecting something that related to the harvest, the figure is broken, and the two members of the sentence have no suitable correspondence to each other.[19]

In that same vein, if Paul switched from figurative to literal language in mid-sentence, as in Murray's example, then like that example, "the figure is broken, and the two members of the sentence have no suitable correspondence to each other."

In short, the term "face to face" should not be considered a literal encounter with Christ at the Second Coming. In keeping with Paul's use of the metaphor concerning the mirror, it must be understood as a figure of speech, like the first (v. 11), about the clarity of understanding that is available to believers. If the statement "now we see in a mirror dimly" is figurative, a fact that is irrefutable, then "face to face" must be considered the conclusion of that metaphor. Just as the distance between Paul's childhood and manhood (v. 11) is relative (adulthood covers a broad range), the time frame between *now* and *then* is undefined, but refers generally to the contextual *now* (the time when information was received through revelatory gifts) and *then* (when information concerning God's will would be complete).

Paul never wrote in extraneous fashion. When he penned something, it served a purpose. With that in mind, it is not insignificant that he employs two analogies in his explanation of the passing of the gifts. If these analogies told the same story, Paul would have omitted one of them. However, each illustration is intended to offer a different perspective regarding Paul's claim that these gifts would eventually disappear. Therefore, a legitimate explanation of the passage requires that the definition of *to teleion* harmonize fully and

---

[19] Murray, Lindley. *Of Figures of Speech, by Lindley Murray*, http://grammar.about.com/od/essaysonstyle/a/MurrayFigures.htm

equally with both examples. Anything short of that demonstrates poor exegesis of the text.

Each of these illustrations serves to highlight a certain characteristic of the passing/replacement of the gifts. The first provides a sense of the progression from revelatory gifts to "the perfect" (v. 10). Growing from childhood to manhood does not take place instantaneously. It occurs over a period of decades. Childhood possessions and adolescent understanding change gradually over time. Therefore, the Corinthians could expect the same when it came to the replacement of the gifts. The failure of the gifts would not be abrupt; nor should they expect the coming of "the perfect" to occur too suddenly.

The obscure mirror image, when compared to "face to face" clarity, demonstrates the contrast in understanding that would be available at each end of the spectrum in the child/man analogy. A distorted mirror image reflects the lack of clarity available both physically (in a bronze mirror) and spiritually (through the gifts) to those in the first century. It is comparable to the undeveloped mental and emotional state of a child. In his "face to face" remark, Paul envisions the clarity that is present at adulthood and the spiritual insight that would eventually be made available to believers through *to teleion*.

It is evident from Paul's words that the information provided through these revelatory gifts (prophecy, tongues, and knowledge) would pale in comparison to the measure of information/understanding that would be available when the time came for their passing. Perusing the words of the prophets, it seems that, while prophecies generated *from* God, they were not typically *about* God, but *about* men. It was through these gifts that, for a time, God's will and/or plans for humanity were revealed. It stands to reason, then, that at the passing of these gifts and the arrival of *completeness*, it is man's knowledge about God's will and/or plans for humankind that would become *fully known*.

Parallel Pauline Passages

A couple of corresponding passages support this view concerning Paul's portrayal of spiritual gifts in Corinthians. For instance, the temporal role of the apostolate is, in part, established by Paul in his words to the Ephesians when he wrote about the foundational structure of the church, with Jesus "being the corner stone" (Ephesians 2: 20).

The foundation is that upon which a structure is built. Where the church is concerned, Jesus serves as the cornerstone of the foundation with apostles and prophets providing the balance of that foundation. All else is built upon that foundation. Once established, the foundation does not change. This passage provides insight into the temporal character of the apostolate. It also gives substance to the notion that prophets, along with the apostles, would be done once the church's foundation was laid.

> [11] And He gave some *as* apostles, and some *as* prophets, and some *as* evangelists, and some *as* pastors and teachers, [12] for the equipping of the saints for the work of service, to the building up of the body of Christ; [13] until we all attain to the unity of the faith, and of the knowledge of the Son of God, to a mature (teleion) man, to the measure of the stature which belongs to the fullness of Christ. [14] As a result, we are no longer to be children, tossed here and there by waves and carried about by every wind of doctrine, by the trickery of men, by craftiness in deceitful scheming; [15] but speaking the truth in love, we are to grow up in all *aspects* into Him who is the head, *even* Christ, [16] from whom the whole body, being fitted and held together by what every joint supplies, according to the proper working of each individual part, causes the growth of the body for the building up of itself in love. (Ephesians 4: 11-16)

These verses offer further insight into Paul's view of what lay ahead for the body of Christ. The focus here is not on the cessation of gifts like knowledge, prophecy, and tongues, but this section does provide a clearer sense of Paul's use of *teleion*, translated in this instance as *mature* (v. 13).

According to Paul, the "building up of the body of Christ" would result in a *united* and *mature* (teleion) state. Where *teleion* is concerned, no one argues in favor of the meaning of the Parousia in this instance, since the words simply will not allow it. Still, there is every reason to believe that the *teleion* state of the church that is mentioned here is the same as that discussed in 1 Corinthians, since Paul uses the term in parallel fashion, referring to the degree of understanding in the church body. Yet, according to this passage, once the church reached this *teleion* state, Christians would still be challenged "by the trickery of men, by craftiness in deceitful scheming" (v. 14). That being the case, *teleion* cannot refer to the Parousia here, since these things will not be present in heaven, which certainly weakens that interpretation in Paul's letter to the Corinthians.

Faith, Hope, and Love

Paul concludes his discourse on love with the words, "But now faith, hope, love, abide these three; but the greatest of these is love" (1 Corinthians 13: 13). Next to love, Paul views faith and hope as matters of great significance. Like love, their import is being compared to the less relevant gifts. They do not rise to the height of love, but they are greater than the gifts. The heart of Paul's message can be found in verses eight and thirteen. The metaphors that lie between these two verses are parenthetical explanatory remarks. They are not intended to affect the lesson, but to help articulate it. The NIV offers the following rendering of verses eight and thirteen, expressing the true sense of Paul's words:

> ⁸ Love never fails. But where there are prophecies, they will cease; where there are tongues, they will be stilled; where there is knowledge, it will pass away...¹³And now these three remain (meno): faith, hope and love. But the greatest of these is love. (1 Corinthians 13: 8, 13 – NIV)

Paul uses the Greek *meno,* translated "remain," which implies a sense of continuity. His choice of words is curious since, if he intended to merely acknowledge the existence of faith, hope, and love, the more appropriate word would seem to be *eimi*, which means *to be.* His reason for using *meno* becomes evident in the context, however, given the fact that he has just introduced the suspension of three things – prophecies, tongues, and knowledge (v. 8). Thus, *meno* is used in juxtaposition to these gifts. In other words, when the former three cease to exist, the latter three will *remain.*

Paul's use of *meno*, in view of the context, necessitates a period during which faith, hope, and love continue while (concurrently) the miraculous gifts mentioned here have ceased. This clashes with the view that the gifts could continue until the Second Coming of Christ, since two of these three virtues will also pass away at that time. At the Parousia, the believer's hope (in Christ's return) will be fulfilled, and faith will be made sight (1 John 3: 2-3). If the gifts continued until the Parousia, a time for faith, hope, and love to coexist absent spiritual gifts would not be possible.

It is highly likely that Paul was unaware of the *exact* timing for the cessation of these gifts. He may not have known when the last tongues would be spoken or when the final prophecy would be offered. Like many others, he may have believed Christ would come sooner rather than later. Neither did he know how long the apostles would remain on earth.

What Paul did know was that his role as an apostle and prophet, along with the role of other apostles, was foundational to the body of Christ (Ephesians 2: 20). The church would be built upon their foundational work with Jesus taking the place of the cornerstone. He was also aware, as was the Apostle Peter, that they were in the process of writing Scripture for the future benefit of believers (2 Peter 3: 16) as a matter of providing more complete insight into the ways of God. Paul was not specifying the exact time of the cessation of these gifts in this passage. He was only pointing to the *fact* of their cessation.

Identifying "The Perfect"

Robert L. Thomas, who was mentioned earlier, writes in defense of cessationism, even though he sees a reference to the Parousia in the words "face to face." However, he also recognizes something significant about this statement by Paul that most tend to overlook. Reflecting on this terminology in his book, *Understanding Spiritual Gifts*, he makes the following observation:

> Paul has not specifically identified the nature of the prophetic vision or the sequel that will replace it, the "face-to-face" encounter (13: 12).[20]

The implications of this statement must be given serious consideration. It is a matter of fact, as Professor Thomas has noted here, that the apostle has not identified a person, object, or event in conjunction with the phrase "face to face." Why? He has not introduced a new character or event because he is still focused on the image in the mirror – revelation from God. Thus, the image has not changed. The prospect of a meeting outside the mirror imagery must be superimposed onto the text since Paul mentions no such *encounter*.

Those who maintain that Paul has the Parousia in view have cultivated the notion that Paul is writing about being face to face *with God* or face to face *with Christ* as a speculative interpretation (while ignoring the figurative context). They insist that Paul has changed his focus from godly revelation to God himself. Yet, it can be said unequivocally that Paul says nothing about a face-to-face *encounter with Christ* in this setting. In fact, introducing the personage of Christ

---

[20] Thomas, Robert L. *Understanding Spiritual Gifts Revised Edition*, 82

as the object of the phrase "face to face" only serves to undermine the mirror analogy to which these words are so intimately linked.

When James, in his epistle, employs his own mirror imagery (James 1: 23-25), his focus is on one's diligence and faithful response to teaching found in Scripture. Also, note that in James's illustration, the man sees himself in the mirror (self-reflection), and not someone or something else. The comparison is between someone seeing himself in a mirror and seeing himself in Scripture. The image is unchanged.

James's use of the word *teleion* to depict the completeness of Scripture provides a measure of support for a comparable meaning in 1 Corinthians. No one can insist that this refers to the formal *canonized* New Testament, however, since it is unknown exactly what Paul anticipated as far as new covenant writings were concerned. Still, it is not unreasonable to believe that Paul has in mind the writings of the apostles that would eventually provide a permanent collection of apostolic teachings upon which the church could build.

Some may ask: *If to teleion is an allusion to the finalization of New Testament writings, why didn't Paul write:* **when Scripture is completed**? Others may wonder: *If to teleion is an allusion to the Parousia, why didn't Paul write:* **when Jesus returns**? The answer to both questions is the same. Paul was not establishing a timeline for the cessation of gifts. He was contemplating the temporal nature of the gifts to emphasize the virtues and permanence of love. In a chapter that focuses on love, that is what should be drawn from this text…nothing more.

Men will continue to disagree about what Paul has in mind with the phrase *to teleion*, but in comparing the temporal character of the gifts (vs. 9-10), he is focused directly on enhancing the manner by which godly instructions are delivered to men. Therefore, the idea of written apostolic instructions fits well as a replacement for, and improvement upon, revelatory spiritual gifts. It is a monumental stretch to presume that Paul has the Parousia in view, since 1) the Parousia is not mentioned in the text, and 2) *teleios* is not used as an eschatological reference in Scripture. This word generally depicts a sense of maturity or completeness elsewhere in God's Word (Matthew 19: 21; Romans 12: 2; Ephesians 4: 13; James 1: 4, 25).

Spiritual Gifts and the Parousia

The view that Paul was connecting the withdrawal of these spiritual gifts to eschatology (end times) seems to be a rather disproportionate proposition considering the magnitude of the

Parousia. The changes believers will experience as they are transformed to a heavenly existence will surpass what anyone can now imagine. Spiritual life beyond this fleshly veil will be so vastly different from life on earth that the two cannot really be compared. John makes this very point in some of his final words:

> [1] Then I saw a new heaven and a new earth; for the first heaven and the first earth passed away, and there is no longer *any* sea. [2] And I saw the holy city, new Jerusalem, coming down out of heaven from God, made ready as a bride adorned for her husband. [3] And I heard a loud voice from the throne, saying, "Behold, the tabernacle of God is among men, and He will dwell among them, and they shall be His people, and God Himself will be among them, [4] and He will wipe away every tear from their eyes; and there will no longer be any death; there will no longer be *any* mourning, or crying, or pain; the first things have passed away." [5] And He who sits on the throne said, "Behold, I am making all things new." And He said, "Write, for these words are faithful and true." (Revelation 21: 1-5)

The elimination of these gifts at or after the Parousia would be inconsequential when compared to the enormity of the transformation that will take place. Unless the gifts were exceedingly relevant to the Parousia, and there is no scriptural reason to believe that is the case, Paul would have no reason to draw attention to their passing in relation to eschatology, since, at that time, God will make "all things new" (v. 5). If *everything* changes, why highlight the ending of a few spiritual gifts at that time? Consequently, the ceasing of these gifts would only be noteworthy if it were to take place within the framework of church life here on earth and prior to the Second Coming.

The apostle has not written these verses (1 Corinthians 13: 8-12) as a teaser about the timing of the cessation of gifts. That is not the message Paul has in mind. His focus is on the worth of Christian love. The gifts are only mentioned to contrast their temporary nature against the permanence of love. Perhaps the reason people remain so divided over the apostle's words is that they are trying to draw more information from these verses than Paul intended.

What is most curious, and even a bit perplexing, is that the doctrine of continuationism has been argued rather successfully based largely on a passage of Scripture that candidly proclaims the passing of these gifts (v. 8). The Corinthians would not have made that mistake when they read Paul's words, since they fully understood the relationship between the apostles and the miraculous works of the Spirit (2 Corinthians 12: 12). It is fascinating that the uncomplicated, biblically established principle of the bestowal of spiritual gifts through the apostles (Acts 8: 18) could be forsaken by many in favor of a doctrine of continuation that lacks biblical support.

Chapter 8

Spiritual Gifts and Biblical Harmony

Miraculous Episodes in Scripture

On occasion, Scripture depicts miraculous works being performed outside the presence of an apostle. At times this occurred even prior to an apostle's appearance on the scene. For instance, Philip performed extraordinary works in Samaria before Peter and John arrived there (Acts 8: 4-8). Also, when writing to the Romans, Paul acknowledged that some believers in the church there had demonstrated miraculous gifts (Romans 12: 4-6) even though there is no record of Paul or any other apostle traveling to that city before he penned his letter.

Passages like this can cause some confusion where the miraculous is concerned, so some time will be spent considering certain episodes involving miraculous works and how they harmonize with the teaching that the power of the Spirit was distributed through the apostles. Such incidents are fully understandable and are explained through complementary passages of Scripture. Paul also takes time, in various passages, to teach the disciples about the use of these gifts.

Acts 6: 8

Shortly after the Day of Pentecost, problems arose within the church in Jerusalem. As a remedy, the believers selected certain men to address these issues. These men were to step in and see to the various needs of the body. For this work, they chose Stephen, Philip, Prochorus, Nicanor, Timon, Parmenas and Nicolas (Acts 6: 5). Having been selected, these men served the church well. As the story unfolds, Luke focuses his attention on a man named Stephen.

> And Stephen, full of grace and power, was performing great wonders and signs among the people. (Acts 6: 8)

With the words "great wonders and signs," it is evident that Luke is writing about miracles since this is the meaning of these words elsewhere in Scripture (Matthew 24: 24; Mark 13: 22; Hebrews 2: 4). Early in the post-Pentecost age, only the apostles performed miracles

(Acts 5: 12). How, then, was Stephen able to perform miracles since he was not an apostle?

Scripture teaches that "...the Spirit was bestowed through the laying on of the apostles' hands" (Acts 8: 18). These words represent more than the words of an observer in Samaria. This is a fundamental biblical truth. With this principle in mind, it could be inferred without further investigation that, at some time, the power to perform miracles was bestowed upon Stephen through the apostles' touch. However, there is additional scriptural support in favor of this view.

> [5] ...they chose Stephen, a man full of faith and of the Holy Spirit, and Philip, Prochorus, Nicanor, Timon, Parmenas and Nicolas, a proselyte from Antioch. [6] And these they brought before the apostles; and after praying, they laid their hands on them. (Acts 5b-6)

Stephen did not perform miracles until after the apostles laid their hands on him. While Luke has not specifically stated that this power was bestowed at this particular time, this is a reasonable conclusion in that it provides biblical harmony between Stephen's performance of miracles and the means by which the power of the Spirit was delivered.

Acts 8: 5-8

Due to the persecution of the church after Stephen's death, the believers fled Jerusalem, dispersing themselves throughout other lands. Philip, who had left Jerusalem, traveled to Samaria. Luke provides the following narrative about Philip's experience.

> [5] Philip went down to the city of Samaria and *began* proclaiming Christ to them. [6] The crowds with one accord were giving attention to what was said by Philip, as they heard and saw the signs which he was performing. [7] For *in the case of* many who had unclean spirits, they were coming out *of them* shouting with a loud voice; and many who had been paralyzed and lame were healed. [8] So there was much rejoicing in that city. (Acts 8: 5-8)

The apostles heard what was happening in Samaria. As a result, Peter and John traveled there where they bestowed the Spirit upon Philip's many converts. In fact, this is the very incident where a man named Simon observed the apostles bestowing the power of the Spirit. What is interesting about the events in Samaria is that Philip performed miracles prior to the arrival of the apostles.

Philip, like Stephen, received his ability to perform miracles from the apostles. Revisiting the list of men who were chosen with Stephen to serve the church in Jerusalem – those upon whom the apostles laid their hands – it seems Philip was among them (Acts 6: 5). It stands to reason, then, that Philip received the power of the Holy Spirit at that time.

Romans 8: 26-27

When a person accepts Jesus as Savior, God's promise of the presence of the Holy Spirit as a helper and teacher for that believer is fulfilled. The Holy Spirit guides people in their walk with God so that they can live lives that honor him. Paul explained to the Romans that, on occasion, the Spirit might intercede in one's prayers when words fail.

> [26] In the same way the Spirit also helps our weakness; for we do not know how to pray as we should, but the Spirit Himself intercedes for us with groanings too deep for words; [27] and He who searches the hearts knows what the mind of the Spirit is, because He intercedes for the saints according to the *will* of God. (Romans 8: 26-27)

What Paul has described is not, as some have suggested, a form of speaking in tongues. The Spirit may intercede, not with words, but with "groanings too deep for words" (v. 26). In other versions they are called "groans that words cannot express" (NIV-1984), "wordless groans" (NIV), "words that cannot be uttered" (KJV), and "groanings that cannot be uttered" (NKJV).

The prayer of apparent turmoil that is pictured here is one where the words necessary to present concerns to God are too difficult to express. It is certainly prayer *in the spirit* as the believer allows the Holy Spirit to lead the way, since the weight of the world can make it difficult to speak the words. However, what Paul does not have in mind in this passage is doctrine concerning speaking or praying in tongues.

Nothing in the eighth chapter of Romans suggests that Paul is addressing spiritual gifts in any fashion. His discourse in this section of Scripture focuses on individuals exhibiting personal perseverance while they await their heavenly reward. He is attempting to teach the Romans what it means to live in the Spirit even as they are surrounded by things of the flesh. Spiritual gifts are not in view. Additionally, the *groanings* by which the Spirit intercedes are not spoken words, such as tongues, but *unuttered* words that have been replaced by the groans that stem from words, perhaps out of grief, anguish, or sorrow, that are too painful to speak.

Romans 12: 4-8

Each Christian has something unique to contribute to the well-being of the body of Christ. This is also true of spiritual gifts. Writing to the Romans, Paul discussed the complementary nature of the gifts. Assorted gifts were given so that the body of Christ would be complete.

> [4] For just as we have many members in one body and all the members do not have the same function, [5] so we, who are many, are one body in Christ, and individually members one of another. [6] Since we have gifts that differ according to the grace given to us, *each of us is to exercise them accordingly*: if prophecy, according to the proportion of his faith; [7] if service, in his serving; or he who teaches, in his teaching; [8] or he who exhorts, in his exhortation; he who gives, with liberality; he who leads, with diligence; he who shows mercy, with cheerfulness. (Romans 12: 4-8)

It stands to reason that Paul was writing to the Romans about gifts with which they were familiar. If they knew nothing of these gifts, his words might be cause for confusion. While most of the gifts mentioned here fall under the headings of service and ministry, the same cannot be said of prophecy, which is considered a miraculous gift.

What is interesting is that, prior to Paul's letter, there is no indication that any apostle had yet traveled to Rome. If the Romans were familiar with the gift of prophecy (and perhaps other miraculous workings of the Spirit), how can this be reconciled with the biblical principle that the power of the Spirit was bestowed by the apostles?

Where the church in Rome is concerned, in his final salutation in his letter to that congregation (Romans 16), Paul takes the time to offer greetings to roughly thirty individuals who were his personal friends. Some, like Aquila and Priscilla, had been his close companions for a considerable length of time. It can be reasoned, then, that the apostle distributed the power of the Spirit to these believers when he was with them.

Still, many in Rome would not have had the opportunity to experience these gifts. That is undoubtedly why Paul was anxious to travel to Rome so that he could impart spiritual gifts (Romans 1: 11). Therefore, it is not out of harmony with the intimacy between the apostles and the miraculous that these gifts were carried off to other locations by those so endowed.

1 Corinthians 1: 4-9

Some have insisted that, in his initial salutation to the Corinthians, Paul linked the spiritual gifts to eschatology when he penned the following greeting:

> [4] I thank my God always concerning you for the grace of God which was given you in Christ Jesus, [5] that in everything you were enriched in Him, in all speech and all knowledge, [6] even as the testimony concerning Christ was confirmed in you, [7] so that you are not lacking in any gift, awaiting eagerly the revelation of our Lord Jesus Christ, [8] who will also confirm you to the end, blameless in the day of our Lord Jesus Christ. [9] God is faithful, through whom you were called into fellowship with His Son, Jesus Christ our Lord. (1 Corinthians 1: 4-9)

The Corinthians were "not lacking in any gift, awaiting eagerly the revelation of our Lord Jesus Christ who will also confirm you to the end, blameless in the day of our Lord Jesus Christ" (vs. 7 & 8). In that case, would it not seem fair for the Corinthians to anticipate the presence of these gifts until Christ's return? A wide range of viewpoints have been offered concerning this passage. Some teach that these verses offer no reference to miraculous spiritual gifts. Others believe miracles are but a single aspect of the text. Still others claim that Paul's focus is *primarily* on the miraculous gifts.

The diversity of views is a decent indicator of the difficulties of the text. However, on this topic, the only relevant question concerning this greeting from the apostle to the Corinthians is whether verses seven and eight serve as testimony that miraculous spiritual gifts would continue until the Parousia. It is unwise to dig too deeply for doctrinal language in a salutation where Paul is preparing his readers for admonition. Yet, these words cannot be ignored since all Scripture is significant.

The bond between the miraculous and the apostles, which has been discussed at length and is well-established, governs this text. Any instruction concerning spiritual gifts must harmonize naturally with this guiding New Testament principle. The fact that miraculous spiritual gifts were intended for the apostolic age does not diminish their importance for those who experienced them. These gifts had confirmed, or authenticated, the gospel message in Corinth (v. 6). The men and women of that city exercised these gifts *even as* they awaited Christ's return (v. 7).

Some insist that verse seven demands the continuation of the miraculous gifts until Christ's return, but that is not what the text says. Literal English Bible translations reveal that Paul is talking, not about the use of the gifts *until* the revelation of Christ, but about the fact that the Corinthians had enjoyed these gifts *while waiting for Christ*. The word "awaiting" in verse seven is not forward-looking as many contend. Instead, the apostle has in mind what the Corinthians *had been and were still doing*. They were practicing their use of spiritual gifts while waiting for Christ. This suggests that they were hoping Jesus might return sooner rather than later. Here are a couple of literal translations offered by some interlinear New Testaments:

> So as you not to be lacking in no gift, having been awaiting the revelation of the Lord of us, Jesus Christ.[21]

> So that you are not lacking in any gift, awaiting the revelation of the Lord of us, Jesus Christ.[22]

Paul then told the Corinthians that Jesus would "also confirm you to the end, blameless in the day of our Lord" (v. 8). In this case, *confirm* does not suggest substantiation or authentication in the manner that the gospel message was confirmed (v. 6), nor is this a reference to miraculous spiritual gifts. Christ's confirming of the Corinthians regards *maintaining their spirituality* or *keeping them strong* in the faith. This is a principle distinct from the gifts of verse seven as indicated by Paul's insertion of the word *also* (Gr. *kai*), meaning this is something that was a benefit of God's grace *in addition to* the gifts. The NIV translation illustrates this point very well.

> [7] Therefore you do not lack any spiritual gift as you eagerly wait for our Lord Jesus Christ to be revealed. [8] He will **also** (kai) **keep you firm** to the end, so that you will be blameless on the day of our Lord Jesus Christ. (1 Corinthians 1: 7-8 – NIV) Emphasis added.

---

[21] Green, J. P., Sr. general editor, *The Interlinear Bible Greek English, Volume IV New Testament*, 450.

[22] Brown, Robert K. and Philip W. Comfort, translators. *The New Greek English Interlinear New Testament*, 579.

1 Corinthians 12: 27-31

Just prior to challenging the Corinthians with his discourse on love in the thirteenth chapter, Paul makes the following comment concerning spiritual gifts:

> [27] Now you are Christ's body, and individually members of it. [28] And God has appointed in the church, first apostles, second prophets, third teachers, then miracles, then gifts of healings, helps, administrations, various kinds of tongues. [29] All are not apostles, are they? All are not prophets, are they? All are not teachers, are they? All are not workers of miracles, are they? [30] All do not have gifts of healings, do they? All do not speak with tongues, do they? All do not interpret, do they? [31] But earnestly desire the greater gifts. (1 Corinthians 12: 27-31)

If word placement means anything, which is generally the case throughout Scripture, apostleship would be considered the greatest of the spiritual gifts. It is listed first here with prophecy coming second. Interestingly, healing and tongues, along with interpretation of tongues, appear last. After educating the disciples concerning the Spirit's equitable distribution of the gifts, Paul encourages his readers to "earnestly desire the greater gifts" (v. 31). *Earnestly desire the greater gifts?* If the gifts were given via the apostles' touch, and Paul was not even nearby (he was writing from Ephesus), why would he encourage such a thing? Furthermore, the greatest gift was apostleship, which was not available to all men. Thus, it would seem fruitless to desire apostleship. What could Paul be thinking?

It is safe to presume that Paul was not encouraging the Corinthians to desire the gift/office of apostle. He, as well as his readers, realized that was something unavailable to the general membership of the body of Christ. It was an office received by appointment directly from the Lord himself. Therefore, as far as spiritual gifts are concerned, apostleship was distinct from all the rest. The apostolate aside, Paul seems to indicate that desiring other gifts such as prophecy was not a bad thing.

According to Scripture, individuals received miraculous spiritual gifts through the apostles' touch. While that statement is true, the process by which gifts were bestowed deserves re-examination to gain greater insight into Paul's words. Individuals received spiritual gifts after the apostles laid hands on them. However, it was the Holy Spirit who distributed the gifts. When an apostle laid his hands on a believer, that person received the outpouring of the Spirit. This is what Luke wrote about and Simon witnessed when Peter and John visited Samaria. At that time, "Simon saw that the Spirit was bestowed through the laying on of the apostles' hands" (Acts 8: 17-18).

The outpouring of the Spirit that was received through the apostles resulted in the miraculous manifestations experienced and witnessed by men. It is reasonable to conclude, and harmonizes fully with biblical instruction, that once the Spirit fell upon someone via the apostles' touch, he would distribute gifts as he saw fit. Also, nothing in Scripture precludes the Holy Spirit from distributing more than one gift, or distributing assorted gifts at various times, to someone who had received the Spirit in this manner. Thus, it would not be unreasonable for Paul to encourage the members at Corinth who had already received the outpouring of the Spirit to "earnestly desire the greater gifts."

1 Corinthians 13: 1-3

The expression "…tongues of angels" is found only once in God's Word. However, that fact has not prevented questionable treatment of this phrase. Many people, convinced that the tongues spoken by so many today are not equivalent to those tongues of the first century, have defended their use by claiming that, rather than *human languages*, they are the *angelic languages* mentioned by the Apostle Paul. Consequently, they are not subject to the same rules (of language) as the tongues of the early church.

> [1] If I speak in the tongues of men or of angels, but do not have love, I am only a resounding gong or a clanging cymbal. [2] If I have the *gift* of prophecy and can fathom all mysteries and all knowledge, and if I have a faith that can move mountains, but do not have love, I am nothing. [3] If I give all I possess to the poor and give over my body to hardship that I may boast, but do not have love, I gain nothing. (1 Corinthians 13: 1-3)

Paul's use of literary devices was discussed earlier, and these verses offer a prime example for consideration. The apostle articulates a clear point in the form of hyperbole. This is an over-the-top statement by Paul to impress on the minds of his readers his point concerning love. Thus, he exaggerated his comments for them to grasp his meaning. John Calvin, a key figure in the Reformation Movement of the sixteenth century, noted the hyperbole Paul had in view, stating:

When he speaks of the tongue of angels, he uses a hyperbolical expression to denote what is singular, or distinguished.[23]

The amplified nature of the statement is further supported as Paul continues in hyperbolic fashion. He contemplates for his readers the possibilities of having the gift of prophecy, fathoming all mysteries, being endowed with complete knowledge, and having faith to move mountains. He talks of giving all possessions to the poor and sacrificing his own body. These overstatements suggest exaggeration heaped on top of exaggeration – all intended to introduce Paul's teaching on the importance of love. All of these, on the heels of a reference to angelic tongues, suggest that Paul is attempting to make a point through what might be considered *exaggerated hyperbole*, if such a thing exists.

This is not the only instance of angelic hyperbole in Paul. This text is comparable to another that Paul wrote to the church in Galatia. He told them, "But even if we, or an angel from heaven, should preach to you a gospel contrary to what we have preached to you, he is to be accursed!" (Galatians 1: 8). It is highly unlikely, and even impossible, that an apostle or an angel from heaven would offer a competing gospel message. Paul's wording here is intended only to solidify for the Galatians the strength of the gospel message they had already received, but from which they had slowly begun to slip away. His point is that if it were wrong to accept another gospel from an angel or an apostle, it would be senseless to accept it from someone else.

Outside of 1 Corinthians 13: 1, there is no verse in God's Word connecting an angelic language with the gift of tongues, which highlights the uniqueness of Paul's remark. In every instance where this gift is discussed in the pages of Scripture, human language is the overt theme. This is equally true in 1 Corinthians 12-14. That is what makes Paul's use of this hyperbole so effective. He is saying that *even* the tongues of angels, if accessible, would be worthless without love.

Those who have developed their religious practice of tongues around this inflated statement by Paul should reconsider the reasonableness of this approach when it comes to biblical interpretation. As with 1 Corinthians 13: 8-13, figurative style must be allowed its place in Scripture without forcing a meaning onto the text that is not intended and has no support elsewhere in God's Word. It is

---

[23] Calvin, John, *Calvin's Commentary on the Bible*, http://www.studylight.org/commentaries/cal/view.cgi?bk=45&ch=13.

unwise to develop a doctrine (i.e., angelic tongues) based upon a single obscure/figurative statement of Scripture.

1 Corinthians 14: 1-5

Paul continues his illumination concerning spiritual gifts as he moves into the fourteenth chapter of his first epistle to the church at Corinth.

> [1] Pursue love, yet desire earnestly spiritual *gifts*, but especially that you may prophesy. [2] For one who speaks in a tongue does not speak to men but to God; for no one understands, but in *his* spirit he speaks mysteries. [3] But one who prophesies speaks to men for edification and exhortation and consolation. [4] One who speaks in a tongue edifies himself; but one who prophesies edifies the church. [5] Now I wish that you all spoke in tongues, but *even* more that you would prophesy; and greater is one who prophesies than one who speaks in tongues, unless he interprets, so that the church may receive edifying. (1 Corinthians 14: 1-5)

Again, Paul encourages his readers to "desire earnestly spiritual *gifts*," although, in this case he specifically has in mind the gift of prophecy (note that he did not encourage them to seek the gift of apostle). The primary reason for Paul's focus on prophecy is also explained. Prophecy was, in Paul's view, the most beneficial and profitable of all spiritual gifts (vs. 2-5) besides apostleship. Additionally, prophets aided the apostles in declaring God's will openly to the people, serving as a foundational element for the church (Ephesians 2: 20). Insight into how they might attain these gifts absent the presence of an apostle was given when considering Paul's instructions in 1 Corinthians 12: 27-31.[24]

1 Corinthians 14: 14-16

Praying in (or with) *the spirit* is a recurring phrase in the epistles. Paul employs the term twice while Jude uses it once in his abbreviated address.

> [14] For if I pray in a tongue, my spirit prays, but my mind is unfruitful. [15] What is the *outcome* then? I will **pray with the spirit** and I will pray with the mind also; I will sing with the spirit and I will sing with the mind also. [16] Otherwise if you bless in the spirit only, how will the one who fills the place of the ungifted say the "Amen" at

---

[24] See pages 122-123

your giving of thanks, since he does not know what you are saying? (1 Corinthians 14: 14-16) Emphasis added.

Many believe that Paul, in these words to the Corinthians, equates praying in the Spirit and speaking in tongues. However, this view fails to account for the fullness of Paul's comments. While his instructions are given in the context of tongues, he is writing about the unfruitfulness of tongues in an assembly where no interpreter is available. The apostle states, "For if I pray in a tongue, my spirit prays, but my mind is unfruitful" (v. 14). As a matter of contrast, Paul follows up with the comment, "I will pray with the spirit and with the mind also" (v. 15). He then adds, "I will sing with the spirit and I will sing with the mind also" (v. 15). Singing and praying in the company of Christians are complementary forms of worship.

When considering the lessons from this text, the Bible student must understand the setting about which Paul writes. His focus is on the gathering of believers. With that in mind, the apostle teaches two valuable lessons. First, speaking/praying in tongues represents *one's spirit praying* (v. 14) or, in other terms, *praying with the spirit* (v. 15). Second, Paul does not *equate* praying with the spirit and speaking/praying in tongues.

There are differences of opinion about what Paul means by *unfruitful*[25] (v. 14). Some believe he means that the mind of the one who is praying lacks understanding when praying in tongues. Others have suggested that a message or revelation delivered through tongues is clear to the person who is praying, but the prayer would bear no fruit to those present without an interpreter. Given the balance of the narrative, where the concern is blessing the *ungifted* (v. 16), the second view probably fits the context best, but the first view is not without merit.

According to the apostle, he could pray *in the spirit* – via tongues – without understanding (v. 14); or he could pray intelligibly *in the spirit* (v. 15) with understanding. This view is supported by the text as Paul distinguishes between praying (or singing) "in the spirit only" (v. 16) and praying (or singing) in the spirit *and* with the mind (v. 15). By praying/singing with the spirit *and* with the mind, the spirit and mind labor jointly. As a result, those present can appreciate the prayer or the song (v. 16).

---

[25] The Greek indicates a lack of comprehension.

1 Corinthians 14: 39

Paul offered what may be a brief glimpse into some of the issues the Corinthians faced with respect to spiritual gifts as he charged the disciples with the following apostolic command.

> Therefore, my brethren, desire earnestly to prophesy, and do not forbid to speak in tongues. (1 Corinthians 14: 39)

Apparently, some in the congregation at Corinth sought to limit, or even prohibit, speaking in tongues in corporate worship. Since this chapter focuses on prophets and tongue-speakers, both seeming to want to dominate the assembly, it could very well be that the prophets sought to muffle the voices of those gifted with tongues. In fact, his words seem to be directed toward those with the gift of prophecy, telling them that they should "desire earnestly to prophesy." However, their eagerness to share prophecy should not be abused to the point where they stifle other giftedness since, according to the apostle, "…to each one is given the manifestation of the Spirit for the common good" (1 Corinthians 12: 7).

Paul's words were written at a time when miraculous spiritual gifts were available to the church. Having already noted the temporal nature of the gifts (13: 8), Paul still recognized them as valuable tools for the edification of the body. Therefore, this verse is not inconsistent with teaching concerning gifts, even though they would only exist for a time. While they were available, the disciples should take every advantage of the complementary character of the gifts for the benefit of the church.

Ephesians 6: 18

Paul sought to foster the prayer lives of the disciples at Ephesus, encouraging them to make prayer a part of their daily walk with God.

> With all prayer and petition **pray at all times in the Spirit**, and with this in view, be on the alert with all perseverance and petition for all the saints. (Ephesians 6: 18) Emphasis added.

Paul encouraged the disciples at Ephesus to "pray at all times in the Spirit." No mention is made of tongues or praying in the spirit *only*; nor is there any implication of prayer in an assembly. The phrase "at all times" suggests that Paul has in mind prayer as a way of life rather than prayer that takes place in a specific setting. Could this not, then, be an encouragement from Paul for the Ephesians to pray (in tongues) in the spirit at all times?

Praying in the spirit, as Paul uses the term, seems to suggest that one should allow the Holy Spirit to guide/lead in prayer. This is akin to his explanation of *walking in the spirit*, which Paul defines as being led by the Spirit (Galatians 5: 16-18). Walking in the Spirit means living a Spirit-led life in the same sense that the Apostle John defined *walking in the light* as *walking with God* (1 John 1: 5-7). This offers insight into the difference Paul sees between praying in spirit *only* (1 Corinthians 14: 16) and praying in spirit *and* mind. It is possible to do both but praying in the spirit *only* seems to indicate that the person who is praying allows the Spirit to fully determine the content of the prayer since the mind is *unfruitful* (1 Corinthians 14: 14). It is a prayer that is completely of the Spirit. On the other hand, praying *intelligibly* (with the mind) involves the productive mind of the individual who allows the Spirit to lead the way as that person shares his/her thoughts with God (and others if they are present).

Such is the case with "prayers and petitions" in the Ephesians passage. Petitions do not come from an unfruitful mind, or a mind without understanding. On the contrary, they come from a person who approaches God with kingdom thoughts. The prayers Paul has in mind are prayers offered consistently and with resolve. In that vein, he asked the Ephesians to allow the Holy Spirit to direct their prayers as they prayed with understanding with "petition for all the saints."

1 Timothy 4: 14; 2 Timothy 1: 6

Some may wonder about a couple of passages in Paul's letters to Timothy. A few have advanced the notion that a miraculous spiritual gift may have been delivered to Timothy through the hands of the presbytery (elders). An honest examination of these passages is required in order to be faithful to the principles of interpretation.

> Do not neglect the spiritual gift within you, which was bestowed on you through prophetic utterance with the laying on of hands by the presbytery. (1 Timothy 4: 14)

> For this reason I remind you to kindle afresh the gift of God which is in you through the laying on of my hands. (2 Timothy 1: 6)

In the first instance, Paul reminds Timothy of a gift he received, *through* prophecy, as the elders laid their hands on him. While some insist that this is an example of Timothy receiving a miraculous spiritual gift through the hands of the elders, that conclusion is difficult to reconcile with the words of the text. First, there is no mention here of any extraordinary manifestation of the Spirit. It is true that the word translated gift (charisma) is often employed to indicate the miraculous, but that is not its sole meaning or even its most common use.

This word for *gifts* appears seventeen times in the New Testament. It is used sixteen times by the Apostle Paul and once by Peter. It is evident from the context that seven of these involve miraculous gifts (Romans 1: 11; 12: 6; 1 Corinthians 12: 4, 9, 28, 30, 31). Note that references to these extraordinary works, or gifts, are limited to Romans and 1 Corinthians. Peter makes reference to spiritual gifts, but he has in mind the gifts of hospitality, stewardship, and service (1 Peter 4: 9-10). He also mentions speaking, which some insist could be an allusion to prophecy and/or tongues, although the word *logos* is not normally used in that manner. Elsewhere, when Paul employs the word *charisma*, his theme is generally God's favor toward mankind or Christians' grace toward one another (Romans 5: 15, 16; 6: 23; 11: 29; 1 Corinthians 1: 7; 7: 7; 2 Corinthians 1: 11). This leaves only the two passages in Paul's letters to Timothy unexplained.

Although it is not stated specifically, it is possible, and perhaps even probable, that Timothy experienced a miraculous manifestation of the Spirit when Paul laid hands on him (2 Timothy 1: 6). Paul, an apostle of Jesus Christ, could distribute the power of the Holy Spirit to believers. That having been said, it can be said conclusively that the incident cited in 1 Timothy as the presbytery participated does not depict a miraculous gift being given via the hands of the elders. Consider these insightful words from Robert Jamieson, A. R. Fausset, and David Brown concerning these verses:

> **Neglect not the gift**—by letting it lie unused. In 2Ti 1:6 the gift is represented as a *spark* of the Spirit lying within him, and sure to smoulder by neglect, the *stirring up* or keeping in lively exercise of which depends on the will of him on whom it is bestowed (Mt 25:18, 25, 27, 28). The *charism* or spiritual gift, is that of the Spirit which qualified him for "the work of an evangelist" (Eph 4:11; 2Ti 4:5), or perhaps *the gift of discerning spirits,* specially needed in his function of ordaining, as overseer [BISHOP HINDS].
> **given thee**—by God (1Co 12:4, 6).
> **by prophecy**—that is, by the Holy Spirit, at his general ordination, or else consecration, to the special see of Ephesus, speaking through the prophets God's will to give him the graces needed to qualify him for his work (1Ti 1:18; Ac 13:1-3).

with ... laying on of ... hands—So in Joshua's case (Nu 27:18-20; De 34:9). The gift was connected with the symbolical act of laying on hands. But the *Greek* "with" implies that the *presbyter's* laying on hands was the mere *accompaniment* of the conferring of the gift. "By" (2Ti 1:6) implies that *Paul's* laying on his hands was the actual *instrument* of its being conferred.

of the presbytery—In 2Ti 1:6 the apostle mentions only *his own* laying on of hands. But there his aim is to remind Timothy specially of the part he himself took in imparting to him the gift. Here he mentions the fact, quite consistent with the other, that the neighboring presbyters took part in the ordination or consecration, he, however, taking the foremost part. Paul, though having the general oversight of the elders everywhere, was an elder himself (1Pe 5:1; 2Jo 1). [26]

The gift that Timothy received at the time the presbytery laid hands on him was likely an ordination to prepare him for his evangelistic role in the church. However, as Jamieson, Fausset, and Brown have indicated, it is quite possible, and even probable, that Paul was also present and, in conjunction with his ordination, granted Timothy a gift through his apostolic hands. Thus, the two references to gifts in Paul's letters to Timothy most likely occurred in concert.

What is important, however, is the *source* of the gift that was given. Unlike the delivery of Paul's signature "with my own hand" or the "signs of an apostle" through "signs and wonders and miracles," the elders' hands accompanied (Gr. *meta*) the gift Timothy received at the time. They were not the vehicle by which the gift was given. This would be in keeping with an ordination, setting aside Timothy for his evangelistic ministry as prophecy was spoken delivering a message of God's blessing/grace upon him. Conversely, Paul's hands were the source (Gr. *dia*) of the gift that Timothy received from the apostle.

Jude 20-21

In a message similar to direction Paul offered the Corinthians and Ephesians, Jude encouraged his readers to strengthen their spiritual walk, through prayer.

[20] But you, beloved, building yourselves up on your most holy faith, **praying in the Holy Spirit**, [21] keep yourselves in the love of

---

[26] Jamieson, Robert, A. R. Fausset, and David Brown. *A Commentary on the Old and New Testaments, Volume 3*, 492-493.

God, waiting anxiously for the mercy of our Lord Jesus Christ to eternal life. (Jude 20-21) Emphasis added.

The first part of Jude's message teaches that prayer builds faith. This is only natural, since answered prayer provides further evidence to substantiate and reinvigorate belief in God. Within the scope of that message, the subtle expression, "praying in the Holy Spirit" (v. 20) suggests an act that is a source of spiritual strengthening. Some also see an allusion to eschatology in the phrase, "waiting anxiously for the mercy of our Lord Jesus Christ to eternal life" (v. 21). They see this as supportive of the proposition that tongues (praying in the spirit) might continue until the Parousia. However, it is clear from the text that praying in the spirit does not equate to speaking or praying in tongues (Ephesians 6: 18). Therefore, there is no reason to insist that Jude has tongues in mind in this passage. Still, tongues cannot be immediately ruled out as part of the equation here since tongues is one form of praying in the Spirit.

Generally, when prayer of any kind is discussed in God's Word, the message is that man is expected to communicate with God through thoughtful prayer. This is certainly the lesson in Jesus' prayer example (the Lord's Prayer) given to his listeners in the Sermon on the Mount (Matthew 6: 9-13). It is also reasonable to conclude that this is the kind of prayer Jude has in mind here.

Jude's message is written, "To those who are the called, beloved in God the Father, and kept for Jesus Christ" (v. 1). This letter is meant to provide encouragement as well as cautions to the general membership of the body of Christ. He urged them to pray in the Holy Spirit, a plea to the many who would read his words. Yet, Paul acknowledged that not everyone spoke in tongues (1 Corinthians 12: 30). Only some were endowed with that gift. Therefore, this could not be a call from Jude for all members to speak in tongues, even though it is a call for all members to pray in the spirit.

What the writer envisions is the same thing Paul discussed in his words to the Ephesians. Jude wants the believers to pray thoughtfully (with understanding), but also with consistency and perseverance. It is simply a matter of letting the Holy Spirit guide their prayer lives in accordance with God's will. That is how they would build themselves up in the faith (v. 20) and keep themselves in the love of God (v. 21).

Summary on Spiritual Gifts

Miraculous spiritual gifts were offered in the church of the first century to provide the apostles with valuable tools that were meant to assist them in laying a foundation upon which the body of Christ could build once the apostles had departed this life. Signs, wonders, and miracles served to demonstrate the unique role of the apostles in establishing and spreading Christ's teachings throughout the world. It was through these men that others would learn what God expected of those who would seek him and how sinners might be reconciled to God.

The case for abeyance of these gifts begins with the fact that what was arguably the greatest gift – apostleship – ended when the Apostle John died. That fact provides powerful precedent and reasoning for the passing of the gifts. These gifts were intimately linked to the apostles as evidence of their authority and confirmation of their message. This is a recurring theme through the entire New Testament with respect to these gifts (Mark 16: 20; Acts 2: 1-4, 43; 3: 7-9; 5: 5, 9, 12; 8: 14-17; 10: 44-46; 14: 3; 19: 6; 28: 3-6, 8; Romans 1: 11; 15: 18-19; Hebrews 2: 4).

Anchoring these examples are Paul's words to the Corinthians where he characterizes miraculous works as a matter of apostolic credential (2 Corinthians 12: 12). Careful study has revealed that all of Scripture harmonizes with Paul's words concerning the relationship between spiritual gifts and the apostolate. Thus, it can be fairly stated that this is the teaching with which beliefs concerning these gifts must agree.

The King James translation of Paul's words in 1 Corinthians 13 has been a primary source of division for the past century where miraculous spiritual gifts are concerned. By translating *to teleion* as "that which is perfect" (1 Corinthians 13: 10), the translators opened a can of worms of which they were undoubtedly unaware. Considering the consistent use of *teleios* in the New Testament to depict maturity or completeness, they had every reason to believe their readers would apply this same meaning in this instance. However, as time passed, the concept of a *flawless state*, which is derived from the English meaning of *perfect*, replaced the biblical meaning of *teleios* in this verse.

When the Apostle Paul passed from this earth, he took his hand with him. It did not remain behind so others who wished to do so could use it to continue to provide Paul's personal mark (cf. 2 Thessalonians 3: 17). Even if someone had severed Paul's hand and kept it to sign additional letters (an obviously disconcerting prospect), the signature would constitute forgery, since the hand would no longer be intrinsic to the apostle. The notion that a signature might outlive its owner is utter foolishness.

God's Word is rich with instruction concerning the critical role of the apostles in the distribution of miraculous spiritual gifts. Paul taught plainly that signs, wonders, and miracles were representative of the Holy Spirit's power and authority, providing a signature unique to the apostles. This pattern throughout the New Testament is undeniable. In other words, the Bible *makes the case*[27] for a unique bond between the apostles and the miraculous. These works were the hand that delivered the apostolic mark. For all practical purposes, they were the apostolic mark. Accordingly, modern-day gifts equivalent to those of the first century would require modern-day apostles, of which there are none.

The claim that the miraculous gifts continue today enjoys no such biblical support. Interestingly, the key passage used to defend the continuation of miraculous spiritual gifts (1 Corinthians 13: 9-12) is introduced by a bold and uncomplicated pronouncement of their passing (1 Corinthians 13: 8). That proclamation complements the apostle's claim that signs, wonders, and miracles were intended to provide apostolic support (2 Corinthians 12: 12).

Just as it is inconceivable that a man's signature might outlive him, the idea that the apostolic signature should outlive the apostles is not only implausible, but it is biblically unfounded. This can only mean that the countless claims of miraculous spiritual gifts in modern times, whether tongues or healings or various other gifts, are not equivalent to the gifts of the first century. Since Scripture can only legitimately support one view concerning these gifts, the only possibility is that the miraculous gifts professed by so many in this modern age are imitations. As disappointing as this may be to those who so eagerly aspire to share in these gifts, this is the doctrine that is sustained by God's Word.

---

[27] See Chapter 2, Systematic Theology: Where Systematic Theology Falls Short, 28.

Section III
Election and Free Will

Chapter 9

The Divide Concerning Election

Elect vs. Elected

The principle of election, which is well established in the pages of Scripture, is as relevant today as it was to the first century church and even prior, as there is much discussion on the subject in the Old Testament. Unfortunately, election has come to mean different things to different people. Those differences have become so pronounced that conflicting doctrinal perspective has, once again, led to division among those who seek salvation through Jesus Christ.

With respect to election, those differences center on contrasting beliefs about what the biblical authors intended by the term *election*. In question is what method God employs to determine who are among the *elect* when the term is used to designate those who can anticipate eternal salvation. In Scripture, these people are often called the *elect* or the *chosen*.

The primary controversy up for consideration here is not *whether* the saved are chosen, but rather *how* they are chosen. Some believe that men and women, of their own unconstrained volition, respond to the gospel call and choose to accept Jesus as their Savior. In so doing, they become members of the elect. According to this view, conditions (primarily the condition of faith) are placed upon humankind and meeting those conditions establishes one among the elect.

Others believe that human free will is not a factor when it comes to attaining spiritual salvation. Instead, they teach that God has predetermined who will receive an eternal heavenly reward without regard for the personal choices people make. This view is often termed *unconditional election* in contrast to *conditional election* where human choice is seen as an intimate component of God's plan of salvation. The discussion centers on whether individuals can *seek* elect status, or they have been pre-selected for salvation by God without regard for human free will.

It seems reasonable, when addressing a topic as broad in scope as the doctrine of election, to start at the beginning. It is obvious that the doctrine of election begins in the Bible, but that is not where the doctrinal departure occurred. The differences of opinion about the election that is discussed in God's Word surfaced roughly three hundred years after the death of John, the last of the apostles.

Early Church Fathers

During the first few centuries following the death of the Apostle John, church leaders spent much of their time upholding the truth of apostolic teaching and fending off assorted heresies (e.g., Gnosticism). According to A. A. Hodge (1823-1886):

> It does not appear that any definite and consistent statements were made in that age, as to the origin, nature, and consequences of human sin; nor as to the nature and effects of divine grace; nor of the nature of the redemptive work of Christ, or of the method of its application by the Holy Spirit, or of its appropriation by faith. As a general fact it may be stated that, as a result of the great influence of Origen, the Fathers of the Greek Church pretty unanimously settled down upon a loose Semi-pelagianism, denying the guilt of original sin, and maintaining the ability of the sinner to predispose himself for, and to cooperate with divine grace.[1]

Men like Hermas (*The Shepherd of Hermas*, A.D. 150), Justin Martyr (*First Apology XVIII*, A.D. 155), and Tertullian (*Treatise on the Soul*, A.D. 204), wrote unambiguously about the innocent state of children. The doctrine of original sin, as it is taught today, did not exist for them. This is important in that the concept of original sin is foundational to Calvinism (a.k.a., Reformed Theology). Man's inherited sinfulness is used to explain, at least in part, why no one can be saved without the *unconditional election* taught by Calvin. The general theological perspective of the early church fathers does not seem to support certain foundational views of Reformed Theology.

Augustine (A.D. 354-430)

In the late fourth and early fifth centuries, a man known as Augustine served as the bishop of Hippo (now Algeria) in the Roman Catholic Church. During his tenure, Augustine introduced, through his writing and preaching, a religious philosophy that altered the course of the church in many ways. It was a viewpoint that dwelt heavily on

---

[1] Hodge, A. A., *Semi-Pelagianism*,
http://monergism.com/thethreshold/articles/onsite/semi-pelagian.html.

God's sovereignty and how, in light of that sovereignty, God relates to his creation.

Augustine spent more than forty years of his life in the Roman Catholic Church. His life experiences are detailed in his most famous work entitled *Confessions*. Mostly autobiographical with hints of theology and philosophy, this work greatly influenced religion in the fifth century. During that time, most of Christ's followers were raised as Roman Catholics where the primary focus was on the corporate church. After reading *Confessions* it seems that many "...began to think of themselves primarily as individuals; Christianity also became more individualistic in emphasis."[2]

A former Manichaean, Augustine converted to Christianity in A.D. 386. Mani (A.D. 216-276), the Persian originator of the Manichaean religion, combined assorted doctrines from Gnosticism (salvation through knowledge), Buddhism, and others into a dualistic view of light and dark where anything that was physical by nature was considered evil. Daryl Aarons describes it as "...a philosophy/religion that assumed two eternal and equal principles of good and evil in constant struggle with one another."[3] The Manichaeans did not place much emphasis on God's sovereignty or omnipotence. They did, however, draw clear lines of distinction between the *elect* and those known only as *hearers*.

Augustine became disillusioned with Manichaean beliefs, at least in part, due to their de-emphasis of God's sovereignty. They taught of a "...God of so untarnished an innocence as to be dangerously shorn of his omnipotence."[4] His studies caused him to turn away from Manichaeism and, for some time, lead a scholar's life focused primarily on philosophy.

Later, under the influence of Bishop Ambrose in Milan, he returned to the Christianity his mother had taught him and became a priest in the Catholic Church five years later. Yet, Augustine did not immediately develop his views of deterministic[5] sovereignty. In his early years as Bishop of Hippo, "...he had taken up his stand on the freedom of the will; his criticism of Manichaeism had been a typical philosopher's criticism of determinism generally."[6] He argued, "It was a matter of common sense that men were responsible for their actions;

---

[2] Aaron, Daryl. *The Forty Most Influential Christians*, 103.
[3] Ibid., 102.
[4] Brown, Peter. *Augustine of Hippo*, 53.
[5] Determinism suggests that humans lack free will and that God makes our decisions for us.
[6] Aaron, Daryl. *The Forty Most Influential Christians*, 148.

they could not be held accountable if their wills were not free."[7] Still, he struggled with the permanence of sin in the world and the fact that men seemed subject to sin.

The Manichaeans, arguing in favor of determinism despite their indifference regarding God's sovereignty, challenged Augustine with the words of Paul where he considered himself, "...sold into bondage to sin" (Romans 7: 14). Augustine took this challenge seriously. After years of study, this led him to a belief that people were not merely born with a propensity to sin, but they were born guilty of sin – Adam's sin.

His changed view on the nature of sin guided Augustine to the perspective that sovereignty was/is necessarily primary in God's relationship with mankind. He determined that God's was not merely a sovereignty of control (God controls all things), but a sovereignty of causation (God causes all things). He surmised that if God, in fact, causes all things, salvation itself must involve choices that come only from God. In other words, man does not make choices about salvation; only God does that.

Augustine argued that if one's salvation depends on independent freewill choices made by mankind it would infringe upon God's sovereignty. Additionally, he believed, due to inherent corruption, that humans were too depraved to even be *able* to respond to an offer from God unless that offer was irresistibly thrust upon them. It is from this premise that the idea of *unconditional election*, as well as other related beliefs, ultimately developed.

Prior to Augustine, there was no serious discussion of sin being *inherited* from Adam. According to Wiggers and Emerson, "All or at least the greater part of the fathers of the Greek church, before Augustine, denied any real original sin."[8] The term *ancestral sin*, depicting humanity as having an *inclination to sin*, was employed on occasion. However, the notion of original, or hereditary, sin was unknown prior to Augustine. His belief concerning original sin came at least in part from his Manichaean background where he was taught that all material things, including inanimate objects, are evil. The Manichaeans especially taught that, because the sinfulness of lust was inherent within the act itself, sin was transmitted through procreation and childbirth.

---

[7] Ibid., 148.
[8] Wiggins, Gusav, F. and Ralph Emerson, *An Historical Presentation of Augustinism and Pelagianism*, 43.

Augustine wrote extensively concerning his perspective of God's relationship with mankind. However, because of Augustine's diminished perception of man's free will, his ideas about salvation were met with broad skepticism and resistance. His views stood in stark contrast to commonly held beliefs up to that point in history.

Some, like Julian, the bishop of Eclanum who was a contemporary, challenged Augustine's views, seeing them as a dramatic departure not only from the position on free will and salvation the church held historically, but also from the teachings offered by the apostles. He accused Augustine of introducing his Manichaean beliefs into the church, stating, "I am amazed that anyone should entertain the slightest doubt as to the equity of God."[9] Similarly, Vincent of Lérins, another contemporary of Augustine, accused him of devoting "…all your time and energy to theological controversies."[10]

Augustine offered a perspective on salvation that provided a different slant to the notion of the *chosen* than had been held prior. The early church fathers occasionally incorporated the apostolic words *foreknowledge, predestination*, and *election* into their writings, but there is no indication that they believed this terminology in any way impeded a person's capacity, through the use of reason, logic, and volition, to participate in God's offer of salvation freely and responsibly. They taught that people could choose to accept Jesus as Savior based on the call and power of the gospel message. For instance, Justin Martyr and Clement of Alexandria made the following statements, respectively.

> We have learned from the prophets, and we hold it to be true, that punishments, chastisements, and rewards are rendered according to the merit of each man's actions. Otherwise, if all things happen by fate, then nothing is in our own power. For if it is predestined that one man be good and another man evil, then the first is not deserving of praise or the other to be blamed. Unless humans have the power of avoiding evil and choosing good by free choice, they are not accountable for their actions—whatever they may be.... For neither would a man be worthy of reward or praise if he did not of himself choose the good, but was merely created for that end. Likewise, if a man were evil, he would not deserve punishment, since he was not evil of himself, being unable to do anything else than what he was made for.

---

[9] Brown, Peter. *Augustine of Hippo*, 393.
[10] Aaron, Daryl. *The Forty Most Influential Christians*, 242.

Neither praise nor condemnation, neither rewards nor punishments, are right if the soul does not have the power of choice and avoidance, if evil is involuntary.[11]

Pelagius (A.D. 354-420/440)

Another contemporary of Augustine, a British monk by the name of Pelagius, was arguably Augustine's chief nemesis, doctrinally speaking. His exact place of birth is unknown, although some believe he hailed from the British Isles. Pelagius was a Culdee monk, a monastic group with communities scattered throughout Ireland, Iceland, Scotland, England, and Wales. In his mid-twenties, Pelagius traveled to Rome in hopes of influentially writing and teaching about his beliefs. He became not only popular, but well-respected, very quickly, no doubt due to "...the integrity of his character and the purity of his morals."[12] He soon gained many followers and what came to be known as Pelagianism spread quickly from Rome to Carthage and beyond.

It is the opinion of not a few scholars that Pelagius's theological views may have been influenced by a presbyter by the name of Rufinus who arrived in Rome around the end of the fourth century. Rufinus hailed from Greece where the church greatly respected teachings of the early church fathers. In contrast to Augustine's teaching about original sin, Rufinus purportedly taught, "...that there is no propagation of sin by generation."[13]

Pelagianism conflicted dramatically with Augustinianism on several counts: 1) original sin, 2) the degree to which people have free will, 3) the manner in which God delivers salvific grace, and 4) the principle of predestination. Augustine believed man's depraved state was a condition each one inherited from Adam's sin. Pelagius, on the other hand, "...ascribed the actual existence and universality of sin to the bad example which Adam set by his first sin."[14] He taught that an infant was as blameless as the newly created Adam prior to his fall.

Augustine believed individuals *could not* choose God, partly due to man's depravity (from the fall) and partly due to God's sovereignty, while Pelagius saw people as independent creatures capable of freely

---

[11] Bercot, David. *What the Early Christians Believed about Free Will*, http://earlychurch.com/freewill.php.

[12] Wiggers, Gustav F., Ralph Emerson, *An Historical Presentation of Augustinism and Pelagianism*, 41.

[13] Ibid., 44

[14] *Pelagius and Pelagianism*, "The Life and Writings of Pelagius," http://www.newadvent.org/cathen/11604a.htm.

deciding whether to follow God's law. Augustine taught that God essentially impressed his grace upon those chosen by him. Since they could not choose God, the only way anyone could be saved was for him to bestow irresistible grace upon them. Pelagius believed God bestowed grace on those who, by choice, decided to accept God's invitation to salvation. Augustine held that predestination for salvation came from God deterministically. Pelagius, on the other hand, insisted that salvific predestination relied on God's foreknowledge of those who would freely choose to accept Jesus as savior.

Pelagius's denial of original sin conflicted with Augustine's view that mankind existed in a depraved state that was inherited from Adam. Yet, Pelagius supported infant baptism, not for cleansing, but for entrance into the kingdom. Unfortunately for Pelagius, his denial of original sin was his undoing. While the concept of original sin was first introduced late in the fourth century, by the early fifth century it had become accepted dogma in the Catholic Church. The church, in turn, condemned Pelagius as a heretic and Pelagians were banished from all Roman cities (A.D. 418).

The Middle-Ages

The doctrine of original sin became a fundamental teaching of the Catholic Church from the early fifth century. However, other aspects of Augustinian principles were not so quickly embraced. On occasion, in the Middle-Ages, Augustine's views were debated by prominent religious leaders like Thomas Aquinas (A.D. 1225-1274), who accepted a rather light version of Augustine's philosophy that involved *infused* free will upon fallen men. Aquinas, like Augustine, believed "...that humans are entirely dependent upon the grace of God for salvation, and even the faith by which this is received is a gift of God."[15] Duns Scotus (A.D. 1256-1308), who was an ardent follower of Augustine, also held similar views. The elaborate philosophy of God's sovereignty and predetermined election that Augustine taught was not immediately recognized by Christianity in general. After a time, however, these teachings took root and developed into a full-blown theology of their own.

---

[15] Aaron, Daryl. *The Forty Most Influential Christians*, 140.

John Calvin (A.D. 1509-1564)

John Calvin was born in Noyon, Picardi (in France) to Catholic parents who raised him staunchly in the Catholic tradition. Encouraged by his father to study law, he went to Orleans (A.D. 1528) and Bourges (A.D. 1529) in keeping with his father's wishes. After his father died (A.D. 1531), Calvin finished his study of the law and earned his *license in law* (A.D. 1532). However, absent the obligation to please his deceased father, he decided to alter course and pursue his first love – religious studies. He returned to France where he entered College de France in Paris.

A younger contemporary of Martin Luther and Huldrich Zwingli, Calvin converted to Protestantism sometime before A.D. 1533. He soon became a staunch critic of the practices of the Catholic Church in France. He considered excessive the ceremonies and great processions of the church. He was infuriated with the pretense of church leaders who "…feigned religion to keep others obedient…but privately among their inmates, they laughed at all these absurdities."[16] As a result, Calvin was branded a heretic by the church. People critical of the church were often hunted down and persecuted, so Calvin spent much time wandering around France, Italy, and Switzerland, writing and teaching, eventually settling in Geneva, Switzerland circa A.D. 1536.

Calvin took Augustine's teaching to heart. In his best-known literary work, *Institutes of the Christian Religion*, Calvin published his Reformed views of God, the Bible, and the church. It was Calvin's belief that every aspect of God's relationship with mankind stems from his sovereignty (or supremacy) and that men and women must appreciate God from that standpoint. Like Augustine, he taught that salvation could not be received as a matter of human free will. God could not allow something so important to infringe upon his sovereignty. For Calvin, the only possible manner by which one might be saved is by God's own righteous judgment as he decides who will be given an eternal heavenly reward and, conversely, who will be eternally condemned.

Calvin ridiculed those who insisted that men should not be held accountable for their sins if sin itself was involuntary. He stated, in defense of Augustine:

> If sin, they say, is necessary, it ceases to be sin; if it is voluntary, it may be avoided. Such, too, were the weapons with which Pelagius assailed Augustine…I deny, therefore, that sin ought to be the less

---

[16] Bouwsma, William J. *John Calvin, A Sixteenth Century Portrait*, 204.

imputed because it is necessary; and, on the other hand, I deny the inference, that sin may be avoided because it is voluntary."[17]

Some may wonder how a just God might be so arbitrary and unfair but, according to Calvin, such reasoning suggests that the God of righteousness *could* be unfair. If God predetermined who would be saved, as Augustine and Calvin proclaimed, it must be a righteous decision because God is righteous. According to Calvin, those who question God's equity in judgment "…are attempting to deprive God of the power of showing mercy."[18]

Calvin's theological system incorporates every aspect of the God/man connection. Unlike Augustine, however, Calvin lived at a time when humanity was ripe for something other than the Catholic teachings of salvation by works. It was time for a Reformation of the church, and Calvin, like Luther and Zwingli, was in the right place at the right time to make the changes he and others believed were long past due.

John Calvin died in A.D. 1564, leaving his indelible stamp on the world of religion. Many of the religious views taught by evangelicals today stem from the work of Calvin. While Augustine, in the fourth and fifth centuries, did much to assist the Reformers by leaving behind volumes of his teaching, it was Calvin who put in place a theological system that would survive through the centuries.

After Calvin's death, believers continued to experience the aftermath of the Reformation that had occurred in the first half of the sixteenth century. However, with the death of Calvin, the originators of the Reformation Movement were no more. It was left to their successors to wade through the sea of theological changes that had, like a wave, overtaken them. The rejection of countless Roman Catholic practices left many confused, wondering exactly what they should believe. While many turned to Calvinism, some did not.

Jacob Arminius (A.D. 1560-1609)

Four years prior to Calvin's death, Jacob Arminius was born in Oudewater, Utrecht in the Netherlands. Raised in the Reformed tradition, in A.D. 1576 he attended the newly founded University of Leiden. He was highly influenced by his professors, especially one named Johann Kolmann, who believed Calvinism depicted God as an unjust tyrant rather than a righteous and loving God.

---

[17] Calvin, John. *Institutes of the Christian Religion*, 197.
[18] Ibid., 632

Arminius enrolled at the Geneva Academy, which had been founded by Calvin in A.D. 1559. However, he found himself at odds with his professors over the strong Calvinist theology taught there. Still, he studied diligently, impressing his professors despite his theological departure on many issues. From A.D. 1588 to A.D. 1603 he served as pastor in a Reformed Church in Amsterdam. His final years (A.D. 1603-1609) were spent as Professor of Divinity at his alma mater, the University of Leiden.

At the University of Leiden, Arminius's teaching was often called into question since his views concerning free will and election conflicted with the convention of Calvinism. Rather than an election that took place within the corridors of heaven before creation, as Calvin taught, like Pelagius, he believed predestination did not interfere with free will but simply demonstrated God's foreknowledge of men. Arminius taught, in competition with Calvinism, that grace was available to all, not just the so-called elect.

His views especially came to light in his teaching on the seventh chapter of Romans where, in contrast to Reformed Theology, he believed the "…wretched man" (v. 24) was simply one's pre-Christian state; and his views concerning the ninth chapter of Romans, as he insisted that believers were God's cooperative covenant partners in salvation. In like manner, he argued against the limited atonement taught in Calvinism, insisting that Christ died for all men. Ironically, it was Augustine's study of the seventh chapter of Romans that led him to his view of original sin and the total depravity of mankind.

Arminius's teachings and writings were blasted by the Protestant church authorities who had embraced Calvin's perception of election/salvation. According to Keith Stanglin and Thomas McCall, "By 1608, the theological debates and accusations against Arminius were escalating to such a degree that the magistrates of Holland could no longer ignore the situation."[19] He was called before the magistrates twice – once in 1608 and once in 1609 – to present his doctrinal views in The Hague. However, through all of this, Arminius's health was failing.

Nothing really came of Arminius's appearances in The Hague and his defense of human free will. Soon after, in October 1609, Arminius died. Nonetheless, his views did take hold in certain circles. After his death, some of his followers developed and published *Five Articles of Remonstrance* in A.D. 1610. These articles stated:

---

[19] Stanglin, Keith D., Thomas H. McCall, *Jacob Arminius, Theologian of Grace*, 33.

Article 1
That God, by an eternal and unchangeable purpose in Jesus Christ his Son, before the foundation of the world, hath determined, out of the fallen, sinful race of men, to save in Christ, for Christ's sake, and through Christ, those who, through the grace of the Holy Ghost, shall believe on this his son Jesus, and shall persevere in this faith and obedience of faith, through this grace, even to the end; and, on the other hand, to leave the incorrigible and unbelieving in sin and under wrath, and to condemn them as alienate from Christ, according to the word of the Gospel in John 3:36: "He that believeth on the Son hath everlasting life: and he that believeth not the Son shall not see life; but the wrath of God abideth on him," and according to other passages of Scripture also.

Article 2
That agreeably thereunto, Jesus Christ the Savior of the world, died for all men and for every man, so that he has obtained for them all, by his death on the cross, redemption and the forgiveness of sins; yet that no one actually enjoys this forgiveness of sins except the believer, according to the word of the Gospel of John 3:16, "For God so loved the world, that he gave his only begotten Son, that whosoever believeth in him should not perish, but have everlasting life." And in the First Epistle of 1 John 2:2: "And he is the propitiation for our sins: and not for ours only, but also for the sins of the whole world."

Article 3
That man has not saving grace of himself, nor of the energy of his free will, inasmuch as he, in the state of apostasy and sin, can of and by himself neither think, will, nor do any thing that is truly good (such as saving faith eminently is); but that it is needful that he be born again of God in Christ, through his Holy Spirit, and renewed in understanding, inclination, or will, and all his powers, in order that he may rightly understand, think, will, and effect what is truly good, according to the Word of Christ, John 15:5, "Without me ye can do nothing."

Article 4
That this grace of God is the beginning, continuance, and accomplishment of all good, even to this extent, that the regenerate man himself, without prevenient or assisting, awakening, following and cooperative grace, can neither think, will, nor do good, nor withstand any temptations to evil; so that all good deeds or movements, that can be conceived, must be ascribed to the grace of God in Christ but respects the mode of the operation of this grace, it

is not irresistible; inasmuch as it is written concerning many, that they have resisted the Holy Ghost, Acts 7, and elsewhere in many places.

Article 5
That those who are incorporated into Christ by true faith, and have thereby become partakers of his life-giving Spirit, have thereby full power to strive against Satan, sin, the world, and their own flesh, and to win the victory; it being well understood that it is ever through the assisting grace of the Holy Ghost; and that Jesus Christ assists them through his Spirit in all temptations, extends to them his hand, and if only they are ready for the conflict, and desire his help, and are not inactive, keeps them from falling, so that they, by no craft or power of Satan, can be misled nor plucked out of Christ's hands, according to the Word of Christ, John 10:28: "Neither shall any man pluck them out of my hand." But whether they are capable, through negligence, of forsaking again the first beginning of their life in Christ, of again returning to this present evil world, of turning away from the holy doctrine which was delivered them, of losing a good conscience, of becoming devoid of grace, that must be more particularly determined out of the Holy Scripture, before we ourselves can teach it with the full persuasion of our mind.[20]

Some statements here seem to reflect aspects of Calvinism. For instance, Article 3 appears to concede mankind's total depravity and Article 4 seems to say that people cannot understand what is good or choose to accept Jesus without first experiencing some godly intercession.

On the other hand, Article 1 recognizes that the decision God made prior to creation was that *believers* would be saved without insisting that God determined who would believe. Article 2 teaches that Jesus died for everyone while many Reformers claim that Jesus died only for those who would be saved. Article 4 denies the irresistibility of God's grace that was taught by Calvin. Also, Article 5 suggests that redeemed people *can* walk away from God – a claim that Calvinism denies.

---

[20] *The Five Articles of Remonstrance.*
http://evangelicalarminians.org/the-five-articles-of-remonstrance//.

Chapter 10

The Principles of Calvinism

God's Sovereignty

Perhaps no one in the past few centuries has left his mark on the religious community as dramatically and as deeply as John Calvin. While others like Martin Luther, Huldrych Zwingli, Jacob Arminius, John Wesley, and Alexander Campbell have influenced many, their achievements, and legacies pale in comparison to that of Calvin. Part of Calvin's success was, no doubt, due to timing. He arrived on the scene on the heels of Luther and others who had recently led the groundswell of rebellion against the Catholic Church, successfully piggybacking his views on their message. Yet, his success was also due in part to the theological system he developed. Luther was more interested in overcoming what he saw as heretical church practices than developing a systematic belief structure, leaving a vacuum that needed to be filled. Calvin filled that vacuum by developing and offering a concise, deliberate system of beliefs that could be ascertained by the most common of men.

The cornerstone of Calvin's theology is the sovereignty (supreme authority) of God. Like Augustine, his teachings ultimately grew from his high view of God's almighty nature. While holiness, righteousness, and other godly characteristics have their place and are not insignificant, it is God's sovereignty, according to Calvin, that most influences his interaction with mankind; and it was on this premise that he developed his theological views.

There should be no doubt among believers that God is all-powerful. This is a truth that is taught in Scripture (cf. Genesis 17: 1; Psalm 115: 3; Daniel 4: 35; Ephesians 1: 11; 1 Timothy 6: 15). The authors of the Bible, led by the Holy Spirit, placed intense emphasis on this attribute of God. The Hebrew word for *sovereign*, which is *adoram*, appears nearly three hundred times in the Old Testament as a testimony to its truth and import.

God has created clever creatures. Mankind is known for attempting to artificially quantify and limit God's sovereignty with absurdity, asking questions like: *Can God create a stone so large he could not lift it?* or *Could God create a being greater than himself?* As whimsical as these may be, they miss the point of sovereignty. Things like these are outside the realm of possibility, not because God is not supreme, but because these actions are contradictory by nature. That is to say, if God could do either of these, it would mean that he is not sovereign. God's sovereignty does not mean that he can do what is naturally contrary. It means there is none greater than God.

While this section focuses on Calvin's view of *unconditional election*, it is impossible to effectively isolate this individual doctrine from the larger view of Scripture that is Calvinism. That is because, with the possible exception of a limited view of the atonement, the various aspects of Reformed Theology are inter-dependent. Each step of Calvin's systemic principles leads fluidly to the succeeding principle and ultimately to a deterministic view of salvation. Therefore, it will help to take some time and consider his teachings and the unavoidable conclusions to which they lead.

The TULIP Philosophy

The easiest and quickest way to present Calvinism is through the TULIP acronym that was developed by Calvin's followers after his death, apparently in an effort to combat the *Five Articles of Remonstrance* the Arminians had adopted. The exact origin of the acronym is unknown. Some attribute its development to the Synod of Dort in early A.D. 1619. Others give it a later date. However, the principles for which the letters stand were generally drawn from the works of John Calvin.

The letters of this acronym represent the core principles of Calvinism, as it is currently taught, which are: (1) Total depravity of man; (2) Unconditional election; (3) Limited atonement; (4) Irresistible grace; and finally (5) Perseverance of the saints. A thorough discussion of these five points would be cumbersome, resulting in a serious distraction from the intended objective; but a brief look is necessary to give honest consideration to the doctrine of election from the Reformed point of view.

Total Depravity of Man

The fall of Adam and Eve in the Garden of Eden had an unquestionable and irrevocable effect on the relationship between God and humanity. This has led to a variety of views about the extent to which Adam's sin directly or indirectly touches his descendants. Some believe in the concept of *original sin*, as discussed earlier, recognizing inheritance of sin by each person born into the human race. Others believe that, due to Adam's sin, human beings are born with a sinful nature. This nature explains why Paul could so boldly proclaim that *all have sinned* (Romans 3: 23). Still, others insist that Adam's sin is the reason each human being must experience physical death. For them, death is the primary effect of Adam's sin on humanity. According to this view, each person is born into this world in a state of complete purity. There are, of course, a multitude of intermediate perspectives that incorporate these three views to varying degrees.

Calvin believed in the concept of original sin that was developed by Augustine. In his work *Institutes of the Christian Religion*, he emphasized the degenerate condition of mankind, devoting five entire chapters to the subject. He regarded Adam's sin as a "…contagious influence…to the whole posterity of Adam. Hence, hereditary corruption, or original sin, and the depravation of a nature which was previously pure and good."[21] He also stated that this depravation was "…communicated not merely by imitation, but by propagation."[22] By propagation, Calvin meant breeding, or procreation.

It is difficult to argue with the contention that mankind is depraved. At the time of Noah, God noted that, "…the wickedness of man was great on the earth, and that every intent of the thoughts of his heart was only evil continually" (Genesis 6: 5). These words depict an extreme situation of sin. Although, in the covenant of grace, many do worship God, it is also true that mankind has not improved much since the days of old. Sin is still rampant and fully consumes most people.

Calvin saw this wickedness, which resulted from the initial fall of Adam (Romans 5: 12), as evidence of the condition of *total depravity*. The depravity of mankind runs so deep, according to Calvin, that no person *can* choose to do what is right in God's eyes. That being the case, neither do individuals have the capacity to choose to serve God. His argument is founded, at least in part, on Paul's words to the Ephesians when he wrote, "Among them we too all formerly lived in the lusts of our flesh, indulging the desires of the flesh and of the mind, and were by nature children of wrath, even as the rest" (Ephesians 2: 3).

Calvin's view of total depravity surpassed the mere notion that a person could not choose to do what is right. He proposed "…that hereditary depravity extends to all the faculties of the soul."[23] Thus,

---

[21] Calvin, John, *Institutes of the Christian Religion*, 146.
[22] Ibid., 146.
[23] Ibid., 147.

mankind had, by virtue of original sin, lost the ability to reason logically to distinguish between good and evil or to even conceive of that which is good. He claimed that man had "...no ability in himself for the study of righteousness."[24] For this reason Calvin believed that the gospel message, delivered to freewill human beings, could have no possible effect.

Since, according to Calvin, free will on the part of totally depraved human beings could not have any role in a person's reconciliation with God, he believed that substantive free will must have been limited after the fall. He postulated, "Having seen that the dominion of sin...has complete possession of every soul, it now remains to consider more closely, whether from the period of being thus enslaved, we have been deprived of all liberty."[25] Additionally, Calvin believed the principle of a person's independent choice to accept Jesus as Savior was incompatible with God's sovereignty. He wondered how the totally depraved man could "...arrogate any thing, however minute, to himself, without robbing God of his honor."[26]

He also taught "...that free will does not enable any man to perform good works, unless he is assisted by grace."[27] That is because, when it comes to man's ability to reason concerning things of a divine nature, his "...discernment...is altogether stupid and blind."[28] He did not deny the existence of perhaps a sliver of human free will pertaining to earthly things (which sins to commit), but concerning things spiritual, free will is simply not an option or all people would remain fully corrupt and lost. Only the elect, according to Calvin, are capable of good works, spiritually speaking. He insisted that godly works lay beyond the reach of human free will, stating that:

> ...free will does not enable any man to perform good works, unless he is assisted by grace; indeed, the special grace which the elect alone receive through regeneration.[29]

In Calvinism, the depravity of mankind prevents human beings from seeking or following God. Calvin stated, "When the will is enchained as the slave of sin, it cannot make a movement toward

---

[24] Ibid., 157.
[25] Ibid.
[26] Ibid.
[27] Ibid., 161.
[28] Ibid., 169.
[29] Ibid., 161.

goodness, far less steadily pursue it."[30] Calvin's arguments about man's inability to reason concerning things spiritual is not without a certain measure of biblical support. Paul told the believers at Corinth that men, in their sinful state, cannot achieve an understanding of godly things.

> But a natural man does not accept the things of the Spirit of God, for they are foolishness to him; and he cannot understand them, because they are spiritually appraised. (1 Corinthians 2: 14)

Man's spiritual state was unquestionably diminished by the fall. However, opinions differ dramatically over the degree to which mankind's ability to differentiate between good and evil was affected. In Calvin's view, the human capacity to reason on a spiritual level – to choose between good and evil – was destroyed resulting in *absolute* spiritual bankruptcy.

Unconditional Election

The doctrine of *unconditional election*, which Calvin termed *predestination* or *election*, lies at the heart of his theology. He believed and taught "...that salvation is spontaneously offered to some, while others have no access to it."[31] In his own words, predestination is "...the eternal decree of God, by which he determined within himself whatever he wished to happen with regard to every man."[32] To this he added, and this is the meat of unconditional election, "All are not created on equal terms, but some are preordained to eternal life, others to eternal damnation; and, accordingly, as each has been created for one or other of these ends, we say that he has been predestinated to life or to death."[33] This is known as *double predestination*.

In the New Testament, beginning with the words of Jesus, it is clear that there exists a class of people known as the *elect*. He occasionally voiced the term *elect*, or *chosen*, as a designation for the saved (Matthew 24: 22-31; Mark 13: 20-27). There is no record of Jesus using any form of the word *predestination*, although the Apostle Paul employed the terms *chosen* (Colossians 3: 12) and *predestined* (Romans 8: 29-30; Ephesians 1: 5, 11). Like Jesus, he referred to believers as the *elect*, or *chosen* of God (2 Timothy 2: 10; Titus 1: 1).

---

[30] Ibid., 180.
[31] Ibid., 607.
[32] Ibid., 610.
[33] Ibid.

Peter (1 Peter 1: 1) and John (Revelation 17: 14) also used these terms in similar fashion.

Calvin's view of the doctrine of election represented a redirection from what the church historically held, notwithstanding the works of Augustine. According to Calvin, the election, or selection, of the saved took place, divinely and irrevocably, prior to the creation of the world. This he derived in part from Paul's words to the Romans and Ephesians.

> [28] And we know that God causes all things to work together for good to those who love God, to those who are called according to *His* purpose. [29] For those whom He foreknew, He also predestined *to become* conformed to the image of His Son, so that He would be the firstborn among many brethren; [30] and these whom He predestined, He also called; and these whom He called, He also justified; and these whom He justified, He also glorified. (Romans 8: 28-30)

> [3] Blessed *be* the God and Father of our Lord Jesus Christ, who has blessed us with every spiritual blessing in the heavenly *places* in Christ, [4] just as He chose us in Him before the foundation of the world, that we would be holy and blameless before Him. In love [5] He predestined us to adoption as sons through Jesus Christ to Himself, according to the kind intention of His will, [6] to the praise of the glory of His grace, which He freely bestowed on us in the Beloved. (Ephesians 1: 3-6)

From these words, Calvin concluded that God selects people to salvation unconditionally, without regard to any good works they might perform or character traits they may possess. To Calvin, this is illustrated in God's choice of Jacob over Esau. He considered God's selection of Jacob to be a model for the biblical doctrine of election.

> [10] And not only this, but there was Rebekah also, when she had conceived *twins* by one man, our father Isaac; [11] for though *the twins* were not yet born and had not done anything good or bad, so that God's purpose according to *His* choice would stand, not because of works but because of Him who calls, [12] it was said to her, " THE OLDER WILL SERVE THE YOUNGER." [13] Just as it is written, " JACOB I LOVED, BUT ESAU I HATED." (Romans 9: 10-13)

John Calvin recognized that his view of election served up a bit of a quagmire since, for many people, it smacked of injustice. Would a just God create most of humankind for the purpose of condemning them to eternal punishment with absolutely no opportunity for reprieve? How could such inequity come from a righteous God? This obvious incongruity was inconsequential where Calvin was concerned. He taught that justification of this doctrine of election is found in the fact that God chooses who will be saved and, since God is righteous, so is election.

He addressed this challenge forthrightly, not just within the doctrinal context of total depravity (the notion that his view of election was the only way anyone *could* know salvation), but also with some cautionary words for those who might seek to reconcile election and justice. He wrote:

> ...it is not right that man should with impunity pry into things which the Lord has been pleased to conceal within himself, and scan that sublime eternal wisdom which it is his pleasure that we should not apprehend but adore...let us willingly abstain from the search after knowledge, to which it is both foolish as well as perilous, and even fatal to aspire.[34]

From Calvin's perspective, no view but his own could be legitimately derived from Scripture. He believed that his doctrine of election was Paul's doctrine of election. He recognized, however, that some believed election, as revealed in God's Word, is simply a consequence of God's prescience, or foreknowledge. In other words, God knew beforehand who would be faithful and, as a result, they are the elect. For Calvin, the notion that predestination might be subordinate to foreknowledge was absurd. If election was in any way reliant on the decisions of men, as he believed the lesson concerning foreknowledge suggested, then salvation would no longer be of grace. Election grounded in foreknowledge would not be salvation by grace, but by works, even if those works had not yet occurred.

Limited Atonement

Limited atonement addresses what Reformers see as the concentrated, and therefore fractional, objective of Christ's sacrifice for sins. They believe when Jesus descended to earth and surrendered his life as a substitute for mankind, his intent was to provide atonement only for those who were previously elected by God to receive salvation/eternal life. In other words, Jesus did not die for all people, but only for those God elected "...before the foundation of the

---

[34] Ibid., 608.

world" (Ephesians 1: 4). Thus, the purpose of Christ's sacrifice was limited in scope.

This doctrine is distinctive in Calvinism in that, at least in his most famous work, *Institutes of the Christian Religion*, John Calvin did not address the topic of limited atonement, *per se*. For the most part, those who studied and followed the beliefs of Calvin after his death inferred this principle from his teaching on the doctrine of election. It stands to reason, they have said, that if only the chosen are to be saved, Jesus' sacrifice made on behalf of all of humanity would be inefficient, since the sins of the reprobate would never be forgiven. Why, then, should he shed his blood for those for whom such a sacrifice could never provide salvation? Still others raise even stronger objections, such as this remark from Jonathon Barlow:

> Believing that Jesus' death was a potential, symbolic atonement for anyone who might possibly, in the future, accept him trivializes Christ's act of atonement.[35]

Some have suggested that Calvin made a stronger point of this doctrine in some of his later commentaries, but if that is the case, his arguments are most subtle. Because the doctrine of limited atonement is, at best, surmised from Calvin's works, not all proclaimed Calvinists find it appealing. They have difficulty reconciling this doctrine with statements like the following one from Calvin's commentary on the most famous verse in the Bible, John 3: 16:

> And he has employed the universal term *whosoever*, both to invite all indiscriminately to partake of life, and to cut off every excuse from unbelievers. Such is also the impact of the term *world*, which he formerly used; for though nothing will be found in the *world* that is worthy of the favour of God, yet he shows himself to be reconciled to the whole world, when he invites all men without exception to the faith of Christ, which is nothing else than an entrance into life.[36]

What is most interesting about this observation by Calvin is that it seems to conflict with his teaching on election. If, after all, Christ died to give an opportunity for salvation to *whosoever* believes, does that not mean such an opportunity could exist? It was apparently

---

[35] Barlow, Jonathan. *Calvinism*, "Limited Atonement (Particular Redemption)," http://www.reformed.org/calvinism/.
[36] Calvin, John. *Commentary on the Gospel According to John*, 125.

contradictions such as this that led to the eventual development of the doctrine of limited atonement.

To be fair, the idea of limited atonement complements Calvin's view of election and can thus be inferred from certain statements in *Institutes*. For instance, in the following remark, which speaks of election rather than limited atonement, it becomes clear that Calvin believed that Christ's sacrifice was effectual for only the elect:

> But it is by Isaiah he more clearly demonstrates how he destines the promises of salvation specially to the elect (Isaiah 8: 16); for he declares that his disciples would consist of them only, and not indiscriminately of the whole human race.[37]

Reformers who challenge the concept of limited atonement, also known as *four-point Calvinists*, make some interesting points. For instance, in response to the question of the efficiency of Christ's sacrifice, some have stated that if, for the same cost (the shedding of his blood), Jesus could die for all rather than merely a few, would that not constitute a more efficient use of the cross? Also, many find it difficult to understand exactly how one's belief in a sacrifice for all of humanity "trivializes Christ's act..." as Mr. Barlow claims.

The schism among Calvinists over *limited atonement* is generally not a deal breaker. That is to say, it does not normally send people scampering off to Arminianism, since acceptance or rejection of this doctrine does not change the overall Reformed perspective on election or salvation. However, it is also not likely that these differences will be resolved soon.

Irresistible Grace

Irresistible grace is deemed necessary in Reformed Theology since moral depravity would naturally prevent anyone from accepting God's grace. This teaching is linked to total depravity in that humans do not have the capacity for good. Therefore, God, having elected certain ones to salvation, bestows them with grace (unmerited favor). Those who receive this grace are unable to resist because they have been chosen. They must respond positively to the grace they have been offered. This, too, is tied to God's sovereignty. If someone could resist a grace for which they have been elected by God, it would mean that he is not fully sovereign. Therefore, when God gives grace to one whom he has elected for salvation, it cannot be rejected or resisted.

---

[37] Calvin, John. *Institutes of the Christian Religion*, 622.

Calvin did not employ the term *irresistible grace* in *Institutes*, but the label is inconsequential. What others call *irresistible grace* Calvin simply called *grace*. He knew of no other kind. The doctrine known today as *irresistible grace*, an expression developed to fit the TULIP acronym, is drawn from what Calvin termed *effectual calling*.

The calling for salvation offered through the gospel of Christ, according to Reformed Theology, distinguishes between the reprobate (those who are eternally condemned), and the elect (those who are eternally saved). This distinction is found in two types of calling. Bruce Ware recognizes that the call provided by the gospel message is meant for all people. On the other hand, he states that:

> Another sense of "the call" to be saved is indicated by several texts, but these passages portray not a general but a "special" call…Hence, this "special call" is sometimes referred to as the "effectual call…"[38]

This *special calling* differs from the general call of the gospel in that it 1) is intended *only* for God's elect, and 2) always results in the salvation of the called. It has become known among the Reformed community as *effectual calling*. The most noted passage from which Reformers derive this doctrine is Paul's reference to "…those who are called according to his purpose" (Romans 8: 28), presumably providing contrast against those who are either *not* called according to his purpose, or possibly, those who are called, but *not* according to his purpose. People "…called according to his purpose" are, through the eyes of Reformed Theology, the elect, and it is these Paul has in mind in this verse.

Effectual calling is attributed to several other passages that identify calling as a matter of salvation. For example, in Jesus' parable of the wedding feast, as he said, "For many are called, but few are chosen" (Matthew 22: 14), it is said that *many* refers to the general call while those who are *chosen* receive an effectual call. Similar teachings are proposed for other passages that refer to the general/effectual call provided through the gospel (cf. 1 Corinthians 1: 9; 1 John 3: 1).

That is not to say that grace is forced upon the individual. At least, that is not the way Calvin understood it. He did not speak of irresistibility, or effectual calling, in terms of force, but in terms of the magnetism of grace. Calvin likened God's bestowal of grace on the elect to Hosea's words concerning the Israelites when he said, "The children of Israel shall fear the Lord and his goodness in the latter

---

[38] Brand, Chad Owen, editor. *Perspectives on Election, Five Views*, 17.

days" (Hosea 3:5).[39] Comparing the elect to Hosea's words about the Israelites' eventual and inevitable fear of God, Calvin noted:

> For not only does piety beget reverence to God, but the sweet attractiveness of grace inspires a man, though desponding of himself, at once with fear and admiration, making him feel his dependence on God, and submit humbly to his power.[40]

Admittedly, the notion that someone might be drawn to grace as a matter of attraction, as opposed to having it thrust upon his/her being with irresistible force, smacks of free will. The difference here is that only those whose eyes have been opened by God through regeneration will be able to understand the charm of God's grace; so, the notion of attraction is suitable to Calvinism in that regard. This is possible in that, according to Reformed theologians, regeneration precedes faith as can be seen in the following remarks:

> In regeneration, God changes our hearts. He gives us a new disposition, a new inclination. He plants a desire for Christ in our hearts. We can never trust Christ for our salvation unless we first desire Him. This is why we said earlier that regeneration precedes faith.[41]

> Only God can bring life to dead souls to enable them to believe. He does this when and where and how He pleases by His Spirit, who regenerates, or gives life leading to faith.[42]

As with other Reformed teachings, irresistible grace is accepted to varying degrees. For instance, some believe that when God bestows his grace on the elect, they are compelled to accept his grace (viz. attraction) without any resistance whatsoever. Others, like John Piper, believe a certain amount of resistance is feasible as long as the ultimate result of salvation for the elect is realized. He wrote:

> The doctrine of irresistible grace does not mean that every influence of the Holy Spirit cannot be resisted. It means that the Holy Spirit can overcome all resistance and make his influence irresistible.[43]

---

[39] Calvin, John. *Commentary on the Gospel According to John*, 370.
[40] Ibid.
[41] Sproul, R. C. *Chosen by God*, 118.
[42] Adams, Jay. *Competent To Counsel*, 70.
[43] Piper, John. *Irresistible Grace*, http://www.monergism.com/thethreshold/articles/piper/irresistable.html.

It is difficult to see how this view differs significantly from irresistible grace as defined by Calvin and other Reformers, except that it seems to suggest a greater measure of free will could be in play in the process of one inevitably accepting God's grace.

Perseverance of the Saints

Perseverance of the saints is the claim that once a person has been elected to salvation, it is a permanent, unalterable condition. Many define it as the doctrine of *once saved always saved*. Those who believe and teach this doctrine deny the existence of apostasy (the notion that someone could lose, or relinquish, his/her salvation). Since, in Calvin's Reformed view, men and women were elected to salvation by God prior to the creation of the world, the suggestion that someone who was predestined to receive God's grace might subsequently see that grace withdrawn is without foundation.

Perseverance of the saints is the natural outcome of the Calvinist perspective on the doctrine of *election*, since apostasy would thwart the salvific decisions God made prior to creation. This is especially true when considered in conjunction with the doctrine of *irresistible grace*. If God's grace is truly irresistible, no elect person would ever be found in a spiritual condition where God might consider withdrawing his grace. God's decision of election is irreversible.

The doctrine is based on the principle that the believer, or saint, is preserved by God. One's preservation does not rely on personal will or actions, but on God's power and authority by which the decree of election has been made. Thus, the elect are sustained by God. Since God has, through Christ's sacrifice, satisfied the debt for the sins of the elect (limited atonement), they can no longer be condemned for sins committed.

Part of the reasoning behind *perseverance* lies in the understanding that eternal life begins the moment a person is saved. For instance, Paul, in discussing God's elect in his letter to the Romans, made the following statement:

> [38] For I am convinced that neither death, nor life, nor angels, nor principalities, nor things present, nor things to come, nor powers, [39] nor height, nor depth, nor any other created thing, will be able to separate us from the love of God, which is in Christ Jesus our Lord. (Romans 8: 38-39).

Similarly, Jesus, while emphasizing the oneness between himself and God the Father, told the Jews in Jerusalem:

> Truly, truly, I say to you, he who hears My word, and believes Him who sent Me, has eternal life, and does not come into judgment, but has passed out of death into life. (John 5: 24)

Do these verses teach that eternal life begins the moment one accepts Jesus as Savior, or is eternal life for those who *hold fast* (Hebrews 3: 6)? In other words, is eternal life *bestowed* here, or is it promised? If eternal life is bestowed while one remains in this human frame, it stands to reason that the believer's life is eternal (spiritually speaking) even as that person's physical life continues. On the other hand, if eternal life is offered as a promise to those who hold fast, it seems reasonable to believe that someone who is legitimately looking forward to his/her promised eternal existence can also choose to walk away from that promise.

Chapter 11

God and Predestination

The Doctrine of Predestination

Predestination essentially means predetermination. With respect to things spiritual, predestination is a doctrine whereby people recognize that God predetermines certain things, especially concerning his relationship with men. The doctrine of predestination is particularly challenging, since people seem to view it from a variety of perspectives. A simple example of predestination is seen in the countless fulfilled prophecies that are found in God's Word. For instance, God warned Noah that he would destroy mankind with a flood (Genesis 6: 17), a prophecy he fulfilled just as he promised (Genesis 7: 6).

The fact that God has historically involved himself intimately in the events of earth, offering prophecies about the future and then overseeing their fulfillment, unequivocally establishes the presence of at least a certain degree of predestination. Early in man's history, God promised Abraham, "...in you all the families of the earth will be blessed" (Genesis 12: 3). Serious students of the Bible generally recognize this as God's promise to Abraham that the Messiah would be his descendant – a prophecy fulfilled in the New Testament. In fact, the Old Testament is essentially thirty-nine books foretelling the coming of the Messiah and the ensuing age of grace. In complement, the New Testament reveals the realization of Jesus' life, death, burial, and resurrection along with the establishment of the church as foretold by the prophets. Therefore, it would be foolish for anyone to deny that God has predetermined many events that have taken place and will take place here on earth. The following are other examples of fulfilled prophecies.

Prophecy about the Virgin Birth (8th Century B.C.)
Therefore the Lord Himself will give you a sign: Behold, a virgin will be with child and bear a son, and she will call His name Immanuel. (Isaiah 7: 14)

Fulfillment (1st Century A.D.)
[18] Now the birth of Jesus Christ was as follows: when His mother Mary had been betrothed to Joseph, before they came together she was found to be with child by the Holy Spirit. [19] And Joseph her husband, being a righteous man and not wanting to disgrace her, planned to send her away secretly. [20] But when he had considered this, behold, an angel of the Lord appeared to him in a dream, saying, "Joseph, son of David, do not be afraid to take Mary as your wife; for the Child who has been conceived in her is of the Holy Spirit. [21] She will bear a Son; and you shall call His name Jesus, for He will save His people from their sins." [22] Now all this took place to fulfill what was spoken by the Lord through the prophet: [23] "BEHOLD, THE VIRGIN SHALL BE WITH CHILD AND SHALL BEAR A SON, AND THEY SHALL CALL HIS NAME IMMANUEL," which translated means, "GOD WITH US." [24] And Joseph awoke from his sleep and did as the angel of the Lord commanded him, and took *Mary* as his wife, [25] but kept her a virgin until she gave birth to a Son; and he called His name Jesus. (Matthew 1: 18-25)

Prophecy about John the Baptist (8th Century B.C.)
A voice is calling, "Clear the way for the LORD in the wilderness; Make smooth in the desert a highway for our God." (Isaiah 40: 3)

Fulfillment (1st Century A.D.)
For this is the one referred to by Isaiah the prophet when he said, "THE VOICE OF ONE CRYING IN THE WILDERNESS, 'MAKE READY THE WAY OF THE LORD, MAKE HIS PATHS STRAIGHT!'" (Matthew 3: 3)

Given these examples, it is evident that God has, at least on occasion, intervened in life here on earth even to the point of predetermining human events, particularly with regard to the life of Jesus Christ, for the benefit of mankind as he fixed his eyes on the covenant of grace. Essentially everything that occurred between the fall of man (Genesis 3: 1-13) and the Day of Pentecost (Acts 2: 1-41) happened in order to lay a foundation, either symbolically (the flood and the Passover) or substantively (the Mosaic Law), for the covenant of grace (Galatians 3: 1-26).

In the New Testament, the Greek word for *predestined*, which is *proōrizo*, appears six times (Acts 4: 28; Romans 8: 29-30; 1 Corinthians 2: 7; Ephesians 1: 5, 11). Peter uses it to describe God's predetermination of Jesus' sacrifice (Acts 4: 28) and Paul wrote of the preordained things of this world as part of the hidden wisdom of God (1 Corinthians 2: 7).

In his letters to the Romans and Ephesians, Paul had some interesting things to say about predestination. He told the Romans that those whom God *foreknew* he also predestined to be conformed to the likeness, or image, of Christ (Romans 8: 29). He uses similar language in his epistle to the Ephesians, writing about those predestined to adoption as God's sons according to his purpose (Ephesians 1: 5-11). These passages will be discussed in greater depth a bit later, but it is clear from Paul's words that God has predestined certain events.

Understanding that a certain level of predestination exists as an undeniable biblical truth, everyone should recognize that God, as a being, possesses certain qualities that make it *possible* for him to carry out such incredible feats. Therefore, in order to have a better understanding of *how* God predestined various events, consideration will be given to those godly characteristics that make it possible for him to do so.

God is Sovereign

The first attribute necessary for God to be able to predestine events and outcomes is his sovereignty, or supremacy. In other words, nothing that exists is greater than God since he is creator of all. Consequently, everything in both the physical and spiritual worlds is subject to him. The topic of God's sovereignty was discussed briefly in the first and tenth chapters of this book when acknowledging that God, as creator, has full authority over his creation. A number of biblical passages point to God's sovereignty establishing it, in keeping with the principle of *sola scriptura*, as a profound biblical truth.

> Yours, O LORD, is the greatness and the power and the glory and the victory and the majesty, indeed everything that is in the heavens and the earth; Yours is the dominion, O LORD, and You exalt Yourself as head over all. (1 Chronicles 29: 11)

> This sentence is by the decree of the *angelic* watchers
> And the decision is a command of the holy ones,
> In order that the living may know
> That the Most High is ruler over the realm of mankind,
> And bestows it on whom He wishes
> And sets over it the lowliest of men. (Daniel 4: 17)

> [15b] He who is the blessed and only Sovereign, the King of kings and Lord of lords, [16] who alone possesses immortality and dwells in unapproachable light, whom no man has seen or can see. To Him *be* honor and eternal dominion! Amen. (1 Timothy 6: 15b-16)

God Is Omnipotent (All Powerful)

The second godly attribute necessary for the doctrine of predestination is the element of omnipotence (God is all-powerful). The teaching that God is omnipotent is proclaimed boldly within the pages of Scripture. The Greek *pantokratōr*, which the New Testament writers used to address God's omnipotence, is most often rendered *Almighty* in English translations. In the Old Testament, the word translated into English as *Almighty* is the Hebrew word *Shadday*. Following are some biblical examples of their use:

> Now when Abram was ninety-nine years old, the LORD appeared to Abram and said to him, I am God Almighty;
> Walk before Me, and be blameless. (Genesis 17: 1)

> He who dwells in the shelter of the Most High
> Will abide in the shadow of the Almighty. (Psalm 91: 1)

> "I am the Alpha and the Omega," says the Lord God, "who is and who was and who is to come, the Almighty." (Revelation 1: 8)

Sovereignty alone would be insufficient without omnipotence. Having the *authority* to do something (predestine events and results) means nothing without the *ability* to do it. God's sovereignty and omnipotence are evidence that he has both the authority and the ability to control, and even preordain, events here on earth and through eternity.

God Is Omniscient (All-Knowing)

The third and final characteristic God must possess in order for the doctrine of predestination to have traction is the quality of omniscience, meaning that God has complete knowledge. Without omniscience, events unknown to him could interfere with his ability to predestine. The omniscient character of God is also taught deliberately in the pages of Scripture. The following passages demonstrate that he knows intimately even the hearts of men:

> ...for the LORD searches all hearts, and understands every intent of the thoughts. If you seek Him, He will let you find Him; but if you forsake Him, He will reject you forever. (1 Chronicles 28: 9b)

> ...for God is greater than our heart and knows all things. (1 John 3: 20b)

Predestination vs. Free Will

Men and women face a multitude of decisions each day, both physical and spiritual. These include decisions about relationships, finances, etc. A person also chooses whom to marry, what vocational paths he/she will take, where to live, and whether or not to believe in God. The invariable assumption, when it comes to making choices, is that there are options. When someone chooses to act a certain way, the presumption is that other choices were available. After all, if no other options were available, no *choice* could be made.

Mankind's free will is understandably limited by human nature. That is to say, there are certain things humans cannot do. Men and women cannot live forever in the physical bodies God has provided since they will eventually fail (Hebrews 9: 27). Nor can someone choose to fly independent of some man-made mechanism, (airplane, helicopter, etc.). People can *invent*, but they cannot *create* in the same manner that God created the world out of nothing. Options like this fall outside human nature. Still, within the boundaries of human nature, it seems men are free to make decisions about how they will live their lives.

Paul was a man in whose life God interceded. He interrupted him on his journey to Damascus where Paul (known as Saul at the time) intended to persecute Christ's followers. Concerning Paul, God told Ananias, "...he is a chosen instrument of Mine, to bear My name before the Gentiles and kings and the sons of Israel" (Acts 9: 15). Yet, this is where the doctrine of predestination gets a bit tricky. Paul's situation begs the question: *Could he have resisted God's call to apostleship?* Did Paul have a choice? Were alternatives available to him?

Judas Iscariot betrayed Jesus, leading to his crucifixion. This was foreseen by God. Zechariah prophesied about this betrayal hundreds of years before it occurred (Zechariah 11: 13). God's plan from the beginning was for Jesus to sacrifice himself in order to provide redemption to a lost creation through his blood. It seems Judas's behavior was a critical component of God's plan.

The biblical discussion concerning man's free will and predestination lies at the heart of the division where the subject of election is concerned. In this life it is unlikely that people will reach common ground when addressing questions such as these. Some teach that God absolutely predetermined Judas's actions as he does the actions of all men. Others teach that God selected Judas for this role, but that it was an exception God made in order to carry out his plan of salvation. Still others insist that God simply foresaw Judas's attitude and actions. There is no question that he did use men like Pharaoh, who was determined to challenge God's will, to achieve a certain outcome (Exodus 7: 3-5).

Jesus' birth was one activity upon which everyone should agree. God decided that Jesus would come to earth and live as a man and then acted upon that decision. This was the manner in which God would redeem men. According to the Apostle Peter, Jesus' life, death, burial, and resurrection were decided before the earth was created.

> [17] If you address as Father the One who impartially judges according to each one's work, conduct yourselves in fear during the time of your stay *on earth*; [18] knowing that you were not redeemed with perishable things like silver or gold from your futile way of life inherited from your forefathers, [19] but with precious blood, as of a lamb unblemished and spotless, *the blood* of Christ. [20] For He was foreknown before the foundation of the world, but has appeared in these last times for the sake of you [21] who through Him are believers in God, who raised Him from the dead and gave Him glory, so that your faith and hope are in God. (1 Peter 1: 17-21)

Notwithstanding the preterist view that Jesus returned in A.D. 70, believers generally anticipate Jesus' Second Coming and the final judgment, confident that these events have been pre-ordained by God and are inevitable. God's plans concerning eschatology cannot be frustrated. Many believe the surety of these things is what Jesus had in mind in his well-known Olivet Discourse:

> [30] And then the sign of the Son of Man will appear in the sky, and then all the tribes of the earth will mourn, and they will see the SON OF MAN COMING ON THE CLOUDS OF THE SKY with power and great glory. [31] And He will send forth His angels with A GREAT TRUMPET and THEY WILL GATHER TOGETHER His elect from the four winds, from one end of the sky to the other. (Matthew 24: 30-31)

What is more difficult to determine is whether Mary, the mother of Jesus, could have refused to be the instrument for the Messiah's entrance into the world or whether her betrothed, a man named Joseph, could have refused to marry her under these circumstances. Did Mary have a choice? Did Joseph make a freewill decision? These and similar questions have plagued Bible scholars for centuries with no resolution in sight.

Chapter 12

Righteousness and Reformed Theology

The God of the Bible

Created in God's image, men and women can be described by the various traits for which they are known. These traits generally break down into three types: 1) ability, 2) character, and 3) status. For instance, athletic prowess describes someone's ability. Honesty, on the other hand, is considered a (quality) character trait. Finally, a person's status as a man or woman says nothing about his/her quality of character or, to a more limited degree, ability (i.e., men cannot give birth). Thus, each one displays various traits and kinds of traits.

While Calvin built his theology by focusing on God's sovereignty, it is fair to say that God's other attributes are no less critical in unpacking the nature of his relationship with mankind. They are just as important as are diverse human traits in building relationships between individuals. As noted in the previous chapter, omnipotence and omniscience are godly traits. However, these are not traits of *character*, but traits of *ability*. Omnipotence is God's ability to *do* all things and omniscience is his ability to *know* all things. Accompanying these is God's omnipresence (Jeremiah 23: 24) – his ability to be present everywhere.

God is also holy (Revelation 4: 8) and righteous (Psalm 71: 15-17). He also bears the fruit of the Spirit in that he is patient, kind, faithful, gentle, self-controlled, etc. (Galatians 5: 22-23). Unlike omnipotence, omnipresence, and omniscience, these are not traits of *ability*, but traits of *character*.

Sovereignty differs from these others in that it is neither an attribute of ability nor of character. Instead, it speaks to the *state* of God. It serves as recognition of his unequaled position of authority. At least two other characteristics also provide insight into the state of God. One is his eternality (Psalm 90: 2). He lives perpetually with no beginning or end. Also, God abides in spiritual rather than physical form (John 4: 24). Like sovereignty, his timelessness and spiritual essence describe who God is, and not what he does or can do.

Admittedly, these characteristics of God are intimately interconnected and, therefore, difficult to categorize. For instance, it is not that God *can* know all things, but that he *is* all-knowing (omniscient). Similarly, God not only *can* be all-present, but he *is* all-present (omnipresent). Therefore, these define who God is as much as they describe what he can do. However, God's trait of omnipotence does not mean he *can* or *does* do all things without exception. Like people, he can do only those things where he is not limited by his nature. For instance, God cannot lie (Titus 1: 2) due to his traits of character. God does only what is in keeping with the holiness and righteousness that are inherent in his being.

One characteristic that must not be overlooked is God's attribute of love. This, too, is an attribute of ability (John 3: 16) and status (1 John 4: 8). It is also treated in Scripture as a character trait (1 John 4: 16). As one contemplates God's creation of, and relationship with, humankind, it is important to recognize that each godly trait plays a distinct and deliberate role in how God interacts with his creation.

God and Righteousness

One of the primary godly characteristics the biblical authors used to reveal him to their readers is the attribute of *righteousness*, which is translated into English from the Greek word *dikaiosunē*. While it is often used in connection with faith (people achieve or realize righteousness through faith), perhaps the best meaning that could be applied to this word is the principle of justice. In other words, God is just in his decision-making.

Fairness is not always in view when it comes to righteousness since fairness is a relative term while righteousness focuses on right and wrong. For instance, in his will, a father may bequeath more to one son than to another. While that may seem unfair to the child who receives less, it cannot be considered unjust since the assets were the father's to give. This does not mean that fairness and righteousness are unrelated. In God's Word, there are times when fairness and justice are used in a way that shows how they are intended to complement each other (cf. Colossians 4: 1). God is both righteous and fair, but these two principles should not be confused.

When God created mankind, he did not establish an arbitrary standard of holiness for men. The kind of holiness God demands from those who would seek to be faithful is the holiness that resides in and exudes from him. It is God's hope that believers will be like him, displaying his holiness. He does not differentiate between his own holiness and the holiness he expects from mankind. The Apostle Peter wrote:

> [15] but like the Holy One who called you, be holy yourselves also in all *your* behavior; [16] because it is written, "YOU SHALL BE HOLY, FOR I AM HOLY." (1 Peter 1: 15-16)

His final phrase in verse sixteen, "You shall be holy, for I am holy," is a citation from Leviticus. The expression seems to be the theme of chapters 17-26 of Leviticus where it appears a number of times. Just as God is holy, he expects holiness from men and women. Each individual will be held accountable for the holiness in his/her life measured against the only possible standard, which is God's holiness.

Similarly, men are to love as God loves. No unreasoned standard of love has been established. The love people are to show toward God and others is the love that emanates from him. In the first of his three epistles, the Apostle John addressed in depth the kind of love God expects from believers when he wrote:

> [7] Beloved, let us love one another, for love is from God; and everyone who loves is born of God and knows God. [8] The one who does not love does not know God, for God is love. [9] By this the love of God was manifested in us, that God has sent His only begotten Son into the world so that we might live through Him. (1 John 4: 7-9)

Just as the holiness and love believers are to practice are the same holiness and love that are attributes of God, so the righteousness, or sense of justice, God expects from Christians is the same righteousness that is found in him. Paul told the Romans that Jesus gave himself to make righteousness available to mankind (Romans 5: 19). This is one of three directives given to mankind through the prophet Micah.

> *...the righteousness, or sense of justice, God expects from Christians is the same righteousness that is found in him.*

He has told you, O man, what is good;
And what does the LORD require of you
But to do justice, to love kindness,
And to walk humbly with your God? (Micah 6: 8)

Three things God requires. Three things are good, and the first is justice. This provides a sense, from God's perspective, of the significance of the justice he expects to see in the lives of believers. It is the same justice God himself exercises. Through the Apostle Paul, God directly compares the justice of men to the justice of God.

> Masters, grant to your slaves justice and fairness, knowing that you too have a Master in heaven. (Colossians 4: 1)

From this verse, it does not seem unreasonable to conclude that an individual could anticipate treatment from God that is at least as just *and* as fair as any slave could expect from a flawed human master. The verse even seems to contain a veiled message that one may well answer to the heavenly master for the manner in which he/she demonstrates fairness and justice toward others here on earth.

God allowed the Israelites to *judge* for themselves his own form of justice, placing himself before them as though he was a defendant making his case. In the eighteenth chapter of the book of Ezekiel, the children of Israel grumbled, claiming that God was unjust, since righteous children were sometimes made to pay in some fashion for the sins of their fathers. The Israelites could not square their perception of justice with what they believed they were seeing around them as good people were forced to suffer seemingly unjust consequences.

God responded, spelling out exactly how he viewed justice. This discourse covers the bulk of the eighteenth chapter of Ezekiel. The message God delivered through the prophet is one of true justice. God told the Israelites that each person would be held accountable for his/her deeds, whether righteous or unrighteous. God's words are clear and stated repeatedly. Those who practice righteousness will live. Those who do not will die. The son is not accountable for the sins of the father; neither is the father held accountable for the sins of the son. If a righteous person turns from God to unrighteousness, he will surely die. However, the unrighteous person who turns to righteousness will live. This same message was delivered through Moses at an earlier date (Deuteronomy 24: 16).

The life and death God has in view must be spiritual, not corporal life and death since all humans die physically. Additionally, God acknowledges that the punishment for one's sins can be, and sometimes is, visited upon his descendants in dramatic fashion (Exodus 20: 5; 34: 6-7; Deuteronomy 5: 9). Sin can have consequences that have a ripple effect, even touching generations. Still, what is most interesting is how God's sense of righteousness is depicted exactly as men perceive justice. The difference is that God's righteousness is more just and more equitable than any righteousness men can muster. God's righteousness is also broader in scope. People see righteousness in terms of life on earth (rewards and punishments) while God looks beyond the physical to the spiritual.

As with holiness and love, God comprehends and administers justice perfectly. This is natural since righteousness comes from God. Just as people have the capacity to understand his holiness and love, they have the ability to grasp the righteousness of God. Given God's explanation to the Israelites of his sense of justice, it becomes noticeably clear that his judgments, as he described them, are based on the manner in which human beings lived their lives. The righteous will live (spiritually) while the unrighteous will die (spiritually). There is nothing ambiguous in his words, nor is there anything subjective about the way God administers justice.

Godly Righteousness and Reformed Theology

It is because of God's perfect righteousness that so many find it difficult to reconcile God's righteousness, as defined by him, with Reformed Theology. According to God, his judgment of humanity takes into consideration individual actions and attitudes. The argument has been made that the seeming contradiction that unfolds within the Calvinist system, where people are judged for carrying out choices God made, has somehow been reconciled in the mind of God and is simply beyond human comprehension. However, it is evident from the episode in Ezekiel, as God presented his case to the Israelites, that his sense of righteousness holds no hidden mysteries. Like humans, God fully recognizes the inherent unrighteousness involved in holding someone accountable for choices made by others. He wanted the Israelites to understand the equitable manner in which he administers justice.

Chapter 13

Unconditional Election: Major Passages

The Dynamics of Unconditional Election

Reformed theologians teach that God irrevocably preselected, prior to creation, who among his creation would be saved and reside with him in heaven. The decision concerning each one's eternal salvation or condemnation was based, not on whether an individual chose to accept Jesus Christ as Savior, but "…according to His purpose who works all things after the counsel of His will' (Ephesians 1: 11). In other words, the decision was God's alone and what he decided prior to creation stands.

According to Calvin and his followers, not only was this decision made prior to the creation of man, and not only was this God's decision, but mankind is not privy to the reasoning that was involved in that process. Part of the reason men cannot know how God chose people for salvation is that this information is *intended* for God alone. The second reason it is not possible to know how God selected those who would be saved is that salvation is unconditional. According to Calvinism, God did not consider the faith, character, or morals of those whom he would save. These are irrelevant to election. Since election has no conditions, at least from man's perspective, there is nothing to understand.

One of the greatest obstacles in reconciling unconditional election with God's Word is that the Bible is a book of conditions. From the moment humankind was created – even before sin entered the picture – God's relationship with his creation has been grounded in conditions. Adam and Eve were given a condition regarding the Tree of Knowledge of Good and Evil. They were told they must not eat of that tree lest they die (Genesis 2: 17). In order to avoid the consequences of the flood, Noah was required to construct an ark (Genesis 6: 11-15). The walls of Jericho would not fall until the Israelites obeyed God's commands (Joshua 6: 1-27). The list of conditions upon which man's relationship with God is founded is virtually endless.

Many scholars agree that, in the New Testament, faith is portrayed as a condition of one's salvation (Ephesians 2: 8; Hebrews 11: 6). Calvinism, on the other hand, teaches that faith is not a condition of salvation, but a result of it. The idea is that God first regenerates a person and, once he/she has been saved, God grants them faith so that they may believe. According to Reformed Theology, this is a necessary progression due to man's total depravity.

Calvinists rely on a number of biblical passages to buttress the doctrine of unconditional election, insisting that these verses fully establish and support their perspective on election. Despite the claim that the Bible speaks boldly on the subject, the doctrine of unconditional election has been developed through the use of inference. The term *elect*, as it appears in Scripture, offers no proof for unconditional election, and the word *unconditional* does not appear anywhere in any context within God's Word. Consequently, in passages of Scripture that are used to argue in favor of unconditional election, the unconditional character of that election must be introduced into the text by the reader/teacher as a matter of speculation. Therefore, it is necessary to study the primary passages from which this doctrine is derived to see if they do, as Reformed tradition teaches, lay a firm foundation for Calvinism, or if something else is in view.

Acts 13: 48

On Paul's first missionary journey, he and Barnabas traveled to the town of Pisidian-Antioch in Asia Minor. While there, Paul was invited to speak in the synagogue. Among his listeners were some Jews as well as certain proselytes among the Gentiles (Acts 13: 14-43). Encouraged by his message, they asked him to return the next week and speak again. The following week, the place was wall-to-wall people as residents of the town, including many Gentiles, came to hear Paul's message. Luke states that "...nearly the whole city assembled to hear the word of the Lord" (Acts 13: 44).

The Jews became angry that the gospel message was given to Gentiles and started giving Paul and Barnabas a difficult time, even slandering and/or cursing them. Paul responded by telling them that the gospel message had first been offered to the Jews. However, they had rejected Christ. As a result, that message was now being offered to Gentiles (v. 46). Luke follows Paul's comments with the following observation:

173

When the Gentiles heard this, they *began* rejoicing and glorifying the word of the Lord; and as many as had been appointed to eternal life believed. (Acts 13: 48)

The issue with this verse is Luke's comment concerning *appointment to eternal life* that seems to place the timing of that appointment prior to one's belief. The translation of *appointed* for the Greek *tasso* is not unreasonable in this setting, although, in keeping with the theme of the passage, which depicts God arranging for eternal life for the Gentiles, an interpretation of *arranged* (Acts 28: 23 – NIV) or *assigned* (Acts 22: 10 – NIV, NRSV) might be preferable. The word literally means: "…to arrange in an orderly manner, i.e. assign or dispose (to a certain position or lot):--addict, appoint, determine, ordain, set."[44] In past perfect mode, as Luke uses it here, various translations have termed it *were ordained* (KJV; RSV), *were appointed* (NIV), *had been appointed* (NASB), etc.

Before delving too deeply into the intricacies of this narrative, two things should be clarified. First of all, appointment to eternal life is, and always has been, of God. People cannot appoint themselves to eternal life. Salvation through faith is not self-appointment, it is submission. On the other hand, that appointment is not unconditional. It is conditioned upon one's faith, which is a fundamental biblical tenet (Ephesians 2: 8).

Calvinists like to underscore Luke's statement, claiming that, with his use of *tasso* in this verse, he has provided an undeniable biblical declaration of the doctrine of unconditional election. To them, this verse erases any doubt that the believers mentioned here were individually predestined to eternal life "…before the foundation of the world" (Ephesians 1: 4). After all, it does say, "…as many as had been appointed to eternal life believed."

At first blush, these words could easily confound non-Calvinists, since they seem to suggest that appointment to eternal life occurs prior to belief. Those who seek to challenge Calvin's philosophy of unconditional election have offered a variety of possible explanations for Luke's comment. For instance, some teach that the word *tasso* could be interpreted *disposed to*. Thus, it is those who were *disposed to,* or *inclined toward,* eternal life who believed.[45]

---

[44] Strong, James. *The New Strong's Exhaustive Concordance of the Bible, Greek Dictionary of the New Testament*, 71.
[45] This was the view of men like Henry Alford (1810-1871), Edward Plumptre (1821-1891), J. W. McGarvey (1829-1911), and others.

Those who make this claim insist that, in this instance, *tetagmenoi*, which is the verb form of *tasso* that appears in the verse, may be an example of what is known as middle voice. In the Greek language, the use of middle voice denotes an action taken by oneself that reflects back upon oneself or an action where the beneficiary is also a participant.[46] Technically speaking, the verb form of *tasso* that is used here can represent either middle voice or passive mode. The application of middle voice in this setting would result in the following translation offered by the *Holy Bible Modern Literal Version:*

And when the Gentiles heard this, they were rejoicing and glorifying the word of the Lord, and they believed as many as were appointing *themselves* toward everlasting life. (Acts 13: 48)

From this perspective, it is argued that *personal disposition* or *inclination* could be in view. However, wording like this seems out of character for Luke, who tended to write unambiguously. Note also that the word *themselves* is italicized because it does not appear in the Greek text. Additionally, one must appreciate the fact that, through the pages of history, translators have consistently avoided applying middle voice in this setting precisely because of the awkwardness involved.

Calvinists are quick to point out that Luke could not be using middle voice in this instance, since *tasso* does not involve one's own mindset or disposition. That is, it does not point to something internal, such as one's inclination, as this argument suggests, but always implies the influence of an outside force. Additionally, a meaning of *inclination* or *disposition* does not reflect the common biblical use of this word. It is true that the Apostle Paul used a form of this same word to describe the personal *devotion* of Stephanas and his household (1 Corinthians 16: 15). Yet, to be fair to Calvinism and diligent where interpretive principles are concerned, it should be noted that, in the Corinthians passage where this occurs, *tasso* appears in active mode, while here in Acts it is passive – a fact that directly affects its meaning.

Reformers are correct in denying a meaning of *inclination* or *disposition* in the current setting. In passive mode, it is safe to say that *tasso* suggests an *arrangement* provided by something or someone other than the believers. Regardless of the nature of this arrangement, the text indicates that those who believed were passively involved.

---

[46] An example of middle voice is seen as Paul was commanded to *be baptized* (middle voice) in Acts 22: 16. It was something he was to do as well as something that would be done to him.

Others have argued that *tasso* is more general, claiming that it depicts God's arrangement (or appointment) for the gospel message to be preached to the Gentiles. The idea is that delivering the gospel to the Gentiles was part of God's timeline...it was scheduled, or set in place, as part of God's plan. This fits well with Paul citing Isaiah (v. 47), who had prophesied concerning inclusion of the Gentiles. It also preserves the true meaning of *tasso* and finds support from the use of this word in other biblical settings.

> But the eleven disciples proceeded to Galilee, to the mountain which Jesus **had designated** (extaxo).[47] (Matthew 28: 16) Emphasis added

> When they **had set** (taxamenoi)[48] a day for Paul, they came to him at his lodging in large numbers. (Acts 28: 23a) Emphasis added

While this explanation seems to have some merit, it does not quite fit the specific phraseology Luke employs. The word *tasso* is written to denote the appointment of people to eternal life. Unless one is willing to disregard legitimate interpretive principles, the expression "...as many as had been appointed' cannot be forced to say *the gospel had been appointed*.

Non-Calvinists have spent much time and energy protesting what many consider to be the difficult wording of Acts 13: 48 – difficult in that it seems to contradict their salvation doctrine. Some have even gone so far as to challenge the arrangement of the words, claiming that Luke meant to say that those who believed were then appointed to eternal life. For instance, *The Simple English Bible* offers the translation:

> ...and many of the people believed. These were the people appointed to have eternal life. (Acts 13: 38)

This rendering of the verse undoubtedly appeals to many non-Calvinists. The problem is that the phrase "many of the people" does not appear in the Greek text. Legitimate biblical analysis requires accepting the words of Scripture as they are written, not as someone wishes they were written to support a specific doctrinal view. On the other hand, it is important to avoid seizing upon a solitary word (tasso) in one verse of the Bible and using it to develop any doctrine, much

---

[47] Aorist Middle Voice Third Person Singular form of tasso
[48] Aorist Middle Voice Nominative Plural form of tasso

less a doctrine of salvation. In order to understand Luke's point concerning appointment to eternal life, the context of his remark must be given full consideration. That requires starting a bit earlier in the passage, where the immediate storyline about Pisidian-Antioch begins (v. 42).

At the request of his listeners, Paul returned to speak in the synagogue, having sparked the interest of many with his words – especially the Gentiles. The Jews made it known that preaching the gospel to Gentiles was, in their view, unacceptable. In Paul's exchange with them, he not only accused the Jews of rejecting that message, but he cited the prophet Isaiah who had prophesied concerning the salvation of Gentiles (Isaiah 49: 6). Actually, Paul only quotes the second half of the verse from Isaiah, but what he failed to cite is equally relevant to this discussion. Here is the verse in its entirety:

> He says, "It is too small a thing that You should be My Servant
> To raise up the tribes of Jacob and to restore the preserved ones of Israel;
> I will also make You a light of the nations
> So that My salvation may reach to the end of the earth."
> (Isaiah 49: 6)

The "Servant" of this passage is a reference to Christ. It was he who would "restore the preserved ones of Israel." He would also be "a light of the nations." God's plan, which he revealed through the prophet and executed through the apostles, was to have an inclusive kingdom. His goal was to expand that kingdom to the Gentiles, since limiting it to the Jews would be "too small a thing."

Paul's remarks as well as Isaiah's prophecy portray God *arranging for eternal life for the Gentiles* – an honor previously reserved for the Jews or Gentile converts. That arrangement was now fully developed, and Gentiles could know salvation without converting to Judaism. When the Gentiles heard this news, "they began rejoicing and glorifying the word of the Lord" (v. 48). Following this, Luke commented, "and as many as had been appointed to eternal life believed."

Upon the Jews' rejection of the gospel, the message was delivered to the Gentiles. In his discussion with the Jews, Paul is speaking in broad terms. He is not talking about the salvation of a select few among the Gentiles. His use of the passage from Isaiah, where the unfettered opportunity for salvation among the Gentiles is in view, speaks to the corporate nature of Paul's words. The prophecy complements the apostle's call to reach out to the Gentile nations with the gospel (Acts 9: 15).

Given the context of Luke's remark about *arranging eternal life*, it is nonsensical to suggest that he is attempting to comment on unconditionally elected Gentiles. He had just penned the words from Paul and Isaiah where they reasoned concerning the unlimited personality of this opportunity for the Gentiles. Isaiah, in prophesying concerning these things, recognized that salvation was intended to sweep across the nations, reaching "to the end of the earth" (v. 47). The phrase *heōs eschatou tēs gēs*, which is translated "to the end of the earth," is all-encompassing, indicating that the gospel message is intended to reach every crevice of the earth. These words literally mean *as far as the limits of the land*. A. T. Robertson (1863-1934) defines this phrase with the words, "Unto the last portion...of the earth."[49] Paul understood that God had *arranged for eternal life* for all people of all nations, and not just the Jews.

Luke also uses the Greek word *hosoi*, which is translated "as many as" in the current text (Acts 13: 48). In Scripture, this word is used to identify people. Generally, the reference is to all those who share a common experience and/or characteristic. For instance, as Jesus traveled through the villages of Israel, certain people were healed simply by touching his cloak.

> Wherever He entered villages, or cities, or countryside, they were laying the sick in the market places, and imploring Him that they might just touch the fringe of His cloak; and **as many as** (tais-from the root word for hosoi) touched it were being cured. (Mark 6: 56) Emphasis added

Many sick people sought healing from Jesus. Of those who were sick, Scripture does not detail how many were actually healed. What it does say is that the healings, at least as they are discussed in this context, involved all those who touched Jesus' cloak. Thus, *hosoi*, which is translated "as many as" speaks to the common experience of all who were healed in this manner.

Writing about the early church in Jerusalem, Luke notes that the believers shared their possessions liberally. Some went so far as to sell property and/or houses and offer the money to the apostles so that it could be used to help those among the believers who were less

---

[49] Robertson, A. T. *Robertson's Word Pictures in the New Testament*, *Acts 13*, http://www.studylight.org/commentaries/rwp/view.cgi?bk=43&ch=13.

fortunate. In this case, *hosoi* identifies all those who found it in their hearts to give up these possessions to help others who were in need.

> For there was not a needy person among them, for **all who** (tas-from the root word for hosoi) were owners of land or houses would sell them and bring the proceeds of the sales. (Acts 4: 34) Emphasis added

In English, the translation "as many as" which appears often in Bible translations as the meaning of *hosoi*, tends to suggest that there is a *hint of exclusion* where this word is concerned. For instance, in the case mentioned here, since *hosoi* depicts those who sold property, it naturally excludes those who did not. This has led many to regard Luke's remark about appointment to eternal life (v. 48) as a statement about exclusivity. In other words, Luke was saying that *only* those who were appointed to eternal life believed, and their pre-appointment (by God) was the reason for their belief.

Although *hosoi* necessarily excludes those who do not share in the experience or circumstance that is in view (e.g., those who did not sell houses and/or land), its focus is more inclusive than exclusive. The use of *hosoi* says nothing about those outside the group that is in view, but simply highlights the connection among those who have something in common. The NIV offers a much better explanation of this word where Acts 13: 48 is concerned.

> When the Gentiles heard this, they were glad and honored the word of the Lord; and **all who** (hosoi) were appointed for eternal life believed. (Acts 13: 48 - NIV) Emphasis added

Having contemplated the specific wording of the text, it is now time to determine Luke's intent. Is he saying that God predestines individuals to eternal life and that *only* these people will be saved? In truth, there is a much simpler explanation for Luke's comment that fully harmonizes with the balance of Scripture, and it is unrelated to the doctrine of unconditional election.

Early in this work the idea of context was addressed. It was noted at that time that "Paying attention to context is vital since, at times a verse may not mean what it plainly says. Context may fully alter the meaning of a verse, so no single verse or passage stands alone."[50] Context involves the subject matter of the text, the circumstances that

---

[50] See Chapter 2, Systematic Theology: Understanding Context, 25.

are being addressed, and the identity of the audience. However, there is one other element that can heavily influence how one might read and understand a verse of Scripture. It is the author's writing style, and this is arguably the most important factor where Acts 13: 48 is concerned.

In Luke's letters there is a literary device known as *metonymy* that he seemed to enjoy using. This is a figure of speech that is used to add effect when identifying people or items. More than sixty metonyms appear in the book of Acts alone. Through his use of metonymy, Luke was able to highlight the circumstances or some other distinct characteristic surrounding people or objects. For instance, when he wrote his first letter, which was the gospel of Luke, he began the letter as follows:

> ¹Inasmuch as many have undertaken to compile an account of the things accomplished among us, ² just as they were handed down to us by **those who** (ton-from the root word for hosoi) from the beginning were eyewitnesses and servants of the word. (Luke 1: 1-2) Emphasis added

These verses may seem wordier than necessary since Luke could have simply said *handed down to us by the apostles* (v. 2). However, he used a metonym, as a matter of effect, to highlight their early and personal involvement with Christ, hence establishing the legitimacy of their authority where doctrine is concerned. Therefore, rather than calling them apostles, he described them as "those who from the beginning were eyewitnesses and servants of the word."

Pisidian-Antioch was not the first time Gentiles heard the gospel message. Peter had, much earlier, introduced the gospel to certain Gentiles in Caesarea. Luke also recorded Peter's visit with those Gentiles. At that time, an extraordinary event occurred, and it was important that it should be shared. Below is Luke's account of the incident.

> ⁴⁴ While Peter was still speaking these words, the Holy Spirit fell upon **all those who** (tou-from the root word for hosoi) were listening to the message. ⁴⁵ **All the** circumcised believers **who** (hoi) came with Peter were amazed, because the gift of the Holy Spirit had been poured out on the Gentiles also. (Acts 10: 44-45) Emphasis added

Again, Luke has used metonymy to identify the two groups present on this occasion. He could have said, *the Holy Spirit fell upon the*

Gentiles, but he did not. Instead, he identified them as "all those who were listening to the message" (v. 44). In similar fashion, where the Jews are concerned, he could have said, *the Jews who were with Peter*, but he did not. He described them as "all the circumcised believers who came with Peter" (v. 45).

In this instance, the metonym, "all those who were listening to the message" corresponds to all of the Gentiles who were present. This was something they all had in common. Similarly, with the words "all the circumcised believers who came with Peter," Luke has in view all of the Jews who were present. Similar use of metonyms by Luke appear elsewhere in the book of Acts. As an example, upon returning to Jerusalem from Caesarea, Peter encountered Jewish believers who questioned his association with Gentiles.

> ² And when Peter came up to Jerusalem, **those who** (hoi) were circumcised took issue with him, ³ saying, "You went to uncircumcised men and ate with them." (Acts 11: 2) Emphasis added

Luke could have said *the Jews took issue with him*, but he did not. As in the earlier episode, he identifies the Jews as "those who were circumcised." Note also that the Gentiles are identified as "uncircumcised men," which is a separate metonym that appears in the same verse. Peter also employed metonymy on the Day of Pentecost, as recorded by Luke.

> ³⁷ Now when they heard *this*, they were pierced to the heart, and said to Peter and the rest of the apostles, "Brethren, what shall we do?" ³⁸ Peter *said* to them, "Repent, and each of you be baptized in the name of Jesus Christ for the forgiveness of your sins; and you will receive the gift of the Holy Spirit. ³⁹ For the promise is for you and your children and for all who are far off, **as many as** (tois-from the root word for hosoi) the Lord our God will call to Himself." (Acts 2: 37-39) Emphasis added

In this excerpt from Peter's sermon on the Day of Pentecost the apostle employs a metonym to echo his own words. He characterizes "you and your children and all who are far off" with the words "as many as the Lord our God will call to Himself." These two phrases identify the same people. In other words, the promise is meant for everyone. Paul later identifies the Gentiles as those who are "…far off" (cf. Ephesians 2: 13, 17), complementing Peter's remarks.

Yea and all the prophets from Samuel and them that followed after, **as many as** (hoi) have spoken, they also told of these days. (Acts 3: 24 - ASV) Emphasis added

Where these prophets are concerned, "as many as have spoken" is a reiteration, in the form of a metonym, of "all the prophets from Samuel and them that followed after." Note also that as with other metonyms (Acts 2: 39; 10: 45), *hosoi* represents those who are already in view in the narrative.

While his use of figurative language is rich and effective, Luke wrote plainly. His writing style was very straightforward and easy to understand. He seemed to try to avoid embellishment and controversial language. He did not entertain deep theological issues, but left that for the apostles, citing their words and allowing the reader to glean doctrine from those words. Consequently, where Luke is concerned, the simplest contextual explanation of a verse is probably the correct one.

The subject matter in the thirteenth chapter of Acts is God's arrangement for the spiritual salvation of the Gentiles. Paul is clear about this message, citing Isaiah's prophecy as a matter of scriptural support. With the words, "all who had been appointed to eternal life believed" (NIV), it is unlikely that Luke has anything in view but the topic and the people that have been the focus of the entire chapter – God's arrangement for salvation for Gentiles. This recent arrangement to eternal life was something all of the Gentiles had in common.

Most people have failed to recognize Luke's statement concerning *appointment to eternal life* as a metonym. As a result, Calvinists have mistakenly ascribed an unintended meaning to an innocent statement by Luke, as though he was uncharacteristically commenting on something beyond the immediate storyline. However, Luke was simply reporting what he had learned from Paul about his visit to Pisidian-Antioch. When he wrote, "all who had been appointed to eternal life" (NIV), as with other metonyms by Luke, he was merely identifying those already in view in the narrative. In this case, he could have said, *and the Gentiles believed*, but he did not. Instead, he portrayed them, in keeping with the theme of Paul's account, as those for whom God had arranged eternal life.

Metonymy adds effect to a storyline. Luke used metonyms to accentuate certain truths about people and/or circumstances. In this case, the Gentiles had been assigned to eternal life – not individually, but collectively. Luke uses that fact to distinguish them. In this case, he used a metonym to not only recognize the Gentiles, but to highlight the opportunity that was now theirs as well as God's role in providing that opportunity. This is a *descriptive* statement about the Gentiles and not a *prescriptive* declaration of unconditional election.

Did all of the Gentiles believe? Just prior to his infamous statement concerning appointment to eternal life, Luke mentions the Gentiles who had come to hear Paul speak, noting their response to his message. According to Luke, they were rejoicing over their newfound opportunity for salvation. Since he does not say that *some* of the Gentiles rejoiced, it can be reasonably inferred that all of the Gentiles who were present participated. Indeed, the very reason they were in attendance was the prospect of eternal life.

In Caesarea, Luke identified all of the Gentiles who were present at Cornelius's house on that day with the words, "all those who were listening to the message" (Acts 10: 44). He also described all of the Jews who were in attendance with the metonym, "All the circumcised believers who came with Peter" (Acts 10: 45).

In like fashion, where Pisidian-Antioch is concerned, there is no reason to look beyond the setting described in the text. The expression *hosoi tetagmenoi* is intended to identify the Gentiles who were present at the time. Luke is focused on the group as a whole, not individuals. Therefore, it is reasonable to conclude that all of the Gentiles who heard the apostle's message on this occasion – those who had been rejoicing – believed. In other words, with Luke-style simplicity he explains that, like the Gentiles in Caesarea, the Gentiles in Pisidian-Antioch responded enthusiastically to the gospel message.

Romans 8: 28-30

God has a plan for mankind. He has always had a plan for mankind, and it is one that predates creation. The design of this plan is spelled out clearly in Scripture. He has invited humanity to celebrate eternal life with him in heaven. This is the meaning behind numerous verses (cf. John 3: 16; 2 Peter 3: 9). It was on this premise that Paul wrote the following:

> [28] And we know that God causes all things to work together for good to those who love God, to those who are called according to *His* purpose. [29] For those whom He foreknew, He also predestined *to become* conformed to the image of His Son, so that He would be the firstborn among many brethren; [30] and these whom He predestined, He also called; and these whom He called, He also justified; and these whom He justified, He also glorified. (Romans 8: 28-30)

These verses have been at the center of much controversy over the past few centuries for rather obvious reasons. Words like *predestined* tend to grab one's attention, especially where the topic of election is concerned. Those who believe in the doctrine of unconditional election insist that, in these verses, the apostle makes the case for that point of view. Exactly how should these verses be read and understood? How do Paul's words influence the election debate?

It should be obvious that this section presents some special difficulties for Bible scholars. Currently, there are a host of conflicting views among theologians about Paul's use of *foreknew* and *predestined* in this text. Even grammarians often disagree over exactly what should be gleaned from Paul's use of these words in this setting. In fact, different explanations often emerge from people of similar theological backgrounds. Therefore, the task is not an easy one.

Due to the abundance of information that these verses offer, and the way that information interconnects, it is best to take small bites in order to digest that message more easily. Therefore, this section will be addressed one verse at a time. Afterward, the message will be tied together in a summary that reflects the apostle's thoughts.

According to Paul, "God causes all things to work together for good to those who love God, to those who are called according to His purpose" (v. 28). This verse is primary. It launches Paul's discourse about God's faithfulness toward those who love him. It is evident that this verse is primary since it is followed by the word "For" (Gr. *hoti*) meaning *because*. In the ensuing verses, Paul expounds upon his initial thought, which is that "God causes all things to work together for good to those who love God."

Paul's goal in these verses is to build confidence among the believers in Rome concerning their relationship with God. That relationship is not just about heaven and an eternal spiritual life. It is also about life on earth. God is in control and cares for men even as they abide in this earthly shell. Thus, he begins with a rather broad statement about God's involvement in the lives of the faithful.

What did Paul mean when he wrote that "God causes all things to work together for good"? For the one who loves him, God always wants and seeks to do that which will more fully develop that person's relationship with him and with others, and not necessarily what is most pleasing or comfortable. For instance, Joseph was sold into slavery by his brothers (Genesis 37: 28), which was not pleasant. However, Joseph later realized that God allowed this to happen so that, in the future, he would be able to care for his family during the famine

(Genesis 45: 4-8). While Joseph's experience was not fun, it was what *God had worked together for good.*

It would be foolish to think that Paul is writing only about earthly circumstances and events, such as Joseph's slavery. First and foremost, he surely has in view man's spiritual condition. In fact, that is undoubtedly his main focus, knowing that God cares infinitely more for a man's spiritual state than his physical well-being.

The *calling* (v. 28) that Paul mentions is, according to Reformed Theology, reflective of a special calling that applies only to the elect – an invitation only they receive. It is the *effectual calling* that was previously mentioned.[51] The lost are not privy to this calling, nor is it intended for them. According to Calvin, this calling is the reason the saved are saved. It is the reason "those who love God" (v. 28) love God.

The word *called*, in this instance (v. 28), is from the Greek *klētos*, which can mean *invited* or *appointed*, depending on the context. In this case, *appointed* is the best solution since, according to Scripture, everyone is invited (Acts 2: 39). Here Paul references "those who love God" (v. 28), not all who have been invited. The *called*, in this case, must be equivalent to the *chosen* in the parable of the wedding feast that was discussed earlier. In the parable, the king called many to the feast, but few attended. In the current setting, Paul appears to be discussing those who have accepted God's invitation.

If the lesson from the parable of the wedding feast is applicable here, which seems reasonable, Paul is using *called* as a term to denote not just an invitation, but acceptance of that invitation. The *called* are those who have decided to respond positively to God's invitation and become a part of the kingdom. They are equivalent to the *chosen* at the feast, although they were not the only invitees. Where Calvinists see an *effectual calling* meant only for the elect, others see a fulfilled invitation.

Many assume that with the phrase, "called according to *His* purpose" (v. 28), Paul is identifying people who are called according to God's *will*, presuming that *purpose* means *will* or *desire*. This presumption has been used to support the proposition that the Romans were *effectually called according to God's will*, but that is not what this verse says. The Greek word for *will*, as in the *will* of God, is *thelēma*. Certain passages of Scripture (cf. Matthew 26: 42;

---

[51] See Chapter 10, The Principles of Calvinism: Irresistible Grace, 156.

Mark 3: 35; Romans 12: 2; Hebrews 10: 36) provide examples of *thelēma* as it is used in God's Word.

If *God's purpose* does not mean *God's will*, what is the apostle Paul teaching? The word translated as *purpose* in the current text (v. 28) is the Greek word *prothesis*. Some of the common meanings of this word include *resolute, goal, intent, purpose, a setting forth, a proposal,* or *a plan*. Here are some biblical examples of its use.

> Then when he arrived and witnessed the grace of God, he rejoiced and *began* to encourage them all with **resolute** (prothesei) heart to remain *true* to the Lord. (Acts 11: 23) Emphasis added

> *This was* in accordance with the eternal **purpose** (prothesin) which He carried out in Christ Jesus our Lord. (Ephesians 3: 11) Emphasis added

> ...who has saved us and called us with a holy calling, not according to our works, but according to His own **purpose** (prothesin) and grace which was granted us in Christ Jesus from all eternity. (2 Timothy 1: 9) Emphasis added

The meaning of *prothesis* relies heavily on the text and context in which it is used. For instance, when Luke writes of a *resolute heart* (Acts 11: 23), he is writing of steadfastness and unwavering devotion. In that case, the meaning is relatively easy to recognize. Yet, when encountering phrases like "eternal purpose" (Ephesians 3: 11) and "His own purpose" (2 Timothy 1: 9), it becomes a bit more difficult to determine exactly what the writer, in these cases the Apostle Paul, has in mind.

Most English versions of the Bible do not help much in determining the meaning of *prothesis* in these settings, since they generally translate them uniformly as *eternal purpose* and *his own purpose*. However, Paul's use of this word in Romans finds a comparable use in his letter to the Ephesians. The NIV delivers a translation that reflects what seems to be a reasonable rendering of this verse.

> In him we were also chosen, having been predestined according to the **plan** (prothesin) of him who works out everything in conformity with the purpose of his will. (Ephesians 1: 11 – NIV) Emphasis added

The translation of *plan*, which the NIV translators deemed appropriate, fits very comfortably in both of the verses cited above (Ephesians 3: 11; 2 Timothy 1: 9). For instance, in Ephesians, substituting the word *plan* for *purpose*, the result is, *in accordance with the eternal plan which He carried out in Christ Jesus our Lord.* Not only does *plan* provide a sensible solution, but the text essentially demands this meaning. The idea of something being *carried out* is generally thought of in terms of a *plan*.

Similarly, the interpretation of *plan* in Timothy fits nicely when incorporated into the phrase "His own purpose," resulting in the words, *according to his own plan and grace which was granted us in Christ Jesus from all eternity*. Once again, *plan* seems to be a most reasonable characterization of *prothesis*. In each case, this word represents something that was carried out (executed) *through* Christ. Those "called according to His purpose" (Romans 8: 28), are *called according to his plan*. This is a reasonable understanding of the first verse of the text.

Paul's use of *hoti* (v. 29), which is translated "For," indicates that his ensuing remarks are intended to reinforce his claim about God's role in the lives of the disciples (v. 28). It is his goal to help them understand *how* they can know that God cares for those who love him. He told them, "For (because) those whom He foreknew, He also predestined to become conformed to the image of His Son" (v. 29).

A couple of questions must be answered to properly understand the passage. First of all: *Whom did God foreknow?* Second: *How do these remarks serve as evidence that God cares for those who love him?* Answering these questions should provide a better understanding of the meaning of this passage.

Many people make the mistake of assuming that Paul has in view God's foreknowledge – his ability to see the future or to know people who have not yet been born. It is easy to understand how that could happen given the English translation "those whom he foreknew." It also lends a tempting sense of mysticism to the passage. However, there is a much simpler, more practical explanation.

Early in this letter Paul began pointing to the people of the Old Testament as examples in order to provide lessons for his audience in Rome. For instance, in the very first chapter he said concerning the people of old that "God gave them over in the lusts of their hearts to impurity" (Romans 1: 24), since they refused to honor him. In the fourth chapter, Abraham serves as an example of one who had a faith-based relationship with God. Paul wrote that, "…faith was credited to

Abraham as righteousness" (Romans 4: 9). In fact, the entire fourth chapter is about Abraham.

He recalls Adam, in the fifth chapter, in order to teach lessons about how sin and death entered the world and how death was overcome through Christ. The ninth chapter covers Isaac, Rebecca, Jacob, and Esau, while, in the eleventh chapter, he discusses Elijah (Romans 11: 2). Paul's letter to the Romans is brimming with Old Testament examples. These characters serve as models for the various lessons Paul hopes to instill in his readers, and the current text seems to follow this pattern.

The Greek *proegnō* (a form of *proginōsko*), which is translated *foreknew* in the text, does not carry the meaning of foreknowledge, or prescience, that translators generally apply in this instance. Instead, it commonly refers to something or someone *known beforehand* or *known at an earlier time* (in the past), which is exactly how it is used in Scripture. It means to have knowledge about something (or someone) prior to a specific time or event. In fact, in this very epistle there is a rather obvious example of this. While most translations use the English word *foreknew* (in the sense of prescience) in the following text, that meaning is not what the apostle intended:

> God has not rejected His people whom He **foreknew** (proegnō). Or do you not know what the Scripture says in *the passage about* Elijah, how he pleads with God against Israel? (Romans 11: 2) Emphasis added

In this text, Paul is again pondering people of the Old Testament. He is writing about those God knew before (in the past). The very example he offers of those he knew previously is that of Elijah and the Israelites (specifically the seven thousand whom the Lord had kept) whom he had known in times past. These words are written in the context of Paul's continued discourse concerning the Israelites of old that permeates the epistle. Fully aware of this weakness of the translation *foreknew*, other versions of the Bible offer the following renderings of this verse:

> [2] God has not rejected his people whom he **knew long ago** (proegnō). Don't you know what Elijah says in the Scripture passage when he complains to God about Israel? He says, [3] "Lord, they've killed your prophets and torn down your altars. I'm the only one left, and they're trying to take my life." [4] But what was God's reply? God said, "I've

kept 7,000 people for myself who have not knelt to worship Baal." (Romans 11: 2-4 – God's Word Translation) Emphasis added.

God has not cast off His People whom He **knew beforehand** (proegnō). Or are you ignorant of what Scripture says in speaking of Elijah--how he pleaded with God against Israel, saying... (Romans 11: 2 – Weymouth New Testament) Emphasis added.

God did not cast away His people whom He **knew before** (proegnō); have ye not known -- in Elijah -- what the Writing saith? how he doth plead with God concerning Israel saying..,(Romans 11: 2 – Young's Literal Translation) Emphasis added.

God's Word Translation seems to offer the most accurate rendering of this verse. Paul is not writing *about* New Testament believers in this text. He is writing *to* New Testament believers, but "His people whom he knew long ago" are the Old Testament faithful, much as they are discussed repeatedly throughout the epistle. These are the ones he *knew before*, Elijah and the seven thousand serving as the example that confirms the meaning of the word. These translations offer a truer sense of the use of *proegnō* in this setting. Additionally, this same use of the word appears in the book of Acts when Paul talks about those who knew him before he converted to Christianity.

> [4] "So then, all Jews know my manner of life from my youth up, which from the beginning was spent among my *own* nation and at Jerusalem; [5] since they have **known about me for a long time** (proginōskontes), if they are willing to testify, that I lived *as* a Pharisee according to the strictest sect of our religion." (Acts 26: 4-5 – NASB) Emphasis added.

> [4] 'The manner of my life then, indeed, from youth -- which from the beginning was among my nation, in Jerusalem -- know do all the Jews, [5] **knowing me before** from the first (proginōskontes), (if they may be willing to testify) that after the most exact sect of our worship, I lived a Pharisee.' (Acts 26: 4-5 – Young's Literal Translation) Emphasis added.

Some form of the word *proginōsko* appears only five times in the New Testament. Three of those instances have already been reviewed. The other two appear in Peter's epistles. On the first occasion, Peter recognizes that Jesus was known (proegnōsmenou) "...before the foundation of the world" (1 Peter 1: 20). In that passage *proginōsko* could simply mean that Jesus *lived* prior to creation or it could be, and most likely is, an allusion to the role he would eventually play in the salvation of men, that role being known beforehand. Later, in his second letter, Peter told his readers that they should beware of those who distort Scripture. Since they had been forewarned and therefore *knew beforehand* (proginōskontes) what to expect, they should be on their guard (2 Peter 3: 17).

It is not Paul's intent, by his use of *proginōsko* (Romans 8: 29), to entreat deep theological mysteries, much less establish the groundwork for the themes of Reformed Theology. When the meaning of a word is in question in a biblical setting, interpretive principles require applying its most common biblical meaning and, if that meaning fits the context, it is likely the correct one. Of the four other instances where this word appears in the New Testament, not once is it used to depict God's foreknowledge *of men*. Paul uses it to depict those who were *known at an earlier time*, including himself. His use of this word in the eleventh chapter of Romans, where Elijah and the Israelites provide the example of those previously known, is essentially identical to the use of this word in the eighth chapter.

Peter employs this word regarding God's knowledge of and plan for Jesus prior to creation. He later uses the same word to note his forewarning to his readers so they would be prepared for those who would twist the lessons of God's Word. For those who are curious, the word that speaks of God's *foreknowledge* where mankind is concerned is the Greek word *prognosis*, a word that appears only twice in the New Testament (Acts 2: 23; 1 Peter 1: 2).

The use of *proginōsko* in secular literature follows the same pattern that is found in its five appearances in Scripture. For instance, Josephus wrote:

> But still God foreshews what is to come upon men, not to grieve them, but that, when they **know it beforehand** (proginōsko), they may by prudence make the actual experience of what is foretold more tolerable.[52] Emphasis added

This better understanding of the use of *proginōsko* in the New Testament will help in understanding what Paul intended in the verses currently under consideration in the eighth chapter of Romans and how this meaning affects the text. On this occasion, the apostle's goal is to

---

[52] Josephus, Flavius. *The Works Of Flavius Josephus, Antiquities Of The Jews*, trans. William Whiston, Ant. ii, v, 6.

offer up the Old Testament faithful (as in the eleventh chapter) as an example for his readers so that they will better grasp his primary thought. That is, they could "know that God causes all things to work together for good to those who love God" (v. 28) because he had done it with those he *knew before* (v. 29). He then explains in the balance of the narrative exactly *how* God was faithful to those he *knew before*.

Another reason to be confident that Paul is not using this word in the prescient sense is that all of the blessings he describes for those he *knew before* took place in history. They are aorist indicative, in this case indicating past tense, which means they describe historical events. Those God previously knew he also *predestined* (past tense) to be like Christ (v. 28). He also *called, justified*, and *glorified* them (v. 30) in an historical sense. In order to fully understand Paul's lesson, consider the exact nature of these blessings and how they serve to make his point to the Romans.

The author of the book of Hebrews draws several clear distinctions between the old and new covenants. For instance, "…the blood of bulls and goats" lacked the power to cleanse from sin (Hebrews 10: 4). True cleansing from sin is available only through the blood of Christ. This is true for everyone, including the Old Testament faithful.

> For this reason He is the mediator of a new covenant, so that, since a death has taken place for the redemption of the transgressions that were *committed* under the first covenant, those who have been called may receive the promise of the eternal inheritance. (Hebrews 9: 15)

God applied Christ's blood retroactively to those who lived faithfully under the first covenant – at least from a human perspective it was retroactive. During their lives, however, it was a cleansing yet to come – one for which they were predestined due to their faithfulness. It was the means by which they could take on the likeness of Christ and know salvation. This, according to God's plan, afforded them the opportunity to be counted among the reborn, Christ being "the firstborn among many brethren" (Romans 8: 29). Hence, the predestination mentioned here is for those he *knew before* as their salvation was brought to fruition through Christ. During their lives, he predestined them to eventually take on Christ's likeness – a promise fulfilled through Christ's death and resurrection – providing a perfect example to the Romans of God's faithfulness toward those who love him.

Not only did God *previously know* these people, and not only had he *predestined* them to Christ's likeness, but he *called* them (past tense). This is in keeping with the passage from Hebrews, cited above, where those of the first covenant were called to "receive the promise of eternal inheritance" (Hebrews 9: 15) to which they were predestined. It was a call to those found faithful under the first covenant to accept the promise of salvation.

Just as they were *predestined* and *called* to salvation in Christ, those God *knew before* – those predestined to Christ's likeness – were justified through Christ's blood. They could not be fully justified without Christ's blood. This is the lesson of the verses in Hebrews. Through Christ, God fulfilled the promise he had made long ago to the Old Testament faithful.

Finally, those who in times past were predestined to salvation in Christ were *glorified*, or given the eternal heavenly existence promised to all who are in Christ. The fact that they were among those untimely born, that is to say they were born prior to the availability of salvation through Christ's blood, did not prevent God from offering them the same salvation.

Paul told King Agrippa that he had lived much of his life as a Pharisee. According to the apostle, those who knew him before (his conversion) could testify to his previous life (Acts 26: 4-5). The shift in Paul's life came when he met Jesus and his life was transformed. Any testimony witnesses might offer about his former life would have concerned his life prior to that moment.

Regarding those whom God *knew before*, that line of demarcation is logically the cross – the death, burial and resurrection of Christ. The faithful who lived and died prior to that moment – those who never had the opportunity to receive Jesus as Savior – were still covered by his blood. They were "predestined to become conformed to the image of His Son" (v. 29).

In summary, the lesson of the text is clear and actually quite simple. Paul told the Romans that "God causes all things to work together for good to those who love God" (v. 28). The Romans could be confident in God's faithfulness and diligence where those who love him are concerned. They could be confident because God has shown historically that he cares for those who love him, always keeping his promises just as he did with those he *knew long ago*. He had promised salvation through Christ's blood to those who were faithful in the first covenant. This was that to which they were predestined. They would receive the *true* justification that was unavailable in their time. In Paul's discourse, the Old Testament faithful serve as an example for

Paul's contemporaries, as well as for all believers everywhere, that God is worthy of trust.

Romans 9: 1-13

The ninth chapter of the book of Romans constitutes a point in Scripture that Calvinists insist provides significant support for some of their doctrinal views, including unconditional election. Although the three sections of this chapter under consideration appear consecutively (vs. 1-13, 14-18, and 19-24), it is necessary to break them into segments for a couple of reasons. First of all, addressing them as a unit may prove a bit overwhelming, since there is much information. Also, while the general theme is God's sovereignty, each section approaches the topic from a slightly different angle.

> [1] I am telling the truth in Christ, I am not lying, my conscience testifies with me in the Holy Spirit, [2] that I have great sorrow and unceasing grief in my heart. [3] For I could wish that I myself were accursed, *separated* from Christ for the sake of my brethren, my kinsmen according to the flesh, [4] who are Israelites, to whom belongs the adoption as sons, and the glory and the covenants and the giving of the Law and the *temple* service and the promises, [5] whose are the fathers, and from whom is the Christ according to the flesh, who is over all, God blessed forever. Amen. [6] But *it is* not as though the word of God has failed. For they are not all Israel who are *descended* from Israel; [7] nor are they all children because they are Abraham's descendants, but: "THROUGH ISAAC YOUR DESCENDANTS WILL BE NAMED." [8] That is, it is not the children of the flesh who are children of God, but the children of the promise are regarded as descendants. [9] For this is the word of promise: "AT THIS TIME I WILL COME, AND SARAH SHALL HAVE A SON." [10] And not only this, but there was Rebekah also, when she had conceived *twins* by one man, our father Isaac; [11] for though *the twins* were not yet born and had not done anything good or bad, so that God's purpose according to *His* choice would stand, not because of works but because of Him who calls, [12] it was said to her, "THE OLDER WILL SERVE THE YOUNGER." [13] Just as it is written, "JACOB I LOVED, BUT ESAU I HATED." (Romans 9: 1-13)

Paul begins the chapter with a lament concerning his Israelite brothers and sisters. The Israelites had rejected Christ. For this reason, the apostle grieved over them, even suggesting that, were it possible, he would prefer himself rather than his fellow Israelites to be cut off from Christ (v. 3). After all, the promise of sonship was originally given to them (v. 4), not in an individual salvific sense as it is with the believers, but in a national sense. Still, that sonship carried with it, certain rights and privileges others did not know, and it was God's desire to have a truly spiritual rather than a law-driven relationship with the Israelites (Luke 13: 34).

Paul's remarks imply that the Israelites were lost to God. What, then, can be said of God's promises? The hypothesis was that in midstream, God supposedly abandoned those he had chosen in the first covenant (the Israelites) for those chosen in the covenant of grace. Thus, the Jews believed that by offering salvation to Gentiles, God was reneging on promises made to the descendants of Abraham, Isaac, and Jacob. Therefore, Paul felt it necessary to address this issue with his audience.

The distinction lay in identifying properly who could be considered the true descendants of the patriarchs. According to the apostle, not every descendant is of fleshly descent. Those of the new covenant are descendants in that they are children of promise rather than flesh (v. 8). As those born of Abraham through Sarah were children of promise (v. 9), so those who are of faith receive the promise of adoption as sons of God (Galatians 3: 26).

Paul reminds the Romans of Rebekah, the wife of Isaac, who bore the twins Jacob and Esau (v. 10). He makes an important point about these twins, and it is a point upon which John Calvin relied heavily when developing his doctrine of unconditional election. The apostle notes that before the twins were born, God selected Jacob over Esau. In fact, he emphasizes the fact that Jacob was selected over his brother before either had "done anything good or bad" (v. 11). What is so significant about this fact? According to Paul, this was done so that God's purpose (or plan) could be fulfilled.

Calvin believed the decision by God to choose Jacob over Esau before they were born underscores two principles. First of all, this remark, as well as the passage in general, speaks to God's sovereignty. Jacob was chosen "that God's purpose according to His choice would stand, not because of works but because of Him who calls" (v. 11). Equally important is the highlighting of God's method of selection. Paul's very focus seems to be on the unconditional character of the choice. Accordingly, Calvin states:

> If foreknowledge had anything to do with the distinction of the brothers, the mention of time would have been out of place. Granted that Jacob was elected for a worth to be obtained by future virtues, to what end did Paul say that he was not yet born? Nor would there have been any occasion for adding, that as yet he had done no good,

because the answer was always ready, that nothing is hid from God, and that therefore the piety of Jacob was before him. If works procure favor, a value ought to have been put upon them before Jacob was born, just as if he had been of full age. But in explaining the difficulty, the apostle goes on to show that the adoption of Jacob proceeded not on works but on the calling of God.[53]

Calvin's point is not only perfectly made, but it is absolutely correct. No better-reasoned conclusion can be drawn from Paul's words. His very focus is on the fact that Jacob was chosen, not as a matter of merit or works – not even as a matter of foreseen faith. His selection was grounded fully in God's sovereign choice. Any other conclusion would require, at the very least, a muddying of the text.

The twins were conceived simultaneously, but Esau was born first. This meant that he should receive his father's blessing as the eldest son. However, God, in his sovereignty, had other ideas. To emphasize the point even further, Paul cites the book of Genesis where God, prior to the birth of the twins, told their mother Rebekah, "The older will serve the younger" (v. 12).

This section climaxes with Paul citing the prophet Malachi with the well-known statement, "Jacob I loved, but Esau I hated" (v. 13). *God hated Esau?* How can this be? Does not Scripture teach that God loves everyone? In fact, the Apostle John states that God *is* love (1 John 4: 8). How, then, can this be reconciled with the statement, "Esau I hated"?

God did not *hate* Esau as men think of hate and it does not take exegetical magic to figure this out. It is true that the form of the Greek *miseō*, translated here as *hated* (emisēsa), can and does at times mean hatred in a caustic sense. Here are some passages where the word is probably intended to depict at least a degree of malice:

> You have heard that it was said, "YOU SHALL LOVE YOUR NEIGHBOR and **hate** (misēseis)[54] your enemy." (Matthew 5: 43) Emphasis added.

> For we also once were foolish ourselves, disobedient, deceived, enslaved to various lusts and pleasures, spending our life in malice and envy, hateful, **hating**[55] (misountes) one another. (Titus 3: 3) Emphasis added.

---

[53] Calvin, John. *Institutes of the Christian Religion*, 617-618.
[54] Future active singular.
[55] Present active plural.

On the other hand, this word does not mean vitriolic hate in every circumstance. There are times when it means to love less, or to love less significantly. Jesus told the disciples, "He who loves his life loses it, and he who hates (misōn)[56] his life in this world will keep it to life eternal" (John 12: 25).

Scripture teaches that individuals, as God's created, are to love themselves as Christ loves the church (Ephesians 5: 28-29). Jesus also taught that one should strive to love his neighbors in equal measure (Matthew 19: 19). The lesson from these two passages is that it is *natural* for one to love and care for oneself. That is a good thing.

Since it is a good and natural thing for a man to love himself, what can be said about Jesus' claim in the gospel of John that one must hate his life in order to keep it? What Jesus meant is that love for one's spiritual life should be deemed much more significant than love for a physical life or physical world. It is a comparative statement. That is also the sense in which *misēi* is intended in the following verse:

> If anyone comes to Me, and does not **hate** (misēi) his own father and mother and wife and children and brothers and sisters, yes, and even his own life, he cannot be My disciple. (Luke 14: 26) Emphasis added.

If God wished someone to hate his parents, he would not have established honoring one's father and mother as the fifth commandment (Exodus 20: 12). Clearly God does not want anyone to hate family, but to love them. However, relatively speaking, love of family must be considerably less significant than love for God and commitment to living a spiritual life that honors him.

As demonstrated in these examples, God's *hatred* of Esau must be viewed in a relative, less significant sense. Still, some may wonder why, if God merely loved Esau less significantly, he highlighted in the Malachi passage the fact that he had "...made his mountains a desolation and appointed his inheritance for the jackals of the wilderness" (Malachi 1: 3). Does this not suggest a measure of malevolence?

When God did these things, he did not do them to Esau *the man*, but to his posterity. Similarly, God told Rebekah that "the older shall serve the younger" (Genesis 25: 23). Yet, Esau never personally served Jacob. God was not referring to these men as individuals, but to their descendants. These are national rather than individual decisions.

---

[56] Present active singular.

Although God chose Jacob over Esau in the womb, it was never about Jacob or Esau.

Paul's point is that God's decisions are his to make. This is fully demonstrated in the Jacob/Esau paradigm. Jesus was a result of Jacob's seed while Esau's seed was ultimately eliminated. God's selection and blessing of Jacob was made to distinguish the lineage of the Messiah. In order to accomplish his plan of salvation, certain choices, like the seed through which the Messiah would be born, were necessary. As creator of all, God was the only one who could make that choice.

It would be a mistake to equate God's selection of Jacob with the unconditional election of Calvinism. The election of Jacob was not salvific in nature and Paul does not depict it as such. His was a patriarchal election in that he would father the tribes of Israel. God did not impart eternal salvation to Jacob by this decision any more than his earthly descendants were appointed to salvation just because they were God's chosen people. Nor did he condemn Esau to everlasting punishment by this choice. Jacob was elected to a position of service as a *step* in God's plan of salvation for mankind and his selection must be viewed in that light.

Like Jacob, each Israelite was *chosen* before birth. Yet, they had misconstrued the nature of that election. Their election was an inheritance of the flesh rather than spirit (Hebrews 10: 1-4). If the election of the Jews as a nation was intended to be election to salvation, one could expect every Jew to know eternal life regardless of his/her personal relationship with God. However, the adoption of the Israelites (Romans 9: 4), which was grounded in the Mosaic Law within the framework of God's covenant with Abraham, was inferior to believers' adoption under the covenant of grace. The Israelites were adopted as the *vehicle* through which salvation came to earth. Still, that adoption must not be discounted since it was/is genuinely relational. The Israelites were not *merely* a vehicle; they enjoyed a covenant relationship with God. He loved and cared for them. However, theirs was not an adoption to salvation.

Not only had the Jews misinterpreted the nature of their election, but they had also misunderstood the character of God's covenant with Abraham. God told Abraham, "…in you all the families of the earth will be blessed" (Genesis 12: 3). That was his covenant promise. In keeping with that promise, salvation was extended to Abraham's *spiritual* descendants through Christ, who was his physical descendant. Salvation is for those *born spiritually* into the kingdom of God

(John 3: 3-5) rather than those born physically into the Israelite nation. Paul's point is that God has, in his sovereignty, chosen to save those who live by faith (Romans 9: 30). These are Abraham's descendants – the children of promise.

Romans 9: 14-18

It is unclear whether someone had asked Paul the following question or if the story of Jacob and Esau simply raised a hypothetical quandary Paul felt compelled to address. The question is this: *If God makes subjective decisions, as he evidently did with the twins, is he an unjust God?* Predetermining that he would bless Jacob rather than Esau without regard to their character or faith could be considered, in the minds of men, an unreasonable method of selection. From a human perspective, it is difficult to see it as anything but arbitrary and unjust.

> [14] What shall we say then? There is no injustice with God, is there? May it never be! [15] For He says to Moses, "I WILL HAVE MERCY ON WHOM I HAVE MERCY, AND I WILL HAVE COMPASSION ON WHOM I HAVE COMPASSION." [16] So then it *does* not *depend* on the man who wills or the man who runs, but on God who has mercy. [17] For the Scripture says to Pharaoh, "FOR THIS VERY PURPOSE I RAISED YOU UP, TO DEMONSTRATE MY POWER IN YOU, AND THAT MY NAME MIGHT BE PROCLAIMED THROUGHOUT THE WHOLE EARTH." [18] So then He has mercy on whom He desires, and He hardens whom He desires. (Romans 9: 14-18)

In answer to the hypothetical question about godly injustice, Paul rebukes the very idea with a resounding "May it never be!" (v. 14). How, then, can God's seemingly unqualified selection of Jacob be reconciled with his sense of justice? Paul does not address the matter directly, at least not initially. Instead, he begins a fascinating discussion about the righteousness of God in conjunction with the sovereignty of God.

Paul begins by reminding his audience of God's words to Moses (Exodus 33: 19) when he stated, "I will have mercy on whom I have mercy, and I will have compassion on whom I have compassion" (v. 15). Note that there is nothing in this statement about God judging or hardening the heart of anyone. This remark is purely about grace and compassion. The reason for this is that Paul was addressing the Jews' resentment over the compassion and grace God so willingly offered the Gentiles. Paul asserts that if God chooses to show compassion to the Gentiles, that is his sovereignty in action.

In the Old Testament incident where this statement originates, Moses had requested to see God's glory (Exodus 33: 18). God was under no obligation to grant Moses's request but, as a God of compassion, he consented by exposing Moses to a small portion of his glory. Paul uses this as an example of God's sovereignty. His point is that God can grant mercy to whomever he chooses whenever he chooses. If God had refused Moses's request, such a refusal would have been a matter of his sovereignty just as granting his request was a matter of sovereignty. Moses could not demand that God reveal his glory. The decision was God's alone. As with the choice concerning the lineage of the Messiah, it was a choice only God could make. No human had the authority or ability to make it happen.

Paul follows the example of Moses with the statement, "So then it does not depend on the man who wills or the man who runs, but on God who has mercy" (v. 16). This quote by Paul seems to emphasize even more vividly the merciful character of God's decision-making. God's mercy is not demanded or earned by men. It can only be given by God. Men cannot make decisions that are reserved for God alone.

Where sovereignty is concerned, the *unspoken reality* in this passage is that if God can show mercy and compassion as he chooses, he can equally withhold mercy and compassion as he chooses. While Paul has not yet openly commented on that aspect of the doctrine, from the balance of the text it is obvious that he understood this to be an inevitable consequence of his remarks.

Paul addresses this unspoken reality by citing a passage from Exodus which, on its face, appears to suggest that God appointed Pharaoh to his role in Egypt so that God could use him for his own purpose. The passage states that Pharaoh was raised up "…for this very purpose" (NIV –Exodus 9: 16). To what end was Pharaoh raised up? This was done that God's name might be proclaimed among men (v. 17). Paul then reinforces his point by reiterating his earlier statement that God "has mercy on whom He desires." However, he adds that God also "hardens whom He desires" (v. 18).

This passage (vs. 14-18) seems to offer a measure of support for the deterministic view of God's sovereignty. If God makes choices about mankind in a seemingly subjective manner based solely on his sovereignty, as these verses suggest, can this principle be expanded to include unconditional election where salvation is concerned? In a word, the answer is *'No!'* This sounds like a bold statement. In fact, it seems contrary to the very point Paul is trying to make. How, then, does this answer make any sense, since Calvinism does appear to be much more in line with Paul's logic? The legitimacy of this answer lies in the fact that these verses do not stand alone.

Paul's discourse on this topic begins in the first chapter of the epistle and he never lets up. Those who single out these verses and set them apart from the balance of Paul's discussion have derived a meaning that was never intended. The poor exegesis of these verses is a result of two primary factors. The first is the disappointing verbiage in certain English translations. The second is an unfortunate disregard for the context of the passage.

Paul, in the first two chapters of the epistle, addresses human culpability where sin is concerned. Human responsibility for sin is grounded in individual choices made. Reading those chapters candidly can lead to no other conclusion. Discussing worshipers of idols, Paul states that God "...gave them over to the lusts of their hearts" (Romans 1: 24). However, it was not because they had no choice. According to the apostle, they had no excuse for ignoring or rejecting God (Romans 1: 20; 2: 1). The complementary character of the first few chapters of Romans does not allow for a doctrine of unconditional election in the current passage. Here is why.

God had a specific purpose in mind for Pharaoh – to make the people aware of God (v. 17). However, that does not address the real question surrounding God's selection of Pharaoh. Where the current discussion is concerned, what really matters is what Scripture means when it says God "raised him up." Does this mean that God placed this man in a position of authority because he was evil, providing God with a prime opportunity to accomplish his goal; or did he raise him up in the sense that he took this man and instilled within him an evil disposition just to make a point in Egypt? Was this the very purpose for which Pharaoh was born into this world...that he might defy God and die a miserable death in the Red Sea? This is what matters when it comes to understanding the lesson of the text.

In his remarks about Pharaoh, Paul was citing the words of Moses, so first consideration will be given to the Hebrew wording to help gain understanding of the phrase, "raised him up," which is translated from the Hebrew word *eomdthi·k* (originating from the Hebrew *amad*). There are two ways of interpreting this word, both of which may be considered legitimate possibilities in this setting. The first suggests that God placed Pharaoh in his position as ruler in order to achieve the goal of making himself known to the people. This meaning is arguably intended in the translations "raised you up" (NIV; ESV) and "raised thee up" (KJV). Those who prefer this interpretation believe that God *placed* Pharaoh in his position of authority, since this served God's purpose.

Pharaoh was as hard-hearted as they come. He was the kind of man God could use to affect his goal in Egypt. Remember that it was not merely God's desire to free the Israelites. He also wanted to have his own name "proclaimed throughout the whole earth" (v. 17).

The other possibility, and in actuality, the more appropriate option, is that *eomdthi·k* is a statement about God's decision to allow Pharaoh to *remain in his position* as ruler of Egypt when he deserved no such consideration. However, God kept him alive and in position in order to use him to realize a greater goal. That is arguably the best understanding of the Hebrew and it is aptly translated in the NASB.

> But, indeed, for this reason I have **allowed you to remain**, (eomdthi·k) in order to show you My power and in order to proclaim My name through all the earth. (Exodus 9: 16) Emphasis added.

The RSV and NRSV provide an even more powerful and accurate sense of God's patience with Pharaoh with the respective translations:

> But this is why I have **let you live** (eomdthi·k): to show you my power, and to make my name resound through all the earth. (Exodus 9: 16) Emphasis added.

> ...but for this purpose have I **let you live** (eomdthi·k), to show you my power, so that my name may be declared throughout all the earth. (Exodus 9: 16) Emphasis added.

The translation "let you live" makes the most sense given the context in which the statement occurs. God had already sent five plagues upon the Egyptians. He then told Moses to go to Pharaoh and explain that more plagues were coming. Moses was to tell him:

> For *if by* now I had put forth My hand and struck you and your people with pestilence, you would then have been cut off from the earth. (Exodus 9: 15).

By "cut off from the earth," God meant death. Had God so chosen, he could have wiped Pharaoh and his people from the face of the earth. However, he chose instead to *allow him to remain*, or *let him live* so that God's name would be proclaimed. In other words, Pharaoh had survived the plagues for God's own purpose.

The Greek word Paul uses in citing Moses, which is *exegeiro*, coincidently provides for this line of reasoning. One of the definitions for this word is *release (from infliction)*. This is in keeping with the notion that God allowed Pharaoh to survive the plagues, withholding his justly deserved destruction. Of the available options, this is the interpretation that fits most naturally and comfortably in this setting where the Hebrew *eomdthi·k* and the Greek *exegeiro* are intended to intimate the same concept. The following excerpt from Adam Clarke makes the point much clearer as he discusses the meaning of *eomdthi·k* in the Exodus setting:

> But truly, on this very account, have I caused thee to subsist - (העמדתיך *heemadticha*), that I might cause thee to see my power, (הראתך את כחי *harotheca eth cochi*), and that my name might be declared throughout all the earth, (or, בכל הארץ *becol haarets*, in all this land). See Ainsworth and Houbigant.
>
> Thus God gave this impious king to know that it was in consequence of his especial providence that both he and his people had not been already destroyed by means of the past plagues; but God had preserved him for this very purpose, that he might have a farther opportunity of manifesting that he, Jehovah, was the only true God for the full conviction both of the Hebrews and Egyptians, that the former might follow and the latter fear before him.[57]

For those who might wonder if Clarke stands alone in his understanding of the words of the text, the same explanation is offered by a host of scholars. Consider the following words from John Gill:

> Or but truly or verily; instead of smiting thee with the pestilence, and cutting thee off out of the land of the living, "I have raised thee up"; made thee to stand, to continue in being; I have preserved thine from perishing by the former plagues, and have reserved thee for greater judgments and sorer punishments.[58]

Since the Jews were familiar with the Old Testament, they would have understood Moses's words as a reprieve for Pharaoh. Everett F. Harrison makes this point well when he states:

---

[57] Clarke, Adam. *Adam Clarke Commentary*, Exodus 9, http://www.studylight.org/commentaries/acc/view.cgi?bk=1&ch=9.
[58] Gill, John. *John Gill's Exposition of the Whole Bible*, Exodus 9, http://www.studylight.org/commentaries/geb/view.cgi?bk=1&ch=9.

"'I raised you up" is not strictly a reference to Pharaoh's emergence in history, but to God's providence in sparing him up to that time.'[59]

If, by his use of *eomdthi·k,* Moses meant that God had allowed Pharaoh to remain alive and in power in spite of himself, it provides a quite different perspective on Paul's comments. From this point of view, God *refrained from destroying* Pharaoh, choosing instead to use his own wickedness against him and, at the same time, accomplishing his goal of making himself known to the people.

How does this relate to Paul's statement, "He has mercy on whom He desires, and He hardens whom He desires" (v. 18)? In the end, Pharaoh received his just desserts. He was a wicked man who paid for his sins with his life. Yet, while many assume that Paul is focusing on the hardening of Pharaoh's heart that is recorded in the Old Testament (Exodus 10: 20), a better argument can be made that Paul was underscoring God's patience and mercy as he allowed Pharaoh to remain in power longer than he deserved.

Why has Paul used the illustration of Pharaoh to make a point about God's justice and mercy? Logic dictates that it is because this is a perfect example of the complementary character of God's sovereignty and justice. He was not saying that Pharaoh was a good man with whom God dealt cruelly and that must simply be accepted as fact. In order to draw that conclusion from the text, one must ignore what Scripture says about Pharaoh in the Old Testament. There is no example in Scripture of God turning the heart of a godly man toward evil.

It is unarguable that Pharaoh was a proud and evil human being. He rebuked Moses, saying, "Who is the LORD that I should obey His voice to let Israel go? I do not know the LORD, and besides, I will not let Israel go" (Exodus 5: 2). Still, God allowed Pharaoh to survive the early plagues and remain in his position of authority in order to use him as God saw fit.

God was not the force behind Pharaoh's malicious deeds, although it is true that he *fortified* (Heb. *chazaq*) the hardness of his heart (Exodus 9: 12) as he saw fit. Where Pharaoh was concerned, God made sovereign decisions to suit his purpose, and those decisions were righteous. It was God's plan to remove the Israelites from Egypt and settle them in the Promised Land where the Messiah would be born. He did not abuse a good man, but he certainly used the wickedness of an evil man to realize his objective.

---

[59] Harrison, Everett F. *The Expositor's Bible Commentary, Romans*, 106.

In order to understand Paul's point, it is important to recognize that God's decision concerning Pharaoh, as with his choice of Jacob, was not salvific in character. Scripture does not say that God elected Jacob to salvation while condemning Esau. God elected Jacob to a *patriarchal* role. Similarly, Scripture does not say that God chose reprobation for Pharaoh. He simply allowed Pharaoh to live on for a time despite his wickedness, which was his sovereign prerogative, in order to further his own plans. It was Pharaoh's own actions by which he was ultimately condemned.

Romans 9: 19-24

If, as Calvin taught, human free will is extremely limited and God makes decisions about individuals, predestining them to act a certain way, why should he hold people accountable? On the heels of his claim that God will show mercy or harden whom he chooses (v. 18), Paul addresses the question: "Why does He still find fault?" (v. 19).

> [19] You will say to me then, "Why does He still find fault? For who resists His will?" [20] On the contrary, who are you, O man, who answers back to God? The thing molded will not say to the molder, "Why did you make me like this," will it? [21] Or does not the potter have a right over the clay, to make from the same lump one vessel for honorable use and another for common use? [22] What if God, although willing to demonstrate His wrath and to make His power known, endured with much patience vessels of wrath prepared for destruction? [23] And *He did so* to make known the riches of His glory upon vessels of mercy, which He prepared beforehand for glory, [24] *even* us, whom He also called, not from among Jews only, but also from among Gentiles. (Romans 9: 19-24)

The first thing to consider in this text is the exact nature of the questions Paul has asked. Why *does* God find fault? Who *can* resist his will? These are legitimate inquiries. However, Paul may not mean by these questions what most believe. Where the query "Why does He still find fault?" is concerned, it may surprise most people to find that this is not the first time Paul has raised this question in his letter to the Romans. Consider the following words from earlier in the epistle:

> [5] But if our unrighteousness demonstrates the righteousness of God, what shall we say? The God who inflicts wrath is not unrighteous, is He? (I am speaking in human terms.) [6] May it never be! For otherwise, how will God judge the world? [7] But if through my lie the truth of God abounded to His glory, why am I also still being judged

as a sinner? ⁸ And why not *say* (as we are slanderously reported and as some claim that we say), "Let us do evil that good may come"? (Romans 3: 5-8)

In a discussion eerily similar to his discourse on Pharaoh, Paul writes about how God uses human unrighteousness (as he used Pharaoh's) to demonstrate his own righteousness. Paul then asks the question: "if through my lie the truth of God abounded to His glory, why am I also still being judged as a sinner?" (v. 7). This is essentially the same question Paul poses in the ninth chapter when he quips, "Why does He still find fault?"

Paul's point in the third chapter is that God often uses sinful actions for his own glory. He is not saying that he controls people in a deterministic sense – like puppets on a string. That being the case, the apostle argues hypothetically that perhaps people should not be held accountable, since God can use even a person's evil deeds as a tool to demonstrate his glory. The lesson is not that one's actions are not freewill actions, but that God sometimes uses those actions for his own purpose. Is this also what Paul has in view in the ninth chapter when he asks, "Why does He still find fault?" Adam Clarke understood that this was Paul's point in Romans 9: 19, remarking:

> The apostle here introduces the Jew making an objection similar to that in Romans 3:7: *If the truth of God hath more abounded through my lie unto his glory*, that is, if God's faithfulness is glorified by my wickedness, *why yet am I also judged as a sinner*? Why am I condemned for that which brings so much glory to him? The question here is: If God's glory be so highly promoted and manifested by our obstinacy, and he suffers us to proceed in our hardness and infidelity, why does he find fault with us, or punish us for that which is according to his good pleasure? [60]

In the ninth chapter of Romans, Pharaoh is given as a perfect example of the discussion that Paul had begun earlier in the epistle. At no time does he teach that God *caused* Pharaoh's wickedness. Did God strengthen the hardness of Pharaoh's heart? He did, as it served his purpose to show his power and proclaim his name. Pharaoh had already made his choice to defy God and God used that defiance to his

---

[60] Clarke, Adam. *Adam Clarke Commentary*, Exodus 9, http://www.studylight.org/commentaries/acc/view.cgi?bk=1&ch=9.

glory. The alternative was that he would destroy Pharaoh. Instead, he kept him around...for a time.

Remember that this lesson is not about Pharaoh, nor is it focused solely on God's sovereignty. Paul is addressing questions about God's treatment of the Jews and whether that treatment was just (vs. 1-13) – a discussion that began in the second chapter of the epistle. Some seemed to be arguing that God failed to keep his promises to the Jews when he made salvation available to the Gentiles. They were, after all, his chosen people and it was through the lineage of Abraham, Isaac, and Jacob that Jesus, the very source of salvation and the corner stone of the new covenant, entered the world (v. 5).

"Why does He still find fault?" Paul offers an answer that probably seems strange to many people. Rather than pointing out the failure of the Jewish community to remain faithful to God and placing the blame on their shoulders, he compares man's relationship with God to that of a lump of clay and the potter who molds the clay into a vessel of some sort. His point is that it is the potter, not the clay, who determines what that shape will be (v. 20).

Those especially skilled in artistry can often take something blank, like an artist's canvas, or unformed, like a lump of clay, and develop it into a thing of beauty. However, the final product is determined, not by the canvas or the clay, but by the artist. In his analogy, where Paul has pictured a potter and his clay, he makes the point that the potter, at his discretion, can form a simple bowl or an elegant vase out of the same lump of clay. Thus, despite their claims, the Jews were in no position to determine how God should relate to those he formed or what form they should take (v. 21).

Paul is not making a general statement about how God deals with people, nor is he explaining how salvation is attained. In fact, this discourse is quite reminiscent of God's discussion with Job when he had complained to God about the suffering he faced, even though he had been faithful. From a modern-day perspective, there was reasoning and logic behind the events in Job's life, as unpleasant as they may have been. The reason for this is that, unlike Job, the reader is privy to the behind-the-scenes details and has the ability to understand that situation from God's point of view (Job 1: 6-12).

When God addressed Job's complaint, he did not explain Satan's role in the hardships he had faced. He did not make excuses or apologize for the suffering Job had experienced. Instead, he rebuked Job, challenging him with regard to his role as the creator and Job's role as the created (Job 38: 1-39). It is unknown whether Job ever learned, prior to his death, the reason for his suffering, but where God was concerned, the reason was irrelevant.

Job's ultimate eternal reward was based on his faithfulness to God. That aspect of the story is couched in the storyline throughout the book of Job. It is the same in the current setting. The potter/clay analogy in the Romans text (vs. 20-21) is essentially the same argument God made to Job and, like Job, it is faithfulness (or unfaithfulness) that will determine each person's eternal fortune.

Paul's analogy of the potter and the clay is not intended to depict the fullness of the God/man relationship. For instance, once formed, the clay vessel is not the image of man. It has no mind, nor does it have a spirit. It cannot reason and it cannot have faith. While the man may cherish the artistry of his formed vessel, the clay pot cannot reciprocate.

Appreciating the context of Paul's words to the Romans is the key to understanding the meaning of this passage. The focus of Paul's lesson is the Jewish complaint that God would offer salvation to Gentiles (and that Jews are not guaranteed salvation through the first covenant). Ironically, in the example given, Pharaoh represents the Jewish nation (v. 17). It was the Israelites who had defied and rejected God. Still, he *let them continue* as a nation while he fulfilled his promise of a Messiah. His patience demonstrated his glory even in the face of their unrighteousness. To that end the comparison served its purpose well.

The apostle is not addressing the grand scheme of God's relationship with mankind. He is not writing about the predestined actions of humans as ordered by a sovereign God. He is simply explaining that the Jews are in no position to complain about the opportunity afforded the Gentiles through Christ's sacrifice.

Some may question whether the fact that they were "vessels of wrath prepared for destruction" (v. 22) indicates that all of this was just a matter of predestination. In other words, was the potter/clay example more than figurative? Did God actually view and treat Pharaoh or the Jews as mere lumps of clay? The answer to this can be found in Paul's second letter to Timothy. In that case, the apostle employs a similar metaphor involving items made of gold and silver. In that instance, he places responsibility on the formed vessel to *choose* to become a vessel of honor. The idea is that, although people are created by God, each one can still choose to honor God, whether Jew or Gentile.

²⁰ Now in a large house there are not only gold and silver vessels, but also vessels of wood and of earthenware, and some to honor and some to dishonor. ²¹ Therefore, if anyone cleanses himself from these *things*, he will be a vessel for honor, sanctified, useful to the Master, prepared for every good work. (2 Timothy 2: 20-21)

Paul understands that people are accountable for the choices they make and that they are not mere lumps of clay where God is concerned. The potter/clay imagery is not meant to be an exact representation. It is intended to provide the Jews with an appreciation for God's decision concerning the Gentiles…nothing more. Given the human responsibility that is depicted in Paul's letter to Timothy, as lifeless vessels are again used to represent humanity just as they are in Romans, it seems clear that the opportunity to become an honorable vessel is available to all who will believe. Paul, in the ninth chapter of Romans, recognizes both God's sovereignty and man's free will.

Ephesians 1: 3-6

Paul wrote a letter to the Christians in Ephesus hoping to teach them about the fundamentals of the Christian way of life. In this letter, he seemed to want to cover certain rather large themes. For instance, *faith* appears eight times in six chapters and *faithful* appears twice. Faith is portrayed both as a matter of salvation (Ephesians 2: 8) and a matter of unity (Ephesians 4: 5, 13).

The term that Paul uses most often in this letter is the phrase *in Christ*, also occasionally written as *in him* or *in Jesus*. This terminology is used more than twenty times in this short epistle. Thus, Paul's focus seems to be the believer's life *in Christ* and those things that occur both *as* one is *in him* and *because* one is *in him*.

Paul sets the stage for the theme of this letter in his opening remarks. After his initial greeting, introducing himself as the author and recognizing the Ephesians – those "…who are faithful in Christ" (v. 1) – as his audience, the apostle offers the following words in order to establish the subject matter of the epistle.

³ Blessed *be* the God and Father of our Lord Jesus Christ, who has blessed us with every spiritual blessing in the heavenly *places* in Christ, ⁴ just as He chose us in Him before the foundation of the world, that we would be holy and blameless before Him. In love ⁵ He predestined us to adoption as sons through Jesus Christ to Himself, according to the kind intention of His will, ⁶ to the praise of the glory

of His grace, which He freely bestowed on us in the Beloved. (Ephesians 1: 3-6)

Two words leap from this text where Reformed Theology is concerned. These words are *chose* (v. 4) and *predestined* (v. 5). Focusing on the phrases "He chose us in Him before the foundation of the world" and "He predestined us," Calvinists proclaim that Paul is addressing God's unconditional election of individuals to salvation, explaining to the Ephesians that this (personal and individual) election took place prior to the creation of all things.

That some sort of election took place prior to creation is not at all up for debate. Denying this would mean denying Scripture. In fact, it would constitute an inexcusable rejection of Paul's words in this very instance. Have people been chosen in Christ? Absolutely! Did this decision occur prior to creation? There is no reason to doubt Paul's unambiguous statement that this did occur before men were created.

What is it, then, that distinguishes Calvinism from other views of election to salvation? Exactly how are they different? When all is said and done, it seems that lines of distinction are drawn based upon a single word, or principle. While Calvinism teaches that God has called individuals to *unconditional* election, others believe that election is, according to Scripture, grounded in a *conditional* plan of salvation with Jesus at its center. How does this square with Paul's claim that "He chose us in Him before the foundation of the world" (v. 4)? That is the question that divides.

While Paul explains when "he chose us" (v. 4), the verse does not say that this choice was *unconditional*. The term *unconditional* must be superimposed onto the text in order to make that case. The apostle is writing to an audience of believers and as is evident throughout the New Testament, believers are *in Christ*. That is Paul's theme in this very epistle. Consequently, the question that arises is much like that of the chicken and the egg, where men have questioned which came first. In other words, are people chosen because they are *in him,* or are they *in him* because they are chosen?

Jesus spent much time teaching the disciples about the kingdom of heaven. Quite often these teachings were given through his use of parables. Thus, most parables begin with the phrase *the kingdom of heaven is like...* Through his use of these parables, Jesus explained to the disciples exactly what it means to be *in him*. When it comes to apostolic instructions in the epistles, the teaching can often be connected with one or more of Jesus' parables. The counterpart to

Paul's words concerning the *chosen* is again found in the parable of the wedding feast (Matthew 22: 1-10).

In this parable, when the king sent invitations, he knew that only those who accepted his invitation would eventually participate in the wedding celebration. This does not mean that he did not genuinely invite everyone, but only those who accepted were included among the *chosen*. Participation was conditional. Thus, being among the chosen was conditional.

There is every reason to believe that this parable is intended to provide a true portrait of the kingdom of heaven and what it means to be chosen of God. However, Jesus does not use the word *chosen* (Gr. *eklektoi*) in the conventional sense. When people think of *chosen*, they generally think one-dimensionally, as in *choosing* to pray or to read Scripture. These are one-sided choices. However, in this context, *chosen* is two-dimensional. Here it refers to those who were *participants*. They were chosen in that they were invited *and* accepted the invitation.

In the parable, the king necessarily would have decided *how* he would invite people to the feast prior to actually inviting them. Similarly, God decided *how* he would invite people to his heavenly kingdom prior to actually inviting them. This is the decision he made "before the foundation of the world." Knowing that mankind would sin and thus be separated from him, he established a plan *in Christ* whereby reconciliation would be possible (the invitation). Like the king in the parable, God knew that some would accept, and others would reject that invitation. Also like the king in the parable, God decided that those who accepted the invitation would be welcome. These he considered the *chosen*. However, given the omnipotence of God, and unlike the king in the parable, it is evident that God knew "before the foundation of the world" the identities of those who would accept.

The use of *chosen* in this parable offers insight into how this word applies to the kingdom. Calvinists teach that the idea of being *chosen of God*, especially with respect to salvation, reflects God's sovereignty and that his sovereignty is the sole matter to be considered. They view election as a one-dimensional, one-sided proposition. However, in the parable, the king, who is undoubtedly representative of God within the kingdom of heaven, did not choose who would attend his feast. He did not decide who would come and celebrate. He merely planned the banquet and invited others to share in a joyous occasion.

Concerning this parable, Reformers believe one of the following: 1) the invitations given to those who did not attend were not genuine, or 2) the invitations were genuine, but God withheld their ability to respond. In other words, where the outcome was concerned, the king's invitations were intended only for those who actually attended the feast, since others could not attend. Yet, that is not the lesson from this parable. Jesus paints a picture of people deliberately rejecting an invitation and a king who was angry with their response.

As discussed earlier in this book, shortly after Pentecost, problems arose within the church in Jerusalem. As a remedy, the believers selected certain men to address these issues. These men were to step in and see to the various needs of the body. To that end, they *chose* (exelexanto, which is a form of eklegomai) Stephen, Philip, Prochorus, Nicanor, Timon, Parmenas, and Nicolas (Acts 6: 5). Having been selected, these men served the church well.

Once again, the implication is that this represents a two-dimensional use of *chosen*. In this case, even though these men were *chosen*, there is no reason to believe they were unconditionally selected. It is reasonable to presume that the church considered whether these men were qualified for, and would consent to, that position. No doubt, there was a willingness on the part of these men to accept the role they were being asked to fill. As with the parable of the wedding feast, being chosen is not the same as being unconditionally elected. The idea of being chosen, as it is presented in the New Testament, does not offer support for a Reformed perspective of election. When encountering the words *chosen* or *elect*, as in Paul's words to the Ephesians, it is necessary to keep in mind the manner in which these words are used in Scripture.

In the New Testament, not only is election portrayed as conditional, but Paul, even within the confines of his letter to the Ephesians, points to the conditional nature of election to eternal life. He states that salvation is *through faith* (Ephesians 2: 8). Calvinists argue that one's salvation precedes his/her faith, leading once again to a chicken/egg paradox. However, those instances in Scripture where salvation is discussed clearly teach that justification is attained *by* faith (cf. Romans 3: 26; 5: 1; Galatians 3: 24), and not *vice versa*.

What Paul means by *chosen* can be explained through assorted New Testament sources. Yet, what can be said about his claim that people are *predestined* (v. 5)? After all, it is one thing to be *chosen*, giving due consideration to the two-dimensional sense with which this word is used in the New Testament. However, is it not a completely separate matter for the apostle to speak of predestination?

Scholars generally recognize that where the original Greek is concerned, a singular thought is in view in Ephesians 1: 3-14. In fact, the ASV presents these verses as a single sentence because the translators believed that was Paul's intent. Others agree, but most translations break these verses into shorter sentences to make them reader friendly.

Paul draws no distinction in this context between the *chosen* and the *predestined*. When Paul stated, "he chose us" (v. 4), it is a statement about eternal life. The *chosen*, or *elect*, are those who have attained or will attain salvation. However, when he comments that "he predestined us" (v. 5), salvation is not his primary focus. Instead, he points to certain other blessings the chosen are *predestined to receive*, much as he did in his epistle to the Romans (Romans 8: 28-30) when talking about the Old Testament faithful.

The chosen, or saved, will receive a number of blessings including spiritual adoption into the family of God (v. 5), forgiveness of sins (v. 7), an understanding of the mystery of his will (v. 9), a spiritual inheritance (v. 11), and assurance/confirmation of salvation as they are sealed with the Holy Spirit (v. 13). This focus on blessings ties in nicely with Paul's initial remark about "spiritual blessings in the heavenlies" (v. 3).

In this instance, predestination does not point toward God deciding *who* will be redeemed; nor is it a statement about *how* people are redeemed. It simply reflects the blessings the *chosen* (those who have been invited and accepted the invitation) are predestined to receive. It reflects God's *promises* for those who believe – that is to say, those who are *in Christ*.

Chapter 14

Unconditional Election: Minor Passages

John 6: 37-39

Jesus told a group in Capernaum, "All that the Father gives me will come to me" (John 6: 37). At a glance, and taken singularly, this statement seems to indicate that God gives people to Jesus before they come to him. For this reason, Calvinists believe this verse affirms their teaching concerning unconditional election. However, as with all Scripture, context is the key. Just preceding this statement by Jesus, he told the crowd, "I am the bread of life; he who comes to Me will not hunger, and he who believes in Me will never thirst" (John 6: 35).

Which comes first? Do believers come to Jesus first or does God give them to Jesus so that they can come to him? The Calvinist would say that God gives believers to Jesus so that they can come to him. Others claim that believers choose to come to him and, accordingly, God gives them to him.

The Greek word *didomi*, translated here as *gives*, is used in a broad sense in the New Testament. It can denote something that is bestowed, such as an endowment or gift (Matthew 7: 11), or it can indicate a blessing or reward (Revelation 2: 10). It can also denote something that is offered (John 4: 15) or delivered (John 7: 19) and may even suggest something that is produced, or yielded, as fruit of one's labor (Matthew 20: 4).

The difficulty with the Reformed view of Jesus' words is that they tend to treat verse thirty-seven as if Jesus has in mind a chronology of events. Such is not the case. These remarks by Jesus are about the *effect* of his obedience to the Father (v. 38). He came to earth to do the Father's will; and what was the Father's will? His will was that Jesus would gather believers for heaven (v. 40).

Souls are not given to Jesus in the sense that God predetermined who would come to him. That is not what Jesus has in view in this verse. They are given in the sense that they are a *gift*. By God's eternal design, believers are the reward, or blessing, Jesus receives from the Father for his sacrifice. The very essence of the plan of salvation is that people might be saved. Thus, believers are the fruit of his labor.

It is also God's will that Jesus would not *lose* any (believers) that he has received (v. 39). Setting aside the Calvinist insistence that these words testify to the doctrine of *perseverance of the saints*, they will now be considered in light of *unconditional election*. Actually, it is difficult to reconcile Jesus' words with the doctrine of unconditional election. After all, if God has given believers to Jesus under the principle of unconditional election, Jesus would have no reason to comment on the possibility of losing anyone. Under the terms of unconditional election, he *could not* lose any believers. It would not be possible.

Jesus' words in John 6: 37 do not fit comfortably with the principle of unconditional election and there is no biblical reason to believe that this is what Jesus had in mind. This verse does not necessarily refute Reformed Theology, but it falls far short of confirming or even lending support to the doctrine of unconditional election.

John 6: 44-45

Who will be saved? According to Jesus, "No one can come to Me unless the Father who sent Me draws him" (John 6: 44). This statement gives rise to a couple of questions. First, there is the matter of the identity of those the Father draws to Christ. According to this verse, it is safe to say that those whom the Father does not draw will have no opportunity to come to Christ. Second, one might question whether all who are drawn by the Father actually do come to Christ.

The next verse complements this one with Jesus teaching, "It is written in the prophets, 'AND THEY SHALL ALL BE TAUGHT OF GOD.' Everyone who has heard and learned from the Father, comes to Me." (John 6: 45). In order to understand these verses, it would help to know who *they* are. It would also be nice to understand "who has heard and learned from the Father." It is these, after all, who come to Christ (those who receive salvation through Christ).

Some believe these verses teach that 1) *all* who are drawn by the Father will come to Christ, and 2) *only* those who are drawn by the Father are able to hear and learn from him. These, they claim, are the elect (chosen by God). The presumption is that God's act of drawing people to Christ is limited to a few. Therefore, it is necessary to determine what Christ has in mind when he speaks of the Father drawing people to him.

The notion that God draws only a few people to Christ and, as a result, redemption is limited to those few, ignores the manner of calling that is spelled out in these verses. Calling comes, not through regeneration, but through teaching (v. 45). It is the instructions found in the gospel message that provide the call (Matthew 24: 14; Mark 13: 10; 1 Corinthians 15: 2; Ephesians 1: 13). No other manner of calling is mentioned. Additionally, John explains exactly *how* this calling (teaching) results in eternal life. Jesus taught that "…he who believes (in this teaching or calling) has eternal life" (John 6: 47). Similarly, he told Nicodemus, "And just as Moses lifted up the serpent in the wilderness, so must the Son of Man be lifted up" (John 3: 14). He further explained to the disciples, "And I, if I am lifted up from the earth, will draw all *people* to Myself" (John 12: 32).

A few short verses prior to this (v. 40, which was mentioned under John 6: 37-39), Jesus stated that the Father's will was that "…everyone who beholds the Son and believes in Him will have eternal life, and I Myself will raise him up on the last day" (John 6: 40). The thought process of this chapter reveals that salvation comes through instruction and belief. This is how, according to Scripture, God draws people to Christ (cf. 1 Corinthians 15: 2; Galatians 1: 11); although not everyone accepts that calling.

John 6: 64-65

In the process of instructing some of the disciples, Jesus told them "…no one can come to Me unless it has been granted him from the Father" (John 6: 65). This verse states purposefully that access to Christ is limited to those who are granted that privilege. Denial of that fact would put one at odds with God's Word. To whom, then, does God grant access?

Reformed Theology teaches that Jesus' words must be interpreted to mean that he is speaking expressly about those unconditionally elected to salvation. Yet, nothing about Jesus' words necessitates that conclusion. In fact, one cannot legitimately read the principle of unconditional election into this text. What Jesus said is that for someone – anyone – to come to him, he/she must be granted permission by the Father. Fortunately, Jesus explains in the preceding verse exactly who could not come to him. It is the unbeliever who is denied access to Christ (v. 64). Consequently, it is the believer who is granted access.

According to Holy Writ, "Jesus knew from the beginning" (John 6: 64) exactly who would not believe. This undoubtedly speaks to his *awareness* rather than *determinism*. Despite the many claims, there is no indication that Jesus *decided* who would not believe…only that he *knew* who would not believe. Those who insist that these verses represent an overt proclamation of unconditional election have eclipsed the message contained within Jesus' words. The real lesson is that access to Christ is granted *on the condition of belief*. No lesson about unconditional election is present here.

John 13: 18

Perhaps one of the best-known Bible stories is the episode where Jesus washed the feet of the disciples. It is a demonstration of Jesus' humility and an example of the kind of benevolent service he expects of his followers.

The foot washing took place at the Passover meal the night before Jesus' death. It was the final meal he would share, prior to his death, with those men who would eventually become his apostles. When he finished washing their feet, Jesus spoke candidly with the disciples. He pointed out that they were to serve others in a manner similar to the way he had served them (John 13: 14-15). They would be his messengers/servants. In that role, they should keep an honest perspective. If they were to be Jesus' messengers (apostles), and he had been willing to wash their feet, they should equally be willing to wash the feet[61] of others.

In his follow-up, Jesus remarked, "I do not speak of all of you. I know the ones I have chosen" (John 13: 18). Many have mistaken this to be a proclamation of election to salvation, which is a mischaracterization of the comment. What Jesus has in mind here is the transformation of these men (the chosen) into his personal messengers as they formed the group eventually known as the apostolate. The word translated messenger (v. 16) is *apostolōs*, which is also translated *apostle*.

It is important to note that Jesus' statement concerning the *chosen* is specific. To begin with, his commentary is not about the chosen, but about the one man, Judas, who was not chosen. Nor is this a statement about the many non-elect who would never know salvation. Rather, Jesus focuses on the one man (from among those present) who would not become an apostle. His statement is introductory in nature, leading to the narrative concerning his betrayer, as the balance of the chapter is about the *one* non-elect.

While it is safe to presume that the apostles were saved, the idea of being *chosen*, in this instance, is not about election to salvation, but election to a role of service. Those chosen (the eleven) were to become

---

[61] Foot washing should be considered symbolic of benevolent service. There is no command given that we must literally wash the feet of others as a matter of obedience to Christ.

Jesus' messengers (apostles). The one not chosen would not become his messenger. He (Judas) would eventually be replaced by a man known as Matthias (Acts 1: 12-26).

Those who seek to characterize Jesus' comment regarding the chosen (v. 18) as support for the Reformed idea of election must completely disregard the context of these words. This represents a limited use of the word *chosen*. It is used to depict certain men who were selected by Christ for an exclusive ministry. The principle of unconditional election to salvation cannot be found in this passage.

John 15: 16

Judas, having been identified as Jesus' betrayer, left the Passover feast Jesus had been sharing with his disciples. The other eleven were evidently unaware of Judas's intentions, so their conversation with Jesus continued. In the course of that conversation, Jesus commented, "You did not choose Me but I chose you" (John 15: 16), where *choose* and *chose* are forms of the word *eklektos*, which means *elect*.

Jesus' audience at this time is undoubtedly the most significant portion of the context. He was speaking to his chosen apostles about the work for which they had been selected. No explanation is given as to *why* Jesus chose these specific men, but it is unlikely that they were selected at random. It may have been something about their character, work ethic, etc. that led Jesus to them.

It is not salvation, but the unique apostolic calling that Jesus has in view in this verse. It is this for which these men were chosen. While it would be foolish to question the redemption of the apostles, it is a considerable leap to suggest that Jesus is talking about their salvation here. The conversation is focused directly and unequivocally on their call to service as apostles, as the balance of the narrative bears out.

2 Thessalonians 2: 13

Paul, writing to the converts in Thessalonica, told them, "God has chosen you from the beginning for salvation" (2 Thessalonians 2: 13). In what sense were they chosen? Were they, as Calvinism teaches, predestined to salvation? Did God select them before creation to become a part of his kingdom?

As discussed at length earlier in this section, Calvinists insist that those who are chosen by Christ receive a special calling that is unavailable to most men. It is what they have termed an *effectual calling* whereby individuals are regenerated so that they may believe. However, in his words to the Thessalonians, Paul gives full consideration to the calling they had received. In the verse following his comment about their chosen state, he notes that they had been called "...through our gospel, that you may gain the glory of our Lord Jesus Christ" (2 Thessalonians 2: 14). It was through that calling that they *gained the glory*. It was the calling of the gospel through which they were saved.

Those passages that are most often cited in support of the doctrine of effectual calling certainly speak of the *called* and the *chosen* (Matthew 22: 14; Romans 8: 28; 1 Corinthians 1: 9). In those instances, the presumption has been made by some that the calling that is in view is the *effectual calling* that is directed only toward those predestined for salvation. However, in this letter to the Thessalonians, where being *called* and *chosen* is similarly Paul's focus, the only call mentioned is the gospel which, according to Scripture, is available to all (Matthew 28: 19; Acts 2: 39). Insisting that God's *call* denotes something other than the gospel message seems to stretch the term beyond its biblical purpose.

What can be said about the fact that God had chosen them *from the beginning*? This particular aspect of the verse will be addressed in a discussion of 1 Peter 1: 1-2 that provides a clearer sense of what God knew and/or decided prior to creation.

2 Timothy 1: 9

In his second epistle to his "...son in the faith" (1 Timothy 1: 1), Paul offers some insight into the unmerited character of salvation. He told the young evangelist that God "...saved us...not according to our works, but according to His own purpose and grace which was granted us in Christ Jesus from all eternity" (2 Timothy 1: 9). This terminology is reminiscent of Paul's discourse in other epistles (cf. Ephesians 1: 4).

As noted earlier in connection with similar passages, Paul's observation to Timothy that grace "...was granted...from all eternity" says nothing about unconditional election or the salvation of specific individuals. According to the apostle, this grace has been given "...according to His own purpose (plan)." Knowing that mankind would sin, God established a means of reconciliation prior to creation. It was his plan that, through their faith in Christ's sacrifice for sins, believers would enter his rest (Hebrews 4: 1-3).

1 Peter 1: 1-2

In a single, rather innocent greeting in his first epistle, Peter has provided a statement that should, in all sincerity, put to rest most

Reformed claims about unconditional election. He first introduces himself as the author of the letter. Quickly, then, he shifts his focus and recognizes his audience as Christians in various locations in Asia Minor. He identifies them as "…aliens, scattered throughout Pontus, Galatia, Cappadocia, Asia, and Bithynia, who are chosen" (1 Peter 1: 1).

Peter has stated here that these believers were *chosen*. Biblically speaking, the apostles often refer to believers as the elect or chosen of God. Therefore, the fact that Peter, in this instance, refers to his audience as chosen is not surprising. It is a fair depiction of the state of the believer. Although that does beg the question: *Chosen for what?*

In the next verse, Peter explains the purpose for which they have been chosen. They are chosen "…by the sanctifying work of the Spirit, to obey Jesus Christ and be sprinkled with his blood" (1 Peter 1: 2b). Can this be unconditional election? Unless valuable information is missing, this certainly seems to depict something eerily akin to Reformed Theology. Then again, perhaps something significant is missing. Here is the entirety of these two verses.

> [1] Peter, an apostle of Jesus Christ,
> To those who reside as aliens, scattered throughout Pontus, Galatia, Cappadocia, Asia, and Bithynia, who are chosen [2] according to the foreknowledge of God the Father, by the sanctifying work of the Spirit, to obey Jesus Christ and be sprinkled with His blood: May grace and peace be yours in the fullest measure. (1 Peter 1: 1-2)

Reading this passage in full not only sheds light on what it means to be chosen, but it also provides greater insight into the various passages that speak of what God knew and/or decided about salvation from "…the foundation of the world" (Ephesians 1: 4; Hebrews 4: 3; Revelation 17: 8). Those "chosen…to obey Jesus Christ" were in God's view prior to creation, not in the sense that God *decided* they would obey, but that he *knew* they would obey. The Greek *prognosis*, translated here as *foreknowledge*, speaks to God's foreknowledge of people and events. Consequently, when reading about election in other New Testament passages, it is important to keep in mind, as Peter has plainly stated in this greeting, that the idea of one's pre-selection to salvation is grounded in God's foreknowledge rather than determinism.

Jude 1: 4

The dark side of Calvinism, which is often overlooked, is the teaching of predetermined reprobation. This is the belief that many, and in fact most, men and women have been born into this world with no hope in Christ. It is their destiny to spend eternity separated from God as punishment for sins that were also predetermined.

In his short epistle, Jude wrote about some evil people "...who were long beforehand marked out for this condemnation" (Jude 1: 4). In this passage, Jude points to the ultimate end of such evildoers. They are condemned and will receive their due. However, from Jude's comment that they were "...long beforehand marked out," Calvinists have concluded that Jude has in view the specific individuals in the singular circumstance he was addressing.

Jude's letter is, to a great extent, comparable to the second chapter of 2 Peter. These two sections of Scripture address the same issues with much the same language. It seems reasonable to believe, given this fact, that apostasy and false teachings were becoming serious problems throughout the kingdom. As such, Jude probably was not writing about one or more individuals in a certain setting, but a general condition in the church. This, in itself, does not invalidate unconditional election to reprobation, but it does suggest that Jude may not have specific individuals in mind.

God has made plans for those who deny Jesus as Savior. These plans are spelled out unambiguously in Scripture. They are, beyond a doubt, predetermined. However, the claim that those who will receive this punishment were individually *pre-selected* by God fails to find support in this verse.

Jude explains fully who the "certain persons" are who have been "marked out for this condemnation." He identifies them as "the ungodly." It is those "...who turn the grace of our God into licentiousness and deny our only Master and Lord, Jesus Christ" (v. 4) who will know his wrath. The Greek word *tis* is translated *certain* in this instance, but the word generally suggests the notion of *any* or *whoever* (John 12: 26; Acts 4: 35; Galatians 6: 3; 1 Timothy 5: 8).

While Jude uses the word *tis* to define *some* (of humanity) in this case, it is his intent to classify certain behavior and attitudes among men. Thus, any and all who, through the choices they make, *turn grace into licentiousness* and fall into the category of *the ungodly* are, indeed, *marked*.

Revelation 17: 8

The book of life, according to Scripture, lists the names of those who are saved. A thorough study of this topic would be extensive and well beyond the scope of this work. However, in John's final work, he makes reference to this book. In this case, he writes about names that have "...not been written in the book of life from the foundation of the world" (Revelation 17: 8).

A candid reading of this verse could leave one with the belief that the names found in this book have been *carved in stone*, so to speak, from the beginning of time, and seems to tilt Scripture toward the view of unconditional election. However, one should not be so quick in drawing conclusions.

The book of life is mentioned occasionally in both the Old Testament and New Testament. Still, little is known about this book, and it is unwise to attempt to draw broad conclusions from a single verse. Some passages, such as the one mentioned here, vaguely suggest that certain names have never appeared in the book, although that point is not always clear. Other passages, two of which appear in the very same book where John wrote the remarks now in question, equally suggest that it is possible for names to be removed from the book of life.

> The LORD said to Moses, "Whoever has sinned against Me, I will blot him out of My book." (Exodus 32: 33)

> May they be blotted out of the book of life and may they not be recorded with the righteous. (Psalm 69: 28)

> He who overcomes will thus be clothed in white garments; and I will not erase his name from the book of life, and I will confess his name before My Father and before His angels. (Revelation 3: 5)

> ...and if anyone takes away from the words of the book of this prophecy, God will take away his part from the tree of life and from the holy city, which are written in this book. (Revelation 22: 19)

While little is known about the book of life, it is safe to say that those passages where this book is discussed fail to provide support for Reformed Theology. While Revelation 17: 8 may seem to harmonize with the idea of unconditional election/condemnation, other verses clearly do not. If it is possible for one's name to be removed from this book, the foundation for the doctrine of *unconditional election*, along with the complementary doctrine of *perseverance of the saints*, crumbles. It is for this reason that singling out certain verses to support a doctrinal view while ignoring others (proof texting) is of little value.

Summary on Election and Free Will

Mankind cannot grasp all there is to know about God, his character, and his actions. He thinks and acts in realms beyond human imagination. All men have to go on with respect to a relationship with him is what Scripture teaches. It is there that he has revealed his will, which is unchanging. It has been established once for all in his Word (Jude 1: 3).

The doctrine of predestination is an undeniable truth of Scripture. It cannot be discounted if the Bible is truly God's Word to mankind. The same is true of the doctrine of election. Similarly, the reality is that people have the ability to make freewill choices. This, too, is an undeniable biblical truth. How, then, can harmony be found between these doctrines that appear, at least on the surface, to be diametrically opposed?

The context of those passages of Scripture that speak of *predestination* and/or *free will* must always be given full consideration. For instance, it is fair to say that God used Pharaoh for his role as an antagonist toward the Israelites. However, God's use of Pharaoh was grounded in the decisions this man made.

God chose Jacob, Mary, and John the Baptist for specific roles of service. In these cases, predestination fully focuses on the earthly roles designed by God for these individuals. They were key elements in God's plan as he looked forward to the covenant of grace. Each one played a critical role in Jesus' life as he came to save the world. Therefore, each was vital to God's plan. That being the case, there is biblical harmony in the notion that God predestined them for service. However, predestining someone for service is not the same as predestining them for heaven or hell.

While it is true that the apostles wrote of predestination (Romans 8: 29-30; Ephesians 1: 5, 11), the elect or chosen of God (Matthew 24: 22; Romans 8: 33), and the election of men in the church age (Romans 9: 11; 11: 28; 2 Peter 1: 10), at no time do they ever relieve anyone of the responsibilities associated with *becoming* one of God's elect. On the contrary, the apostles boldly proclaimed the need for faith born of free will (1 Timothy 1: 5; 1 Peter 5: 9). According to Scripture, the *chosen* status shared by those who are saved is based, not on decisions made by God, but on his complete foreknowledge concerning the hearts and minds of men (1 Peter 1: 2). This is the underpinning upon which those known as the elect were chosen before the foundation of the world (Ephesians 1: 4).

It is important to differentiate between God's decisions and his foreknowledge. Just because God knows something, it does not mean he has decided it. If God made every choice that could be made, it stands to reason that he would have chosen everyone to be saved since, according to Scripture, it is not God's desire that any should perish (2 Peter 3: 9).

Section IV
Baptism

Chapter 15

The Baptism Dialogue

The Baptism Debate

Immersion in water is a controversial biblical topic, garnering numerous beliefs from many perspectives. Not only do views differ about the significance of baptism, but the mode of baptism and the legitimacy of the one performing the rite are also often called into question. Even the use of water as a medium for baptism has been challenged in modern times by those who insist that New Testament baptism is a purely spiritual experience, absent any physical activity.

The topic of baptism is much too extensive to address it satisfactorily in a single section of a single book, since there are numerous issues that could be considered. For those who would like to delve more deeply into this subject, some helpful works are available at most online bookstores.[1]

The primary disagreement where baptism is concerned is whether it is essential to one's salvation, so this will be the focus in this section. The challenge is, through the application of interpretive principles discussed earlier, to understand what Scripture has to say about the relationship between baptism and salvation. Following is a list of common beliefs held on this topic.

Salvation by Immersion in Water

Some people believe that immersion in water is the only legitimate form of baptism, claiming that this is the baptism practiced in the earliest days of the church, and that it is an essential component of the plan of salvation revealed in God's Word. Most who advocate this view believe that the decision to submit to baptism rests with each person who has matured physically and mentally to a point where they have the capacity to make a reasoned decision to follow Christ.

In this view, baptism and repentance are complementary. That is to say, it is through the combination of repentance and baptism that a

---

[1] *Baptism in the New Testament* (Beasley-Murray), *Baptism, a Biblical Study* (Cottrell), *Baptism and the Battle for Souls* (Carlson), and *Baptism and the Plan of Salvation* (Carlson) are good sources to begin a study of baptism.

believer receives forgiveness of sins and is regenerated (given new life). The water, in itself, has no power to regenerate a person. Baptism is simply the time appointed by God for the Holy Spirit to apply the blood of Christ to a person's sins, cleansing him/her of all guilt.

This view was advocated strongly by the early church fathers. While some continued in this vein in certain parts of Europe and the Middle East, many elected to dismiss the precept of immersion as a matter of salvation beginning in the early to mid-sixteenth century with the advent of the Reformation Movement. In the early United States, where Baptists and Presbyterians were predominant, baptism was vastly ignored as a salvific matter.

Early in the nineteenth century, Alexander Campbell (1788-1866) and Barton W. Stone (1772-1844) helped to resurrect teaching about the redemptive character of baptism. These are considered the fathers of what is known as the Restoration Movement in America. It was their belief that the church should be *restored* to both the design and the ordinances that were established for the church of the first century as depicted in Scripture.

Salvation by Immersion, Sprinkling, or Pouring

Others teach that water baptism is essential to salvation, but that methods other than immersion are also acceptable. For instance, many teach that sprinkling or pouring water over an individual constitutes legitimate baptism. Most people who hold this view also believe that baptism can and should take place as early as infancy in order to affect *original sin* (the notion that even the newborn is burdened with the guilt of Adam's sin).

A work entitled the *Didache*, also called *The Teaching of the Twelve Apostles*, suggests that pouring and sprinkling, as forms of baptism, may have existed as early as the second century. However, it is highly unlikely that the apostles were involved in its publication since certain teachings found there do not harmonize with apostolic practices. For instance, there is a call within the *Didache* to religiously recite the Lord's Prayer three times daily. Additionally, specific prayers were to be quoted both before and after partaking of the Lord's Supper.

Where baptism is concerned, the *Didache* calls for a two-day fast by the candidate for baptism and the one who would perform the baptism, along with any other willing believers, prior to the event. However, scriptural accounts (Acts 2: 38-41; Acts 8: 36-39; 16: 31-33; 19: 1-5) fail to provide support for this teaching. It was the practice of the apostles and first century evangelists to baptize immediately those who wished to accept Jesus as Savior.

The *Didache* suggests that sprinkling or pouring could be regarded as acceptable methods of baptism when water sufficient for immersion is not accessible. However, if any substitutions for immersion occurred in the second century, they are not recorded. No such incidents were documented until the middle of the third century.

Interestingly, it is this view that most closely resembles Martin Luther's perspective on baptism even as he championed a doctrine of salvation by *faith only*. He did not see a conflict between the efficacy of baptism and salvation by faith. His primary concern was the Roman Catholic Church's promotion of sacraments that were *not* established in Scripture.

Baptism as a Sign of Salvation

Some see baptism as an exercise that is pleasing to God but unrelated to one's salvation. Any physical activity, such as baptism, must be deemed a human *work* and, as such, can have no *direct* bearing on one's spiritual state. Instead, it is taught that baptism is a covenant sign that serves as testimony that a believer has made a decision to follow Christ. Salvation, on the other hand, takes place prior to water baptism. This doctrinal view stems from a belief in a correlation between baptism in the New Testament and infant circumcision as it was practiced under the Old Testament law.

Some historical figures who advocated this view include William Tyndale (1484-1536), an Englishman who was an early translator of the Bible, and John Wycliffe (1324-1384), the first man to translate the Bible into English. Later, a man by the name of Huldrych Zwingli, a contemporary of Martin Luther who was mentioned earlier in this work, was the first of sufficient renown to effectively promote the belief that baptism was merely an outward sign of salvation.

John Calvin saw baptism as an initiatory rite during which one was admitted into the fellowship of the body of believers. He saw some spiritual value in baptism as a new covenant sign just as circumcision was a sign of the Abrahamic covenant. He believed baptism to be a matter of one publicly *accepting* the promises of God. John Wesley's (1703-1791) perspective on baptism paralleled Calvin's, though they agreed on little else. Wesley denied that baptism was the new birth of which Jesus and the apostles spoke, contending in favor of infant baptism based on the belief that it represented a rite of admission into the church.

Baptism Is Spiritual – Not Physical

Insisting that baptism is not *of water*, there are those who regard *baptism with the Holy Spirit* as the moment of salvation. The assumption is that the outpouring of the Holy Spirit that is recorded in the book of Acts is, by definition, baptism with the Holy Spirit, and that this experience corresponds with one's salvation. Through this outpouring of the Holy Spirit, one receives the seal of salvation. This (Holy Spirit) baptism is characterized by the bestowal of spiritual gift(s) – most notably the gift of speaking in tongues – as a sign of salvation.

The popularity of this view of baptism with the Holy Spirit has risen significantly in Pentecostalism, a movement that had its beginnings within the United States in the early twentieth century. Still, this is not a universal Pentecostal teaching. Some within that movement, while teaching that the outpouring of the Spirit in this manner constitutes baptism with the Holy Spirit, do not deem this to be the moment of salvation. To them this kind of episode simply reflects a second blessing God uses to confer miraculous gifts of the Spirit. In fact, many within these circles insist on immersion in water as a matter of salvation.

Baptism in Water Is Irrelevant

Baptism in water is considered inconsequential by many others who proclaim belief in Jesus as the Messiah. For instance, Christian Scientists do not participate in water baptism. It is their belief that the baptism of the Bible is not immersion in water, but immersion into the study of God's Word and immersion into the Christian life in a manner that most effectively honors God. Forgiveness of sins is received as believers are bathed in the Holy Spirit. Quakers have a similar view in that they believe formal observances (viz. baptism and the Lord's Supper) are unnecessary. They teach that how one lives his/her life – living in constant *communion* with God and continually being *immersed* in the Spirit – provides a level of spiritual fulfillment that cannot be achieved in ceremony.

Is Baptism an Essential Doctrine?

Like faith and repentance, baptism is discussed in association with salvation/forgiveness of sins repeatedly throughout the New Testament. In God's Word, when a doctrinal topic is discussed in a passage that also mentions salvation, it is incumbent on believers to learn how the issue relates to salvation.

A number of New Testament passages link baptism directly to forgiveness of sins (Acts 2: 38; 22: 16; Colossians 2: 11-14), salvation (Mark 16: 16; 1 Peter 3: 21), membership in the body of Christ (Acts 2: 41; 1 Corinthians 12: 13), and spiritual renewal (John 3: 5; Romans 6: 4; Titus 3: 5). These are but a few of the verses that establish baptism as an essential doctrine. This explains why baptism always took place immediately upon one's belief. Scripture offers no example of baptism being delayed by days or weeks. Consequently, understanding baptism in apostolic terms is essential, since getting it wrong could affect one's salvation.

Baptism and the Principles of Interpretation

Historically, even fair-minded Bible scholars have too easily abandoned legitimate interpretive principles when it comes to determining baptismal doctrine. When it comes to understanding baptism, the student of Scripture must remain faithful to the numerous rules that have been discussed to this point. For example, out of respect for hermeneutic principles, one must: 1) be sure to fully consider the context of the material under examination, 2) determine the author's intent, and 3) seek to understand how the author's audience would have viewed the teaching that is being examined.[2] These principles are often neglected when it comes to addressing biblical passages that link baptism and salvation.

Additionally, in keeping with the *principles of interpretation* (see Chapter 3), it is important to 1) remain objective when interpreting a passage of Scripture and 2) allow Scripture to harmonize naturally rather than forcing a view that conflicts with other biblical teaching. Many attempt to drive a wedge between passages that speak of baptism and salvation (e.g., Acts 2: 38; 22: 19) and those that speak of faith and salvation (e.g., Ephesians 2: 8; Romans 3: 22) as though they are diametrically opposed. If the doctrines derived from separate passages do not complement each other, it is fair to say that one of those views falls short of trustworthy exegesis. It is necessary to determine how the two passages harmonize rather than insisting that the doctrine gleaned from one passage invalidates the doctrine clearly taught in another.

Finally, it is important to keep in mind the principle of repetitiveness. When the same apostolic instruction is given openly and unswervingly multiple times in the pages of God's Word, it is

---

[2] See Chapter 2, Systematic Theology: Considering the Results/Audience Response, 27.

impossible to sweep that teaching aside without trampling upon the meaning God intended. The topic of baptism is addressed roughly one hundred times in the New Testament. It is discussed in each of the gospels. The book of Acts is filled with teaching about baptism and examples of people who were baptized as they accepted Jesus as their personal Savior (Acts 2: 38-41; 8: 12-13, 36-38; 10: 48; 16: 15, 33; 22: 16). Paul offers instruction about baptism in most of his epistles and Peter dwelt heavily on the topic in his sermons and his first epistle. This kind of emphasis by the apostles suggests that baptism is something that should be taken very seriously. The instructions of the apostles must be respected, especially when it comes to those teachings that they saw fit to repeat time and again.

Chapter 16

The Effects of Baptism

Baptism and Forgiveness of Sins (Justification)

In Scripture, baptism is introduced through the life of a man by the name of John the Baptist. Through the books of gospel (Matthew, Mark, Luke, and John), the water baptism John performed is depicted as baptism for the forgiveness of sins.

> John the Baptist appeared in the wilderness preaching a baptism of repentance (metanoias) for the forgiveness of sins. (Mark 1: 4)

> And he came into all the district around the Jordan, preaching a baptism of repentance (metanoias) for the forgiveness of sins. (Luke 3: 3)

The term *baptism of repentance* may sound a bit awkward, but it is not difficult to understand. The Greek *metanoias* indicates that people submitted to baptism *with a changed mind*. Matthew states that, as with baptism in the church age, during John's ministry repentance and baptism worked in harmony. Matthew wrote about John the Baptist, saying:

> ...and they were being baptized by him in the Jordan River, as they confessed their sins. (Matthew 3: 6)

It seems more than reasonable to surmise that by confessing their sins, these people were repenting of those sins. This is in keeping with the term *baptism of repentance*. With a changed mind, they were baptized for the forgiveness of confessed sins. This purifying character of John's baptism is plainly established in an episode involving John the Baptist and some of his disciples, as recorded by the Apostle John.

> [22] After these things Jesus and His disciples came into the land of Judea, and there He was spending time with them and baptizing.
> [23] John also was baptizing in Aenon near Salim, because there was much water there; and *people* were coming and were being

baptized— ²⁴ for John had not yet been thrown into prison. ²⁵ Therefore there arose a discussion on the part of John's disciples with a Jew about purification. ²⁶ And they came to John and said to him, "Rabbi, He who was with you beyond the Jordan, to whom you have testified, behold, He is baptizing and all are coming to Him." (John 3: 22-26)

Evidently the Jew with whom John's disciples spoke told them that Jesus' disciples were baptizing more people than John and his disciples. By inference, it is evident that their conversation about purification equates to a discussion of baptism. This is clear from a couple of angles. First of all, the word *therefore* (v. 25) indicates that the discussion about purification that ensued was based upon the topic of baptism found in the previous verses. Second, this incident receives support from other passages where the purifying effect of John's baptism is revealed. As reported in the other gospels, it was for the forgiveness of sins.

The baptism John performed was not Christian baptism, despite the fact that the combination of repentance and immersion are depicted as resulting in forgiveness. This is evident from Paul's encounter with several believers at Ephesus where it is established that baptism *in Jesus' name* offers at least one blessing that John's did not – namely, the gift of the Holy Spirit. Consequently, given their lack of understanding, Paul baptized them in Jesus' name even though they had previously received the baptism of John (Acts 19: 1-7).

When it comes to the covenant of grace, a key passage that links baptism with forgiveness of sins is found in the first sermon recorded after Christ's ascension into heaven. On the Day of Pentecost, when asked by the crowd how they might avail themselves of the salvation offered by the apostles, Peter replied by telling them to "Repent, and …be baptized in the name of Jesus Christ for the forgiveness of your sins" (Acts 2: 38).

Peter's sermon to the crowd is a simple one. Those who wished to know forgiveness need only repent and submit to baptism. For those who believe and teach, as this verse does, that forgiveness comes at the time of repentance and baptism, these words are cherished. This commandment, spoken by the apostle, represents God's initial offering of salvation to mankind in the covenant of grace.

Peter's words do not stand alone in teaching baptism as the time of forgiveness. When Saul, who later became the Apostle Paul, was confronted by Jesus on the road to Damascus, he faced a turning point in his life. He later told the Jews in Jerusalem how Ananias had come to him to provide instruction from God. Saul was to be God's messenger to the Gentiles. However, when Ananias first approached him, Saul was still outside of Christ. He had not heard the gospel message and his sins were not yet forgiven. Baptism was offered to Saul as a matter of purification from sins (Acts 22: 16), confirming Peter's instructions on the Day of Pentecost.

The connection between baptism and forgiveness shines through in certain other passages, too. For instance, in his first epistle, Peter calls baptism "...an appeal to God for a good conscience—through the resurrection of Jesus Christ" (1 Peter 3: 21). Other passages by Paul also point to the purifying effect of baptism (1 Corinthians 6: 11; Ephesians 5: 26; Titus 3: 5). These do not use the word *baptism*, but that is unquestionably Paul's focus. Similarly, in writing to the Colossians, Paul provides details about how God strips away the sinful state of those who submit to him (Colossians 2: 11-14).

How could Paul write so confidently about the forgiveness of the Colossians? While these disciples knew forgiveness (the removal of the body of flesh) by the power of Christ's death, Paul also offers insight into the timing of this forgiveness. He explained that they had experienced this forgiveness, "...having been buried with Him in baptism" (Colossians 2: 12). This connection between "...the removal of the body of flesh" (forgiveness) and baptism is unmistakable. In much the same way, Paul explained to the Romans that Christians cannot and must not continue in sin since, having been baptized, they were dead to sin (Romans 6: 1-4).

The complementary makeup of passages that demonstrate the purifying nature of baptism is plain to see. Baptism is boldly regarded in the New Testament as a time of cleansing. Peter called upon the crowd on the Day of Pentecost to submit to baptism "...for the forgiveness of sins" (Acts 2: 38). Ananias urged Paul to be baptized and *wash away his sins* (Acts 22: 16). Paul's remarks in Titus 3: 5 and Colossians 2: 11-14 harmonize fully with what he told the Jews about his own baptism experience. The message concerning the role of baptism for forgiveness of sins rings loud and clear in the pages of Scripture.

Baptism is boldly regarded in the New Testament as a time of cleansing.

Baptism and Regeneration

It can be challenging to distinguish clearly between the numerous blessings attributed to immersion in water, since they are so closely related. While baptism is defined as the moment of forgiveness, it is also a time of renewal, or regeneration, as one becomes a new creature in Christ. Without forgiveness, regeneration is not possible since unremitted sin keeps one separated from God. On the other hand, once sins have been forgiven, reconciliation with God through regeneration is both certain and immediate. In that sense, forgiveness, and regeneration at the time of baptism go hand in hand.

Several passages of Scripture regard baptism as a time of renewal. Even before his death, Jesus addressed the spiritual rebirth (regeneration or renewal) that occurs during baptism. In his conversation with Nicodemus, the issue of rebirth arose, and Jesus took the opportunity to teach this Jewish leader just what it means to be reborn.

In his words to Nicodemus, Jesus indicates that to be *reborn* is to be *born spiritually* or regenerated. However, the passage says more than this. Jesus did not say one who is not born of Spirit cannot enter the kingdom. He states that "…unless one is born of water and the Spirit he cannot enter into the kingdom of God" (John 3: 5). That begs the question: *What does it mean to be born of water and the Spirit?*

That the term *water*, in this instance, points to baptism is supported in certain other passages. For instance, Peter, on the Day of Pentecost, connects baptism and the receiving of the Holy Spirit. Paul also linked baptism and the Spirit (1 Corinthians 12: 13). Additionally, in his letter to the Romans, he explains that "…all of us who have been baptized into Christ Jesus have been baptized into His death" (Romans 6: 3), and it is this that allows an individual to "…walk in newness of life" (Romans 6: 4).

Scripture paints a doctrinal picture concerning regeneration. It is a portrait of renewal that occurs during the penitent believer's immersion in water. Baptism is the moment God has chosen to apply the blood of Christ to one's sins through the work of the Holy Spirit (Colossians 2: 11-12). Having shared in Christ's death through burial in baptism, the believer rises from the water to live a renewed life, as these verses demonstrate.

Baptism and Sanctification

The concept of sanctification is not far removed from the idea of regeneration. While regeneration defines one's transformation into a new creature in Christ, sanctification depicts a setting apart of someone or something for a specific purpose. In spiritual terms, it means being separated from the world of corruption (as a new creature) and consecrated unto God and to his purpose, much like Noah, via the ark, was separated from the evil that surrounded him. Sanctification for the believer in the church age is realized in baptism as taught in God's Word (Ephesians 5: 25-27).

While believers are in the world, they cannot be part of the world (John 17: 14). That is because Christ is holy. As such, he requires holiness in his bride. Sanctification for the church involves being *made holy* by God (the work of sanctification belongs to him) that she might be presented to Jesus *holy and blameless* (Ephesians 5: 27). However, mankind is not innocent (Romans 3: 23), so all who would take their place as a part of that bride must submit to spiritual cleansing in baptism, designated in this Ephesians passage as "…washing of water with the word" (Ephesians 5: 26).

Similar instructions were offered to the Corinthians as Paul linked both sanctification and justification to the rite of baptism, even as the disciples in Corinth were overtly focused on their baptizer (1 Corinthians 1: 13-16).

It is evident from both Ephesians and 1 Corinthians that, biblically speaking, sanctification and cleansing go hand in hand. The church consists only of those who have been sanctified. The unsanctified cannot be presented to the Lord as holy. Paul makes that clear in these verses. His audience was comprised of men and women who had been sanctified. Therefore, one's sanctification should never be taken lightly. Having been sanctified, the believer is called to live a life that is as distinct and separate from the world as were Noah and his family during the flood.

Baptism and Adoption/Inheritance

Jesus is the only begotten of God (John 3: 16). However, believers share in the heavenly inheritance, having been adopted as children of God (Romans 8: 15; Galatians 4: 5). No one may be saved without experiencing the adoption process, since it is the very means by which an individual becomes an heir to the kingdom of God. Like justification and sanctification, adoption is available by faith, through the blood of Christ, at the time of baptism.

Adoption, and all that it involves, is essential to salvation. No one may "…see the kingdom of God" without being transformed by the *spiritual birth* of which Jesus spoke (John 3: 1-6). No one may be saved without becoming a true child of God (Romans 8: 14-17). While there is considerable disagreement regarding the moment at which this adoption occurs, Scripture is teeming with testimony that God has set aside baptism for that very purpose.

Baptism and the Body of Christ

The church, also identified as Christ's body, was initially established on the Day of Pentecost. It did not exist during the time period covered by the gospels. While there were believers prior to Pentecost, they were not bonded together in Christ in the same sense that believers in the church age are united. On the Day of Pentecost, those who believed and submitted to immersion in water were joined together as a unit (Acts 2: 41). Luke does not refer to them as the body of Christ at the time, but Paul introduces this term later, using it to identify the same organization of believers that Luke has in view (cf. Ephesians 4: 12; Colossians 1: 18).

Through the book of Acts, baptism in Jesus' name is commanded for those who wished to follow Christ (Acts 2: 38; 19: 4-5; 22: 16). In the epistles, baptism is generally discussed in retrospect fashion. That is to say, it is addressed as something believers had previously experienced. The retrospective treatment of baptism within the epistles highlights a clear presumption by these authors that those to whom they were writing had been baptized. It is not insignificant that, in Paul's words to the Galatians, he confines those who are *clothed with Christ* to those who *have been baptized* (Galatians 3: 27). He also explained to the Corinthians that baptism is the manner of entry into the body of Christ (1 Corinthians 12: 13), complementing Luke's observation from the Day of Pentecost (Acts 2: 41). It becomes evident in reading the epistles that, in the eyes of the apostles, membership in the body of Christ is inseparable from baptism.

Baptism and Salvation

It is the ultimate goal of every believer to attain eternal salvation. Yet, all do not agree on the path to salvation, despite the fact that everyone reads the same Bible. Given the portrayal of baptism in God's Word, it is difficult to ignore the fact that the authors consistently link baptism and salvation just as they consistently link grace, faith, and repentance to salvation. How, then, is salvation associated with baptism?

On the Day of Pentecost, which was discussed earlier, Peter joined repentance and baptism with forgiveness of sins (Acts 2: 38). Few would deny, given the context of Peter's words, that forgiveness of sins, in complement with the gift of the Holy Spirit that he promised, was intended to reflect the principle of salvation/eternal life. In other words, those who followed his instructions concerning repentance and baptism would be forgiven and saved.

Salvation in the book of Acts is connected intimately to immersion in water. Detailed evangelistic episodes that resulted in belief by those listening concluded with baptism (Acts 8: 4-13, 26-39; 9: 10-19; 10: 34-48; 16: 14-15, 31-34). Water baptism is portrayed as the anticipated response of someone who believes. Belief and baptism in the book of Acts are depicted as natural steps to salvation.

Baptism is also tied intimately to salvation frequently and convincingly in the epistles of the New Testament. Paul calls it "…the washing of regeneration" (Titus 3: 5), a matter of justification and sanctification (1 Corinthians 6: 11; Ephesians 5: 26), and the manner of entry into the body of Christ (1 Corinthians 12: 13). In his letter to the Romans, he identifies baptism as the moment one attains "…newness of life" (Romans 6: 4). Peter states unequivocally that "…baptism now saves you" (1 Peter 3: 21). The apostolic portrayal of baptism as the time of salvation is too prominent to ignore.

Baptism and the Holy Spirit

The link between baptism and the Holy Spirit was first introduced by John the Baptist as he promised that the coming Messiah would baptize with the Holy Spirit (Matthew 3: 11; Mark 1: 8; Luke 3: 16). Later, Jesus described spiritual rebirth as a birth of water and the Spirit (John 3: 5). Then, on the Day of Pentecost, Peter proclaimed that those who repented and submitted to baptism could anticipate receiving the gift (presence) of the Holy Spirit (Acts 2: 38).

Scripture speaks of baptism with the Spirit that involved an outpouring of the Spirit (Acts 2: 4; 10: 44-46), resulting in the recipients performing miraculous feats. However, this form of baptism with the Spirit seems to have been quite limited. According to Scripture, this was not the usual manner by which people received the Holy Spirit. At Ephesus, while speaking to some disciples of John the Baptist, Paul associated the Holy Spirit (Acts 19: 1-7) with immersion in water in much the same way Peter did on the Day of Pentecost.

A number of other passages also join the Spirit with baptism. The Corinthians "…were washed…in the name of the Lord Jesus Christ and in the Spirit of our God" (1 Corinthians 6: 11). Similarly, speaking of the unity of the body, Paul told them that "…by one Spirit we were all baptized into one body" (1 Corinthians 12: 13). Defining the manner of salvation, Paul told Titus, "He saved us…by the washing of regeneration and renewing by the Holy Spirit" (Titus 3: 5), and the Apostle John describes the (Holy) Spirit, the water (of Jesus' baptism), and the blood (of Jesus' sacrifice) as equal witnesses that Jesus is the Son of God (1 John 5: 5-8). Receiving the Holy Spirit is one additional extraordinary blessing that occurs at the time of one's baptism in Jesus' name.

Chapter 17

Christian Baptism in the Gospels

Matthew 28: 18-20

The Great Commission, as recorded by Matthew, represents some of Jesus' final words to the disciples prior to his ascension. With these words, he commissioned them to bring people into the kingdom of heaven.

> [18] And Jesus came up and spoke to them, saying, "All authority has been given to Me in heaven and on earth. [19] Go therefore and make disciples of all the nations, baptizing them in the name of the Father and the Son and the Holy Spirit, [20] teaching them to observe all that I commanded you; and lo, I am with you always, even to the end of the age. (Matthew 28: 18-20)

Although no form of the words *salvation* or *redemption* appears in the narrative, it seems clear that eternal life for mankind is intended as the ultimate outcome of Jesus' instructions. This was the very purpose of his life and ministry on earth, which culminated in these words to the disciples. In issuing his commission, Jesus instructed the disciples to do three things. They were to 1) make disciples (Gr. *mathēteusate*), 2) baptize (Gr. *baptizontes*), and 3) teach (Gr. *didaskontes*). With these words, Jesus charged them with establishing his kingdom on earth.

Two specific forms of teaching are depicted here. The first (mathēteuo; lit., *make learners*) means they were to offer basic instruction (the gospel) that would be necessary for one to gain sufficient knowledge (and faith) to become a disciple of Christ. This primary set of instructions, if accepted, would evidently lead to baptism, since that is what Jesus anticipates on the heels of *mathēteuo* (v. 19). Baptism is presented as an element of *mathēteuo,* a fact that receives support from the book of Hebrews where baptism is included, along with faith, among the "...elementary teachings about the Christ" (Hebrews 6: 1-2). Baptism, then, is a matter of *initial* discipleship.

It is one thing to *become* a follower (disciple) of Christ. It is another to live a life that meets the elevated level of devotion and spiritual growth Jesus seeks in his followers. This requires instruction well beyond one's initial belief in the Lordship of Christ and submission to baptism. For one to fully appreciate the Christian way of life, much more involved and in-depth teaching is necessary. From the moment of baptism, each believer must seek to understand and "observe all that I have commanded you" (v. 20). These are the instructions given through God's Word about how to live the renewed life that one has been given, honoring God with that life by 1) worshiping him on a high spiritual plane (Philippians 3: 3), and 2) doing good works, the very purpose for which men were created (Ephesians 2: 10).

The Great Commission constitutes some of Jesus' final words prior to his ascension. In fact, this is his last recorded directive to the disciples by Matthew. That fact attaches a sense of gravity to these instructions. What is remarkable about these verses is that, in a setting where Jesus is clearly establishing a foundational commission for the establishment of his church on earth, baptism is one of only three instructions given. Faith and repentance, which are not minor factors in discipleship, are conspicuously absent (although they would be included in both *mathēteuo* and *didasko* as matters of instruction), giving even greater weight to the presence of baptism in the text. The implication is that Jesus considered *baptizing* to be as important as *mathēteuo* and *didasko* in the execution of his commission.

While all agree that the Great Commission provides a foundation for evangelism given to the disciples as they embarked on the adventure before them, modern scholarship has invested much into diminishing the prominence of baptism in this setting. That portion of the Great Commission has been effectively abandoned by those who challenge the salvific role of baptism. Some believe baptism, while significant in the first century, is not relevant in the current age. Others deny that the baptism of the Great Commission is baptism in water. This is, of course, indefensible since, through the book of Acts, water is the vehicle used in fulfilling these instructions.

It is of utmost importance that believers, respecting the principles of interpretation, treat the words of Scripture reverently. One cannot ignore the distinction that is bestowed upon baptism in Jesus' final words to the disciples and still claim the high road of principled and fair-minded biblical analysis. If baptism is so critical that Jesus would prescribe it in his final instructions as a matter of Christian discipleship, the faithful must seek to honor his words.

Mark 16: 15-16

Mark has offered what appears to be his own version of the Great Commission. The wording is a bit different from that found in Matthew's gospel, but the import surrounding baptism is still present. The time frame for the end of Mark seems to combine the events at the end of Matthew with those in the first few verses of Acts where Jesus' ascension is in view.

> [15] And He said to them, "Go into all the world and preach the gospel to all creation. [16] He who has believed and has been baptized shall be saved; but he who has disbelieved shall be condemned." (Mark 16: 16)

These verses are not without their share of controversy. Perhaps the greatest issue involving this passage is the fact that many scholars question whether it should have been included in canonized Scripture. The last twelve verses of this final chapter of Mark's gospel (vs. 9-20), it is argued, may have been a later addition to the text and were probably not penned by Mark. That is the viewpoint of many well-respected textual critics, although others are equally confident of the authenticity of this passage. In this work, these verses will be treated as genuine since they appear in most Greek manuscripts and English translations.

Through his words in these verses (Mark 16: 15-16), Jesus establishes a direct link between baptism and salvation, stating "He who has believed and has been baptized shall be saved." Many insist that it was not Jesus' intent to make a connection between baptism and salvation since, in the ensuing comment, only disbelief results in condemnation. It is argued that this comment demonstrates that baptism is not essential to salvation. To derive from Scripture what God intends, honest consideration must be given to this verse to determine exactly what effect Jesus' remark about condemnation might have on his assertion about belief and baptism.

When Jesus stated that someone who does not believe will be condemned, the word translated into English as "disbelieved' is *apistēsas*. This word derives from the Greek for *belief* (pistēuo). Placing an *'a'* at the beginning of a word, as in this case, results in the inverse of the original word. In English, placing an *'a'* before the word *theist* renders the word *atheist* (this principle carried over from the Greek). The same is true in this current verse. In this case, it is belief or disbelief in the gospel message. However, the disbelief of this passage indicates more than mere *lack of* belief, as in the case of one who had not yet heard the gospel. Just as the theist and atheist make conscious decisions about what they will or will not accept, the belief and disbelief mentioned here is based on deliberate individual choice. It is a choice made on the heels of hearing the gospel message (v. 15).

Note that Jesus does not make the claim that one who is baptized will be saved. Rather, he states that one who *believes* and *is baptized* will be saved. These two responses to the gospel are inseparable in this verse. In fact, they are not two responses, but two elements of one's response. This contradicts the claim by some that, since Jesus did not disqualify the un-immersed in his follow-up comment "he who has disbelieved shall be condemned," this somehow unravels the fabric of his initial remark concerning baptism.

Those who deny the efficacy of baptism claim that, since disbelief alone brings condemnation, Jesus left the door open to the possibility of believers who remained un-immersed. The reason for this omission is that the very concept of an un-immersed believer would run contrary to New Testament instructions and examples. Regardless of what one believes about the meaning of baptism, it is impossible to escape the fact that New Testament believers, beginning with the Day of Pentecost, were immersed. This is supported in the detailed conversions in the book of Acts where baptisms are recorded along with the fact that Paul recognized the *baptized* status of his readers (Romans 6: 3-4; 1 Corinthians 1: 14-16; Galatians 3: 27; Colossians 2: 12). According to G. R. Beasley-Murray:

> Had an early Christian teacher handed on in writing a systematic treatment of this subject, which alas none ever did, it is conceivable that he could have included in his discussion all six aspects we have considered, viz. baptism and grace, faith, the Spirit, the Church, the good life, and hope. But I cannot think it would have entered his head to round it off with a section entitled, 'The necessity of baptism.' Who would have wished to raise the question? It would have sounded as strange to a first generation Christian as many other queries characteristic of our time such as, 'Is it necessary for a Christian to join the Church? Is it necessary to pray? Is corporate worship necessary? Is preaching necessary? Is the Lord's Supper necessary? Is the Bible necessary?' Such matters are self-evident, for they belong to the very structure of the Christian life.[3]

---

[3] Beasley-Murray, G. R. *Baptism in the New Testament*, 296-297.

Many people continue to insist that Mark 16: 16 fails to demonstrate the critical role of baptism in God's plan of salvation. Rather than adjusting their point of view to conform to Jesus' teaching, they have recast his words to conform to their point of view. This gives rise to a serious dilemma. Those who reject the redemptive character of baptism that is presented in this passage are, by the very nature of their position, claiming that the following two remarks are identical in meaning:

He who has believed and has been baptized shall be saved.

He who has believed and has _not_ been baptized shall be saved.

The first statement is biblical. The second is not. Yet, those who seek to neutralize the clear baptismal instruction found in Jesus' words are, in essence, equating these two antithetical statements, insisting that his instruction concerning baptism is extraneous. If Jesus' comment regarding disbelief was truly intended to negate his directive concerning baptism, these two statements must be granted equal weight. Where salvation is concerned, they must be deemed to render *precisely* the same meaning despite the glaring contradiction. In fact, modern scholarship tends to insist that the unbiblical statement is true while the biblical statement is false.

Many choose to disregard what Jesus has stated about baptism in Mark 16: 16, but it is a flimsy foundation, exegetically speaking, to deny that he meant what he said. The heart of Jesus' directions to the disciples, that an individual must *believe and be baptized* to be saved, is straightforward and he has stated it in such plainspoken terms that no one should have trouble understanding these instructions. Consequently, men have no excuse to misconstrue the teaching that is offered here.

Luke 23: 39-43

When Jesus hung on the cross, he was crucified between two thieves who were paying for their crimes with their lives. One thief was unrepentant. He hurled insults at Jesus and even mocked him. However, the other thief saw things a bit differently.

> [39] One of the criminals who were hanged *there* was hurling abuse at Him, saying, "Are You not the Christ? Save Yourself and us!" [40] But the other answered, and rebuking him said, "Do you not even fear God, since you are under the same sentence of condemnation? [41] And

we indeed *are suffering* justly, for we are receiving what we deserve for our deeds; but this man has done nothing wrong." [42] And he was saying, "Jesus, remember me when You come in Your kingdom!" [43] And He said to him, "Truly I say to you, today you shall be with Me in Paradise." (Luke 23: 43).

Some may wonder what this episode has to do with the topic of baptism. The truth is most discussions about the redemptive role of baptism eventually drift to this incident in Scripture. Pointing to the fact that baptism cannot be found in the narrative regarding the thief, who was promised a place in Paradise, the assumption is that anyone may be saved in like manner, without submitting to water baptism. The fact that the thief lived at a time prior to the covenant of grace is often deemed meaningless by those who either do not understand or, worse yet, do not care.

Some have suggested that *perhaps* this thief was baptized by either John the Baptist or Jesus' disciples. While it is possible, since he did recognize who Jesus was, it is highly unlikely. Little is known about this man, but there is no question that he was a thief. His guilt is never in doubt. The likelihood of a baptized thief fades even more in that his petition to Jesus was not made on the basis of a baptism that he might have received. Yet, it was not just the good fortune of being nailed next to Christ that brought salvation to this man. Two thieves were present but only one was saved. It was his willingness to recognize Jesus as the Son of God and his request to be remembered in Jesus' coming kingdom that saved him.

Since the thief was saved without even an inference to baptism, why should anyone submit to baptism as a matter of salvation? He believed and was saved; therefore, salvation today must be achieved in the same manner. This is the case presented by those who turn to the thief as a New Testament example of salvation without baptism. In order to give this episode its due, it is necessary to give honest consideration to how the salvation of the thief reflects upon salvation in the church age.

In his epistle to the Romans, Paul expressed his hope that Israelites who still continued to live under the law would soon come to understand the covenant of grace (Romans 10: 1-13). In his discourse, he regards belief in the resurrection as essential to salvation both for the Israelites and for the Romans. In the church age, belief in, and acceptance of, Jesus' resurrection is deemed by all to be an indispensable element of redemption. This faith lies at the very heart of the plan of salvation.

Those who believe that the thief's salvation – sans baptism – might serve as a model for salvation in the church age should take note that the thief did not, and in fact could not, believe in the resurrection. Jesus had not yet died when he told him, "you will be with Me in Paradise." Based on this principle, the thief would not have been saved in the covenant of grace.

Who would accept that anyone could be saved without the Holy Spirit? Few would ever discount the value of the work of the Spirit. In his own words Jesus taught that no one may enter the kingdom without first experiencing spiritual birth (John 3: 5). The Holy Spirit plays a significant part in the lives of the saved (Acts 2: 38; Ephesians 2: 18; 1 Thessalonians 1: 6). While some insist that the thief must have received the Holy Spirit prior to his death, the claim finds no scriptural support, nor is it implied in the text. Scripture indicates that people would not receive the Holy Spirit until after Jesus had returned to heaven (John 7: 39).

Paul spends much of his time teaching disciples about the body of Christ. As with baptism and the Holy Spirit, he describes the body of Christ as one of the unique unifying elements of Christianity (Ephesians 4: 4). According to Scripture, all who are saved are integrated into Christ's body (1 Corinthians 12: 13). For a saved person, membership in that body is automatic. Foregoing membership is not an option, since, according to Paul, it is the members of that body who are heirs to the kingdom (Ephesians 3: 6). Yet, the thief on the cross was not a part of the body of Christ (the church) in the covenant of grace. He could not have held membership in *the church*, since it was not established until Pentecost, weeks after his death.

While many who wish to be saved *like the thief* may consider these disparities insignificant, it is fair to say that God does not. If inheritance of the kingdom of God in the church age is limited to those who 1) believe in the resurrection, 2) receive the Holy Spirit, and 3) are part of the body of Christ, conversion in the likeness of the thief is not something to which those in the church age should aspire.

Baptism in Jesus' name was not introduced until after Jesus' resurrection (Mark 16: 16, Acts 2: 38, 1 Peter 3: 21) and well after the death of the thief. Relying on the gospel account of the thief to support a doctrine of salvation without baptism is equivalent to offering Abraham, Isaac, or Jacob as suitable examples. It is true that, in the end, even these great men of God were saved by the grace made available through Christ (Romans 8: 29). However, it is also true that their salvation (grounded in the *promise* of a coming Savior) has no direct impact on the call to baptism in the covenant of grace.

John 3: 3-5

When Nicodemus, a Pharisee, approached Jesus, the Lord knew what was troubling him. Like the rich young ruler (Luke 18: 18-23), Nicodemus had some spiritual questions and chose to address Jesus directly so that he might receive some answers. As Nicodemus spoke, recognizing Jesus as having come from God, Jesus responded in anticipation of his question.

> ³ Jesus answered and said to him, "Truly, truly, I say to you, unless one is born again he cannot see the kingdom of God." ⁴ Nicodemus said to Him, "How can a man be born when he is old? He cannot enter a second time into his mother's womb and be born, can he?" ⁵ Jesus answered, "Truly, truly, I say to you, unless one is born of water and the Spirit he cannot enter into the kingdom of God. (John 3: 3-5)

Jesus' conversation with Nicodemus establishes terms for entering the kingdom of God (i.e., salvation). The statement concerning *seeing the kingdom* is straightforward enough, but Nicodemus, who apparently got lost in the *rebirth* phraseology, wished to know just *how* one might be "born again" (v. 3). Jesus responded with, "unless one is born of water and the Spirit he cannot enter into the kingdom of God" (v. 5).

John began his thoughts on spiritual birth a bit earlier (John 1: 13). The topic resurfaces in Jesus' words here. Yet, scholars differ greatly in their understanding of what constitutes the spiritual birth that Jesus has in view in this conversation. One truth in which all can be confident is this: Jesus, in this passage, likens being "born again" (v. 3) to being "born of water and the Spirit" (v. 5) The Lord makes two statements in his conversation with Nicodemus that are intended to teach the same lesson. Consider the parallel character of the following remarks:

> Truly, truly, I say to you, unless one is born again he cannot see the kingdom of God. (John 3: 3)

> Truly, truly, I say to you, unless one is born of water and the Spirit he cannot enter into the kingdom of God. (John 3: 5)

In this passage, Jesus considers the expression "born of water and the Spirit" (v. 5) a suitable substitute for the phrase "born again" (v. 3). Since he was responding to Nicodemus's query about how one might be reborn (v. 4), it stands to reason that the words "born of water and the Spirit" (v. 5) are intended to clarify for the Pharisee exactly what Jesus meant by the phrase "born again" (v. 3). There is a general consensus that to be "born of…the Spirit" (v. 5) speaks to spiritual renewal/redemption), but there is considerable disagreement over the meaning of the expression "born of water" (v. 5).

Some believe *water*, in this instance, points to childbirth, and that Jesus was telling Nicodemus that a person must first be born into this life physically and later be born spiritually. The theory is that the water in this passage represents the amniotic fluid of the womb. However, this view carries with it some exegetical difficulties. First of all, Jesus would have no reason to introduce the topic of physical childbirth in an explanation of what it means to be "born again" (v. 3) Second, if "born again" (v. 3) equals "born of water and the Spirit" (v. 5), then childbirth does not fit the context, since it is not a component of rebirth.

When human childbirth is addressed in God's Word, it is described with phrases like "…born of women" (Matthew 11: 11), "…born of flesh" (John 3: 6), "…birth *through the* woman" (1 Corinthians 11: 12), "…born of woman" (Galatians 4: 4), "…born according to the flesh" (Galatians 4: 23), etc. It is not defined as "born of water" (v. 5). Consequently, there is no reason to think that meaning might apply in this setting. This is especially true since, in the very next verse, Jesus contemplates "…born of flesh" (John 3: 6) drawing a clear distinction between earthly and spiritual births.

Others teach that this represents a symbolic use of the term *water*. In other words, Jesus was not introducing literal H_2O into the conversation, but something comparable to *living water* that is mentioned occasionally in God's Word. A number of times the New Testament authors use the term *water* symbolically. The first is the incident with the Samaritan woman (John 4: 10-15). The next occurs at the end of the Feast of Booths (John 7: 37-39). Others appear in John's apocalyptic vision (Revelation 7: 16-17; 21: 6; 22: 1, 17).

Two distinct patterns arise from these passages. First of all, when *water* is discussed symbolically in the New Testament, its divine nature is revealed within the narrative. Speaking to the Samaritan woman, Jesus called the water that would quench all thirst *living water*. Any water that quenches an eternal/spiritual thirst could not be a physical substance. In fact, in that episode Jesus distinguishes between *living water* and physical water. Also, at the Feast of Booths, Jesus again refers to water as *living water*. Similarly, in the book of Revelation, the reference in each case is to what the apostle calls *living water* or *water of life*.

The second pattern that emerges in those instances where symbolic/spiritual water is in view is the manner in which the water is applied. Symbolic water is offered to quench a spiritual thirst. That is the case with the Samaritan woman, Jesus' words at the Feast of Booths, and the assorted references in Revelation that are mentioned above.

There are a few other instances in Scripture where the term *water* is used symbolically without reference to *living water* or *waters of life*. In his second epistle, Peter refers to *water* in an illustration. He references Balaam, an Old Testament character (Numbers 22: 5), stating that pseudo-prophets like him were "…springs without water and mists driven by a storm" (2 Peter 2: 17). This (lack of) water is intended to represent *prophets without substance*. It is similar to Jude's remark about men who are like "…clouds without water" (Jude 1: 12). Revelation also has some colorful apocalyptic references to water (Revelation 12: 15; 17: 15), but the eschatological character of these passages suggests that they are unrelated to the rebirth Jesus discusses with Nicodemus. There is nothing in these passages from 2 Peter, Jude, and Revelation that *could* apply to John 3: 5.

Water is also linked to baptism in the New Testament. For instance, John the Baptist baptized with water (Matthew 3: 6). Consequently, when the Bible discusses the baptism performed by John, it is most reasonable to presume that immersion in water is in view. Additionally, the baptism performed and taught by the apostles and others in the first century church also involved immersion in water (Acts 8: 35-38; 10: 47-48).

When baptism in water is discussed in the New Testament, it is often recognized for its spiritual efficacy. Baptism was practiced on and after the Day of Pentecost as a matter of forgiveness of sins (Acts 2: 38; Colossians 2: 9-14), membership in the church (Acts 2: 41; 1 Corinthians 12: 13), spiritual renewal (Romans 6: 1-4; Colossians 2: 9-14), salvation (1 Peter 3: 21), and access to the Holy Spirit (Acts 2: 38; 19: 1-7).

In Paul's first letter to the Corinthians, he introduces water in metaphoric fashion. In that instance, Paul points to himself as one who *planted*, Apollos as one who *watered*, and God as one who brings growth, referring to the spiritual growth of the Corinthians both individually and as a group (1 Corinthians 3: 6-8). Even though the apostle uses the imagery of farming, it is easy to recognize that the idea of baptism is being depicted since, a mere two chapters earlier (1 Corinthians 1: 12-17), Paul portrayed himself as a preacher (planter) and Apollos as a baptizer (one who waters).

Water has two primary functions. It is used to quench thirst (in that sense it sustains life) and it is used for cleansing. In the pages of Scripture, these attributes of water are given spiritual applications. It is a well-established biblical principle that when water is addressed symbolically in the New Testament (i.e., living water, water of life), it is associated with quenching spiritual/eternal thirst. However, where baptism/rebirth is concerned, it is not the thirst-quenching character of water, but its cleansing nature that is in view. This is what Jesus has in mind in his discussion with Nicodemus.

Purification, water, and baptism form a triangular bond in Scripture, with purification/renewal being the *primary* matter in water baptism. Consequently, when purification and water are discussed in the New Testament (cf. Ephesians 5: 26), there is reason to be confident that baptism is in view. Similarly, when water and baptism are the topic, spiritual purification is implicated (cf. Romans 6: 1-4). Finally, when purification is discussed in conjunction with baptism, immersion in water is under consideration (cf. Acts 2: 38). This is a pattern that is consistent throughout the New Testament.

Paul's letters to the Romans and Colossians are particularly relevant to Jesus' conversation with Nicodemus. In those epistles he tells the believers:

> [3] Or do you not know that all of us who have been baptized into Christ Jesus have been baptized into His death? [4] Therefore we have been buried with Him through baptism into death, so that as Christ was raised from the dead through the glory of the Father, so we too might walk in newness of life. (Romans 6: 3-4)

> [12] ...having been buried with Him in baptism, in which you were also raised up with Him through faith in the working of God, who raised Him from the dead. [13] When you were dead in your transgressions and the uncircumcision of your flesh, He made you alive together with Him, having forgiven us all our transgressions, [14] having canceled out the certificate of debt consisting of decrees against us, which was hostile to us; and He has taken it out of the way, having nailed it to the cross. (Colossians 2: 12-14)

Paul saw baptism as a matter of forgiveness/renewal/rebirth. He told the Romans that, rising from the waters of baptism, the penitent believer experiences "newness of life" (v. 4). Similarly, he explained to the Colossians that, "having been buried with Him" the baptized believer is "raised up with Him" (v. 12) from the baptismal water. At that moment, that person is "made...alive with Him," his sins having been forgiven (v. 13).

The connection between baptism and rebirth in these verses is clear. He identifies baptism as the moment one attains newness of life – the time when sins are forgiven (purification). Based on these complementary verses, it is easy to see why Jesus considered "born of water and spirit" (v. 5) a fitting explanation of what it means to be "born again" (v.3). He was explaining to Nicodemus that one must be spiritually renewed – in baptism.

Some may balk at the presumption that the combination of water and rebirth in John 3: 5 necessarily points to immersion in water. However, there is additional evidence that baptism is in view here. The Apostle John recorded Jesus' visit with Nicodemus. Is it possible, then, that John connected "born of water and the Spirit" with the rite of baptism? There is a strong argument for this when comparing the same apostle's words in his first epistle.

> [6]This is the One who came by water and blood, Jesus Christ; not with the water only, but with the water and with the blood. It is the Spirit who testifies, because the Spirit is the truth. [7] For there are three that testify: [8] the Spirit and the water and the blood; and the three are in agreement. (1 John 5: 6-8)

Most Bible scholars recognize that the water mentioned in this passage refers, at least in part, to the baptism of Christ, and the case can be made that, where this water is concerned, baptism is John's primary focus. Jesus' baptism by John the Baptist took place as he prepared for his ministry on earth (Matthew 3: 13-17). In *Zondervan Illustrated Bible Backgrounds Commentary* it is written, "Jesus' identity is gauged by both his baptism ("water") and crucifixion ("blood")...Jesus therefore "came," embodied and revealed God's presence, not only at his baptism by the Spirit...but also in his death on the cross."[4]

---

[4] Arnold, Clinton E. general editor. *Zondervan Illustrated Bible Backgrounds Commentary*, Volume 4, 205.

The fact that the water of this passage from 1 John points to Jesus' baptism was recognized by Tertullian in the early third century. It is similarly acknowledged in many other respected works.[5] The consensus, derived from the writings of early church fathers like Tertullian, is that John was refuting the claims of a Gnostic by the name of Cerinthus who insisted that Jesus came *only by water* (his baptism). John denied that claim, insisting that Jesus came by *water* (baptism) and *blood* (crucifixion) with the Spirit providing the final witness.

Since John (1 John 5: 6-8) and Paul (1 Corinthians 3: 6-8) used the term *water* as a deliberate substitute for baptism, a powerful case can be made for the same use of *water* in the gospel of John, especially since rebirth is in view in the text. In fact, it is not unreasonable to believe that John drew his alternate wording for baptism in his epistle from the conversation between Jesus and Nicodemus, which he had recorded.

There is additional evidence to consider that strongly favors the meaning of baptism in John 3: 5. Irenaeus, one of the early church fathers, was born around A.D. 130 and died early in the third century. When confronted with those who, in his time, tried to deny the salvation value of immersion in water, he wrote the following in his work titled *Against Heresies*:

> And when we come to refute them, we shall know in its fitting-place, that this class of men have been instigated by Satan to a denial of that baptism which is regeneration to God, and thus to a renunciation of the whole faith...For the baptism instituted by the visible Jesus was for the remission of sins.[6]

He also wrote the following when comparing baptism to the healing of leprosy experienced by Naaman in the Old Testament:

> As we are lepers in sin, we are made clean from our old transgressions by means of the sacred water and the invocation of the Lord. We are thus spiritually regenerated as newborn infants, even as the Lord declared: "Except a man be born again through water and the Spirit, he shall not enter the kingdom of heaven."[7]

---

[5] Barnes Notes on the Bible, Clarke's Commentary on the Bible, Gill's Exposition of the Entire Bible, Wesley's Notes, Robertson's Word Pictures of the New Testament, and countless others.
[6] Irenaeus. *Against Heresies (Book I, Chapter 21)*, http://www.newadvent.org/fathers/0103121.htm.
[7] Irenaeus. *Fragment 34*, catholic.com, http://www.catholic.com/tracts/born-again-in-baptism.

Irenaeus believed strongly in the efficacy of baptism. To him, baptism was the moment of one's purification (forgiveness) and regeneration. In his view, those who denied the salvific character of baptism were heretics – a "class of men...instigated by Satan." It is also evident from his words that Irenaeus considered Jesus' instructions to Nicodemus an unapologetic call to baptism.

Certain facts about Irenaeus give his claim concerning Jesus' talk with Nicodemus even greater force. Irenaeus was a student of a man by the name of Polycarp (A.D. 69-155). This man was one of the apostolic fathers and a student and friend of the Apostle John. That means Irenaeus was one generation removed from the very man who recorded the expression, "born of water and the Spirit." Raised in a Christian home, some estimate that he may have learned under Polycarp for as much as the first twenty years of his life.

No doubt his teacher, Polycarp, shared with Irenaeus much of the personal insights he received from the apostle. That this conversation was among those discussions is highly likely since Irenaeus considered it a matter of critical importance. It would seem only natural for them to discuss in-depth the meaning of a passage where Jesus openly taught that one's salvation is predicated on being "born of water and the spirit." In fact, it would be essentially impossible for them to avoid that conversation in the time they spent together. Irenaeus was certainly confident that, by his words, Jesus proclaimed the necessity of baptism.

Birth of water and the Spirit does not, as many like to teach, depict two separate births, one of water and one of Spirit. In his statement to Nicodemus, Jesus is identifying two elements of rebirth. Being reborn (spiritually) involves both water (baptism) and the (Holy) Spirit's indwelling presence as proclaimed by Peter on the Day of Pentecost (Acts 2: 38). With all the authority that was his, Jesus told the Pharisee that one must be baptized to *enter the kingdom.*

It has been suggested by some that Jesus could not have been proposing immersion in water to Nicodemus, since Christian baptism was not yet instituted when Jesus spoke these words. Thus, they insist that Jesus could only have a spiritual birth in view – undoubtedly that foreseen by John the Baptist (Matthew 3: 11). What most tend to overlook, however, is that when Jesus said, "unless one is born of water and the Spirit," the Holy Spirit had not yet been given. People in general did not have access to the filling of, or renewal by, the Spirit any more than they had access to Christian baptism. Rebirth through water and Spirit was yet to come. Thus, Jesus' lesson is necessarily forward-looking.

Nicodemus was undoubtedly familiar with the baptism of John the Baptist (Matthew 3: 4-6) and would have taken that to be the frame of reference where water is concerned. However, during his ministry, Jesus continually offered lessons about the coming covenant of grace, proclaiming the blessings men would experience at that time. Just as John explained that the thirst-quenching Spirit Jesus proclaimed during the Festival of Booths was not yet accessible to men (John 7: 39), so the Christian baptism he taught to Nicodemus would apply in the coming covenant of grace.

With the words "unless one is born of water and the Spirit," Jesus has plainly established an edict for entering the kingdom of God. Yet, many seek to discount the portraiture of baptism that is found in this verse, insisting that Jesus' meaning is unclear. In other words, it is not possible to know what Jesus meant even though he plainly teaches that, short of being "born of water," no one will see heaven. As a result, Nicodemus's query, "how can a man be born when he is old?" (v. 4) remains unresolved for many people despite the fact that Jesus has provided the answer – an answer that was clear enough for the early church fathers.

Chapter 18

Christian Baptism in Acts

Acts 2: 38

The Day of Pentecost stands alone as a pivotal moment in the history of mankind. It was on that day that two distinct, but related events took place. The first was the inspiring entrance of the Holy Spirit into the world of humanity at a level previously unknown. The resulting miracle of tongues, experienced by the apostles, led to the next critical event, which was the establishment of the church of Christ.

In the midst of the coming of the Spirit and the establishment of the church, something happened that tied these phenomena together. On that day the gospel message, in its fullness, was first presented to mankind. Peter, speaking on behalf of the apostles, revealed to the crowd in Jerusalem exactly who Jesus was, recalled the prophecies that had been fulfilled, and explained to all that Jesus had risen and returned to heaven.

Realizing the gravity of their situation, the people pleaded with the apostles for direction. They wished to know how they might escape their well-deserved punishment for what they had done. They asked Peter and the other apostles what they should do. Peter's response is clear and concise as he offered instruction about what they must do to be forgiven and saved.

> Peter *said* to them, "Repent, and each of you be baptized in the name of Jesus Christ for the forgiveness of your sins; and you will receive the gift of the Holy Spirit." (Acts 2: 38)

Peter's words combined power and authority with pure simplicity. His directive to those in the crowd was uncomplicated. If they repented of their sins and submitted to baptism in Jesus' name, they would be forgiven. In addition, they would experience an individual relationship with God, through the Holy Spirit, that was unavailable before that day.

Despite the forthrightness of Peter's words, this verse has become one of the most disputed in all of Scripture. Peter's call for submission to baptism for those who seek forgiveness has been a matter of animated debate for the past several centuries and it is a doctrinal fracture that will not easily mend.

Many arguments have been raised to counter Peter's depiction of baptism as a matter of forgiveness. One line of reasoning that has been offered is the claim that forgiveness, while linked to repentance, is grammatically disconnected from baptism due to the singular/plural nuances found in the text. Below is a breakdown of the verse where the details of the grammar used to support this position are noted:

> Peter *said* to them, "Repent (second person plural), and each (singular) of you (second person plural) be baptized (third person singular) in the name of Jesus Christ for the forgiveness (singular) of your (second person plural) sins; and you (second person plural) will receive the gift of the Holy Spirit." (Acts 2: 38)

It has been argued that, since *repentance* and *your*[8] (sins) appear in second person plural and *be baptized* is third person singular, only repentance is required for forgiveness. The short answer to this challenge is that the impact of the verb *be baptized* is shaped by the expression *each of you*. The Greek *humōn* (of you) is second person plural and identifies those to whom the command of baptism was given. According to Cottrell:

> Those who use this argument seem to deliberately ignore the fact that the singular verb "be baptized" is emphatically pluralized by the immediately-following words, hekastos humōn, "each one OF YOU" (plural). True, the verb "be baptized" is grammatically singular because its immediate subject is "each one" (hekastos), but the addition of the plural "of you" (humōn) clearly shows that the application of this verb is intended to be plural.[9]

It is easy to get so distracted by the linguistic gymnastics of this debate that people lose sight of the picture the apostle is attempting to paint. In response to their query about how they should respond to Peter's message, he told those in the crowd to repent and be baptized. This would result in forgiveness for those who followed Peter's

---

[8] Certain Greek manuscripts simply say *for the remission of sins*.
[9] Cottrell, Jack. *Answering a false interpretation of Acts 2: 38*, http://jackcottrell.com/notes/answering-a-false-interpretation-of-acts-238/.

instructions. This is the simple yet powerful message an unbiased person would naturally derive from a candid reading of the text. Peter had no intention of severing the connection between baptism and forgiveness. In the New Testament, repentance and baptism are consistently linked to forgiveness of sins (Mark 1: 4; Luke 3: 3; Acts 3: 19; 22: 16; Romans 6: 1-4; Colossians 2: 11-14).

Peter had just concluded a sermon where he had accused the Jews before him of murdering the Messiah. When the crowd, recognizing their guilt, asked what they should do, Peter told them to *repent*. It makes sense that this word should be plural. Peter was talking about corporate sin in this setting – specifically, Jesus' crucifixion. Therefore, the demand for collective repentance makes sense.

Christian baptism, on the other hand, is a personal matter and Peter recognized the individualism that is involved. Thus, the people in the crowd were instructed to be baptized, "each of you." The lesson of the text is simple. When Peter told the crowd that they must "Repent and…be baptized…for the forgiveness of your sins," that is exactly what he meant.

The second objection to this verse of Scripture has developed from assorted opinions about the meaning of *for* (Gr. *eis*) as it is used in this setting. Peter told the crowd to repent and be baptized *for* the forgiveness of sins. Insisting that baptism could not possibly be a factor with respect to forgiveness, some believe that it would be more accurate to interpret *eis* as *because of* rather than *for*. The claim is that people should submit to baptism *because* they have been forgiven.

On its face, this position is riddled with problems. First of all, if *eis* means *because of*, what is the purpose of repentance? God's Word makes clear that forgiveness does not precede repentance (Mark 1: 4; Luke 3: 3; Acts 3: 19). Could this word carry two distinct meanings in a single appearance – one in relation to repentance and another where baptism is concerned? The proposal is certainly strained. Yet, some of the same individuals who insist that *eis* must be interpreted *because of* also employ the singular/plural line of reasoning discussed earlier. Thus, Peter was telling the crowd that they should repent *for* (eis) *the forgiveness of sins* and submit to baptism *because* (eis) *they had been forgiven*. In doing so, they apply two meanings to the same word in this setting.

Despite claims to the contrary, *eis* is consistently forward-looking. In other words, forward movement *to*, or *into*, a time, place, setting, or circumstance is in view. This is found not only in the definition of the word, but also among scholars. A. T. Robertson, a well-known Greek grammarian of the Baptist persuasion, struggled heavily with his discussion of *eis*. Convinced that baptism could not be *for* forgiveness, he claimed that *because of* might be considered a legitimate interpretation for *eis* in Acts 2: 38, even though the context does not really fit that usage. Ultimately, he concluded that a person's doctrine will be the judge of the meaning of *eis*. He stated, "One will decide the use here according as he believes that baptism is essential to the remission of sins or not."[10] This results in the dilemma of doctrine driving interpretation rather than interpretation driving doctrine.

The word *eis* appears nearly 1,800 times in the New Testament. In every case where it is used in conjunction with imperatives, as it is in this instance (*repent* and *be baptized* are imperatives), it carries the meaning of *objective* or *result*. Consider the following examples:

> And saith unto him, See thou say nothing to any man: but go (imperative) thy way, shew (imperative) thyself to the priest, and offer (imperative) for thy cleansing those things which Moses commanded, for (eis) a testimony unto them. (Mark 1: 44 – KJV)

> Repent (imperative), then, and turn (imperative) to God, so that (eis) your sins may be wiped out...(Acts 3: 19 - NIV)

A comparable use of *for the forgiveness of sins* (eis aphesin hamartion) occurs in Matthew's gospel. At the time, Jesus was, through the introduction of the emblems of the Lord's Supper, explaining the purpose of his impending death. In this case, it is clear that Jesus was offering himself as a sacrifice, and that offering was for a specific purpose.

> ...for this is My blood of the covenant, which is poured out for many for (eis) forgiveness of sins. (Matthew 26: 28)

This same use of the phrase applies in Acts 2: 38. The people were told to repent and be baptized *eis aphesin hamartion* (for the forgiveness of sins). Any attempt to alter that sense of the text does harm to the apostle's message.

There is no need to reinvent the wheel when it comes to discussing the meaning of *eis*. This debate has raged for centuries, so there is sufficient material on the subject. Perhaps the finest exposition of this

---

[10] Robertson, A. T. *Robertson's Word Pictures in the New Testament*, http://www.studylight.org/commentaries/rwp/view.cgi?bk=43&ch=2.

word, as it appears in Acts 2: 38, was given by J. W. Willmarth late in the nineteenth century. His view of *eis* was as follows:

> Its general English equivalent is, *Into*. But *unto, in order to, for, until*, and other English prepositions translate it better in certain cases, owing to difference of idiom.[11]

Mr. Willmarth expressed sincere disappointment toward those among his own brotherhood who refused to acknowledge the true meaning of *eis* in this text. His frustration was grounded in what he saw as a dogmatic interpretation rather than one based on the actual words of Scripture. Of those who chose to teach a causal use of *eis* (because of) in this passage, Willmarth stated:

> This interpretation was doubtless suggested, and is now defended, purely on dogmatic grounds. It is feared that if we give eis its natural and obvious meaning, undo importance will be ascribed to Baptism, the Atonement will be undervalued, and the work of the Holy Spirit disparaged...
>
> Such methods of interpretation are unworthy of Christian scholars. It is our business, simply and honestly, to ascertain the exact meaning of the originals, as the sacred penmen intended to convey it to the mind of the contemporary reader. Away with the question – 'What *ought* Peter to have said in the interest of orthodoxy?' The real question is, 'What *did* Peter say, and what did he *mean*, when he spoke on the Day of Pentecost, under the inspiration of the Holy Spirit?'[12]

Finally, some attempt to overcome Peter's words concerning baptism by insisting that earlier in his message, while citing the prophet Joel, he had proclaimed that "...everyone who calls on the name of the Lord will be saved" (Acts 2: 21). Thus, it is calling on his name, and not baptism, that saves. This is a curious proposal that also raises some interesting questions. For instance, exactly what does it *mean* to call on his name? Where is it defined in Scripture? It cannot simply be a matter of calling out to him. Jesus put that notion to rest early in his ministry (Matthew 7: 21). Consequently, calling on his name must involve more.

---

[11] Bales, James D. *The Case of Cornelius*, 88-89, citing J. W. Willmarth from *The Baptist Quarterly*, July 1877, 298.
[12] Ibid., 89.

When the crowd asked the apostles, "...what shall we do?" (Acts 2: 37) they were seeking direction that would lead them to salvation. Despite the fact that Peter had cited *calling on the name of the Lord*, they did not know what to do. They did not know *how* to call on his name. In response, the apostle told them to repent and be baptized. It is reasonable to believe, then, that the command to be baptized *in Jesus' name* is how Peter applied the words of the prophet to the instructions he had received from Jesus (Matthew 28: 19; Mark 16: 16).

An important step, when it comes to interpreting Scripture, is to consider how the immediate audience responded to the instructions they received. A look at the response of those in the crowd on the Day of Pentecost offers additional insight into how they understood Peter's words.

> So then, those who had received his word were baptized; and that day there were added about three thousand souls. (Acts 2: 41)

Every person who believed was baptized. Additionally, Luke notes a connection between those who were *baptized* and those who were *added* (to the church). All who were immersed were added. Similarly, all who were added were immersed. Luke draws no distinction between believers (who received his word) and people who were baptized. While *only* those who "received his word" were baptized, Luke indicates that *all* who "received his word" were baptized. They accepted the apostles' teaching and having submitted to baptism, were counted among the believers. On the other hand, those who remained un-immersed were not believers. Consequently, they were not added. This very point, that all believers were immersed, was made earlier during a discussion of Jesus' words in his evangelistic commission to the disciples (Mark 16: 16).

Notice also what Luke conspicuously omitted. He did not say that it was those who *repented* who were added, but those who were *baptized*. Did some fail to repent? Was repentance unnecessary? That would be a foolish notion since Peter had just instructed them to repent and be baptized. His words demonstrate the harmonious relationship between the two. Those who "received his word" (believed) would not have hesitated to repent. Yet, if Peter intended to dissociate baptism and forgiveness as many people claim, it would have made sense for Luke to recognize the repentance of those who were added. However, in his ensuing remarks, Luke highlights their baptism. That is because other aspects of the gospel message, such as belief and repentance, culminate in baptism – the final decisive step *into* the kingdom. Immersion in water defines the *moment* when they were added.

Many have attempted to wrest baptism from Peter's message on the Day of Pentecost, a position it has held for two millennia, claiming that the apostle intended to tie forgiveness to repentance alone. If that was Peter's goal, he and Luke have masked it well. The challenge to the biblical principle that baptism is *for the forgiveness of sins* in Acts 2: 38 is a prime example of *disputes about words* that was discussed in the preface of this book and about which Paul warned Timothy when he wrote:

> ³ If anyone advocates a different doctrine and does not agree with sound words, those of our Lord Jesus Christ, and with the doctrine conforming to godliness, ⁴ he is conceited *and* understands nothing; but he has a morbid interest in controversial questions and disputes about words, out of which arise envy, strife, abusive language, evil suspicions, ⁵ and constant friction between men of depraved mind and deprived of the truth, who suppose that godliness is a means of gain. (1 Timothy 6: 3-5)

Acts 10: 44-48

God called Peter to attend the house of Cornelius, a Gentile, in the town of Caesarea near the coast of the Mediterranean Sea. He coaxed Peter with a vision involving unclean animals (Acts 10: 9-16). When the opportunity to speak to the Gentiles presented itself, Peter understood the vision to mean that he should go.

As Peter began to preach to the Gentiles, he witnessed the Holy Spirit come upon them much as he had enveloped the apostles on the Day of Pentecost. The apostle and those with him were astonished that God would offer the Holy Spirit to Gentiles. Yet, they knew this was genuine because, "...they were hearing them speaking with tongues and exalting God" (v. 46).

Peter soon realized the significance of this occasion. The gospel message was no longer to be given to Jews only. God was offering to the Gentiles the same redemption through Christ's blood that had been taught among the Jews. As a result of these events, Peter said, "Surely no one can refuse the water for these to be baptized..." (v. 47). In fact, in his explanation to the Jews in Jerusalem as to why he would allow the Gentiles into the body of Christ, he remarked, "...who was I that I could stand in God's way?" (Acts 11: 17).

The Gentiles were ready to believe. This can be inferred from the fact that they invited Peter to Caesarea. When the Spirit came upon them, it seems that their readiness was turned to full-fledged faith. To Peter, the offer of baptism to the Gentiles in Jesus' name was the obvious next step. Actually, it was the obvious first step since they were plainly ready to accept Jesus as Savior.

God had made clear to Peter that it was time to address the lost souls of the Gentile nations, and Peter knew that, as with the Jews, it must begin with baptism for those who believed (Acts 2: 38). Peter apparently remained with the Gentiles for a time following their conversion, taking the opportunity to further instruct them concerning the things of Christ.

This episode provides a sterling example of the execution of the Great Commission (Matthew 28: 19-20). Peter first taught the Gentiles so that they would know *what* they must believe to be saved. He then baptized them in accordance with Jesus' instructions. Afterward, he remained so that he could provide further insight into Christ's teachings.

Acts 16: 30-34

Paul's encounter with the Philippian jailer and his family has received considerable attention in the debate over the efficacy of baptism (Acts 16: 22-34). The jailer, realizing his life would be spared since his prisoners Paul and Silas had not attempted to escape during an earthquake, posed a simple question. He asked them, "Sirs, what must I do to be saved?" (Acts 16: 30).

The beauty and simplicity of the question reflect the beauty and simplicity of the gospel message. In response, Paul remarked, "Believe in the Lord Jesus, and you will be saved, you and your household" (Acts 16: 31). While the earnestness of both the jailer's question and the apostle's response can be appreciated by all, for a long time now a dark cloud has hung over this passage. It has been employed time and again in an attempt to refute the spiritual worth of baptism that is taught throughout the New Testament. The line of reasoning is that, since baptism is absent from Paul's response, its redemptive value must be denied. Those who hang their salvation instruction here seem to want to place brackets around the first fourteen words Paul spoke to the jailer, insisting that these words, and only these words, may be used in teaching people how to attain eternal life.

One characteristic of this passage that makes it enticing is the specificity and clarity with which the jailer phrased his question to Paul and Silas. This is the only instance in the New Testament where someone seeking salvation asked in full, "What must I do to be saved?" This specific phraseology is found nowhere else in Scripture. A comparable question offered by the rich young ruler comes relatively close (Matthew 19: 16), but the context is different in that it was asked prior to the establishment of the church and the introduction of baptism in Jesus' name. Consequently, certain men insist that the answer Paul gave the jailer should be considered the biblical standard regarding conditions for salvation. However, in doing so, they ignore the equivalence of the question asked of Peter by the Jews in Jerusalem on the Day of Pentecost (Acts 2: 37). While those Jews did not ask what they must do *to be saved*, it can be inferred from Peter's answer that this was the meaning behind their question.

Some may wonder why anyone would even attempt to limit the message of salvation to a single biblical statement. It seems that the motivation is ardent dogmatism intended to silence any teaching that connects baptism and salvation. Some even believe that it is wrong to teach repentance or confession in connection with redemption, since they are also lacking in this specific setting. They believe that allowing other passages of Scripture to interfere dilutes the purity of the message of salvation that is presented in these words. They are correct in their assumption since, when other New Testament passages are given consideration in ascertaining the plan of salvation, the claim that the jailer was saved by belief alone begins to unravel.

The New Testament is filled with salvation-centered instructions. Jesus instructed the apostles on salvation. Peter preached to the Gentiles, Philip taught the Samaritans and the Ethiopian eunuch, and Paul's epistles are steeped in salvific instruction. Resting the whole of the message of redemption on a single event and then limiting it to one verse within that episode purely as a matter of doctrinal bias, turns earnest biblical analysis on its ear.

By any measure, a line of reasoning that consciously dissects and even eliminates portions of a biblical account to derive a certain doctrinal outcome represents a poor application of hermeneutic principles. It reflects not only an enthusiastic blindness to the surrounding text and complete disregard for interpretive principles, but also an eagerness to superimpose one's own beliefs onto the narrative. When taken in context, the jailer's conversion not only refutes the

> *When taken in context, the jailer's conversion ... actually shines a favorable light on the baptismal instruction Paul offered this man and his family.*

teaching of salvation by belief only, but it actually shines a favorable light on the baptismal instruction Paul offered this man and his family.

When the jailer asked Paul and Silas what he must do to be saved, Paul responded by telling him that he must believe. That is true, and it would be disingenuous and unbiblical to discount that answer in any fashion. However, it is, at the very least, misleading for anyone to suggest that Paul's instructions ended with that statement. Taking in the balance of Luke's account, it is evident that beyond the initial call to believe, "...they spoke the word of the Lord to him together with all who were in his house" (Acts 16: 32). If the message Paul sought to deliver ended with belief, exactly what could Luke mean by "the word of the Lord?" What else did Paul say to this man?

The expressions *the word of the Lord* and *the word of God* are metonyms commonly used in the New Testament to depict the gospel. Luke uses these terms often. They appear six times in the gospel he wrote (cf. Luke 8: 11; 22: 61) and twenty-one times in the book of Acts (cf. Acts 8: 25; 11: 1; 15: 36; 19: 20). Paul used these terms several times in his epistles (cf. Colossians 1: 25; 1 Thessalonians 1: 8) as did the apostles Peter (cf. 1 Peter 1: 23, 25; 2 Peter 3: 5) and John (cf. 1 John 2: 14; Revelation 1: 2; 20: 4).

When Luke states that "they spoke the word of the Lord" (v. 32) to the jailer and his family, it means they shared with them the gospel message. The ensuing text indicates that what Paul and Silas had to say eclipsed the idea of belief only. What happened next is very telling. When Paul finished speaking "the word of the Lord" to the jailer and his family, Luke reported the following sequence of events:

> [33]And he took them that *very* hour of the night and washed their wounds, and immediately he was baptized, he and all his *household*. [34]And he brought them into his house and set food before them, and rejoiced greatly, having believed in God with his whole household. (Acts 16: 33-34)

Paul's instructions to this man not only exceeded belief, but he taught him about baptism in practically the same breath. In his teaching, Paul would have explained exactly what the jailer should believe where Jesus was concerned and what form his response should take. Luke does not specifically say how long Paul talked. However, if Luke's timing is literal (and there is no reason to doubt it), all of these events, from the jailer's initial query to his baptism, occurred within an hour or so, since they went "...that *very* hour of the night" (v. 33) to wash their wounds and submit to baptism. At most, it was a matter of minutes between the words *believe* and *be baptized* in Paul's instructions to the jailer.

The necessary inference that can be drawn from this text is that baptism was a component of "the word of the Lord" (the gospel message) that they shared with this family. Once Paul and Silas had their wounds cleaned, baptism was the first order of business, just as it was on the Day of Pentecost and other conversion accounts.

Acts 19: 1-7

Upon his arrival in Ephesus, Paul sought out the local believers. He eventually encountered some men who were disciples of John the Baptist. As they talked, it became apparent to Paul that something was missing. It is reasonable to believe that these men may have referenced the *coming* Messiah or made some other comment that indicated to Paul that they did not know Jesus.

Paul did not wonder whether these disciples had been immersed. They had been John's disciples, so their submission to baptism was a given. Yet, he had reason to doubt that they had been baptized *in Jesus' name*. However, in his query concerning them he simply asked, "Did you receive the Holy Spirit when you believed?" (Acts 19: 2a). This may appear to be a curious approach, but it makes sense when the balance of the narrative is given honest consideration.

In itself, Paul's question to the Ephesians concerning the Holy Spirit does not seem remarkable. However, when they told Paul, "No, we have not even heard whether there is a Holy Spirit" (Acts 19: 2b), his response is unexpected. Paul asked them, "Into what then were you baptized?" (Acts 19: 3) What lesson can be learned from Paul's exchange with these disciples?

Only those who are most dogmatic in their rejection of baptism as a matter of salvation will deny the connection between belief, baptism, and the Holy Spirit that unfolds here. Even though he had asked if they had received the Spirit *when they believed*, when Paul discovered that these disciples had not received the Spirit, he did not question their belief, but their baptism. That is because, in accord with Peter's words on the Day of Pentecost, the Spirit they did not know would have been received when they were baptized in Jesus' name. This is the essence of Paul's remarks.

This episode provides clearer understanding about what it means to *believe* according to Scripture. Since these men had not received the Holy Spirit when they believed, Paul presumed that in their belief they had not been baptized in Jesus' name. The sentient act of belief alone would not suffice. The lesson from this text is that immersion in water is an element of saving belief. Like Peter on the Day of Pentecost (Acts 2: 38), Paul portrays baptism as that moment in the plan of salvation when a believer connects with the Holy Spirit.

Acts 22: 16

Saul, who later became the Apostle Paul, was an early opponent of the first century church. He is first introduced by Luke as he recorded the events surrounding the death of Stephen, a man who had been chosen as one of seven servants in Jerusalem. Stephen's teaching angered the Sanhedrin and other Jews in Jerusalem to such a degree that they killed him. Luke wrote:

> When they had driven him out of the city, they began stoning *him*; and the witnesses laid aside their robes at the feet of a young man named Saul. (Acts 7: 58)

How much this episode influenced Saul, Luke does not say; although he does indicate that Saul "…was in hearty agreement with putting him to death" (Acts 8: 1). After Stephen's death, Saul was resolute in his persecution of believers. He "…began ravaging the church, entering house after house, and dragging off men and women, he would put them in prison" (Acts 8: 3).

What was interesting about Saul is that he was religiously sincere. He believed he was doing God's will by attacking the church. To him, the believers were spewing lies that countered everything he believed about God and his relationship with the Jewish nation. Hence, they must be dealt with quickly and severely.

After Stephen's death, the disciples scattered to other regions in Judea and Samaria. Anxious to hunt them down, Saul sought and received permission to extend his search for believers beyond the immediacy of Jerusalem. His first stop was to be Damascus, where he had received permission from the synagogues located there to round up any believers who might be seeking refuge in the area.

God had other plans for Saul. He was a chosen vessel through whom God would present his gospel message to the Gentile nations. As he traveled toward Damascus, the Lord intercepted Saul, blinding him with a bright light. Realizing he had been on the wrong side of a spiritual battle Saul asked the Lord what he should do. He was told to continue to Damascus where he would receive instructions. There he later received his sight and was immersed into Christ.

According to Paul, as he recounted his own conversion experience for some Jews in Jerusalem, after three days in Damascus, and while he was still blind, a man by the name of Ananias came to see him. Through this man, God restored his eyesight. Not only did Ananias explain the gospel message to Saul, but he told him that he (Saul) was a chosen vessel of God. The conversation culminated in these words from Ananias to Saul:

> Now why do you delay? Get up and be baptized, and wash away your sins, calling on His name. (Acts 22: 16)

It seems clear, and well in keeping with other passages that tie baptism to purification (Matthew 3: 6; Acts 2: 38; Ephesians 5: 25-26; Hebrews 10: 22), that Ananias was telling Saul to be baptized for the forgiveness of his sins. That is the basic understanding one derives from a candid reading of this verse. Still, as with other passages that offer a salvific view of baptism, Ananias's instructions have faced a spirited challenge.

The protest against these words by Ananias is two-fold. Some believe that the baptism mentioned in this setting is not immersion in water, but a purely *spiritual* baptism that Saul was commanded to experience. However, a biblical three-way connection between water, baptism, and purification was established earlier, and that principle applies here. In this case, baptism and forgiveness are linked, helping the reader to understand that what Ananias has in mind is immersion in water.

Others teach that, while Saul may well have been immersed, his forgiveness came by "calling on His name," with baptism as a separate matter of obedience. In other words, what Ananias told Saul is that, in addition to baptism, he must wash away his sins *by* calling on the name of the Lord. As with the claim that Saul was not instructed to submit to immersion in water, this proposition challenges even-handed analysis. The claim that Saul's forgiveness was unrelated to his participation in baptism requires innovative exegesis that ignores some basic principles of interpretation.

The use of the middle voice (be baptized...wash away...calling) is indicative of Saul's active participation in the commands (imperatives) that are given while the actions are also conferred upon him. The imperatives of this verse carry the same meaning as those spoken by Peter on the Day of Pentecost (Acts 2: 38). At that time, Peter told the crowd to be baptized for the forgiveness of sins. In similar fashion,

Ananias explained to Saul that he must be immersed (in water), washing away his sins. The phrase *apolousai tas hamartias sou* literally means *have your sins bathed off*. Ananias was telling Saul: *Get yourself baptized, bathing away your sins*. The language provides a natural connection between the *bathing away* of sins and the water of baptism. This is in keeping with the purifying nature of the rite of baptism that was discussed earlier where it was identified as the time of forgiveness.[13]

One thing that is prevalent in baptismal instruction in the New Testament, but seems to be absent from this verse, is the teaching that Saul should be baptized *in Jesus' name*...or is it absent? On the Day of Pentecost, Peter, citing the prophet Joel, noted that the day would come (and this was it) when all who called on the name of the Lord would be saved (Acts 2: 21). Subsequently, when those in the crowd asked what they should do, Peter told them to first repent and then submit to baptism *in Jesus' name*. Since no other means of calling on his name is depicted in Scripture, it is apparent that Peter considered baptism the very manner in which sinners should *call on his name*.

Ananias did not tell Saul to *call on* or *call out to* the Lord. Instead, he was to *call on his name*. The command to call on Jesus' *name* is a subtle but important distinction. This difference becomes even more evident and more significant by more closely examining the Greek word that most interpreters translate as *calling on*.

The word *epikaloumenos* does not suggest the idea of *calling out to* someone, as some might suspect. It is the same word Peter used in citing Joel's prophecy about those who *call on* the name of the Lord (Acts 2: 21), and it means to *invoke*. To invoke a name is to *reference* that name or person in some fashion. For instance, when Paul stood before Festus, he invoked (epikaloumai) Caesar's name (Acts 25: 11). He did not call out to Caesar directly, but appealed to his authority in order to seek justice for himself. He petitioned Festus *in Caesar's name*.

By whatever means Saul's sins would be forgiven, it involved *invoking* the Lord's name. However, calling on his name is not the same as *calling on him* any more than invoking the name of Caesar involved speaking to him directly. The path to forgiveness involves *invoking/applying* Jesus' name, not calling out to him. It is a matter of making an appeal *in his name*. This indicates that neither Peter nor

---

[13] See Chapter 16, The Effects of Baptism: Baptism and the Forgiveness of Sins (Justification), 232.

Ananias told their listeners to pray to Jesus for forgiveness as a matter of salvation, as so many have suggested.

Ananias did not tell Saul to *call on the Lord*, but to *invoke his name*. He did not tell him to *be baptized* and, as a separate matter, *wash away his sins*. In a true rendering of this text – *Get up and be baptized, and wash away your sins, invoking His name* – it is clear that, as on the Day of Pentecost, baptism in Jesus' name results in forgiveness of sins.

Notice that the Sinner's Prayer is conspicuously and necessarily absent from the text. It is conspicuously absent in that many believe this is what Ananias meant by the expression "calling on His name." It is necessarily absent because Ananias knew nothing of the Sinner's Prayer. He had not heard of the Sinner's Prayer because it was not introduced into the world of religion until the late 1800's.[14] The timing of this doctrine indicates that it did not originate with the apostles.[15]

One can gain valuable insight into the lesson of a text by giving consideration to the audience response.[16] In the book of Acts, Luke describes people responding to the command to *call on the name of the Lord* (cf. Acts 2: 21-41; 9: 17-18; 22: 16).[17] Yet there is no moment on these occasions when anyone prayed a prayer seeking forgiveness. In each episode, those listening to the message responded by submitting to baptism in (invoking) Jesus' name.

In this passage, "calling on His name" represents the faith involved in the process of forgiveness as one is immersed into Christ. This phrase appears here in aorist form rather than imperative. In other words, Saul was to be baptized (imperative/command) and get his sins washed away (imperative/command) *while* invoking (aorist) the name of the Lord.

A sinner cannot seek forgiveness from God on his own. Humans have no standing that God should grant forgiveness or even hear the plea from an unrighteous person. Therefore, one must rely on Jesus as mediator and seek cleansing through his blood or remain lost. Those are the choices. Invoking (trusting in) Jesus' name as a matter of faith is what positions the sinner for forgiveness during baptism. The down-to-earth translations of *The Simple English Bible, The Bible in Basic*

---

[14] See Appendix B, The Sinner's Prayer, 322.
[15] See Preface: The Timing of Doctrine, 12.
[16] See Chapter 2, Systematic Theology: Considering the Results/Audience Response, 27.
[17] Acts 9 and Acts 22 record the same episode and must be combined to read the complete account of Saul's conversion.

English, the *Common English Bible*, and *The Jerusalem Bible*, cited here respectively, make this point abundantly clear.

> Now, don't wait any longer. Rise up, get yourself immersed and get your sins washed away, trusting in his name.

> And now, why are you waiting? Get up, and have baptism, for the washing away of your sins, giving worship to his name.

> What are you waiting for? Get up, be baptized, and wash away your sins as you call on his name.

> And now why delay? It's time you were baptized and had your sins washed away while invoking his name.

When someone submits to baptism *in Jesus' name*, God no longer sees a sinner. Rather, he views that person through the prism of Christ's blood by which sins are washed away. This is the lesson from the words of Peter on the Day of Pentecost (Acts 2: 38). It is also what Ananias had in mind when he told Paul to *be baptized and bathe away his sins* (Acts 22: 16).

Chapter 19

Christian Baptism in the Epistles

Romans 6: 1-4

One passage that defines the relationship between baptism and freedom from sin in no uncertain terms is found in the book of Romans. Early in the sixth chapter of Romans, Paul writes about forgiveness and regeneration (vs. 1-4). However, Paul does not end his discourse there. He continues his train of thought through the balance of the chapter. Through the course of the chapter, he ties everything back to the believer's participation in baptism, employing the words "For" (Gr. *gar* meaning *because*) eight times and "Therefore" twice in his effort to maintain the connection with his comments on baptism. The final verse of the chapter (v. 23) joins together the entire passage concerning the theme of forgiveness of sins that permeates these verses. Note the connection (below) between the first four verses and the final verse of Paul's words on forgiveness.

> ¹What shall we say then? Are we to continue in sin so that grace may increase? ² May it never be! How shall we who died to sin still live in it? ³ Or do you not know that all of us who have been baptized into Christ Jesus have been baptized into His death? ⁴ Therefore we have been buried with Him through baptism into death, so that as Christ was raised from the dead through the glory of the Father, so we too might walk in newness of life… ²³ For the wages of sin is death, but the free gift of God is eternal life in Christ Jesus our Lord. (Romans 6: 1-4, 23)

Paul's thoughts from beginning to end focus not only on forgiveness, but on the newness of life the believer experiences. He compares freedom from sin to freedom from slavery. On the heels of his comments on forgiveness and newness of life at the time of baptism (vs. 1-4), Paul says this:

> ⁵ For if we have become united with *Him* in the likeness of His death, certainly we shall also be *in the likeness* of His resurrection, ⁶ knowing this, that our old self was crucified with *Him*, in order

that our body of sin might be done away with, so that we would no longer be slaves to sin; ⁷ for he who has died is freed from sin. (Romans 6: 5-7)

The figure of slavery continues through the chapter. From Paul's perspective, the Romans' freedom from slavery to sin came through obedience in baptism.

¹⁷ But thanks be to God that though you were slaves of sin, you became obedient from the heart to that form of teaching to which you were committed, ¹⁸ and having been freed from sin, you became slaves of righteousness. (Romans 6: 17-18)

To what "form of teaching" (v. 17) had these believers been obedient? Paul's initial thoughts in this section tie relief from sins to burial in baptism. Forgiveness at the time of baptism is the very heart of his message early in the chapter. It is an inescapable truth that the apostle links baptism with one's *new life* (v. 4).

It is important to note one especially intriguing aspect of the relationship between baptism and forgiveness/salvation that is revealed in Paul's words. While the apostle points to baptism as the time of one's renewal (v. 4), that does not affect his characterization of eternal life as a free gift (v. 23). Evidently Paul did not see a contradiction between baptism as a condition of salvation and God freely *gifting* salvation through Jesus Christ.

1 Corinthians 1: 12-17

The problems facing the local church at Corinth were formidable. Divisions in the body had arisen over assorted issues. Interestingly, one item that was causing problems was baptism. This is surprising given Paul's extensive teaching on the subject. However, a close look at the nature of the division reveals that the Corinthians had taken Paul's teaching on baptism in a direction the apostle did not intend. Rather than questioning the necessity or significance of baptism, these people had formed cliques based on the name of their baptizer. Those baptized by Paul considered that to be a matter of pride. Others who were baptized by Apollos identified themselves as such.

Paul was frustrated by the situation. He did not want the fact that he had baptized someone to be a matter of division. Baptism was not about Paul, or about any individual who *performed* baptism. It was always and only about Christ. Paul responded by contending the insignificance, not of baptism, but of the one who performed the rite.

He expressed relief that he personally had baptized few, thus averting claims of baptism in the name of Paul.

What is most interesting is Paul's view of the role of baptism as a matter of identification. He believed and taught that baptism had the *effect* of association.

> [12] Now I mean this, that each one of you is saying, "I am of Paul," and "I of Apollos," and "I of Cephas," and "I of Christ." [13] Has Christ been divided? Paul was not crucified for you, was he? Or were you baptized in the name of Paul? [14] I thank God that I baptized none of you except Crispus and Gaius, [15] so that no one would say you were baptized in my name. [16] Now I did baptize also the household of Stephanas; beyond that, I do not know whether I baptized any other.
> (1 Corinthians 1: 12-13)

The people of Corinth believed they were "of Paul" or "of Cephas" based on the baptism they had received. Paul made it clear that those he had baptized should not identify with him, but his explanation tells a deeper story. Paul and the Corinthians understood that baptism was a matter of identification with the one who had died for them and the one in whose name they were baptized. However, neither of these stipulations applied to Paul. It was Christ who had died for them and it was in his name that they were baptized, making them "of Christ."

> For Christ did not send me to baptize, but to preach the gospel.
> (1 Corinthians 1: 17a)

A number of modern-day scholars have taken considerable liberty with Paul's follow-up statement respecting his role as a preacher. They have concluded that, with this remark, Paul effectively neutralizes any biblical link between baptism and the gospel message. This is neither a fair nor honest assessment of the text since the apostle is not addressing the content of the gospel message at this time. It also gives rise to conflict between this statement and those passages where baptism is clearly identified as an element of the gospel message (cf. Matthew 28: 19-20; Mark 16: 15-16; Acts 2: 38; 1 Peter 3: 21).

Insisting that Paul is attempting to differentiate between baptism and the gospel for the Corinthians, many like to place the emphases of the statement on *baptize* and *gospel*. This approach ignores Paul's point of the narrative. He is distinguishing, not between an action (baptize) and a subject (the gospel), but between two actions. In that case, Paul wrote, "For Christ did not send me to *baptize*, but to *preach* the gospel" (emphasis added). Thus, he contrasts the *action* of baptizing against the *action* of preaching. In fact, accenting these two actions, which is where the emphasis belongs, leaves a strong impression that the *gospel* would be associated with both *baptizing* and *preaching*.

Paul's reflection upon his assigned role of preaching is an example of an elliptical statement, a form of Greek syntax that is used in Scripture to offer emphasis. Specifically, the speaker/writer uses the phrase *ou...alla* (not...but), or something comparable, to accentuate one matter over another. Paul's remark, "For Christ did not (ou) send me to baptize, but (alla) to preach..." simply punctuates his primary focus. This would not preclude Paul from baptizing, which he clearly did, but highlights his role as a teacher.

Similar use of the ellipsis can be found in a number of passages in the New Testament. Later in the same epistle, Paul offered the following words of wisdom:

Nobody should seek his own good, but the good of others. (1 Corinthians 10: 24)

This is another fine example of elliptical language. Paul was not telling the Corinthians that they should not seek their own good but was highlighting the responsibility of Christians to seek the good of others. In this instance, Paul is comparing one's *own good* to the *good of others*. What he is not doing is contrasting *seeking* and the *good of others*. One is an action, the other an ideal. They cannot be compared. *Seeking* is related to both one's *own good* and the *good of others*. The same is true in his remark in the first chapter where his call to *baptize* is contrasted against his call to *preach*. Baptizing cannot be compared to the *gospel*, but it can be compared to preaching, which was Paul's point.

The use of an elliptical statement can be powerful. It is a method by which the writer seemingly overshadows something significant with the one where emphasis is placed. The point is not to diminish the former but to accentuate the latter. The assumption that Paul's remark somehow eliminates baptism from the gospel message can be summarily dismissed. The elliptical nature of the statement, accenting one element without excluding another, is confirmed by the very fact that Paul did, indeed, baptize many believers.

1 Corinthians 12: 13

One of the many blessings men receive upon submission to baptism is membership in the body of Christ (the church). This connection was established on the Day of Pentecost when those who were baptized were *added to* the church (Acts 2: 41).

Paul's words support what Luke wrote in the book of Acts. Because of the divisions that had formed in the congregation in Corinth, Paul sought to deliver words of unification. He did not want the church to be separated by petty disagreements and jealous wrangling. In the first chapter of 1 Corinthians, Paul addresses the fact that the Corinthians had formed cliques founded solely upon the identity of the individual by whom they had been baptized (1 Corinthians 1: 11-17), voicing his disappointment with their misdirected devotion toward people rather than Christ.

Continuing with his concerns over the discord that had cropped up, beginning in the twelfth chapter Paul addresses the resentment that had evidently invaded the church there with respect to spiritual gifts. While the exact details are not given, the narrative suggests that those with rather modest gifts may have become envious of others who had received what they considered to be some of the more colorful gifts (i.e., speaking in tongues, prophesying, healing, etc.).

Paul's goal was to dissolve these rifts by focusing on unity within the body. Using his gift of discourse, Paul uses figurative language in order to explain spiritual truths in a way the Corinthians could appreciate. He likens the church to the human body, noting that the individual members of the church should serve to provide balance within Christ's body just as the various parts of the human body complement each other (1 Corinthians 12: 12-26). As he begins, Paul makes an observation that establishes the foundation for the truth he is about to share, stating:

> [12] For even as the body is one and *yet* has many members, and all the members of the body, though they are many, are one body, so also is Christ. [13] For by one Spirit we were all baptized into one body. (1 Corinthians 12: 12-13a)

All Christians are baptized into one body. This is a profound statement that provides support for a couple of powerful biblical principles. First of all, Paul explains that *all* believers are immersed, noting that "we were all baptized" (v. 13). No Christian is excluded here. There is nothing about this statement that addresses the un-immersed. Second, and equally important, he recognizes the fact that baptism provides entry "into one body" (v. 13).

Some have proposed that the baptism of this verse does not represent immersion in water, but that Paul is writing of the same outpouring of the Holy Spirit that was experienced by the apostles on the Day of Pentecost (Acts 2: 1-4) and later by the Gentiles in Caesarea (Acts 10: 44-46). Perhaps the primary reason for this claim is that the surrounding discussion addresses spiritual gifts, including tongues, such as occurred on those occasions. This seems to be a significant leap, however. There is no other occasion in his epistles where Paul wrote about those incidents (the outpouring of the Spirit). Also, Scripture establishes no direct connection between the outpouring of the Spirit that is depicted in those episodes and membership in the body of Christ.

Others believe and teach that it is not the outpouring of the Spirit or immersion in water that is in view in this passage, but a salvific presence of the Spirit that begins at the time of one's regeneration and takes place prior to immersion in water. It is presumed that this spiritual baptism (sans water) supplanted immersion in water at some enigmatic moment during the ministry of the apostles, effectively rescinding Jesus' words in the Great Commission (Matthew 28: 19-20) and superseding Peter's instructions on the Day of Pentecost (Acts 2: 38). There is no scriptural support for this teaching, although there is ample biblical evidence that spiritual baptism occurs when one is immersed in water in Jesus' name (Acts 2: 38; 19; 1-6; 22: 16).

The idea that baptism in the epistles might represent something other than immersion in water originated in the nineteenth century with an Anglican clergyman by the name of E. W. Bullinger (1837-1913). Prior to Bullinger, the word *baptism* in the New Testament epistles was consistently recognized as water baptism unless the context demanded a figurative application (i.e., 1 Corinthians 10: 2). It is difficult to credit Paul with a baptismal doctrine that was not conceived until nearly two thousand years after his death.

Others insist that baptism *by the Spirit*, or *in the Spirit* (in the Greek the wording is the same), generally designates the presence of the Holy Spirit within the believer and that this presence begins when one is immersed in water (Acts 2: 38). The connection between immersion in water and membership in the body, which was discussed earlier, was established on the Day of Pentecost (Acts 2: 41).

Nothing within the confines of this epistle directs the reader away from immersion in water in 1 Corinthians 12: 13. Indeed, the very first topic Paul addresses with the Corinthians is the rift over water baptism (1 Corinthians 1: 10-17). The baptism mentioned earlier in the epistle could only be immersion in water since Paul acknowledges that he had occasionally taken on the role of baptizer.

Later, Paul wrote about a washing in the Spirit (clearly pointing to a spiritual cleansing) that takes place *in Jesus' name* (1 Corinthians 6: 11). Scholars generally acknowledge the influence of immersion in water upon this verse. The consensus is grounded in the fact that Scripture conjoins cleansing and the rite of baptism, leading to the conclusion that immersion in water is in view. This point is reflected in various commentaries on this verse.

> St. Paul...presumes that baptism realizes its design, and that those outwardly baptized inwardly enter into communion with Christ (Gal. iii: 27). He presents the grand ideal which those alone realize in whom the inward and the outward baptism coalesce.[18]

> Ye are washed, απελουσασθε; ye have been baptized into the Christian faith, and ye have promised in this baptism to put off all filthiness of the flesh and spirit.[19]

Baptism is also mentioned figuratively earlier in 1 Corinthians as Paul notes that the Israelites of old had been baptized into Moses (1 Corinthians 10: 2). By this, it seems Paul viewed the Israelites following Moses through the sea as recognition of, and submission to, his leadership and authority. Finally, Paul wrote briefly about the practice of baptism for the dead (1 Corinthians 15: 29), which appears to portray people being baptized (immersed in water) on behalf of the souls of the dead.

None of Paul's other references to baptism in this epistle suggests that he steered away from water in 1 Corinthians 12: 13. Other than the figurative *baptism into Moses*, every time Paul regards baptism in this epistle, he speaks of immersion in water. Consequently, remaining true to apostolic doctrine requires accepting the meaning of immersion in water, which is what Paul intended.

When Paul states, "by one Spirit we were all baptized," he directs the readers' attention to membership in the body. The correlation, then, is not to the outpouring of the Spirit or a spiritual regeneration at

---

[18] Jamieson, Robert, A. R. Fausset, and David Brown. *A Commentary on the Old and New Testaments, Volume 3*, 298.

[19] Clarke, Adam. *Adam Clarke Commentary*, 1 Corinthians 6, http://www.studylight.org/commentaries/acc/view.cgi?bk=45&ch=6.

some unidentified moment in time, but to the words of Peter and Luke from the Day of Pentecost. Peter promised the Holy Spirit to those who were baptized (Acts 2: 38) and Luke depicted baptism as the defining moment when believers were added to the body of Christ (Acts 2: 41).

Galatians 3: 23-27

Paul often contrasted the covenants of law and grace in his letters. Nowhere does he outline their differences more clearly than in his words to the Galatians. Perhaps the most significant distinction, in Paul's view, is that the old covenant was a covenant of law while the new covenant is one of promise (Galatians 3: 16-18). What Paul brings to light is that the covenant of grace was actually arranged prior to the law. The promise of this covenant, which is in essence the covenant itself, was given to Abraham. The law was delivered centuries later as an interim step until the preparations for fulfillment of the promise could be completed (Galatians 3: 19).

As a provisional measure, the law was limited. Its rules and regulations essentially imprisoned the Israelites (Galatians 3: 23), since the sacrifices stipulated under the law could not provide the cleansing from sin that would be necessary for mankind to be reconciled to God (Hebrews 10: 11). The law simply served as a stop-gap platform for worship until the time came when believers could experience true justification, worshiping God through faith in Christ (Galatians 3: 24).

Paul recognized that he was living the promise Abraham had been given. The law had been fulfilled and the covenant of grace established. His words to the Galatians are meant to provide them with some insight into that covenant and some perspective on their status before God.

The apostle places considerable emphasis on baptism in this passage even though faith is recognized as the means of justification. Modern scholarship has attempted to isolate baptism from faith, but Paul does not. Instead, he binds them together. Even in the presence of faith, baptism is relevant according to Paul. Prior to the covenant of grace, even the faithful were kept under guard by the law. However, when it comes to faith in the new covenant, baptism is a central matter in the design of God's plan. People are baptized into (the name of) Christ (v. 27). Like Peter, Paul saw baptism as a passageway through which a person could find his/her way into Christ.[20] Rather than portraying baptism as merely *a* passageway, Paul states that it is *the* passageway into Christ.

The apostle makes two important points in this passage. First, he notes that *all* of his readers were "...sons of God through faith" (v. 26). The word *pantes* (a form of *pas*), translated *all*, is inclusive. It indicates that *all* of those to whom he was writing (the Christians in Galatia) could consider themselves to be God's children.

He also explains that *clothing oneself* with Christ is limited to "...all of you who were baptized" (Galatians 3: 27). The term *hosoi,* translated "all of you," indicates those who shared a common trait or experience – a point made in Chapter 14 when discussing Acts 13: 48. What Paul is saying is that those who had been baptized into Christ had been *clothed with Christ* (become a child of God). However, it is *only* those who have been baptized who had clothed themselves with Christ. Nothing in Paul's statement suggests that those who had not been immersed had so clothed themselves.

Having explained that justification comes through faith (vs. 23-26), Paul begins verse twenty-seven with an interesting word. It is the word *for*, which is translated from the Greek word *gar* and as discussed earlier, this word *assigns a reason* to the statement(s) made. Reviewing the text with this in mind, take note of the careful manner in which Paul designed his remarks:

> [23] But before faith came, we were kept in custody under the law, being shut up to the faith which was later to be revealed. [24] Therefore the Law has become our tutor *to lead us* to Christ, so that we may be justified by faith. [25] But now that faith has come, we are no longer under a tutor. [26] For (the reason is) you are all sons of God through faith in Christ Jesus. [27] For (the reason is) all of you (hosoi) who were baptized into Christ have clothed yourselves with Christ. (Galatians 3: 23-27)

If earnest consideration is given, it is not possible to misconstrue Paul's message. The bond he establishes between the Galatians' baptism and their relationship with God is unmistakable. According to Paul, the reason the Galatians had been justified *by* faith (v. 24) and were no longer under a tutor (v. 25) is that they were now sons of God *through* faith (v. 26). The reason they were deemed to be sons of God *through* faith is that having been baptized *into* Christ, they had *clothed*

---

[20] See also 1 Corinthians 12: 13. Baptism serves as an *entranceway* into the body of Christ.

themselves with Christ (v. 27). Paul points to their baptism as the very reason they were justified by faith. Here are some insights on this passage from some learned men:

> He clothes us with the righteousness of Christ by means of Baptism, as the Apostle says in this verse: "As many of you as have been baptized into Christ have put on Christ." With this change of garments, a new birth, a new life stirs in us.[21]

> Ye *did, in that very act* of being baptized into Christ, *put on,* or clothe yourselves with, Christ: so the *Greek* expresses…This proves that baptism, *where it answers to its ideal,* is not a mere empty sign, but a means of spiritual transference from the state of legal condemnation to that of living union with Christ, and of sonship through Him in relation to God (Ro 13:14).[22]

According to the apostle, it is not those who have faith who are "sons of God" and "clothed with Christ," but those who have been "baptized into Christ" as a matter of faith. This is the only reasonable explanation for this verse, primarily because it is not an interpretation. There is no need to interpret anything since there is nothing mysterious or ambiguous in Paul's words.

Many have attempted to transform this verse. Some have insisted that immersion in water is not in view. Others place *clothing oneself with Christ* before baptism, but with baptism in view. Yet, every such attempt necessitates the use of some innovative scheme that ultimately harms the flow of the text. As written, Paul stipulates here that it is the immersed individual who has been clothed with Christ.

Ephesians 5: 25-26

More than once the Bible compares the human marital relationship and the bond between Christ and the church. The church is depicted as the bride of Christ numerous times in Revelation. Similarly, the Apostle John reported a conversation between John the Baptist and his disciples during which the bride/bridegroom correlative is rendered in conjunction with their discussion of purification through baptism (John 3: 25-29). Also, these words from the Apostle Paul offer the same analogy:

---

[21] Luther, Martin. *Galatians Commentary* (3:20-29), Project Wittenberg, http://www.iclnet.org/pub/resources/text/wittenberg/luther/gal/web/gal3-20.html.
[22] Jamieson, Robert, A. R. Fausset, and David Brown. *A Commentary on the Old and New Testaments, Volume 3,* 385.

> ²⁵ Husbands, love your wives, just as Christ also loved the church and gave Himself up for her, ²⁶ so that He might sanctify her, having cleansed her by the washing of water with the word. (Ephesians 5: 25-26)

The bride/bridegroom portraiture is figurative, but Paul uses it to make his point here in Ephesians. He seems to be delivering a dual message about the relationship. Certainly, the idea is that a man should love his wife as Jesus loves the church, focusing on the sacrifice he made on her behalf. However, there is also a powerful statement about the moment the bride is presented to the groom "having cleansed her by the washing of water with the word, that He might present to Himself the church in all her glory, having no spot or wrinkle or any such thing; but that she would be holy and blameless" (vs. 26-27).

Paul reminds the believers in Ephesus that they had received "washing of water with the word." The fact that he is reminding them of their participation in baptism is supported by many scholars who embrace Paul's imagery in this verse:

> **and cleanse** (katharisos, *contemporaneous with hagiase*) 'cleansing,' without the "and." **with the washing of water** (τω λοντπω) -- "by the *laver* of *the* water," viz., *the* baptismal water.[23]

> All commentators of repute in all bodies refer this to baptism. All in the church pass through the waters of baptism. But the washing of the water would be of no avail without the *word*. The power is in the word of the Lord which offers the gospel and commands baptism.[24]

> With the washing of water - Baptism, accompanied by the purifying influences of the Holy Spirit.
> By the word - The doctrine of Christ crucified, through which baptism is administered, sin canceled, and the soul purified from all unrighteousness; the death of Christ giving efficacy to all. [25]

> The allusion is to baptism.[26]

> That he might sanctify it through the word - The ordinary channel of all blessings. Having cleansed it - From the guilt and power of sin.

---

[23] Ibid., 418
[24] Johnson, B. W. *The People's New Testament*, 203.
[25] Clarke, Adam. *Adam Clarke Commentary*, Ephesians 5,
http://www.studylight.org/commentaries/acc/view.cgi?bk=48&ch=5.
[26] Vincent, Marvin R. *Vincent's Word Studies*, Ephesians 5,
http://www.studylight.org/commentaries/vnt/view.cgi?bk=48&ch=5.

By the washing of water - In baptism; if, with the outward and visible sign, we receive the inward and spiritual grace.[27]

The three-way connection between water, baptism, and purification must be given its due when considering Paul's words. Where water and purification are joined together, the reference is consistently to immersion in water. This is true in the gospels as John the Baptist baptized countless Jews. It is also true in the book of Acts where Luke records the baptism of many believers. The same pattern appears in the epistles, albeit in retrospect fashion.

Colossians 2: 11-14

It seems the Colossians were facing issues similar to those faced by the Galatians. They were perhaps on the precipice of falling for some false teachings. In the case of the Colossians it appears, given some subtle and not so subtle remarks in the first chapter of the epistle, that certain Gnostic teachings had infiltrated the body in Colossè. Gnostics placed more emphasis on knowledge than on faith. According to the Gnostics, they were more enlightened than other believers, claiming a special revelatory knowledge of God's truth. They denied that Christ took on absolute human form, also insisting that the God of the Old Testament, who created the world, was subordinate to another truly Supreme Being. Some at Colossè were apparently being influenced by these claims.

As the second chapter unfolds, Paul explains his great concern for the believers in Colossè and quickly moves to the reason for his concern. He did not want them to be swayed by false teachings (v. 4). From there he spells out the kind of teachings of which they should beware. He wanted them to avoid being derailed by "…philosophy, empty deception, tradition of men, and elementary principles of the world" (v. 8). All of these were contrary to the teaching of the apostles. Having laid out what they should reject, Paul reminds them of the teachings they had received.

> [11] …and in Him you were also circumcised with a circumcision made without hands, in the removal of the body of the flesh by the circumcision of Christ; [12] having been buried with Him in baptism, in which you were also raised up with Him through faith in the working of God, who raised Him from the dead. [13] When

---

[27] Wesley, John. *Wesley's Explanatory Notes*, Ephesians 5, http://www.studylight.org/commentaries/wen/view.cgi?bk=48&ch=5.

you were dead in your transgressions and the uncircumcision of your flesh, He made you alive together with Him, having forgiven us all our transgressions, ¹⁴ having canceled out the certificate of debt consisting of decrees against us, which was hostile to us; and He has taken it out of the way, having nailed it to the cross. (Colossians 2: 11-14)

With vivid imagery, Paul portrays believers as having been *under the knife*, so to speak, as their old life of sin was removed, likening the operation to the circumcision of the Old Testament (v. 11). He then continues, explaining exactly how and when this had occurred. They had experienced this operation, "having been buried with Him in baptism" (v. 12). The aorist *having been buried* places the timing of the removal of sins no earlier than one's submission to baptism. Other passages portray forgiveness taking place during baptism (Acts 2: 38; 22: 16; Romans 6: 4).

Paul is describing the work of God that takes place during one's immersion in water. Just as they were buried with him (in baptism), so they were raised with him. While the act itself is physical in nature, it is God who is at work performing the aforesaid operation. For him it is a spiritual work, but for the believer it is an act of faith in his work (v. 12). The disciples had been (sinfully) dead but were made alive, having been forgiven (v. 13). The aorist "having forgiven us" connects to "having been buried" as additional support for the view that forgiveness occurs during the burial and resurrection of baptism.

As with teaching on baptism in other epistles, this one is retrospective. Paul is writing about something his readers had previously experienced. In this case, he portrays sin being surgically removed as one submits to the waters of baptism in Jesus' name. He reminds them of their experience of baptism, picturing Christ's death, burial, and resurrection, and describing baptism as the time when:

- the body of the flesh had been removed by the circumcision of Christ (v. 11)
- they had been buried with him (v. 12)
- they had been raised with him (v. 12)
- they had done this through faith in God's work (v. 12)
- they were made alive with him (v. 13)
- their sins were forgiven (v. 13)
- their debt had been canceled (v. 14)
- their debt/transgressions had been nailed to the cross (v. 14)

Many people struggle with the notion that a physical act such as baptism might have spiritual results. This passage should alleviate those concerns. Just as Jesus' death, which was a physical act, had significant spiritual effect, so during baptism, as he is "buried with Him through faith," the believer is transformed spiritually into one of God's own through the work of the Spirit.

Titus 3: 5-7

A number of times in his epistles Paul expounds upon the cleansing character of baptism, depicting it as a *washing*, or *bath*. His letter to Titus is one such occasion. What is interesting about this text is that Paul calls to mind so many elements of baptism in so few words. For instance, he portrays it as a regenerative washing (cleansing). He also notes the spiritual renewal that occurs during baptism along with the Holy Spirit's role as one who affects that renewal (John 3: 5; Acts 2: 38).

> ⁵ He saved us, not on the basis of deeds which we have done in righteousness, but according to His mercy, by the washing of regeneration and renewing by the Holy Spirit, ⁶ whom He poured out upon us richly through Jesus Christ our Savior, ⁷ so that being justified by His grace we would be made heirs according to *the* hope of eternal life. (Titus 3: 5-7)

Paul begins by recalling that God "saved us, not on the basis of deeds which we have done" (v. 5). Here he echoes his claim that people are saved "not as a result of works" (Ephesians 2: 9). The fact that salvation is not by works begs the question: *On what basis are men saved?* In the Ephesians text, Paul answers the question by stating, "But God, being rich in mercy… made us alive together with Christ (by grace you have been saved)" (Ephesians 2: 4-5). He reiterates that point a few verses later, claiming, "For by grace you have been saved through faith" (Ephesians 2: 8). How, then, does he answer that same question here? He explained to Titus that "He saved us…according to His mercy, by the washing of regeneration and renewing by the Holy Spirit…being justified by his grace" (v. 5, 7).

Two principles of biblical interpretation come into play when explaining Paul's seemingly contradictory words about salvation in these two epistles. The first is the context in which Paul writes. In accord with this principle, one must consider the subject matter of the chapter and book under consideration, the situation behind the writing, and the identity of those being addressed.[28] The second principle is biblical harmony.[29] In other words, what Paul wrote to the Ephesians cannot contradict what he wrote to Titus. If these principles are applied honestly, what Paul has in mind in these two passages should become evident.

In his letter to the Ephesians, Paul was writing to the body of believers in Ephesus. These were people who had accepted Jesus as Savior. They had an understanding of the significance of baptism. They had experienced baptism in Jesus' name, which is why Paul was able to effectively refer to the church metaphorically as a bride who received "...the washing of water with the word" (Ephesians 5: 26). Consequently, Paul's words to the Ephesians, when writing about their salvation, centered on the grace/faith aspect of that salvation (Ephesians 2: 8-9).

The topic of conversation in the Ephesians letter prior to Paul's words about salvation centers on the changed lives of the believers in that congregation, which were grounded in faith (Ephesians 1: 15-23), contrasted against the lives they lived prior, when they were "...dead in your trespasses and sins" (Ephesians 2: 1). According to Paul, it was God's mercy and grace that made the difference.

In his words to the Ephesians, Paul recognizes *mercy* and *grace* as the means of salvation just as he does in his letter to Titus. In Titus he points to *mercy* as the principle whereby salvation is made available to those who seek him (v. 5) while stating in essentially the same breath that justification is by grace (v. 7). *Mercy* and *grace* are not identical ideas, but they are complementary. Through God's mercy a person is rescued from deserved punishment. He then bestows an undeserved eternal reward by his grace. Both are crucial to salvation. These two terms express with great clarity the unmerited nature of salvation.

As with his Ephesians teaching, Paul also reiterated for Titus the *path* to salvation, although the emphasis differs slightly. He taught the Ephesians that they are saved "...through faith." However, in his words to Titus, Paul claimed that salvation comes "by the washing of regeneration and renewing by the Holy Spirit." This seems a rather odd departure. Why would Paul, in these two settings, proclaim what appear to be separate paths to salvation – one of faith and one of baptism?

Titus was an evangelist. It was his role to preach the gospel message to unbelievers and to help believers grow in the faith. This is

---

[28] See Chapter 2, Systematic Theology: Disciplined Theology, 24.
[29] See Chapter 3, Principles of Interpretation: Apostolic Repetition and Biblical Harmony, 46.

likely a big part of the difference in these two discussions about salvation. Paul wrote to the Ephesians, who were already saved, not about how to become a Christian, but what it means to be a Christian. In his letter to Titus, Paul focuses on two specific issues. The first item Paul addresses with Titus is leadership in the church (chapter 1). He did this so that Titus could understand what constitutes godly leadership.

Beginning with the second chapter, Paul addresses the importance of teaching sound doctrine. Indeed, he plainly states that he wanted Titus to understand the doctrine he should teach (Titus 2: 1). The apostle then spends the balance of the epistle discussing that doctrine (Titus 2: 2 - 3: 11). With that in mind, Paul recalls for Titus not only what it means to be a Christian, but the process involved in becoming a Christian. He could have reaffirmed faith as the path to salvation, as he did with the Ephesians, but he chose instead to direct Titus's attention to the salvific character of baptism as he did in certain other epistles (Romans 6: 1-4; Galatians 3: 27).

Faith and baptism are knitted together tightly in the New Testament, and their complementary character, like the harmony between mercy and grace, is expressed in these verses. Faith reflects the circumcised heart of the convert in conjunction with his/her acceptance of Christ's sacrifice as a propitiation for sins. Baptism represents the consummation of that faith as one is buried (in water) and raised in Jesus' name. At that time God cleanses the believer of his/her sins with Christ's blood serving as the cleansing agent.

Paul seems to be saying that what is achieved "through faith" (Ephesians) is accomplished during "the washing of regeneration" (Titus). The apostle exchanges *salvation through faith* in Ephesians with *salvation in baptism* in Titus. Baptism is the instrument by which, through faith, people gain access to God's mercy and grace and accept/receive the regenerating work of the Spirit. Indeed, the apostle emphasizes the point that the change in one's life comes at the time of baptism (Titus 3: 3-7).

These two statements by Paul, one to the Ephesians and one to Titus, depict the same process of salvation. In Titus, "the washing of regeneration" (baptism) complements *faith* in Ephesians. If that is not the case, then Paul has contradicted himself by telling Titus that salvation comes other than through faith, but that cannot be true. The only possible explanation, then, is that Paul sees *salvation through faith* and *salvation by the washing of regeneration* as equivalent doctrine.

Some have insisted that this passage does not address water baptism, but scholarship is against them. Bible scholars generally recognize that, in Paul's words to Titus, the apostle has baptism in view with the term *loutrou*. Here are some examples of comments by learned men:

> The word in itself would naturally be understood as referring to baptism.[30]

> By the *washing of regeneration* I have no doubt that he alludes, at least, to baptism, and even I will not object to have this passage expounded as relating to baptism.[31]

> No statement of the New Testament, not even John 3: 5, more unambiguously represents the power of baptism to lie in the operation of the Holy Spirit.[32]

> In light of other New Testament uses of the word *loutron*, and its verb form, *louo*, it would be unreasonable to deny that this is a reference to baptism.[33]

> ...so he speaks of baptism on the supposition that it answers to its idea...whatever is realized when baptism fully corresponds to its original design.[34]

> The phrase laver of regeneration distinctly refers to baptism, in connection with which and through which as a medium regeneration is conceived as taking place.[35]

> By the washing of regeneration and renewing of the Holy Spirit. Two elements enter into the saving; these are referred to in John as the birth of water and of the Spirit (John 3:5). God's spirit effects the renewal of the spirit of man by bringing him to faith and repentance through the preaching of the gospel; thus the renewal of

---

[30] Barnes, Albert. *Barnes' Notes on the Whole Bible*, Titus 3, http://www.studylight.org/commentaries/bnb/view.cgi?bk=55&ch=3.
[31] Calvin, John. *Calvin's Commentary on the Bible*, Titus 3, http://www.studylight.org/commentaries/cal/view.cgi?bk=55&ch=3.
[32] Beasley-Murray, G. R. *Baptism in the New Testament*, 250.
[33] Cottrell, Jack. *Baptism, A Biblical Study*, 135.
[34] Jamieson, Robert, Fausset, A. R., and Brown, David, *Commentary Critical and Explanatory on the Whole Bible*, Titus 3, http://www.studylight.org/commentaries/jfb/view.cgi?bk=55&ch=3.
[35] Vincent, Marvin R. *Vincent's Word Studies*, Titus 3, http://www.studylight.org/commentaries/vnt/view.cgi?bk=55&ch=3.

the Holy Spirit is begun, and the gift of the Holy Spirit is promised as a sequence of baptism (Ro 6:1-8) shows that the sinner dies to sin, is buried by baptism, rises to a new life, and is a new creature. Washing of regeneration is literally, bath of regeneration. All commentators of reputation refer this to baptism, such as Meyer, Olshausen, Lange, Plumptree, Schaff, Canon Cook, Wesley, etc. Regeneration is due to the Holy Spirit, but baptism is an outward act that God requires to complete the fact. The term regeneration only occurs here and Mt 19: 28.[36]

It is difficult to circumvent the apostle's portraiture of baptism in conjunction with God's act of "regeneration and renewing by the Holy Spirit." Paul's words to Titus appear to offer a fuller explanation of what Jesus meant when he told Nicodemus one must be "...born of water and the spirit" (John 3: 5). This explains *how* and *when* one is saved "by grace...through faith" (Ephesians 2: 8), leading to better appreciation of the emphasis that Jesus (Matthew 28: 19), Paul (Romans 6: 1-4; Galatians 3: 27; Colossians 2: 11-12; Titus 3: 5), and Peter (Acts 2: 38; 1 Peter 3: 21) placed on the rite of baptism. Where the plan of salvation is concerned, baptism is a demonstration of faith to which God responds with his regenerating work. Thus, one is saved by grace through faith during submission to baptism.

Hebrews 10: 22-23

The letter of Hebrews, written to Christians of Jewish descent, is wall-to-wall doctrine. From instruction concerning the changing of the covenants to historical examples of faith, little is left unaddressed, and that includes the topic of baptism. The tenth chapter carries a strong allusion to this rite.

> [22] ...let us draw near with a sincere heart in full assurance of faith, having our hearts sprinkled *clean* from an evil conscience and our bodies washed with pure water. [23] Let us hold fast the confession of our hope without wavering, for He who promised is faithful. (Hebrews 10: 22-23)

The phrase, "our bodies washed with pure water" (v. 22) is used in the context of people drawing near (to God). This movement toward God involves four distinct but related features, and it begins with a "sincere heart." Note that it is sincerity of heart and not purity of heart that is required in one's approach to God. All have sinned

---

[36] Johnson, B. W. *The People's New Testament*, 290.

(Romans 3: 23), so purity of heart occurs only when a person has been forgiven. Second, it is necessary to approach God "in full assurance of faith." Third, when the penitent believer approaches in faith, he is cleansed (forgiven) of his sins. This forgiveness entails the fourth feature. It occurs as the heart is "sprinkled clean from an evil conscience" (by the agency of Christ's blood) and the body is "washed with pure water."

Not only is it difficult to escape the portraiture of baptism that is displayed here, but this verse openly depicts the very essence of the ceremony. The author has drawn a picture of baptism as the vehicle of submission to Christ. Despite the refusal of a few to accept the portrayal of baptism that is found here, most readily admit that the author has baptism in view. Here are noteworthy comments from some well-respected men concerning this verse:

> The washing of the body with pure water is surely a reference to baptism.[37]

> The meeting place of the sanctifying power of Christ's death and the individual is the baptism wherein the believer turns to God in faith for cleansing through Christ.[38]

> 'having...hearts *sprinkled*...body [*to soma*] *washed*,' implying a *continuing state* by a once-for-all accomplished act – viz., our justification by faith through Christ's blood and consecration to God...by baptism.[39]

> That there is an allusion to baptism is clear.[40]

> The apostle probably alludes to this in what he says here, though it appears that he refers principally to baptisms, the washing by which was an emblem of the purification of the soul.[41]

> Our bodies washed with pure water, that is, with the water of baptism (by which we are recorded among the disciples of Christ, members of his mystical body).[42]

---

[37] Morris, Leon, and Donald Burdick. *Expositor's Bible Commentary, Hebrews – James*, 104.
[38] Beasley-Murray, G. R. *Baptism in the New Testament*, 250.
[39] Jamieson, Robert, A. R. Fausset, and David Brown. *A Commentary on the Old and New Testaments – Volume 3*, 563.
[40] Barnes, Albert. *Barnes' Notes on the Whole Bible*, Hebrews 10, http://www.studylight.org/commentaries/bnb/view.cgi?bk=57&ch=10.
[41] Clarke, Adam. *Adam Clarke Commentary*, Hebrews 10, http://www.studylight.org/commentaries/acc/view.cgi?bk=57&ch=10.

And our body washed with pure water is beyond all doubt a reference to Christian baptism.[43]

Only a few, like John Calvin and John Gill, have sought to deny that water baptism is referenced in this setting. Yet even Calvin conceded that the comment regarding pure water "…is generally understood of baptism."[44]

In complement to the reports of these many scholars, take note that this passage involves the combination of water and cleansing that, where Scripture is concerned, points deliberately to baptism as discussed earlier.[45] There is every reason to apply that same principle to the current text, since the author causally links spiritual cleansing with a physical washing in water.

That the ceremony of baptism is in view here becomes even more evident in the next verse where the author complements his remarks about the rite (v. 22) with recognition of the confession of Jesus as Lord that historically and naturally accompanies immersion in water (Acts 8: 37; 22: 16). On the heels of "having our hearts sprinkled…and our bodies washed with pure water" he reminds his readers to "hold fast the confession of our hope without wavering" (v. 23).

The author's poetic imagery of the rite of baptism, in juxtaposition with Old Testament rituals, is too forthright to simply fail to notice. He describes baptism as the moment when one draws near to God with an anxious heart, in faith, seeking forgiveness through Christ's blood. In complement with other passages of Scripture (cf. Acts 2: 38; Romans 6: 1-4), the book of Hebrews offers what can only be seen as a detailed portrayal of New Testament baptism as the moment of forgiveness and spiritual renewal.

1 Peter 3: 21

The Apostle Peter was never one to beat around the bush. While his sermons and letters display a degree of eloquence, Peter's words were very much to the point. When he wrote about the suffering believers could anticipate, he did not sugarcoat the message (1 Peter 2: 19-20). Similarly, when he taught about submitting to those in authority, he was quite frank (1 Peter 2: 13). It was just Peter's way.

---

[42] Henry, Matthew. *Matthew Henry's Commentary on the Whole Bible*, 2396.
[43] Coffman, James. *James Burton Coffman Commentaries - Hebrews*, p. 213.
[44] Calvin, John. *Calvin's Commentary on the Bible*, Hebrews 10, http://www.studylight.org/commentaries/cal/view.cgi?bk=57&ch=10.
[45] See Chapter 17, Christian Baptism in the Gospels: John 3: 3-5.

When it came to the plan of salvation, Peter was equally forthright. He did not mince words. When asked on the Day of Pentecost, "What shall we do?" Peter responded with a straightforward "Repent and...be baptized" (Acts 2: 38).

Peter picks up the topic of baptism in his first epistle. Recalling for his readers the flood of Noah's day, Peter notes that at that time, eight people were saved. He drew the attention of his audience to the fact that Noah and his family "...were brought safely through the water." Other translations are even more direct, stating that they "...were saved through water" (NIV, NKJV) or "...saved by water" (KJV). The apostle takes the opportunity to liken baptism to the waters of the flood, claiming that, just as that family was saved through (or by) water, "...baptism now saves you" (1 Peter 3: 21).

Many have insisted that Peter was not proposing in this passage that the *baptism that saves* is immersion in water, since Noah was saved in the ark. Yet, Peter's words are not blurred. The baptism intimated in the twenty-first verse is openly compared, not to the ark, but to the water. Those on the ark "...were saved through water." This is hardly a timid suggestion that baptism might be likened to the waters of the flood. It is a bold proclamation of the fact that, just as Noah and his family were saved through water, so those in the church age are saved in baptism.

It is important to understand that water in itself did not save Noah and his family. There was nothing mystical or magical about the flood waters that caused this family to be rescued. Water was simply the vehicle God used to accomplish his purpose. He provided for the safety of Noah and his family, using the water to separate them from the sinful world that surrounded them. The same is true of baptism. The water itself does not have the ability to save anyone. Still, God has chosen the waters of baptism as the vehicle through which he separates the faithful from the sins of their past.

Peter employed some form of the word *baptism* six times in the New Testament. He commanded it on the Day of Pentecost in conjunction with repentance as a matter of forgiveness (Acts 2: 38). That case involved immersion in water. He also used the word twice when he instructed the Gentiles at the house of Cornelius to be baptized (Acts 10: 47-48). This, too, was immersion in water. Later in Jerusalem, he recalled Jesus' statement about baptism with the Holy Spirit. In that episode the word appears twice, once in reference to the baptism performed by John the Baptist (immersion in water) and once depicting the *outpouring of the Holy Spirit* that the apostles had experienced on the Day of Pentecost and that Peter had witnessed among the Gentiles in Caesarea (Acts 11: 16).

Immersion in water is further evidenced in 1 Peter 3: 21 by the fact that the apostle has spiritual purification in view. He offers a parenthetical remark that is intended to highlight the cleansing character of baptism, stating, "…not the removal of dirt from the flesh, but an appeal to God for a good conscience—through the resurrection of Jesus Christ." That is to say, baptism does not provide physical, but spiritual cleansing. Additionally, Peter claims that baptism draws its efficacy directly from Jesus' resurrection.

This is not the first time in the New Testament that Peter links baptism to redemption (cf. Acts 2: 38), and that fact is not insignificant. It is also noteworthy that Peter's instructions about the redemptive character of baptism echo Paul's instructions on this same topic (cf. Acts 22: 16; Romans 6: 1-4; Colossians 2: 11-12). This is important in that it speaks to apostolic repetition – another interpretive principle. Two Spirit-inspired apostles teaching the same lessons time and again about the redemptive activity that takes place within the framework of baptism could not be wrong.

Chapter 20

Baptism and the Reformation Movement

The Historical View of Baptism in the Church

For the first fifteen centuries of the church, the incontrovertible viewpoint among believers concerning baptism was founded upon Peter's instructions on the Day of Pentecost. It was understood from this and many other passages of Scripture that baptism was intended to serve as the appointed time when one experienced a transformation to a renewed state, receiving forgiveness/salvation. However, during the time of the Reformation Movement in the sixteenth century, men like Luther, Zwingli, and Calvin were seeking to separate themselves from the Roman Catholic Church. They believed the church was traveling an unscriptural path...observing rituals and teaching doctrine not found in God's Word.

Unfortunately, when these men rejected the ways of the RCC, they also discarded certain teachings that had a solid biblical foundation. This was the case with baptism. While Luther never denied baptism as a matter of forgiveness and salvation, Zwingli and Calvin did. In fact, Zwingli candidly boasted that after fifteen centuries of mistaken teaching on baptism, he was the first to understand that baptism lacked efficacy.

> "In this matter of baptism -- if I may be pardoned for saying it -- I can only conclude that all the doctors have been in error from the time of the apostles. . . . All the doctors have ascribed to the water a power which it does not have and the holy apostles did not teach."[46]

In fairness to Zwingli, the RCC had arguably "ascribed to the water a power which it does not have." The church taught that one among the clergy could *bless* water and make the water, in itself, holy. This *holy water*, then, was seen as possessing a power that Scripture does not recognize. Once blessed, the water ostensibly contained

---

[46] Bromiley, G. W. editor and translator. Zwingli, Huldreigh, *'Of Baptism,'* in Zwingli and Bullinger, *'Library of Christian Classics,' Vol. 24*, 153.

intrinsic spiritual power to forgive sins in baptism as well as providing a number of other benefits (healings, etc.).

Zwingli's words had a powerful impact among the believers of his day and beyond. It was at this point that many began to deny the spiritual effect of baptism that is taught in the New Testament. Over a period of time, more and more people began to show contempt for Peter's words from the Day of Pentecost, insisting that they are deceiving and heretical. Many claim that the message found in Acts 2: 38 is inconsistent with the balance of biblical teaching concerning salvation; and yet, these words came, not *from* Peter, but *through* Peter. There is every reason to believe that he was still speaking in an unknown tongue at the time. Consequently. his frank response to the crowd on the Day of Pentecost must be embraced as Spirit-inspired. His words came from the Holy Spirit and must be afforded the same respect and acceptance as the balance of Scripture.

The Reformation and Faith Only

The teaching of *faith only* has dominated the doctrinal landscape for approximately four hundred years; yet the meaning of this phrase, as it was originally proposed, seems to have been lost on most people. The confusion surrounding this term has resulted in a mystifying sectarianism among most evangelicals when it comes to the terms *belief* and *faith* as they appear in God's Word. A brief study of this topic will hopefully shine the light of Scripture upon a creed that has clouded the perception of so many for so long.

Martin Luther, in A.D. 1517, posted his *Ninety-Five Theses* on the door of the castle church in Wittenberg. This document condemned the selling of indulgences and other actions by the Roman Catholic Church that Luther deemed contrary to the biblical theme of salvation as a matter of faith. In this work he focused on the need for true repentance, insisting that these practices were damaging the church, since those who were paying for indulgences were no more sincere about grace and repentance than those who were selling them. This was the beginning of what has come to be known as the Reformation Movement.

Luther's document was quite cumbersome. After all, it did consist of ninety-five charges against the church and few could remember them all. Eventually, five Latin phrases came to epitomize the core principles of the Protestant Reformation. Known as the *Five Solae*, they stood in stark contrast to the Roman Catholic belief system that had developed over more than a millennium. The phrases and their meanings were as follows:

Phrase	Meaning
• Sola Scriptura	Scripture alone.
• Soli Deo Gloria	The Glory of God alone.
• Solus Christus	Christ alone.
• Sola Gratia	Grace alone.
• Sola Fide	Faith alone.

Although it is popular to attribute authorship of the *Five Solae* to Martin Luther, there is no evidence that he wrote them. While the message they contain clearly derived from the Protestant Reformation arguments, the fact that they are not cited directly in sixteenth century literature suggests a later date. An individual or group likely developed these terms at some point in time after men like Luther and Calvin had laid the groundwork for these principles. Some believe that, like the TULIP philosophy, the *Five Solae* were developed by Calvinists sometime after the sixteenth century based primarily on the *Westminster Confession of Faith*, first published in 1646, in which these kinds of ideas were disseminated.

The idea behind the final three solae is that salvation is *in Christ alone*, *by grace alone*, and *through faith alone*. That is to say, Christ is the *source* of salvation, grace is the *means* of salvation, and faith is the *condition* of salvation (or the *result* of salvation according to Reformed Theology). This language served a specific purpose where the Reformers were concerned, and that objective is what led them to this precise terminology. They hoped to counter the practices of the RCC by highlighting scriptural instruction concerning redemption. The idea was that *Christ*, *grace*, and *faith* were biblically *true* and the current practices of the church, (e.g., the sale of indulgences and the pope's pardoning of the deceased), which were not scripturally based, should not be added to them.

The introduction of the *Five Solae* had a dramatic effect on Christendom in that they led to a new mindset among some believers resulting in philosophies that men like Luther probably never imagined. The problem was the specific wording that was employed by the Reformers to express their ideas. After some time, rather than focusing on Christ, grace, and faith, which was the intent, many began to center their attention on the word *sola*, meaning *alone*. This word came to overshadow the biblical principles that the *Five Solae* sought to advance.

Paul wrote, "For by grace you have been saved through faith...not as a result of works" (Ephesians 2: 8-9), and his words are absolutely true. However, it is one thing to say that salvation comes by grace through faith as this passage indicates. It is an entirely different matter to say that salvation comes by grace *alone* through faith *alone*, a philosophy many have encapsulated in the phrase *faith only*. The use of this term, and what it has come to mean over the centuries, depicts faith in a limited sense that the apostles never intended.

The focus on *sola* rather than the biblical pillars of grace and faith eventually caused many to view God's plan of salvation through a tinted lens. Once the doctrine of *faith only* took hold, saving faith became more narrowly defined. In short, faith as a matter of salvation came to mean (and this is a summarization): *intellectual assent to the fact that Jesus is Lord* (God's only begotten)*, trusting in his substitutive sacrifice for remission of sins, and making an honest commitment to live a life devoted to God.* While this is a decent description of what it means to be a faithful believer, it does not articulate the plan of salvation that is presented in God's Word.

Paul told the Ephesians that they had been saved *through* faith (Ephesians 2: 8-9). However, there is no mention of the time of their salvation. Stating *that* they were saved through faith does not explain *when* they were saved through faith. The timing of initial salvation is depicted in other passages (Acts 2: 38; Romans 6: 1-4; 1 Peter 3: 21), but it is not detailed in the Ephesians narrative. Deriving a doctrine from this text that someone outside of Christ is saved instantaneously at the moment of initial belief in Jesus forces a meaning upon the passage that is not there.

Another principle that must be given serious consideration relative to the doctrine of *faith only* is the time when the doctrine was first introduced. Despite insistence that this doctrine, as currently defined, constitutes apostolic teaching, salvation by *faith only* (or *faith alone*) is not found in Scripture[47] and was not introduced until sometime after the Reformation Movement of the sixteenth century. Given these facts, one can only conclude that this is an extra-biblical doctrine derived by men.

Zwingli, Calvin, and others in the early to mid-sixteenth century had already begun to discount the salvific role of baptism, and the *Five*

---

[47] The term appears in the Bible, but not as a matter of salvation (cf. James 2: 24).

Solae simply added fuel to that fire. Over the ensuing centuries, to a large number of people, the term *faith only* came to mean *salvation without baptism*. Today *faith only* is the primary argument given to deny the efficacy of baptism. However, his own writings indicate that Martin Luther did not expect the concept of salvation by faith to develop into the meaning it now holds. According to Luther:

> Baptism is no human plaything but is instituted by God himself. Moreover, it is solemnly and strictly commanded that we must be baptized or we shall not be saved. We are not to regard it as an indifferent matter, then, like putting on a new red coat. It is of the greatest importance that we regard baptism as excellent, glorious, and exalted.[48]

Baptism as a Covenant Sign

John Calvin considered baptism to be a covenant sign. His belief was drawn primarily from Paul's letter to the Colossians that was discussed earlier.

> [11] ...and in Him you were also circumcised with a circumcision made without hands, in the removal of the body of the flesh by the circumcision of Christ; [12] having been buried with Him in baptism, in which you were also raised up with Him through faith in the working of God, who raised Him from the dead. (Colossians 2: 11-12)

When Peter wrote that certain of Paul's writings could be difficult to grasp (2 Peter 3: 16), a passage he may have had in mind is this one from Paul's letter to the Colossians. The teaching itself is straightforward enough when considered in light of other Pauline epistles. Yet, on its own, at least in English translations, it is a bit awkward. However, the message here is powerful and meaningful, so it is important to understand it fully.

Calvin, along with many others, believed Paul was establishing a connection between baptism and circumcision in this passage, leading him to label baptism a *sign* of the new covenant. As a sign, Calvin believed baptism had no real spiritual effect. To him it was a matter of a person publicly accepting God's promises in baptism. Calvin was so confident in his view of baptism that he stated, "...everything

---

[48] Luther, Martin. *The Necessity of Baptism*, http://www.catholic.com/tracts/the-necessity-of-baptism.

applicable to circumcision applies also to baptism, excepting always the difference in the visible ceremony."[49]

Like Calvin, a number of believers seem to be confounded by the reference to circumcision in Paul's letter to the Colossians. The fact that circumcision and baptism both appear in this passage has led them to regard baptism as a covenant sign in the likeness of circumcision. However, this is not a true reflection of Paul's remarks; nor does it harmonize with other biblical teachings.

A significant principle of literary interpretation is to allow for and recognize figures of speech. Paul was known for his colorful language. The Colossians passage involves an analogy much like what Paul used in his letter to the Galatians. He told the disciples there that they had *clothed themselves with Christ* (Galatians 3: 27). The Galatians knew what it meant to clothe oneself, but they would not have taken Paul's words to mean that clothing themselves with Christ was in any way commensurate with physically donning a coat. Neither would they, having been told that they had clothed themselves with Christ at the time of baptism, have likened their baptism to a physical wardrobe. They understood, as does the modern-day reader, the analogous character of Paul's words.

In his letters to the Galatians and the Colossians, Paul offered analogies to which he believed his audiences could relate. The believers in Colossè were aware of circumcision. Some, and perhaps many of the membership were converted Jews,[50] but the Gentiles would have learned of the Israelite sign of circumcision through the Old Testament instruction they undoubtedly received. When Paul pictured for them "removal of the body of flesh by the circumcision of Christ," they would have understood this in figurative terms. Their old state of sinfulness was removed *much like* the Israelites removed the foreskin of a male infant. They would not have thought that baptism was a new covenant replacement for circumcision any more than the Galatians would have considered it a substitute for a physical cloak.

The fact that baptism was not seen as a replacement for circumcision is confirmed in an incident that involved the believers in Antioch. Some Jews in Antioch were insisting that the Gentile believers should be physically circumcised to participate in the covenant of grace (Acts 15: 1). Unable to resolve the issue, the

---

[49] Calvin, John. *Institutes of Christian Religion*, 874.
[50] Adam Clark and others have claimed that the majority of believers at Colosse and other Asiatic and Grecian communities may have been converted Jews, which explains the use of an analogy grounded in Jewish history.

question was taken to the elders and apostles in Jerusalem (Acts 15: 2). Luke wrote that there was *much debate* over this issue (Acts 15: 7) and that it was finally determined that physical circumcision was irrelevant in the covenant of grace.

If Jesus had taught the apostles that baptism was a new covenant replacement for circumcision, it is safe to say that the topic would not have required *much debate*. It seems more likely that it would have involved *no debate*. In fact, throughout the entire ordeal, Luke offers no hint that the topic of baptism surfaced at all. Baptism was not equated with circumcision in that decision or anywhere else in the New Testament.

Another important point is that, in the first century, the practice of circumcision was common among the Jews even after the introduction of baptism. John the Baptist practiced immersion in water in the Jewish community without ever addressing the topic of circumcision. Furthermore, the Jews in Antioch argued for the necessity of circumcision even after baptism in Jesus' name was introduced on the Day of Pentecost (Acts 2: 38).

The post-Pentecost church consisted of both circumcised and uncircumcised believers as the Jews remained faithful to the old covenant. Beyond Paul's analogous remarks to the Colossians, no relationship between baptism and circumcision was ever proposed in the early church and, in the pages of Scripture, the word *sign* is never used in connection with baptism.

Synecdoche

Having discovered the origins of the doctrine of *faith only* as it developed during and after the Protestant Reformation, consideration must be given to the use of the terms *belief* and *faith* as they are presented in Scripture. Certainly, many passages depict the redemptive character of belief and faith. Some of the better-known examples in addition to Ephesians 2: 8 include:

> For God so loved the world, that He gave His only begotten Son, that whoever believes in Him shall not perish, but have eternal life. (John 3: 16)

> They said, 'Believe in the Lord Jesus, and you will be saved, you and your household.' (Acts 16: 31)

> For I am not ashamed of the gospel, for it is the power of God for salvation to everyone who believes. (Romans 1: 16)

For we maintain that a man is justified by faith apart from works of the Law. (Romans 3: 28)

This is the only thing I want to find out from you: did you receive the Spirit by the works of the Law, or by hearing with faith? (Galatians 3: 2)

What did Jesus mean when he said, "whoever believes in Him shall not perish, but have eternal life"? What did Paul have in mind when he stated that "a man is justified by faith"? These are important questions that require sound biblical answers.

It is safe to say that these comments by Jesus and Paul do not mean *faith only*, at least not in the sense discussed in the previous section. There is too much additional information in Scripture about what it means to believe to insist that these statements are comprehensive. What, then, can be said about these Spirit-inspired words?

Peter proclaimed, "Repent and...be baptized...for the forgiveness of your sins" (Acts 2: 38), delivering a powerful message to his audience. Later, at the temple, he reiterated the need for repentance (Acts 3: 19). In his second epistle, Peter again linked repentance and salvation, telling the disciples that God does not wish "...any to perish but for all to come to repentance" (2 Peter 3: 9). Paul complemented Peter's words, stating, "For the sorrow that is according to the will of God produces a repentance without regret, leading to salvation" (2 Corinthians 7: 10). Who would deny, then, that salvation is unattainable without repentance?

If a person professes to believe in salvation by *faith only,* as many do, what about repentance? Where does it fit into the redemptive scheme of Scripture? The limited view of the doctrine of *faith only* to which most people subscribe does not call for repentance prior to salvation even though Peter and Paul do. Faced with this dilemma, many will acquiesce, admitting the necessity of repentance. However, in doing so, they have automatically broadened the constitution of their doctrine from salvation by *faith only* to salvation by *faith*.

Synecdoche [si-**nek**-d*uh*-kee] is a figure of speech where a part of something represents the whole or vice versa. It is rather common in Scripture. One very well-known example is found in those passages where the biblical writers wrote about the *breaking of bread*. This phrase actually holds two distinct meanings in the Bible. For instance, at times it means simply having a meal (Acts 2: 46; 20: 11). Other times when the *breaking of bread* is mentioned, it is a reference to the

Lord's Supper...both the loaf and the cup (Acts 2: 42; 20: 7). In these cases, the *bread* represents the entire meal.

When the apostles wrote about belief and/or faith in Christ, it was usually in a broad sense much like the *breaking of bread*. That is because these terms generally appear in the form of a synecdoche. That is to say, they represent more than the narrowest meaning of the word itself. This becomes obvious even when one accepts the definition of *faith only* that was presented earlier. Even those who teach salvation by *faith only* generally recognize that believers of the first century were not people who merely believed, but who also repented of their sins and made a commitment to live for Christ; so, believing means more than *only* believing even among the *faith only* crowd.

When Paul wrote to those whom he called believers, he recognized certain common traits among them. The first and most obvious trait is that they believed in Jesus Christ as the Son of God and their personal Savior. He also recognized that they had repented of their sins in keeping with apostolic instruction. It can be inferred that they had confessed Jesus as Lord (Romans 10: 10). They had also been immersed in Jesus' name. Believers were those who had been true to *the faith* as it was presented in apostolic teachings (1 Timothy 6: 21; Jude 1: 3).

When the attempt is made to isolate baptism from redemption, the biblical plan of salvation fails to harmonize. Passages that emphasize baptism as a matter of salvation must be overcome through lumbering methods of biblical analysis, reshaping instructions found in God's Word. Peter called for baptism for the remission of sins (Acts 2: 38). Paul confirmed this (Colossians 2: 11-12) and taught that new life in Christ begins during baptism (Romans 6: 4). Peter tried to make the lesson as simple as possible when he stated boldly that *baptism saves* (1 Peter 3: 21). The vast wealth of Scripture depicting the redemptive role of baptism is overwhelming.

Baptism is no small thing when it comes to salvation, despite the fact that salvation is by faith. When a verse or text speaks of salvation by faith, even though baptism may not be mentioned overtly, like repentance, it is always couched within the message. Passages that link baptism to salvation are crystal clear (Acts 2: 38; Galatians 3: 26-27) and leave no room for maneuvering. If taken as they are written, they harmonize fully with salvation by grace through faith when faith is viewed as a synecdoche.

Chapter 21

Biblical Classification of Baptism

Salvation by Grace Through Faith

The opportunity for salvation via God's grace has been offered because Jesus sacrificed himself on behalf of mankind. Jesus' crucifixion represents the essence of God's grace to his fallen creation. Taking upon his being the punishment for sins served as a true expression of love. Absent God's grace, salvation for mankind would be unknown. Without it, any discussion concerning the method of salvation would be futile.

Grace, in the context of man's relationship with God, is the presence of God's favor on humankind. It is an *unmerited* manifestation of God's favor upon men. Thus, salvation by grace is unmerited salvation. Numerous New Testament passages speak of the grace of God by which men are saved.

> But we believe that we are saved through the grace of the Lord Jesus. (Acts 15: 11)

> But I do not consider my life of any account as dear to myself, so that I may finish my course and the ministry which I received from the Lord Jesus, to testify solemnly of the gospel of the grace of God. (Acts 20: 24)

> ...being justified as a gift by His grace through the redemption which is in Christ Jesus. (Romans 3: 24)

> ...even when we were dead in our transgressions, made us alive together with Christ (by grace you have been saved). (Ephesians 2: 5)

> For the grace of God has appeared, bringing salvation to all men. (Titus 2: 11)

Generally, those who accept Jesus as Savior also accept the teaching that men are saved by means of God's grace. Similarly, a majority agree that salvation is through faith. Grace may be the means of salvation, but faith is the path one must follow to receive God's grace. The Bible, then, is the roadmap that God has provided to direct those who wish to follow him. As with grace, the Bible addresses extensively the truth that salvation is a matter of faith.

> [1] Therefore, having been justified by faith, we have peace with God through our Lord Jesus Christ, [2] through whom also we have obtained our introduction by faith into this grace in which we stand. (Romans 5: 1-2)

> But the Scripture has shut up everyone under sin, so that the promise by faith in Jesus Christ might be given to those who believe. (Galatians 3: 22)

> ... not having a righteousness of my own derived from *the* Law, but that which is through faith in Christ, the righteousness which *comes* from God on the basis of faith. (Philippians 3: 9)

> ...obtaining as the outcome of your faith the salvation of your souls. (1 Peter 1: 9)

It is clear, then, that salvation by grace through faith is a pillar of Christian doctrine. It passes the test of biblical truth on a number of levels including original intent of the author, apostolic repetition, etc. It is safe to say that anyone who teaches salvation that is not a matter of the combination of grace and faith is guilty of misrepresenting the plan of salvation that has been delivered in God's Word.

This was Paul's very point to the Galatians. He was disappointed, and even exasperated, that the Galatians were in the process of discarding the gospel he had delivered to them (Galatians 1: 6-7). Instead, they were seriously contemplating a form of salvation by works. Late in the epistle it is suggested that they were considering the necessity of circumcision as a matter of salvation (Galatians 5: 1-4). This, according to Paul, was inconsistent with salvation by grace through faith and constituted a return to the law where salvation by grace was inaccessible.

Baptism Is God's Work

The loudest and most prolonged protest against the redemptive character of baptism is that it is a *good work* or *human work*. Since, according to Paul, one cannot be saved by works, the notion that baptism might have a role in the plan of salvation is appalling to those who view it as such. The very suggestion, it is said, diminishes the work of Christ on the cross. All that is necessary for salvation is faith in Jesus. A claim that anything else may be required (i.e., baptism) constitutes preaching another gospel, against which Paul vehemently warned the first century church (Galatians 1: 8-9). The argument stems in part from Paul's words to the Ephesians as he told them:

> [8] For by grace you have been saved through faith; and that not of yourselves, *it is* the gift of God; [9] not as a result of works, so that no one may boast. (Ephesians 2: 8-9)

The apostle's message is clear. People are not saved by human works, but through faith. Anyone who claims that someone can earn his/her way to heaven has not taken these words to heart. The truth is, most people who appreciate that the Bible casts baptism in a redemptive role also understand that salvation comes, not by works, but by grace through faith.

...most people who appreciate that the Bible casts baptism in a redemptive role also understand that salvation comes, not by works, but by grace through faith.

Why, then, do people not see eye to eye when it comes to baptism? The heart of the matter seems to lie in one's approach to Scripture and a misconception of baptism as a meritorious work. Those who believe baptism is salvific do not consider it to be a work. This rite cannot be considered a *work* in the vein of feeding the hungry or caring for those in need. Instead, baptism is a vehicle God has established through which a penitent believer re-enacts the death, burial, and resurrection of Christ. During submission to baptism, God performs his spiritual circumcision (Colossians 2: 11), removing an individual's old, sinful self and providing spiritual renewal (Romans 6: 4).

The divisiveness over the role of baptism has had some very unfortunate consequences. Paul's words to the Ephesians, as he explained that salvation is "...not a result of works," have become so fused to the debate over baptism that it is as though he had said *not as a result of baptism*. In modern times this verse is often used to dispute any teaching that highlights baptism's redemptive character. This is far removed from Paul's intent. In fact, the passage carries an allusion to baptism even as Paul teaches the futility of attempting to earn salvation. He states the following just prior to the verses cited above:

⁵ ...even when we were dead in our transgressions, made us alive together with Christ (by grace you have been saved), ⁶ and raised us up with Him, and seated us with Him in the heavenly *places* in Christ Jesus, ⁷ so that in the ages to come He might show the surpassing riches of His grace in kindness toward us in Christ Jesus. (Ephesians 2: 5-7)

These words echo the very sentiments Paul shared time and again in teaching the intricacies and importance of baptism (Romans 6: 1-4; Colossians 2: 12; 3: 1). This is actually less like an allusion to baptism and more like a preamble to his teaching on the subject later in the epistle (Ephesians 4: 5; 5: 25-26).

Baptism has been called a human work based on the fact that it is a physical activity (albeit passive). However, focusing on the physicality of the act does not do justice to biblical instruction concerning baptism. While it is true that in baptism a person is physically buried in water, the apostles placed stronger emphasis on the spiritual side of baptism. This is an activity where man's humanity and God's spirituality meet. It is the point when a person is buried with Jesus (Romans 6: 4) in both a physical and spiritual sense.

It seems a bit awkward to identify baptism as a human work when Scripture does not. The only work that is discussed relative to baptism is the work that God performs (Colossians 2: 12). The passive nature of baptism (it is something to which one submits rather than something one *does*) demonstrates that this is not a human work, but God's work.

That is not to say that the apostles did not classify baptism. Indeed, they did, but they never called it a work of man or a deed of merit. Several times in the New Testament the apostles categorize baptism. Consider what Scripture has to say about how these writers viewed the rite of baptism.

The Bible contains many lists. In the New Testament alone there are lists of the apostles and other groups, genealogies (lists of descendants), assorted lists of spiritual gifts, the fruit of the spirit, etc. Lists are important in that they help to classify people and things. For instance, when given a list of the apostles, their chosen status as apostles and their unique role in the church stands out. The fruit of the Spirit depict the kind of traits one can expect to see in those who share the same Spirit. Spiritual gifts are manifestations of the Holy Spirit, and genealogies identify important lineages.

Lists like these are intended to demonstrate the connection and likeness inherent among the individual members contained in the list. Did the authors of Scripture classify baptism in any way? Indeed, they did. It is often measured against other matters of faith. To gain a biblical perspective, here is a brief examination of these authors' points of view concerning baptism.

Baptism Is Fundamental to the Faith

For several hundred years, the scholarly consensus was that the letter to the Hebrews was penned by the Apostle Paul. However, of late, textual critics have raised serious questions about Paul's authorship. This is based partly on the lack of any salutation that seems to be so prominent and eloquent in Paul's work. The second argument against Paul is what many consider to be a writing style very unlike the apostle.

Who wrote Hebrews? It could well be that this work was written by Paul. That has not been disproven, only effectively questioned. Some attribute the letter to Paul's companion, Barnabas, while others believe it could have been written by Apollos or another first century evangelist known to the apostles. While authorship remains a mystery, the doctrinal instruction found there is viewed as some of the most informative and valuable teaching in the New Testament.

It seems the Jews to whom this letter was addressed were finding it difficult to grow in the faith. Their attention was fixed on the fundamentals and they were unable to move past them. The author of the letter was concerned about their stagnation and hoped to encourage them to advance in understanding and spiritual maturity.

The letter offers a list of the foundational elements of Christianity that had so captivated the believers' attention that they had failed to move forward in their relationship with God and each other. That list details the topics that the author identifies as "…elementary teaching about the Christ" (Hebrews 6: 1). These would be the same elemental doctrinal matters involved in the initial discipleship (mathēteuo) that Jesus commanded in The Great Commission (Matthew 28: 19). Due to their focus on these basic principles, these Jews remained infants in Christ, unable to deepen their understanding of spiritual things.

> [1]Therefore leaving the elementary teaching about the Christ, let us press on to maturity, not laying again a foundation of repentance from dead works and of faith toward God, [2] of instruction about washings and laying on of hands, and the resurrection of the dead and eternal judgment. (Hebrews 6: 1-2)

Six specific items are deemed to be foundational teachings where discipleship is concerned. The first of these fundamentals is identified as *repentance* (v. 1). In the initial gospel message delivered on the Day of Pentecost, Peter responded to those who sought spiritual direction by commanding them to repent. The reasoning behind Peter's statement is that, absent a penitent mind-set, conversion is not possible.

The second matter the author identifies as foundational is *faith toward God* (v. 1). Unlike comprehensive doctrinal faith that is discussed elsewhere in the New Testament (cf. Jude 1: 3), this seems to be the initial belief that God is supreme, and Jesus is Lord.

Instruction about baptisms (v. 2) follows faith among these elementary teachings. The NASB translation of *washings* should not be cause for confusion. The translation is *baptisms* (ASV; KJV; NIV-1984; NKJV) and *cleansings* (NIV) in other versions. In the Greek, the word used (baptizō) is the same word that is translated as *baptism* throughout the New Testament.

It is curious that the author uses the plural form of baptism, calling it *the doctrine of baptisms* (KJV). What could be behind such an overt contradiction of Paul's claim of *one baptism* (Ephesians 4: 5)? The most reasonable explanation is the fact that there is but one baptism (immersion in water), as Paul claims, but the efficacy of that single experience is two-fold. The consequents of baptism, as discussed in Chapter 16, include forgiveness, regeneration, adoption, etc. However, there is one other baptism that also occurs during one's immersion in water.

On the Day of Pentecost, Peter promised those who repented and submitted to baptism in Jesus' name that they would also experience the Holy Spirit's presence in their lives. While baptism with the Holy Spirit is depicted as the whelming of the Spirit on the apostles (Acts 2: 4) and the Gentiles at the house of Cornelius (Acts 10: 44), these are remarkable exceptions to what took place in the first century. The normal manner in which Christians received the (baptism with the) Spirit is defined in Peter's words from the Day of Pentecost. Thus, *baptisms* would seem to point to immersion in water and the baptism with the Spirit that accompanies it.

It is also possible that the author might be referencing assorted historical baptisms. For instance, Gentiles who wished to convert to Judaism submitted to a spiritual cleansing in water. Also, the baptism provided by John the Baptist served as a forerunner to Christian baptism. Thus, the author could have a plurality of baptisms in view.

The writer points to the *laying on of hands* (v. 2) as a fundamental element of Christianity. This is the method generally used to bestow a gift or blessing on another. For instance, miraculous spiritual gifts were distributed through the apostles' touch in the first century. Similarly, the laying on of hands is used as a matter of ordination, or setting someone aside to a specific ministry (Acts 6: 6; 24: 23; 1 Timothy 4: 14). Also, James taught that the elders should lay hands on the sick (James 5: 14).

Other than the distribution of miraculous gifts, which is unavailable today due to the absence of apostles in modern times, these practices still apply today. New believers were taught about the spiritual authority of the apostles, and that may well be part of the explanation for this reference. However, the early church was also told about the care they were to take in this practice where ordination to ministry is concerned (1 Timothy 5: 22). Thus, the application here is logically to the governance and organization of the church as much as to the spiritual power given through the apostles.

Resurrection of the dead (v. 2) as a basic Christian teaching needs no real explanation. Eternal existence beyond this corporal life lies at the very heart of Christian doctrine. Similarly, all new believers would have been instructed about the coming *eternal judgment* (v. 2) all must face.

Baptism, according to the author of Hebrews, is deemed to be an *elementary teaching about the Christ* (v. 1). Here baptism is placed on the same spiritual plane as repentance and faith, and even eternal judgment. In other words, it is fundamental. Thus, it cannot be regarded merely as a good work without completely disregarding the perspective of the author of Hebrews.

Baptism as the Time of Regeneration

Writing to Titus, Paul distinguished between baptism and works in no uncertain terms. The apostle told Titus to remind those disciples under his watch to constantly remember the foolishness of their lives prior to Christ and to live according to godly principles. He also wanted them to remember the character of their conversion…that it was not by works.

> [5] He saved us, not on the basis of deeds which we have done in righteousness, but according to His mercy, by the washing of regeneration and renewing by the Holy Spirit, [6] whom He poured out upon us richly through Jesus Christ our Savior, [7] so that being justified by His grace we would be made heirs according to *the* hope of eternal life. (Titus 3: 5-7)

This passage expresses two important principles when it comes to baptism. First of all, baptism is contrasted with deeds (v. 5). This is an unequivocal statement by Paul that baptism is not a work as defined by those who teach faith only. Second, the fact that initial salvation occurs during baptism does not contradict the apostolic teaching that justification comes by grace (v. 7). The heart of the message in this passage is that "He saved us...by the washing of regeneration and renewing by the Holy Spirit...so that being justified by grace we would be made heirs..." In that statement Paul connects several aspects of baptism including cleansing, the Holy Spirit, justification, and adoption.

Where works are concerned, unlike modern day scholars, Paul contrasts baptism and works, or deeds. Not only does he distinguish between them, but he depicts them as opposites. According to Paul, salvation, the very thing that cannot be gained through deeds, is achieved in baptism. This in itself should put to rest the impression that baptism could be considered a good work.

Baptism and Christian Unity

In his letter to the Ephesians, Paul has included a list of specific kingdom-related entities and concepts that he considered unique, unifying elements within the kingdom. Their uniqueness is highlighted as Paul points to the *oneness* associated with each.

> ⁴ *There is* one body and one Spirit, just as also you were called in one hope of your calling; ⁵ one Lord, one faith, one baptism, ⁶ one God and Father of all who is over all and through all and in all. (Ephesians 4: 4-6)

As noted earlier, the purpose of a list is to demonstrate commonality. Here Paul has provided a record of distinctive elements, each one holding a *unique* place within the construct of the kingdom. This means there is nothing else like these, either in or out of the kingdom of God. They constitute the configuration of the kingdom that has been designed by God and revealed through the gospel.

First, he mentions *one body* (v. 4). This can only be the church, which is often called the body of Christ (cf. 1 Corinthians 12: 27). The import of the body of Christ is underscored at various times in a number of New Testament passages (1 Corinthians 12: 12; Ephesians 4: 12). It is the bride of Christ (Revelation 21: 2), and its members are the saved. Membership is not optional for believers since they are added to the body by God (Acts 2: 41). Next, Paul mentions *one Spirit* (v. 4). This is the Holy Spirit whose uniqueness and magnitude need no explanation.

Paul follows this with what he calls *one hope* (v. 4). While the world is filled with hopes of all sorts, when it comes to the kingdom of God, all rests on one hope. It is the hope of salvation and eternal life in heaven (1 Thessalonians 5: 8). The apostle also recognizes *one Lord* (v. 5). With these words he has in mind Jesus Christ who is lord of all. None in heaven or on earth can compare to him. He is like no other.

Next comes *one faith* (v. 5). This is probably not just a basic faith in Christ that Paul has in view. It is more likely a statement about *the faith*, a term used repeatedly in the New Testament (Acts 6: 7; Colossians 2: 7; Jude 3). In this sense, it points to all that faith in God encompasses and all those teachings that fall under the umbrella of apostolic doctrine.

Paul also points to *one baptism* (v. 5). Like one Lord and one faith, baptism holds a singular position within the kingdom. Because it represents the death, burial, and resurrection, it is understandable that baptism would hold a special place with God. However, it is not merely baptism's physical personality that is in view. Like these others, it has spiritual value with respect to the kingdom. It represents an appeal for forgiveness (Acts 2: 38). It is defined as the moment of spiritual circumcision (Colossians 2: 12) and the time when a person becomes clothed with Christ (Galatians 3: 27). It is God's provision for cleansing (Titus 3: 5) and renewal (Romans 6: 4) through which an individual enters the *one body* (1 Corinthians 12: 13).

The apostle closes his remarks (his list) by identifying that which is greatest in the kingdom, noting that there is but "one God and Father of all" (v. 6). The entirety of *the faith* rests on him, including each of these unique elements of the kingdom.

Quite often in Scripture, the construction of a list may indicate a measure of diminishing importance among the members. When this occurs, the first item mentioned is generally considered most significant, each subsequent member being deemed a bit less consequential. However, that does not seem to be the case here since that would mean the *body* would hold the highest position with God the Father being the least significant. It may well be that Paul was not concerned with weighing these members against one another, since his focus is unity in the kingdom and the uniqueness of each in relation to the kingdom. The distinctiveness ascribed to these spiritual figures indicates that he considered each one vitally important where the kingdom is concerned.

Paul identifies baptism as a unique and honorable element of the kingdom of God. In a single sentence he gives *one baptism* equal footing with *one Lord* and *one faith* (v. 5). It seems a bit presumptuous, then, for those who are not apostles to supersede his call and recast baptism as a human work. If baptism is unique, labeling it a *good work* conflicts with Paul's perception of this rite.

When Jesus offered the Great Commission, he told the disciples to 1) *disciple*, 2) *baptize*, and 3) *teach them to observe all that I have commanded* (Matthew 28: 19-20). He saw baptism through the same lens as Paul, recognizing its unique value. By relegating baptism to the status of *good works*, men have removed it from the notable position Paul has depicted here and lumped it in with "all that I have commanded you," (Matthew 28: 20) which was not the intent of either Jesus or Paul.

The Witness of Baptism

Baptism is again classified by the Apostle John. In the first of his three epistles, the oldest-living apostle discusses at great length the identity of Jesus. In that vein, he mentions three stalwart witnesses to Christ's deity. Who are these three witnesses who testify on Christ's behalf? According to John, they are "...the Spirit and the water and the blood, and these three are in agreement" (1 John 5: 7).

In this text, there is near unanimity among theologians in identifying these witnesses. The Spirit is recognized as the Holy Spirit. This is recorded by men like Adam Clark, John Darby, John Wesley, and a host of others. It is also generally accepted that the blood points to Jesus' blood sacrifice on the cross with perhaps an allusion to the Lord's Supper.

Generally speaking, most theologians believe the water mentioned here represents Christ's baptism by John (Matthew 3: 13-17). That was the beginning of Jesus' ministry. It was the moment of his introduction to mankind as the long-awaited Messiah. It was also the moment when God the Father lauded Jesus as the Spirit, in the form of a dove, descended to him.

The witness of blood, on the other hand, is said to epitomize the end of Jesus' ministry on earth. His death was the culmination of all that had occurred since Adam sinned thousands of years earlier. Thus, the water and the blood serve as bookends of Christ's ministry on earth.

The Spirit needs little explanation. The Holy Spirit descended upon Jesus at his baptism marking the beginning of his ministry. He was also there at the beginning as the church was established on the Day of Pentecost. The Spirit aided the apostles in establishing the church and documenting God's doctrine for the covenant of grace. He is also the seal of salvation given to believers as a teacher, comforter, and helper (Ephesians 1: 13-14).

Like so many other New Testament verses, this one speaks volumes about mankind's attempt to categorize baptism as a work. What is common about these witnesses? What is it that makes them credible witnesses? Throughout the New Testament, these three are identified as critical where salvation is concerned. This is evident in numerous passages where baptism, cleansing through the blood of Christ, and the indwelling presence of the Spirit are bound together.

> Jesus answered, "Truly, truly, I say to you, unless one is born of water and the Spirit he cannot enter into the kingdom of God. (John 3: 5)

> Peter said to them, "Repent, and each of you be baptized in the name of Jesus Christ for the forgiveness of your sins; and you will receive the gift of the Holy Spirit. (Acts 2: 38)

> let us draw near with a sincere heart in full assurance of faith, having our hearts sprinkled *clean* from an evil conscience and our bodies washed with pure water. (Hebrews 10: 22)

It is a bit disconcerting that the view of baptism as a human work has so deeply penetrated the psyche of those who wish to serve God. It should be obvious that the apostles never identified baptism as a work of merit. John, in his first epistle, writes of three witnesses for Christ. These are the Spirit, the water, and the blood. Interestingly, in the plan of salvation, each of these witnesses has a significant role. The Holy Spirit provides the labor necessary for regeneration (Titus 3: 5); the blood of Christ is the cleansing agent by which sins are remitted (Hebrews 10: 22); and baptism provides the occasion for God to make this happen.

The Biblical Measure of Baptism

Peter compared Christian baptism to the Old Testament flood (1 Peter 3: 20-21). The connection is understandable. During those days God "...saw that the wickedness of man was great on the earth, and that every intent of the thoughts of his heart was only evil continually" (Genesis 6: 5). But for Noah, no one on earth was remotely righteous. It is not surprising, given the circumstances, that God regretted creating humanity and set out to destroy his creation.

With Noah and his family safely in the ark, God sent an unprecedented calamity upon the earth in the form of a flood. It rained without ceasing for forty days. With that rain, which covered even the highest mountain (Genesis 7: 20), God not only saved Noah, but he cleansed the earth, removing all that was evil. He literally baptized the planet such that, as the waters receded, the earth was regenerated, and life began anew.

This is the connection Peter was making. He saw immersion in water as corresponding to the flood. As noted earlier, many people struggle mightily with this comparison, since Noah and his family were not immersed in water but were actually lifted above the water. However, given Peter's characterization of the relationship between the flood and baptism, his description is quite appropriate. He did not say that baptism is *like* the flood, but that baptism is actually the mirror image of the flood. The word Peter uses to compare the two is *antitupon*. Drue Freeman describes this specific kind of relationship in the following excerpt from his work:

> There is a distinct vocabulary found in the New Testament that references the Old Testament. The Greek word HUPODEIGMA means that which is shown privately as an example or pattern. TUPOS is an impression that is left from the blow of a hammer... An ANTITUPON is a counterpart like an echo.[51]

This portraiture sheds a slightly different light on Peter's words. However, for those who may still be scratching their heads, perhaps the following explanation from a rather popular commentary series will help explain in even simpler terms the principle of *antitupon*:

> Opposite of imagery which pictures those who floated safely above the waters within the ark is that of a complete immersion which "saves us."[52]

---

[51] Freeman, Drue. *Hermeneutics: The Science and Art of Biblical Interpretation*, http://www.realtime.net/~wdoud/topics/hermeneutics.html.
[52] Speer, L. L., Founder. *The General Epistles: A Practical Faith*, 174.

In comparing baptism to the flood, Peter describes immersion in water as an appeal (Gr. *eperōtēma*) to God for a good (clean) conscience. Baptism is an intimate, moving experience. These words describe the personal nature of both forgiveness and the rite of baptism. Individual submission is another manner in which baptism is a mirror image (opposite) of the flood. At the time of Noah, through the instrument of water, God addressed the sins of everyone in one act. Today, baptism is conferred individually upon those who believe.

Some may be wondering exactly what all of this has to do with repudiation of the claim that baptism should be considered a good work, or a work of man. The correlation actually features two lines of reasoning, and each is equally relevant to the debate. First of all, where works are concerned, it is difficult to imagine any *good work* or *human work* that could be measured so vividly against a world altering event like the flood. Feeding the hungry and caring for the sick simply do not rise to that level of distinction within the kingdom. That is not to say that these works should be trivialized, but they cannot be compared to the plagues of Egypt or any other momentous historical event the way Peter compares baptism to the flood. Good works have no cataclysmic counterpart, nor are they considered baptism's equivalent when it comes to salvation by grace through faith.

Second, it is worth noting exactly *who* was at work during the flood. Noah did not bring forty days of rain upon the earth. This was done by God's hand. Noah simply submitted to God's command and was "saved through water." Similarly, when it comes to baptism, Paul explained that it is God who is at work during baptism (Colossians 2: 11-12). It was God, and not Noah, who cleansed the earth *in the water*. In similar fashion, *in the water* he spiritually cleanses the person who submits. The believer offers/presents himself for cleansing by submitting to baptism. The proposition that something of this magnitude that is *of God* should be cast as a good work is completely unfounded where Scripture is concerned.

Baptism – A Unique Calling

In the nation of Ethiopia, many people, including countless children, are starving to death. Few if any would argue that going to Ethiopia and feeding those hungry people could not be considered a good work. This is the kind of selflessness Jesus had in mind when explaining the character of his followers (Matthew 25: 31-46). In fact, many Christians have done much to feed the hungry in Ethiopia and other parts of the world.

It is also true that those outside of Christ have done much to feed the hungry. Despite the fact that they are unbelievers, many have compassion for the needy and do what they can to help. Feeding the hungry is a good work whether done by a believer or an unbeliever. The difference is that, when done by a believer, God gets the glory.

If traveling to Ethiopia to feed the hungry can be considered a good work, should not every believer hop the next plane with a suitcase full of food and partake in that good work? The thought is nice, but not really feasible. Yet, like taking on such a mission, it is easy to think of hundreds and even thousands of good works in which Christians could participate. The opportunities are essentially infinite.

Not everyone has the opportunity to go and feed the children in a foreign land or help those in another country dig out from a disaster. While some do more good works than others, no one person does every good work that could be done. Those who do not travel to foreign countries often avail themselves of opportunities much closer to home.

This brings to the forefront an aspect of baptism that sets it apart. One of the primary differences between baptism and those actions that would be considered charitable is the fact that, while no one is called to do *every* good work, each one is called to submit to baptism without exception just as each one is called to believe or repent.

This is an important distinction that is generally overlooked. The examples of good works that are presented in God's Word are unselfish actions that benefit others. Nothing about baptism benefits *others*, but it is still something to which every person is called. The focus in baptism is on establishing a personal relationship with God and, unlike a trip to Ethiopia, it is expected of every believer. A classification of *just another good work* completely discounts this unique and universal call to baptism.

Summary on Baptism

J. W. Willmarth was correct when he stated that challenges to the efficacy of baptism are founded on a persistent doctrinal bias rather than sound biblical exegesis. This is evidenced by the fact that, when it comes to denying the redemptive role of baptism, a painfully awkward set of interpretive principles are employed offering markedly forced results. For instance, *believe and be baptized* does not really mean *believe and be baptized*; nor does *for the forgiveness of sins* mean *for the forgiveness of sins*; and *baptism now saves you* could not possibly mean *baptism now saves you*. Nothing about the context of each of these statements suggests that they should not be taken at face value. Applied to any other doctrine, this same reasoning would undoubtedly be derided as spurious and unreliable.

Jesus highlighted the import of baptism in some of his final words to the disciples (Matthew 28: 19). Peter told the crowd on the Day of Pentecost to "Repent, and...be baptized...for the forgiveness of your sins" (Acts 2: 38). Paul explained to the Romans, Corinthians, Galatians, Ephesians, Colossians, and Titus the transformation that takes place during immersion in water. Peter stated in no uncertain terms that *baptism saves* (1 Peter 3: 21). The purifying nature of baptism is discussed boldly through the entire New Testament.

Several episodes of conversion from the book of Acts have been reviewed. These include the Day of Pentecost, the Gentiles in Caesarea, the Philippian jailer, the disciples in Ephesus, and the Apostle Paul's own conversion in Damascus. On each of these occasions, baptism was the first order of business for those who wished to accept Christ. Unlike modern-day conversions where baptism may be delayed for days, or even weeks, baptism in the New Testament immediately followed a person's belief in Jesus as Lord and Savior.

The same is true of other conversions in Acts that were not discussed including the Samaritans (Acts 8: 9-13) and the Ethiopian eunuch (Acts 8: 26-39), each responding to Phillip's preaching by being baptized immediately. In like manner, Lydia's direct response to

Paul's teaching was obedience in baptism (Acts 16: 13-15). In Corinth, after hearing Paul's teaching, Crispus and others "...were believing and being baptized" (Acts 18: 8).

It should be a difficult thing to ignore the many passages of Scripture that link baptism and redemption. The Bible is so bold in its instruction concerning the role of baptism within the plan of salvation that it seems it should take considerable resolve to come to any conclusion that denies this teaching. Yet, where the plan of salvation is concerned, it has become common practice in modern times to simply insert an asterisk after belief and footnote baptism at the bottom of the page as an extra option that pleases God.

In essence, men derive their denial of baptism's redemptive character by assuming that biblical instruction regarding faith (e.g., John 3: 16; Ephesians 2: 8) effectively nullifies those passages that teach about the role of baptism (e.g., Matthew 28: 19; Mark 16: 16; 1 Peter 3: 21). However, in doing so they end up pitting the Bible against itself, insisting that one passage is true, and another is false. Only when these passages are treated harmoniously (e.g., Acts 2: 38; 16: 31) can one gain true understanding of God's Word. Recognizing the complementary character of these words will help each believer appreciate how faith and baptism work jointly within the framework of the gospel.

In the plan of salvation, grace is subordinate to Christ, who is Lord. Without Christ's sacrifice mankind would not know God's grace. Indeed, Christ's sacrifice was his demonstration of that grace. Similarly, faith is subordinate to grace since, without grace, no measure of faith could reconcile the sinner to God. Also, baptism and repentance are subordinate to faith since neither one can occur independent of faith. This, however, does not mean that baptism and repentance are less important than faith any more than faith is less important than grace where redemption is concerned. According to Scripture, each has a distinctive role in God's plan of salvation.

Does salvation come by grace through faith (Ephesians 2: 8)? Of course, it does. What, then, is the role of baptism according to Scripture? It is simply that instrument of surrender designed by God and combined with repentance, all within the framework of faith, during which a person is cleansed of sins and receives the promised gift of the Holy Spirit (Acts 2: 38). It is the water of the new birth through which an individual enters the kingdom of God (John 3: 5).

Baptism is the normal manner through which men and women are admitted into the kingdom of God in the church age. That is the lesson of Scripture. The biblical writers have portrayed baptism as a unique unifying element in the kingdom of God (Ephesians 4: 5) and an "...elementary teaching about the Christ" (Hebrews 6: 2). They never entertained the notion that baptism was a means of earning salvation. Instead, baptism is an act of faith – the very faith by which men are saved.

Appendix A
The Gift of Apostle

The term *apostle* is designated as a spiritual gift twice by Paul (1 Corinthians 12: 28; Ephesians 4: 1). Given the distinct appointment of men like Peter and Paul as apostles of Christ, some may wonder whether the *spiritual gift* of apostle might reference something other than their unique office. Perhaps by the *gift* of apostle, Paul was introducing a distinct spiritual gift available to other Christians through the apostles' touch. For instance, on his missionary journey with Paul, Barnabas was also called an apostle (Acts 14: 14). Yet, Scripture specifically distinguishes between Barnabas and those known as the apostles of Christ (Acts 4: 36).

Scholars have varying opinions when it comes to identifying the apostle by the name of James whom Paul met on his visit to Jerusalem (Galatians 1: 19).[53] Some are convinced this was James, the son of Joseph and Mary who was a leader in the church in Jerusalem. Others believe this was James, the son of Alpheus who was counted among the twelve (Matthew 10: 3), and that he was a *kinsman* of Jesus.

Scripture does not state that James, the son of Alphaeus, was related to Jesus in any way. That fact does not rule out the possibility that he was a *near kinsman* (i.e., cousin) to Jesus, as some believe, but it does seem more likely that Jesus' half-brother is in view in this instance. If Paul was writing about Jesus' half-brother, then this man must have been considered an apostle in the same sense that Barnabas was an apostle. This leaves the student of Scripture wondering whether men like James and Barnabas were endowed with the spiritual gift of apostle or if the gift mentioned twice by Paul was specific to the twelve.

Unlike other gifts that Paul discusses, which focus on specific *tasks* (e.g., speaking in tongues, prophesying, etc.), apostleship was actually a *position* armed with a degree of authority. If the gift of apostle existed outside the twelve and Paul, it is curious that God's Word offers no insight into how this gift might have manifested itself.

---

[53] Reese, Gareth L. *New Testament History – Acts*, See Special Study # 2, p. 39 for full explanation.

The twelve were selected by Christ to be his special ambassadors. This would not have been true of other apostles, nor would they necessarily have met the qualifications for the special office of apostle. For instance, James (Jesus' half-brother) and Barnabas did not travel with Jesus during his ministry (Acts 1: 21).

The term apostle means *one who is sent* and is frequently used in conjunction with missionaries. Throughout the New Testament it is regularly translated as *messenger* rather than apostle, often in connection with churches. Barnabas was a messenger (apostle) in that he, along with Paul, was sent to represent the Antioch church in spreading the gospel (Acts 13: 2-3). Thus, the word appropriately applies to him. Similarly, Epaphroditus was a messenger (apostle) of the church in Philippi (Philippians 2: 25).

There is some rather reliable evidence suggesting that when Paul was discussing the gift of apostle, he was referring specifically to himself and the twelve. First of all, on the two occasions when Paul called apostleship a spiritual gift, he mentioned it first followed by other gifts such as prophets, teachers, etc. Scholars generally agree that the gifts were given by Paul in order of diminishing significance, arguably making apostleship the gift of greatest import, at least in Paul's view.

Scripture says much about the role of the apostles of Christ in the first century. Yet, no instruction is given concerning the gift of apostle separate from the twelve. Scripture offers much insight into other gifts such as prophecy and tongues, but nothing is taught about *other* apostles. Scripture even offers teaching about the positions of elder and deacon, but nothing is said about the role of apostles outside the twelve. This fact suggests that where *apostolōs* is linked to other men, such as Barnabas, the spiritual gift is not in view. Instead, it stands to reason that the word is being employed in its generic sense of ambassador or messenger.

Second, where the apostolic and early church fathers were concerned, they had little to say about spiritual gifts. What is most interesting, however, is that when they did write about spiritual gifts, they tended to focus on prophecies, healings, and miracles, and occasionally the gift of tongues. Yet, when it came to apostleship, they knew nothing of the spiritual gift of apostle save the twelve plus Paul. If a gift of apostleship (other than the twelve) had existed in the first century, and it carried such weight that Paul would list it first among spiritual gifts, it seems logical that such an extraordinary gift might have been recognized by those early Christian writers in the second and third centuries.

The twelve apostles along with Paul received the spiritual gift of apostleship directly from the Lord (Luke 12: 13-16; Acts 9: 15). They were established by Christ as his authoritative representatives on earth. It is more than reasonable, given the biblical and external evidence, that theirs is the spiritual gift Paul had in view when writing about the *gift of apostle*.

Appendix B

The Sinner's Prayer

Whether on the Day of Pentecost (Acts 2: 1-41), the episode involving the Philippian jailer (Acts 16: 31-40), the Ethiopian eunuch's conversion (Acts 8: 26-39), or any other time in Scripture where the narrative depicts people being saved, the Sinner's Prayer is absent. At no time in the post-Pentecost era is prayer defined in Scripture as a matter of salvation for those outside of Christ. Those who claim to derive the Sinner's Prayer from the pages of Scripture insist that, while this teaching is not found in the Bible, it can be inferred from certain passages.

> [13] But the tax collector, standing some distance away, was even unwilling to lift up his eyes to heaven, but was beating his breast, saying, 'God, be merciful to me, the sinner!' [14] I tell you, this man went to his house justified ..." (Luke 18: 13-14)

The prayer of the tax collector (above) is perhaps the closest thing Scripture has to the Sinner's Prayer. Notice, however, that there is no mention here of salvation through Jesus Christ or forgiveness through his blood. This man (the tax collector) did not ask Jesus *into his heart*, which is the essence of the Sinner's Prayer. It is noteworthy that, as with his conversation with Nicodemus (John 3: 1-5), Jesus offered this parable prior to his own death/resurrection and well before baptism in his name was ever commanded (Acts 2: 38).

What Jesus has provided for his disciples in this parable is an example of the humility God hopes to see in every person. He is not, as many suppose, presenting a model for the plan of salvation in the covenant of grace. The passage simply portrays the repentant heart that is essential for those who seek forgiveness.

> [19] Those whom I love, I reprove and discipline; therefore be zealous and repent. [20] Behold, I stand at the door and knock; if anyone hears My voice and opens the door, I will come in to him and will dine with him, and he with Me. (Revelation 3:19-20)

This verse, written by the Apostle John, is a verse highly favored by many who seek to dismiss Scripture's portrayal of baptism as a matter of forgiveness and salvation. It is considered an evangelical appeal to men everywhere, suggesting that by simply opening their hearts to Jesus, they can commune with Him. The greatest irony about this passage is that it is not written to the lost multitudes, but to the church at Laodicea where they were '...neither hot nor cold' (Revelation 3: 15). It is not an appeal to a lost and dying world, but a petition to those in the church who, at one time, had been faithful but were now tepid in their service to the Lord.

The Sinner's Prayer was conceived out of necessity as a result of the Reformation Movement of the sixteenth century. At that time men began to reject the notion that salvation occurred at the time of baptism, which was a staple of Christian doctrine. As a result, a void developed within the plan of salvation that was taught among Protestant denominations. For a considerable length of time after the Reformation Movement, many became confused about the time of salvation. As more people determined that baptism should not be seen as the moment that they knew salvation, the confusion broadened, and it became necessary to replace baptism with something else. A new moment of salvation needed to be established.

Evangelists in the seventeenth and eighteenth centuries, relying heavily on passages like Revelation 3: 20 for support, sought to establish a time of redemption. In the 1700's, many preachers settled on a time of confession that was considered the moment of salvation. Sometimes called the Mourners Seat, although other names were used, individuals were highlighted throughout the service with the challenge for them to accept Christ. According to Steve Staten:

> It is documented that in 1741 a minister named Eleazar Wheelock had utilized a technique called the Mourner's Seat. As far as one can tell, he would target sinners by having them sit in the front bench (pew). During the course of his sermon "salvation was looming over their heads." Afterwards, the sinners were typically quite open to counsel and exhortation.[54]

This practice continued for roughly two centuries as the *way* to salvation. It was the plea for *salvation without activity on man's part* that served as the force behind these doctrinal changes. Still, it is

---

[54] Staten, Steve. *Where Did We Get the Sinner's Prayer? Is It Biblical?* http://www.s8int.com/sinnersprayer.html.

interesting that, once baptism was dismissed as the moment of salvation, every attempt to replace it ultimately laid the responsibility at the feet of the sinner, requiring him to *do* something in response to the gospel message. So it is with the Sinner's Prayer.

The Sinner's Prayer, as it is known today, began to develop in the second half of the nineteenth century. A minister by the name of Dwight Moody (1837-1899), along with Billy Sunday (1863-1935), who was a converted baseball player, and other notables were responsible for its widespread approval. According to David Malcolm Bennett:

> It is clear…that a theology that could support the use of the Sinner's Prayer emerged in the middle of the nineteenth century.[55]

Today, despite the lack of biblical support, the Sinner's Prayer is predominantly preached and accepted as the time of salvation. While this is an abbreviated history of the development of the Sinner's Prayer, it is a history that deserves serious consideration. Since it did not exist for the first 1,800 years of the church age, along with its complete lack of biblical endorsement, the Sinner's Prayer must be dismissed as the moment of salvation. It should more aptly be considered one of the *traditions of men* against which Paul offered the Colossians solemn warning (Colossians 2: 8).

---

[55] Bennett, David M. *The Sinner's Prayer: Its Origins and Dangers*, 150.

Bibliography

Aaron, Daryl. *The 40 Most Influential Christians Who Shaped What We Believe Today*. Minneapolis: Bethany House, 2013.

Adams, Jay. *Competent To Counsel*, Grand Rapids, MI: Zondervan Publishing House, 1970.

Anderson, J. G. C. *Dictionary of National Biography 1931-1940*, "Sir William Mitchell Ramsay," London: Oxford University Press, 1949.

Arnold, Clinton E. general editor. Zondervan Illustrated Bible Backgrounds Commentary, Volume 4, Grand Rapids, MI: Zondervan Publishing House, 1973, 1978, 1984.

Bales, James D. *The Case of Cornelius*, Delight, AR: Gospel Light Publishing Company, 1964.

Barlow, Jonathan. *Calvinism*, http://www.reformed.org/calvinism/index.html, Accessed June 3, 2012.

Barnes, Albert. *Barnes' Notes on the Whole Bible*, studylight.org., http://www.studylight.org/com/bnb/view.cgi?bk=55. Accessed July 8, 2012

Barnes, Albert. *Barnes' Notes on the Whole Bible*. studylight.org., http://www.studylight.org/com/bnb/view.cgi?bk=57. Accessed July 8, 2012

Basinger, David and Randall, editors, *Predestination & Freewill,* Downers Grove, IL: Intervarsity Press, 1986.

Beasley-Murray, G. R., *Baptism in the New Testament*, Grand Rapids, MI: William E. Eerdmans Publishing Company, 1962.

Bennett, David M. The Sinner's Prayer: Its Origins and Dangers, Capalaba, Qld: Even Before Publishing

Bercot, David. *What the Early Christians Believed about Free Will*, http://earlychurch.com/freewill.php. Accessed August 20, 2012

Bouwsma, William J., *John Calvin A Sixteenth Century Portrait*. New York: Oxford, 1988.

Brand, Chad Owen, editor. *Perspectives on Election – Five Views*, Nashville, TN: Broadman & Holman Publishers, 2006.

Bromiley, G. W., editor, and translator, 'Huldreigh Zwingli, "Of Baptism," in *Zwingli and Bullinger*, "Library of Christian Classics,"' Vol. 24, Philadelphia, PA: Westminster Press, 1953.

Brown, Peter. *Augustine of Hippo*, Berkeley, and Los Angeles: University of California, 1967.

Brown, Robert K., Comfort, Philip W. translators. *The New Greek English Interlinear New Testament*, Wheaton, IL: Tyndale House Publishers, 1990.

Byrum, Russell R., *Christian Theology*, Anderson, IN: Gospel Trumpet Company, 1925.

Calvin, John. *Commentary on the Gospel According to John*, Grand Rapids, MI: Wm. E. Eerdmans Publishing Co., 1949.

Calvin, John. *Calvin's Commentary on the Bible*, studylight.org., http://www.studylight.org/com/cal/view.cgi?bk=55. Accessed January 14, 2013

Calvin, John. *Calvin's Commentary on the Bible*. studylight.org., http://www.studylight.org/com/cal/view.cgi?bk=57. Accessed January 15, 2013

Calvin, John. *Calvin's Commentary on the Bible*. studylight.org., http://www.studylight.org/commentaries/cal/view.cgi?bk=45&ch=13.

Calvin, John. *Institutes of the Christian Religion*, Peabody, MA: Henrickson Publishers, 2008.

Clarke, Adam. *Adam Clarke Commentary*. studylight.org., http://www.studylight.org/com/acc/view.cgi?bk=1. Accessed January 30, 2013

Clarke, Adam. *Adam Clarke Commentary*. studylight.org., http://www.studylight.org/com/acc/view.cgi?bk=44. Accessed January 30, 2013

Clarke, Adam. *Adam Clarke Commentary*. studylight.org., http://www.studylight.org/com/acc/view.cgi?bk=45. Accessed February 13, 2013

Clarke, Adam. *Adam Clarke Commentary*. studylight.org., http://www.studylight.org/com/acc/view.cgi?bk=48. Accessed February 13, 2013

Clarke, Adam. *Adam Clarke Commentary*. studylight.org., http://www.studylight.org/com/acc/view.cgi?bk=57. Accessed February 13, 2013

Coffman, James Burton. *James Burton Coffman Commentaries, 1 & 2 Corinthians*, Abilene, TX: ACU Press, 1984.

Coffman, James Burton. *James Burton Coffman Commentaries, 1 & 2 Thessalonians, 1 & 2 Timothy, Titus, Philemon*, Abilene, TX: ACU Press, 1984.

Coffman, James Burton. *James Burton Coffman Commentaries, Hebrews*, Abilene, TX: ACU Press, 1984.

Cottrell, Jack, *The Faith Once For All*, Joplin, MO: College Press Publishing Company, 2002.

Cottrell, Jack. Answering a false interpretation of Acts 2: 38, jackcotrell.com, http://jackcottrell.com/notes/answering-a-false-interpretation-of-acts-238/.

Flavius Josephus, William Whiston translator. *The Works of Flavius Josephus*, "Antiquities of The Jews," Grand Rapids: Associated Publishers and Authors.

Freeman, Drue. *Hermeneutics*, realtime.net., http://www.realtime.net/~wdoud/topics/hermeneutics.html. Accessed March 17, 2012

Gill, John. *John Gill's Exposition of the Whole Bible*. studylight.org., http://www.studylight.org/com/geb/view.cgi?bk=1. Accessed September 10, 2013

Glueck, Nelson. *Rivers in the Desert*, New York, NY: Farrar, Straus, & Cudahy, 1960.

Green, J. P., Sr., general editor. *The Interlinear Bible Greek English Volume IV New Testament*, Peabody, MA: Hendrickson Publishers, 2005.

Grudem, Wayne. *Systematic Theology – An Introduction to Biblical Doctrine*, Grand Rapids, MI: Zondervan Publishing House, 1994.

Guralnik, David B., editor in chief. *Webster's New World Dictionary Second College Edition*, William Collins + World Publishing Company, 1978.

Harrison, Everett F. *The Expositor's Bible Commentary: Romans*, Grand Rapids, MI: Zondervan Publishing House, 1995.

Henry, Matthew, *Matthew Henry's Commentary on the Whole Bible*, Hendricksen Publishers, Inc., 2001.

Hodge, A. A. *Semi-Pelagianism*. monergism.com, http://monergism.com/thethreshold/articles/onsite/semi-pelagian.html. Accessed February 13, 2013

Irenaeus. *Against Heresies (Book I, Chapter 21)*. CHURCH FATHERS: Against Heresies, I.21 (St. Irenaeus), newadvent.org., http://www.newadvent.org/fathers/0103121.htm. Accessed October 13, 2013

Irenaeus. *Tracts*. "Born Again in Baptism," catholic.com http://www.catholic.com/tracts/born-again-in-baptism. Accessed May 4, 2012

Jamieson, Robert, A. R. Fausset, and David Brown. *Commentary Critical and Explanatory on the Whole Bible*. studylight.org. http://www.studylight.org/com/jfb/view.cgi?bk=55. Accessed February 22, 2013

Jamieson, Robert, A. R. Fausset, and David Brown. *A Commentary on the Old and New Testaments – Volume 3*, Peabody, MA: Hendrickson Publishers, 2008.

Johnson, B. W. *The People's New Testament*, Delight, AR: Gospel Light Publishing.

Lewis, A. Allison. *The Ceasing of the Charismata*, christianbeliefs.org. http://www.christianbeliefs.org/books/cm/cm-charisma.html. Accessed February 22, 2013

Lindner, William. *John Calvin*, Minneapolis: Bethany House, 1998

Lockhart, Clinton. *Principles of Interpretation – Revised Edition*, Delight, AR: Gospel Light Publishing Company.

Longnecker, Richard N. *The Expositor's Bible Commentary – Acts*, Grand Rapids, MI: Zondervan Publishing House, 1965.

Luther, Martin. *Galatians Commentary* (3:20-29) – Martin Luther, Project Wittenberg, Iclnet.org. http://www.iclnet.org/pub/resources/text/wittenberg/luther/gal/web/gal3-20.html. Accessed April 24, 2013

Luther, Martin. *Tracts. The Necessity of Baptism*, http://www.catholic.com/tracts/the-necessity-of-baptism. Accessed January 17, 2013

Mare, W. Harold, and Murray J. Harris. *The Expositor's Bible Commentary – 1 & 2 Corinthians*, Grand Rapids, MI: Zondervan Publishing House, 1995.

McGarvey, J. W. *A Commentary on Matthew and Mark*, Delight, AR: Gospel Light Publishing Company.

McGarvey, J. W. *New Commentary on Acts*, Delight, AR: Gospel Light Publishing Company.

McGarvey, J. W., Pendleton, Philip Y. *A Commentary on Thessalonians, Corinthians, Galatians, and Romans*, Gospel Light Publishing Company.

Mare, W. Harold and Murray J. Harris, *The Expositor's Bible Commentary – 1 & 2 Corinthians*, Grand Rapids, MI: Zondervan Publishing House, 1965.

Morris, Leon, and Donald Burdick. *Expositor's Bible Commentary – Hebrews – James*, Grand Rapids, MI: Zondervan Publishing House, 1996.

Murray, Lindley. *About.com Grammar & Composition* "Of Figures of Speech, by Lindley Murray (page Two)," about.com. http://grammar.about.com/od/essaysonstyle/a/MurrayFigures_2.htm. Accessed March 21, 2013

Pelikan, Jaroslav, *The Emergence of the Catholic Tradition (100-600) Christian Tradition # 1*, Chicago, IL, The University of Chicago Press, 1971.

Piper, John. *Irresistible Grace*, monergism.com, http://www.monergism.com/thethreshold/articles/piper/irresistable.html. Accessed March 30, 2013

Reese, Gareth L. *New Testament History Acts*, Moberly, MO: Scripture Exposition Books, 2002.

Robertson, A. T. *Robertson's Word Pictures in the New Testament*, studylight.org, http://www.studylight.org/commentaries/rwp/view.cgi?bk=43&ch=2. Accessed April 2, 2013

Schneider, Thomas R., and Bruce A. Ware. *The Grace of God, The Bondage of the Will, Vol. 2*, Grand Rapids, MI: Baker Books, 1995.

Society of Evangelical Arminians. *The Five Articles of Remonstrance*, evangelicalarminians.org., http://evangelicalarminians.org/the-five-articles-of-remonstrance/. Accessed April 8, 2013

Speer, L. L., Founder. *The General Epistles: A Practical Faith*, Practical Christianity Foundation, Green Key Books .

Sproul, R. C. *Chosen by God*, Wheaton, IL: Tyndale Publishers, 1986.

Stanglin, Keith D. and Thomas H. McCall. *Jacob Arminius Theologian of Grace*. New York: Oxford, 2012.

Staten, Steve. http://www.s8int.com/sinnersprayer.html. Accessed March 24, 2013

Strong, Augustus Hopkins. *Systematic Theology*, Philadelphia, PA: The Judson Press, 1946.

Strong, James. *The New Strong's Exhaustive Concordance of the Bible, Greek Dictionary of the New Testament*, Kansas City, MO: Thomas Nelson Publishers, 1990.

Strong, James. *The New Strong's Exhaustive Concordance of the Bible, Hebrew and Chaldee Dictionary*, Kansas City, MO: Thomas Nelson Publishers, 1990.

Tacitus, A. *Tacitus on the Christians*. livius.org., http://www.livius.org/cg-cm/christianity/tacitus.html. Accessed March 14, 2013

Taylor, Gene. *Calvinism | Unconditional Election | John Calvin*, centervilleroad.com., http://www.centervilleroad.com/articles/calvinism-3.html. Accessed June 30, 2013

Tertullian. *Tracts*. "Born Again in Baptism," catholic.com., http://www.catholic.com/tracts/born-again-in-baptism. Accessed July 22, 2013

Thomas, Robert, L. *Understanding Spiritual Gifts – Revised Edition*, Grand Rapids, MI: Kregel Publications, 1978.

Vincent, Marvin R. *Vincent's Word Studies*, studylight.org., http://www.studylight.org/com/vnt/view.cgi?bk=48. Accessed March 19, 2013

Wesley, John. *Wesley's Explanatory Notes*. studylight.org. http://www.studylight.org/com/wen/view.cgi?bk=48. Accessed March 3, 2013, 2013

Wiggers, Gustav F. and Ralph Emerson. *An Historical Presentation of Augustinism and Pelagianism from the Original Sources*. Andover, NY: Gold, Newman, and Saxton, 1840.

Zwingli, Huldreigh, G. W. Bromiley, editor. *Library of Christian Classics, Vol. 24*, "Of Baptism, in Zwingli and Bullinger," Philadelphia. PA: Westminster Press, 1953.

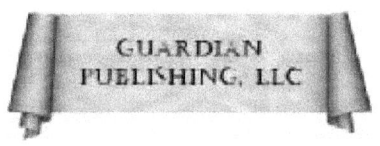

www.ingramcontent.com/pod-product-compliance
Lightning Source LLC
Chambersburg PA
CBHW031603110426
42742CB00037B/824